# MICROECONOMICS

Avi J. Cohen and Harvey B. King

**PEARSON**

Toronto

flexText

Editorial Director: Claudine O'Donnell
Acquisitions Editor: Megan Farrell
Marketing Manager: Claire Varley
Program Manager: Emily Dill
Project Manager: Richard di Santo
Developmental Editor: Heather Sangster/Strong Finish Editorial Design
Composition: Cenveo® Publishing Services

Vice-President, Cross Media and Publishing Services: Gary Bennett

---

10 9 8 7 6 5 4 3 2 1  [V0TX]

**PEARSON**

ISBN: 978-0-13-454429-8

# Contents

*Introduction    iv*

Chapter 1. What Is Economics?    1
Appendix: Graphs in Economics    25
Chapter 2. The Economic Problem    51
Chapter 3. Demand and Supply    85
Chapter 4. Elasticity    127
Chapter 5. Efficiency and Equity    155
Chapter 6. Government Actions in Markets    181
Chapter 7. Global Markets in Action    211
Chapter 8. Utility and Demand    237
Chapter 9. Possibilities, Preferences, and Choices    263
Chapter 10. Organizing Production    295

Chapter 11. Output and Costs    319
Chapter 12. Perfect Competition    345
Chapter 13. Monopoly    377
Chapter 14. Monopolistic Competition    413
Chapter 15. Oligopoly    433
Chapter 16. Externalities    457
Chapter 17. Public Goods and Common Resources    481
Chapter 18. Markets for Factors of Production    505
Chapter 19. Economic Inequality    535

# Introduction

## Before You Begin …

Our experience has taught us that what first-year economics students want most from a *FlexText* is help in mastering course material to do well on examinations. We have developed this *FlexText* to respond specifically to that demand. Using this *FlexText* alone, however, is not enough to guarantee that you will do well in your course. In order to help you overcome the problems and difficulties that most first-year students encounter, we have some general advice on how to study, as well as some specific advice on how to best use this *FlexText*.

## Some Friendly Advice

The study of economics requires a different style of thinking from what you may encounter in other courses. Economists make extensive use of assumptions to break down complex problems into simple, analytically manageable parts. This analytical style, while not ultimately more demanding than the styles of thinking in other disciplines, feels unfamiliar to most students and requires practice. As a result, it is not as easy to do well in economics simply on the basis of your raw intelligence and high school knowledge as it is in many other first-year courses. Many students who come to our offices are frustrated and puzzled by the fact that they are getting A's and B's in their other courses but only a C or worse in economics. They have not recognized that the study of economics is different and requires practice. In order to avoid a frustrating visit to your instructor after your first test, we suggest you do the following:

*Don't rely solely on your high school economics.* If you took high school economics, you will have seen the material on demand and supply, which your instructor will lecture on in the first few weeks. Don't be lulled into feeling that the course will be easy. Your high school knowledge of economic concepts will be useful, but it will not be enough to guarantee high marks on exams. Your college or university instructors will demand much more detailed knowledge of concepts and ask you to apply them in new circumstances.

*Keep a good set of lecture notes.* Good lecture notes are vital for focusing your studying. Your instructor will only lecture on a subset of topics from the textbook. The topics your instructor covers in a lecture should usually be given priority when studying. Also give priority to studying the figures and graphs covered in the lecture.

Instructors do differ in their emphasis on lecture notes or the textbook, so early on in the course ask which is more important in reviewing for exams—lecture notes or the textbook. If your instructor answers that both are important, then ask the following, typically economic question: at the margin, which will be more beneficial—spending an extra hour rereading your lecture notes or an extra hour rereading the textbook? This question assumes that you have read each textbook chapter twice (once before lecture for a general understanding and then later for a thorough understanding); that you have prepared a good set of lecture notes; and that you have worked through all of the problems in the appropriate *FlexText* chapters. By applying this style of analysis to the problem of efficiently allocating your study time, you are already beginning to think like an economist!

*Use your instructor and/or teaching assistants for help.* When you have questions or problems with course material, come to the office to ask questions. Remember, you are paying for your education and instructors are there to help you learn. We are often amazed at how few students come to see us during office hours. Don't be shy. The personal contact that comes from one-on-one tutoring is professionally gratifying for us as well as (hopefully) beneficial to you.

*Form a study group.* A useful way to motivate your studying and to learn economics is to discuss the course material and problems with other students. Explaining the answer to a question out loud is an effective way of discovering how well you understand the question. When you answer a question only in your head, you often skip steps in the chain of reasoning without realizing it. When you are forced to explain your reasoning out loud, gaps and mistakes quickly appear, and you (with your fellow group members) can quickly correct your reasoning. The true/false and explain questions in the *FlexText* and the questions at the end of each textbook chapter are good study-group material. You might also get together after having worked the *FlexText* problems, but before looking at the answers, and help each other solve unsolved problems.

*Work old exams.* One of the most effective ways of studying is to work through exams your instructor has given in previous years. Old exams give you a feel for the style of questions your instructor may ask and give you the opportunity to get used to time pressure if you force yourself to do the exam in the allotted time. Studying from old exams is not cheating, as long as you have obtained a copy of the exam legally. Some institutions post old exams online; others keep them in the library, the department, or at the student union. Upper-year students who have previously taken the course are usually a good source as well. Remember, though, that old exams are a useful study aid only if you use them to understand the reasoning behind each question. If you simply memorize answers in the hopes that your instructor will repeat the identical question, you are likely to fail. From year to year, instructors routinely change the questions or change the numerical values for similar questions.

## Using the *FlexText*

Each *FlexText* chapter contains the following sections:

**Key Concepts**    This first section is a one- to two-page summary, in point form, of all key definitions, concepts, and material from the textbook chapter. The summary is organized using the same major section headings from the textbook chapter. Key terms from the textbook appear in bold. This section is designed to focus you quickly and precisely on the core material that you must master. It is an excellent study aid for the night before an exam. Think of it as crib notes that will serve as a final check of the key concepts you have studied.

**Helpful Hints**    When you encounter difficulty in mastering concepts or techniques, you will not be alone. Many students find certain concepts difficult and often make the same kinds of mistakes. We have seen these common mistakes often enough to have learned how to help students avoid them. The hints point out these mistakes and offer tips to avoid them. The hints focus on the most important concepts, equations, and techniques for problem solving. They also review crucial graphs that appear on every instructor's exams. We hope that this section will be useful, since instructors always ask exam questions designed to test these possible mistakes in your understanding.

**Self-Test**    This should be one of the most useful sections of this *FlexText*. The questions are designed to give you practice and to test skills and techniques you must master to do well on exams. You are encouraged to write directly in the *FlexText*. There are plenty of the multiple-choice questions (25 for each chapter) you are most likely to encounter on course tests and exams. There are also other types of questions, described below, each with a specific pedagogical purpose.

Before we describe the three parts of the Self-Test section, here are some tips that apply to all parts:

Use a pencil. This will allow you to erase your mistakes and have neat, completed pages from which to study. Draw graphs wherever applicable. Some questions will ask explicitly for graphs; many others will not, but will require a chain of reasoning that involves shifts of curves on a graph. *Always draw the graph.* Don't try to work through the reasoning in your head—you are much more likely to make mistakes that way. Whenever you draw a graph, even in the margins of this *FlexText,* label the axes. You may think that you can keep the labels in your head, but you will be confronting many different graphs with many different variables on the axes. Avoid confusion: label! As an added incentive, remember that on exams where graphs are required, instructors will deduct marks for unlabelled axes.

Do the Self-Test questions as if they were real exam questions, which means do them without looking at the answers. This is the single most important tip we can give you. Struggling for the answers to questions that you find difficult is one of the most effective ways to learn. The athletic adage "No pain, no gain" applies equally to studying. You will learn the most from right answers you had to struggle for and from your wrong answers and mistakes. Only after you have attempted all the questions should you look at the answers. When you finally do check the answers, be sure to understand where you went wrong and why the right answer is right.

If you want to impose time pressure on yourself to simulate the conditions of a real exam, allow two minutes for each true/false and multiple-choice question. The short answer problems vary considerably in their time requirements, so it is difficult to give time estimates for them. However, we believe that such time pressure is probably not a good idea for *FlexText* questions. A state of relaxed concentration is best.

There are many questions in each chapter, and it will take you somewhere between two and four hours to answer all of them. If you get tired (or bored), don't burn yourself out by trying to work through all of the questions in one sitting. Consider breaking up your Self-Test over two (or more) study sessions.

One other tip about the Self-Test: *Before* you jump in and do the questions, be sure to read through the Key Concepts and Helpful Hints. This will save you the frustration of getting wrong answers to questions. When you do get wrong answers, you will often find an explanation of the right answers in the Key Concepts or Helpful Hints. The three parts of the Self-Test section are as follows:

**True/False and Explain**   These questions test basic knowledge of chapter concepts and your ability to apply the concepts. Some challenge your understanding, to see whether you can identify mistakes in statements using basic concepts. These questions will quickly identify gaps in your knowledge and are useful to answer out loud in a study group. There are 15 of these questions, organized using the same major section headings from the textbook. The Test Bank that your instructor will likely use to make up tests and exams also contains true/false questions like those in the Self-Test.

When answering, identify each statement as *true* or *false*. Explain your answer in one sentence. The space underneath each question should be sufficient in every case for writing your answer.

**Multiple-Choice**   These more difficult questions test your analytical abilities by asking you to apply concepts to new situations, manipulate information, and solve numerical and graphical problems.

This is the most frequently used type of test and exam question, and the Self-Test contains 25 of them for each chapter organized using the same major section headings from the textbook. Your instructor's Test Bank contains all of the *FlexText* multiple-choice questions, numerous questions that closely parallel the *FlexText* questions, plus many similar questions.

Before you answer, read each question and all five choices carefully. Many of the choices will be plausible and will differ only slightly. You must choose the one *best* answer. A useful strategy is to first eliminate any obviously wrong choices and then focus on the remaining alternatives. Be aware that sometimes the correct answer will be "none of the above." Don't get frustrated or think that you are dim if you can't immediately see the correct answer. These questions are designed to make you work to find the correct choice.

**Short Answer Problems**   The best way to learn to do economics is to do problems. Problems are also a popular type of test and exam question—practise them as much as possible! Each Self-Test concludes with eight short answer, numerical, or graphical problems, often based on economic policy issues. In many chapters, this is the most challenging part of the Self-Test. It is also likely to be the most helpful for deepening your understanding of the chapter material. We have, however, designed the questions to teach as much as to test. We have purposely arranged the parts of each multipart question to lead you through the problem-solving analysis in a gradual and sequential fashion, from easier to more difficult parts.

Problems that require critical thinking are marked with the symbol ⓒ, to alert you to the need for extra time and effort. This symbol gives you the same indication you would have on a test or exam from the number of marks or minutes allocated to a problem.

**Answers**   The Self-Test is followed by a section that gives answers to all the questions. But do not look at any answer until you have attempted the question.

When you finally do look, use the answer to understand where you went wrong, and think about why the answer is right. Every true/false and multiple-choice answer includes a brief, point-form explanation to suggest where you might have gone wrong and the economic reasoning behind the answer. At the end of each answer are page references to the textbook, so you can read a more complete explanation.

Answers to critical thinking questions are marked with ⓒ to indicate why you might have struggled with that question! (We purposely did not mark which true/false and multiple-choice questions were critical thinking, to stay as close as possible to a real test or exam format. In an exam, all multiple-choice questions, for example, are worth the same number of marks, and you would have no idea which questions are the more difficult ones requiring critical thinking.)

The detailed answers to the short answer problems should be especially useful in clarifying and illustrating typical chains of reasoning involved in economic analysis. Answers to critical thinking problems are marked with ⓒ.

If the answers alone do not clear up your confusion, go back to the appropriate sections of the textbook and to the Key Concepts and Helpful Hints in this *FlexText*. If that still does not suffice, go to your instructor's or teaching assistants' office or to your study-group members for help and clarification.

## Pearson *FlexText*...setting you up for success in school and at work

Regardless of the course you're taking — whether you are in a Business, Practical Nursing, ECE, or Police Foundations program — you want to leave with skills that can help you get the job you want. Some of these skills will be specific to your course of study or major. These are basic skills your employers will want you to have. An accountant, for example, will be expected to know how to read a balance sheet and use Microsoft Excel. But there are other skills essential to your success in the workplace that might not seem so obvious but are important enough that the many governments call them "Essential" Employability Skills. The Conference Board of Canada goes even further, calling them "the skills you need to enter, stay in, and progress in the world of work — whether you work on your own or as a part of a team." (http://www.conferenceboard. ca/topics/education/learning-tools/employability-skills. aspx)

This Pearson *FlexText* was designed to help you develop these skills.

What are Essential Employability Skills? They can be grouped into six broad categories: Communication, Numeracy, Critical Thinking & Problem Solving, Information Management, Interpersonal, and Personal. The Government of Ontario thinks that these skills are so important that they expect that everyone who graduates with a certificate or diploma should have them. Other provincial governments place an equal emphasis on them. Many of these skills could also be called "soft skills," or "21st century skills," and represent areas such as writing that are not specific to the core content of any one course but are important to your success in *all* courses, and in the working world. Being able to show prospective employers that you have these skills can make a huge difference in your ability to get the job that you want.

Pearson *FlexText* is designed with the needs of college students in mind, including the need to develop and demonstrate Essential Employability Skills. Here's how:

### Communication Skills   *Defining skill areas: reading, writing, speaking, listening, presenting, and visual literacy*

One of the reasons why students don't develop their reading skills is simply because they have not bought their textbook. *FlexTexts* are affordable, and available at a price that will encourage as many students as possible to buy — and read — their course materials. *FlexTexts* often include chapter summaries and outlines to help support reading comprehension and many will include short answer questions or writing activities that provide opportunities for students to practise their writing and develop their written communication skills.

### Numeracy Skills   *Defining skill areas: understanding and applying mathematical concepts and reasoning, analyzing and using mathematical data, and conceptualizing*

*FlexTexts* in disciplines such as Accounting, Economics and Finance, which require students to understand and apply mathematical concepts to the course content, will include practice questions. The spiral-bound *FlexText* format encourages their use as in-class activity workbooks, where faculty can provide instructional support to students as they work through these problems.

### Critical Thinking & Problem Solving Skills   *Defining skill areas: analyzing, synthesizing, evaluating, decision making, and creativity and innovative thinking*

The exercises and activities found in Pearson's *FlexTexts* are not simply factual, recall, or "skill and drill" type activities. They are created to engage students at many different levels of Bloom's Taxonomy to help them develop their critical thinking and problem solving skills. And because the *FlexText* is affordable, a greater number of students will have the opportunity to develop these skills through practice because they have purchased their course materials.

### Information Management Skills   *Defining skill areas: gathering and managing information, selecting and using appropriate tools and technology for a task or project, computer literacy, and internet skills*

Not all of the exercises in a *FlexText* are pen and paper activities. Many also require students to engage with online multimedia assets, with applications such as Microsoft

Excel, or to explain how they would bring these tools to bear to the solution of a problem.

**Interpersonal Skills**   *Defining skill areas: teamwork, relationship management, conflict resolution, leadership, and networking*

Because *FlexTexts* are designed to be brought to class, they facilitate group work and collaborative problem solving. Activities that, in the past, would have been assigned as homework and be done individually can now be implemented in ways that help students develop their interpersonal skills.

**Personal Skills**   *Defining skill areas: managing self, managing change and being flexible and adaptable, engaging in reflexive practice, and demonstrating personal responsibility*

Making the decision to purchase course materials and actively engage with course content is one of the first steps toward demonstrating a degree of personal responsibility for your own success in school. The page layout of a *FlexText* also encourages note taking and supports the development of good study skills.

# 1 What Is Economics?

## Key Concepts

### Definition of Economics

All economic questions arise from **scarcity**.

- Because wants exceed the resources available to satisfy them, we cannot have everything we want and must make choices.

  - Choices depend on **incentives**—rewards that encourage actions and penalties that discourage action.

- **Economics** is the social science that studies the choices people make to cope with scarcity.

  - **Microeconomics** studies choices of individuals and businesses.
  - **Macroeconomics** studies national and global economies.

### Two Big Economic Questions

Two questions summarize the scope of economics:

- How do choices determine *what*, *how*, and *for whom* **goods and services** are produced, and in what quantities?
- How can choices made in the pursuit of self-interest also promote the social interest?

The **factors of production** used to produce goods and services are

- **land** (shorthand for all natural resources), which earns **rent**.
- **labour** (includes **human capital**—knowledge and skills from education, training, experience), which earns **wages**.
- **capital** (machinery), which earns **interest**.
- **entrepreneurship,** which earns **profit**.

Choices made in **self-interest** are best for the person making them. Choices that are in the **social interest** are best for society as a whole. Society achieves **efficiency** when available resources are used to produce goods and services at the lowest cost.

- Markets often provide incentives so that the pursuit of our self-interest also promotes the social interest; but self-interest and social interest sometimes conflict.
- Economic principles allow us to understand when self-interest promotes the social interest, when they conflict, and policies to reduce those conflicts.

## The Economic Way of Thinking

A choice is a **tradeoff**—we give up one thing to get something else—and the **opportunity cost** of any action is the highest-valued alternative forgone. Opportunity cost is the single most important concept for making choices.

- A **rational choice** compares costs and benefits and achieves the greatest benefit over cost.
- **Benefit**—gain or pleasure of a choice, is determined by a person's **preferences**—likes and dislikes and their intensity.
- The **big tradeoff** is between equality and efficiency. Government redistribution using taxes and transfers weaken incentives, so a more equally shared pie results in a smaller pie.

We make choices in small steps, or at the **margin**, and choices are influenced by incentives.

- Economic choices are made by comparing the *additional* benefit—**marginal benefit**—and *additional* opportunity cost—**marginal cost**—of a small increase in an activity. If marginal benefit exceeds marginal cost, we choose to increase the activity.

- By choosing only activities that bring greater benefits than costs, we use our scarce resources in the way that makes us as well off as possible.

## Economics as Social Science and Policy Tool

Economics, as a social science, distinguishes between

- *positive* statements—statements about what *is;* they can be tested by checking them against the facts.
- *normative* statements—statements about what *ought* to be; they depend on values and cannot be tested.

Economics attempts to understand the economic world and is concerned with positive statements. Economists try to discover positive statements that are consistent with observed facts by

- unscrambling cause and effect.
- creating **economic models**—a simplified description of the economic world that includes only features needed for purpose of explanation.
- testing economic models, comparing predictions with the facts, using

  - natural experiments—where one factor is different in real world; other things are equal.
  - statistical investigations—correlations between variables.
  - economic experiments—putting people in decision-making situations and changing one variable to see the response.

Economics is a useful toolkit for

- personal decisions
- advising businesses on economic policy
- advising government on economic policy

For any *normative* policy objective, economics provides a method of evaluating alternative solutions—evaluate marginal benefits and marginal costs to find solutions that make the best use of resources.

# Helpful Hints

1. The definition of economics (explaining the choices we make using limited resources to try to satisfy unlimited wants) leads us directly to two important economic concepts: choice and opportunity cost. If wants exceed resources, we cannot have everything we want and therefore must make *choices* among alternatives. In making a choice, we forgo other alternatives, and the *opportunity cost* of any choice is the highest-valued alternative forgone.

2. Marginal analysis is a fundamental tool economists use to predict people's choices. The key to understanding marginal analysis is to focus on *additional*, rather than total, benefits and costs. For example, to predict whether or not Taejong will eat a fourth Big Mac, the economist compares Taejong's *additional* benefit or satisfaction from the fourth Big Mac with its *additional* cost. The total benefits and costs of all four Big Macs are not relevant. Only if the marginal benefit exceeds the marginal cost will Taejong eat a fourth Big Mac.

3. In attempting to understand how and why something works (e.g., an airplane, a falling object, an economy), we can try to use description or theory. A description is a list of facts about something. But it does not tell us which facts are essential for understanding how an airplane works (the shape of the wings) and which facts are less important (the colour of the paint).

   Scientists use theory to abstract from the complex descriptive facts of the real world and focus only on those elements essential for understanding. Those essential elements are fashioned into models—highly simplified representations of the real world.

   In physics and some other natural sciences, if we want to understand the essential force (gravity) that causes objects to fall, we use theory to construct a simple model and then test it by performing a controlled experiment. We create a vacuum to eliminate less important forces like air resistance.

   Economic models are also attempts to focus on the essential forces (competition, self-interest) operating in the economy, while abstracting from less important forces (whims, advertising, altruism). Unlike physicists, economists cannot easily perform controlled experiments to test their models. As a result, it is difficult to conclusively prove or disprove a theory and its models. Economists rely on naturally occurring experiments, statistical investigations of correlations between variables, and artificial laboratory economic experiments about choices.

4. Models are like maps, which are useful precisely because they abstract from real-world detail. A map that reproduced all of the details of the real world (street lamps, fireplugs, electric wires) would be useless. A useful map offers a simplified view that is carefully selected according to the purpose of the map. Remember that economic models are not claims that the real world is as simple as the model. Models claim to capture the simplified effect of some real force operating in the economy. Before drawing conclusions about the real economy from a model, we must be careful to consider whether, when we reinsert all of the real-world complexities the model abstracted from, the conclusions will be the same as in the model.

5. The most important purpose of studying economics is not to learn what to think about economics but rather *how* to think about economics. The "what"—the facts and descriptions of the economy—can always be found in books. The value of an economics education is the ability to think critically about economic problems and *to understand how* an economy works. This understanding of the essential forces governing how an economy works comes through the mastery of economic theory and model-building.

# Self-Test

## True/False and Explain

### Definition of Economics

1. Economics explains how we use unlimited resources to satisfy limited wants.

2. Economics studies the choices people make to cope with scarcity and the institutions that influence and reconcile choices.

### Two Big Economic Questions

3. In economics, the definition of "land" includes nonrenewable resources but excludes renewable resources.

4. In economics, the definition of "capital" includes financial assets like stocks and bonds.

5. Entrepreneurs bear the risks arising from the business decisions they make.

6. "How do choices determine *what*, *how*, and *for whom* goods and services are produced?" is one of the big economic questions.

7. "When do choices made in the pursuit of the social interest also promote self-interest?" is one of the big economic questions.

8. Choices made in the pursuit of self-interest always promote the social interest.

## The Economic Way of Thinking

**9.** When the opportunity cost of an activity increases, the incentive to choose that activity increases.

**10.** Tradeoffs and opportunity costs are the key concepts for understanding the economic way of thinking.

**11.** Economists assume that it is human nature for all people to act selfishly.

## Economics as Social Science and Policy Tool

**12.** A positive statement is about what is, while a normative statement is about what will be.

**13.** Economists test positive statements about how the world works to weed out those that are wrong.

**14.** The main economics policy tool is to compare total costs and total benefits to find the solution with the greatest gain.

**15.** Economics is a useful policy tool for governments and businesses, but not for individuals.

# Multiple-Choice

## Definition of Economics

1. The fact that human wants cannot be fully satisfied with available resources is called the problem of
   a. opportunity cost.
   b. scarcity.
   c. normative economics.
   d. what to produce.
   e. who will consume.

2. The problem of scarcity exists
   a. only in economies with government.
   b. only in economies without government.
   c. in all economies.
   d. only when people have not optimized.
   e. now, but will be eliminated with economic growth.

3. Scarcity differs from poverty because
   a. resources exceed wants for the rich.
   b. wants exceed resources even for the rich.
   c. the rich do not have to make choices.
   d. the poor do not have any choices.
   e. the poor do not have any wants.

4. The branch of economics that studies the choices of individual households and firms is called
   a. macroeconomics.
   b. microeconomics.
   c. positive economics.
   d. normative economics.
   e. home economics.

**5.** Microeconomics studies all of the following *except* the
   **a.** decisions of individual firms.
   **b.** effects of government safety regulations on the price of cars.
   **c.** global economy as a whole.
   **d.** prices of individual goods and services.
   **e.** effects of taxes on the price of beer.

## Two Big Economic Questions

**6.** The two big economic questions
   **a.** arise from scarcity.
   **b.** summarize the scope of economics.
   **c.** describe choices we make.
   **d.** examine incentives that influence choices.
   **e.** are all of the above.

**7.** The first big economic question about goods and services includes all of the following *except*
   **a.** *what* to produce.
   **b.** *why* produce.
   **c.** *how* to produce.
   **d.** *what* quantities to produce.
   **e.** *who* gets what is produced.

**8.** The trends over the past 60 years in what we produce show that _____ has expanded and _____ has shrunk.
   **a.** manufacturing; services
   **b.** manufacturing; agriculture
   **c.** agriculture; services
   **d.** agriculture; manufacturing
   **e.** services; agriculture

**9.** All of the following are resources *except*
    **a.** natural resources.
    **b.** tools.
    **c.** entrepreneurship.
    **d.** government.
    **e.** land.

**10.** The knowledge and skill obtained from education and training is
    **a.** labour.
    **b.** human capital.
    **c.** physical capital.
    **d.** entrepreneurship.
    **e.** technological know-how.

**11.** Which statement about incomes earned by factors of production is *false*?
    **a.** Land earns rent.
    **b.** Natural resources earn rent.
    **c.** Labour earns wages.
    **d.** Capital earns profit.
    **e.** Entrepreneurship earns profit.

**12.** When boats fish in international waters, that is certainly a(n)
    **a.** self-interested choice.
    **b.** altruistic choice.
    **c.** globalization choice.
    **d.** factor of production choice.
    **e.** choice in the social interest.

## The Economic Way of Thinking

**13.** When the government chooses to use resources to build a dam, those resources are no longer available to build a highway. This illustrates the concept of
   **a.** a market.
   **b.** macroeconomics.
   **c.** opportunity cost.
   **d.** a "how" tradeoff.
   **e.** the big tradeoff.

**14.** The opportunity cost of attending university
   **a.** depends on what you expect to earn with your degree.
   **b.** must be greater than the money cost of attending university.
   **c.** must be less than the money cost of attending university.
   **d.** depends on your major.
   **e.** depends on what you could earn now.

**15.** Renata has the chance to either attend an economics lecture or play tennis. If she chooses to attend the lecture, the value of playing tennis is
   **a.** greater than the value of the lecture.
   **b.** not comparable to the value of the lecture.
   **c.** equal to the value of the lecture.
   **d.** the opportunity cost of attending the lecture.
   **e.** zero.

**16.** Which of the following sayings best describes opportunity cost?
   **a.** "Make hay while the sun shines."
   **b.** "Money is the root of all evil."
   **c.** "Boldly go where no one has gone before."
   **d.** "There's no such thing as a free lunch."
   **e.** "Baseball has been very good to me."

**17.** Marginal benefit is the
   a. total benefit of an activity.
   b. additional benefit of a decrease in an activity.
   c. additional benefit of an increase in an activity.
   d. opportunity cost of a decrease in an activity.
   e. opportunity cost of an increase in an activity.

**18.** Monika will choose to eat a seventh pizza slice if
   a. the marginal benefit of the seventh slice is greater than its marginal cost.
   b. the marginal benefit of the seventh slice is less than its marginal cost
   c. the total benefit of all seven slices is greater than their total cost.
   d. the total benefit of all seven slices is less than their total cost.
   e. she is training to be a Sumo wrestler.

**19.** Economists assume that
   a. self-interested actions are all selfish actions.
   b. consumers and producers pursue their self-interest while politicians and public servants pursue the social interest.
   c. incentives are key in reconciling self-interest and the social interest.
   d. all people pursue the social interest.
   e. human nature changes as incentives change.

## Economics as Social Science and Policy Tool

**20.** A positive statement is
   a. about what ought to be.
   b. about what is.
   c. always true.
   d. capable of evaluation as true or false by observation and measurement.
   e. **b** and **d**.

**21.** Which of the following is a positive statement?

  **a.** Low rents will restrict the supply of housing.

  **b.** High interest rates are bad for the economy.

  **c.** Housing costs too much.

  **d.** Owners of apartment buildings ought to be free to charge whatever rent they want.

  **e.** Government should control the rents that apartment owners charge.

**22.** A normative statement is a statement regarding

  **a.** what is usually the case.

  **b.** the assumptions of an economic model.

  **c.** what ought to be.

  **d.** the predictions of an economic model.

  **e.** what is.

**23.** Which of the following statements is normative?

  **a.** Scientists should not make normative statements.

  **b.** Warts are caused by handling toads.

  **c.** As compact disc prices fall, people will buy more of them.

  **d.** If income increases, sales of luxury goods will fall.

  **e.** None of the above.

**24.** Which of the following statements is *false*?
An economic model

  **a.** is tested by comparing predictions with the facts.

  **b.** is difficult to test because of the simultaneous operation of many factors.

  **c.** tests only positive economic statements.

  **d.** can be tested using natural and economic experiments

  **e.** includes all aspects of the economic world.

**25.** The common element to making personal, business, and government policy decisions is to evaluate

  **a.** total benefits and total costs to find greatest gain.

  **b.** marginal benefits and marginal costs to find greatest gain.

  **c.** marginal benefits and marginal costs to find highest marginal benefit.

  **d.** marginal benefits and marginal costs to find lowest marginal costs.

  **e.** average benefits and average costs to find greatest gain.

## Short Answer Problems

**1.** "If all people would only economize, the problem of scarcity would be solved." Agree or disagree, and explain why.

2. Ashley, Doug, and Mei-Lin are planning to travel from Halifax to Sydney. The trip takes one hour by airplane and five hours by train. The air fare is $100 and train fare is $60. They all have to take time off from work while travelling. Ashley earns $5 per hour in her job, Doug $10 per hour, and Mei-Lin $12 per hour.

Calculate the opportunity cost of air and train travel for each person. Assuming they are all economizers, how should each of them travel to Sydney?

3. Suppose the government builds and staffs a hospital to provide "free" medical care.

   a. What is the opportunity cost of the free medical care?

   b. Is it free from the perspective of society as a whole?

**4.** Branko loves riding the bumper cars at the amusement park, but he loves the experience a little less with each successive ride. In estimating the benefit he receives from the rides, Branko would be willing to pay $10 for his first ride, $7 for his second ride, and $4 for his third ride. Rides actually cost $5 apiece for as many rides as Branko wants to take. This information is summarized in Table 1.

| TABLE 1 | | | |
|---|---|---|---|
| Ride | 1st | 2nd | 3rd |
| Marginal benefit | 10 | 7 | 4 |
| Marginal cost | 5 | 5 | 5 |

**a.** If Branko chooses by comparing total benefit and total cost, how many rides will he take?

**b.** If Branko chooses by comparing marginal benefit and marginal cost, how many rides will he take?

**c.** Is Branko better off by choosing according to total or marginal benefit and cost? Explain why.

Ⓒⓣ **5.** Assume Branko's benefits are the same as in Short Answer Problem **4**. Starting fresh, if the price of a bumper car ride rises to $8, how many rides will Branko now take? Explain why.

**6.** Indicate whether each of the following statements is positive or normative. If it is normative (positive), rewrite it so that it becomes positive (normative).

   **a.** The government ought to reduce the size of the deficit to lower interest rates.

   **b.** Government imposition of a tax on tobacco products will reduce their consumption.

**7.** Perhaps the biggest economic question is "How can we organize our lives so that when each of us makes choices in our self-interest, these choices also promote the social interest?" When Nike builds a factory in Malaysia and pays workers far less than North American wages, it is acting in its own corporate self-interest. What questions do you need to ask to decide if this is also in the social interest?

**8.** Suppose your friend, who is a history major, claims that economic models are useless because they are so unrealistic. He claims that since the models leave out so many descriptive details about the real world, they can't possibly be useful for understanding how the economy works. How would you defend your decision to study economics?

# Answers

## True/False and Explain

1. **F** Limited resources and unlimited wants. (1–2)

2. **T** This is the full definition of economics—the institutional aspect is often omitted for brevity. (1–2)

3. **F** "Land" includes all natural resources, whether non-renewable (oil) or renewable (forests). (3–7)

4. **F** "Capital" only consists of physical equipment like tools and buildings used in production. (3–7)

5. **T** Entrepreneurs earn profits in return for bearing the risks of organizing labour, land, and capital. (3–7)

6. **T** See text discussion. (3–7)

7. **F** When do choices made in the pursuit of self-interest also promote the social interest? (3–7)

8. **F** Markets often provide incentives so that pursuit of self-interest also promotes social interest, but self-interest and social interest sometimes conflict. (3–7).

9. **F** Incentive decreases because activity is now more expensive. (8–9)

10. **T** Scarcity requires choice, choice involves tradeoffs, and tradeoffs involve opportunity cost. (8–9)

11. **F** Economists assume people act in their self-interest, but self-interested actions are not necessarily selfish actions, if what makes you happy is to help others. (10)

12. **F** Normative statements are about what *ought* to be. (10)

13. **T** Test *positive* statements. (10)

14. **F** Compare *marginal* benefits and *marginal* costs. (10)

15. **F** Useful for personal, business, government policy. (10)

## Multiple-Choice

1. **b** Definition. (1–2)

2. **c** With infinite wants and finite resources, scarcity will never be eliminated. (1–2)

3. **b** Poverty is a low level of resources. But wants exceed resources for everyone, necessitating choice. (1–2)

4. **b** Definition. (1–2)

5. **c** Macroeconomic topic. (1–2)

6. **e** Economics explains choices created by scarcity and incentives that help reconcile self-interest and social interest. (3–7)

7. **b** *Why* is not part of first big question. (3–7)

8. **e** Services have expanded; agriculture and manufacturing have shrunk. (3–7)

9. **d** Government is a social institution. (3–7)

10. **b** Definition. (3–7)

11. **d** Capital earns interest. (3–7)

ⓒⓣ 12. **a** Certainly in the fishing company's self-interest; not altruistic or in social interest depending on benefits and costs. (3–7)

13. **c** Highway is forgone alternative. (8–9)

14. **e** What you must give up, *not* what you will earn. May be more or less than money cost. (8–9)

15. **d** Choosing lecture means its value > tennis. Tennis = (highest-valued) forgone alternative to lecture. (8–9)

16. **d** Every choice involves a cost. (8–9)

17. **c** Definition; **e** is marginal cost, **b** and **d** are nonsense. (8–9)

18. **a** Choices are made at the margin, when marginal benefit exceeds marginal cost. (8–9)

19. **c** Assume human nature is given and all people pursue self-interest. When self-interested choices are not in the social interest, there are wrong incentives. (8–9)

20. **e** Definition. (10)

21. **a** While **a** may be evaluated as true or false, other statements are matters of opinion. (10)

22. **c** Key word for normative statements is *ought*. (10)

23. **a** Key word is *should*. Even statement **b** is positive. (10)

24. **e** Includes only relevant aspects and ignores others. (10)

25. **b** See text discussion. (10)

## Short Answer Problems

1. Disagree. If everyone economized, then we would be making the best possible use of our resources and would be achieving the greatest benefits or satisfaction possible, given the limited quantity of resources. But this does not mean that we would be satisfying all of our limitless needs. The problem of scarcity can never be "solved" as long as people have infinite needs and finite resources for satisfying those needs.

2. The main point is that the total opportunity cost of travel includes the best alternative value of travel time as well as the train or air fare. The total costs of train and air travel for Ashley, Doug, and Mei-Lin are calculated in Table 2.

   On the basis of the cost calculation in Table 2, Ashley should take the train, Mei-Lin should take the plane, and Doug could take either.

| TABLE 2 | | |
|---|---|---|
| **Traveller** | **Train** | **Plane** |
| **Ashley** | | |
| (a) Fare | $ 60 | $ 100 |
| (b) Opportunity cost of travel time at $5/hr | $ 25 | $ 5 |
| **Total cost** | **$ 85** | **$ 105** |
| **Doug** | | |
| (a) Fare | $ 60 | $ 100 |
| (b) Opportunity cost of travel time at $10/hr | $ 50 | $ 10 |
| **Total cost** | **$ 110** | **$ 110** |
| **Mei-Lin** | | |
| (a) Fare | $ 60 | $ 100 |
| (b) Opportunity cost of travel time at $12/hr | $ 60 | $ 12 |
| **Total cost** | **$ 120** | **$ 112** |

**3. a.** Even though medical care may be offered without charge ("free"), there are still opportunity costs. The opportunity cost of providing such health care is the highest-valued alternative use of the resources used in the construction of the hospital, and the highest-valued alternative use of the resources (including human resources) used in the operation of the hospital.

**b.** These resources are no longer available for other activities and therefore represent a cost to society.

ⓒ **4. a.** If Branko rides as long as total benefit is greater than total cost, he will take 3 rides.

Total benefit (cost) can be calculated by adding up the marginal benefit (cost) of all rides taken. Before taking any rides, his total benefit is zero and his total cost is zero. The first ride's marginal benefit is $10, which when added to 0 yields a total benefit of $10. The first ride's marginal cost is $5, which when added to zero yields a total cost of $5. Total cost is less than total benefit, so Branko takes the first ride. For the first and second rides together, total benefit is $17, which is greater than total cost of $10. For all 3 rides together, total benefit is $21, which is greater than total cost of $15.

**b.** If Branko compares the marginal benefit of each ride with its marginal cost, he will only take 2 rides. He will take the first ride because its marginal benefit ($10) is greater than its marginal cost ($5). After the first ride, he will still choose to take the second ride because its marginal benefit ($7) is greater than its marginal cost ($5). But he will quit after the second

ride. The third ride would add a benefit of $4, but it costs $5, so Branko would be worse off by taking the third ride.

**c.** The marginal rule for choosing will make Branko better off. It would be a mistake to pay $5 for the third ride when it is only worth $4 to Branko. He would be better off taking that final $5 and spending it on something (the roller coaster?) that gives him a benefit worth at least $5.

You will learn much more about applying marginal analysis to choices like Branko's in Chapters 2 and 5.

ⓒ **5. a.** If the price of a bumper car rises to $8, Branko now takes only 1 ride. He will take the first ride because its marginal benefit ($10) is greater than its marginal cost ($8). After the first ride, he will quit. The marginal benefit of the second ride ($7) is now less than its marginal cost ($8).

**6. a.** The given statement is normative. The following is positive: If the government reduces the size of the deficit, interest rates will fall.

**b.** The given statement is positive. The following is normative: The government ought to impose a tax on tobacco products.

**7.** Questions must identify benefits and costs that need to be compared. Some of the many possible questions are: Even though the Malaysian workers earn less than North Americans, are they better off or worse off with these jobs? As consumers in North America, are we better off or worse off with shoes being produced more cheaply in Malaysia? Are workers in North America better off or worse off with the Malaysian

Nike plant? How do we define the social interest when people from many countries are involved?

You don't yet have enough information to answer these questions, but economics provides a way of thinking about them that makes it easier to come to a well-reasoned conclusion.

©⊕ **8.** A brief answer to your friend's challenge appears in Helpful Hint **3**. Models are like maps, which are useful precisely because they abstract from real-world detail. A useful map offers a simplified view, which is carefully selected according to the purpose of the map. No mapmaker would claim that the world is as simple as her map, and economists do not claim that the real economy is as simple as their models. What economists claim is that their models isolate the simplified effect of some real forces (like optimizing behaviour) operating in the economy, and yield predictions that can be tested against real-world data.

Another way to answer your friend would be to challenge him to identify what a more realistic model or theory would look like. You would do well to quote Milton Friedman (a Nobel Prize winner in economics) on this topic: "A theory or its 'assumptions' cannot possibly be thoroughly 'realistic' in the immediate descriptive sense.... A completely 'realistic' theory of the wheat market would have to include not only the conditions directly underlying the supply and demand for wheat but also the kind of coins or credit instruments used to make exchanges; the personal characteristics of wheat-traders such as the color of each trader's hair and eyes, ... the number of members of his family, their characteristics,... the kind of soil on which the wheat was grown,... the weather prevailing during the growing season;... and so on indefinitely. Any attempt to move very far in achieving this kind of 'realism' is certain to render a theory utterly useless." From Milton Friedman, "The Methodology of Positive Economics," in *Essays in Positive Economics* (Chicago: University of Chicago Press, 1953), p. 32.

# 1 Appendix: Graphs in Economics

## Key Concepts

### Graphing Data

Graphs represent quantity as a distance. On a two-dimensional graph,

- horizontal line is *x-axis*.
- vertical line is *y-axis*.
- intersection (0) is the *origin*.

A **scatter diagram** shows the relationship between two variables, one measured on the *x*-axis, the other measured on the *y*-axis. Correlation between variables does not necessarily imply causation.

Misleading graphs often break the axes or stretch/compress measurement scales to exaggerate or understate variation. Always look closely at the values and labels on axes before interpreting a graph.

### Graphs Used in Economic Models

Graphs showing relationships between variables fall into four categories:

- **Positive (direct) relationship**—variables move together in same direction: upward-sloping.
- **Negative (inverse) relationship**—variables move in opposite directions: downward-sloping.

- Relationships with a maximum/minimum:
  - Relationship slopes upward, reaches a maximum (zero slope), and then slopes downward.
  - Relationship slopes downward, reaches a minimum (zero slope), and then slopes upward.
- Unrelated (independent) variables—one variable changes while the other remains constant; graph is a vertical or horizontal straight line.

## The Slope of a Relationship

**Slope** of a relationship is change in value of a variable on *y*-axis divided by change in value of a variable on *x*-axis.

- $\Delta$ means "change in."
- Formula for slope is $\Delta y / \Delta x$ = rise/run.
- Straight line (**linear relationship**) has a constant slope.
  - A positive, upward-sloping relationship has a positive slope.
  - A negative, downward-sloping relationship has a negative slope.
- A curved line has a varying slope, calculated
  - *at a point*—draw straight line tangent to curve at that point and calculate slope of the line.
  - *across an arc*—draw straight line across two points on curve and calculate slope of the line.

## Graphing Relationships Among More Than Two Variables

Relationships among more than two variables can be graphed by holding constant the values of all variables except two. This is done by making a ***ceteris paribus*** assumption—"other things remain the same."

# Helpful Hints

1. Throughout the text, relationships among economic variables will almost invariably be represented and analyzed graphically. An early, complete understanding of graphs will greatly facilitate your mastery of the economic analysis in later chapters. Avoid the common mistake of assuming that a superficial understanding of graphs will be sufficient.

2. If you have limited experience with graphical analysis, this appendix is crucial to your ability to understand later economic analysis. You will likely find significant rewards in occasionally returning to this appendix for review. If you are experienced in constructing and using graphs, this appendix may be "old hat." Even so, you should skim it and work through the Self-Test in this *FlexText Workbook*.

3. Slope is a *linear* concept since it is a property of a straight line. For this reason, the slope is constant along a straight line but is different at different points on a curved (nonlinear) line. For the slope of a curved line, we actually calculate the slope of a straight line. The text presents two alternatives for calculating the slope of a curved line: (1) slope at a point and (2) slope across an arc. The first of these calculates the slope of the *straight line* that just touches (is tangent to) the curve at a point. The second calculates the slope of the *straight line* formed by the arc between two points on the curved line.

4. A straight line on a graph can also be described by a simple equation. The general form for the equation of a straight line is

$$y = a + bx$$

If you are given such an equation, you can graph the line by finding the y-intercept (where the line intersects the vertical y-axis), finding the x-intercept (where the line intersects the horizontal x-axis), and then connecting those two points with a straight line:

To find the y-intercept, set $x = 0$.

$$y = a + b(0)$$
$$y = a$$

To find the $x$-intercept, set $y = 0$.

$$0 = a + bx$$
$$x = -a/b$$

Connecting these two points $((x = 0, y = a)$ and $(x = -a/b, y = 0))$ or $(0, a)$ and $(-a/b, 0)$ allows you to graph the straight line. For any straight line with the equation of the form $y = a + bx$, the slope of the line is $b$. Fig. A1 illustrates a line where $b$ is a *negative* number, so there is a *negative* relationship between the variables $x$ and $y$.

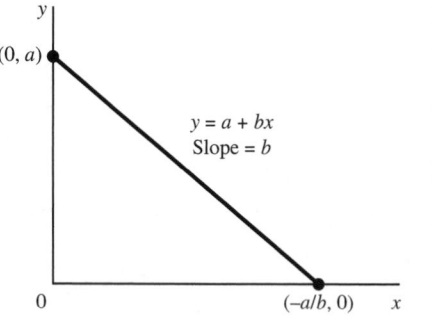

▲ **FIGURE A1**

To see how to apply this general equation, consider this example:

$$y = 6 - 2x$$

To find the $y$-intercept, set $x = 0$.

$$y = 6 - 2(0)$$
$$y = 6$$

To find the $x$-intercept, set $y = 0$.

$$0 = 6 - 2x$$
$$x = 3$$

Connecting these two points, $(0, 6)$ and $(3, 0)$, yields the line in Fig. A2.

The slope of this line is $-2$. Since the slope is negative, there is a negative relationship between the variables $x$ and $y$.

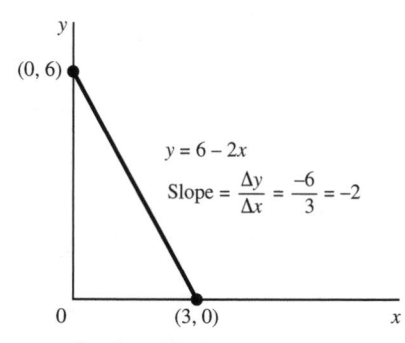

▲ **FIGURE A2**

# Self-Test

## True/False and Explain

### Graphing Data

1. Stretching or compressing the scale on an axis can be misleading.

2. A graph with a break in the axes must be misleading.

3. If a scatter diagram shows a clear relationship between variables $x$ and $y$, then $x$ must cause $y$.

### Graphs Used in Economic Models

4. If the graph of the relationship between two variables slopes upward (to the right), the graph has a positive slope.

5. The graph of the relationship between two variables that are in fact unrelated is always vertical.

## The Slope of a Relationship

**6.** In Fig. A3, the relationship between $y$ and $x$ is first negative, reaches a minimum, and then becomes positive as $x$ increases.

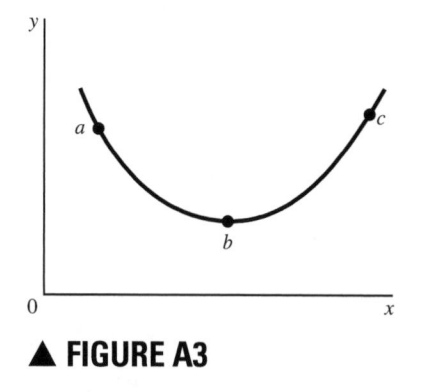

**▲ FIGURE A3**

**8.** In Fig. A3, the slope of the curve is increasing as we move from point $b$ to point $c$.

**7.** In Fig. A3, the value of $x$ is a minimum at point $b$.

**9.** In Fig. A3, the slope of the curve is approaching zero as we move from point $a$ to point $b$.

**10.** The slope of a straight line is calculated by dividing the change in the value of the variable measured on the horizontal axis by the change in the value of the variable measured on the vertical axis.

**11.** For a straight line, if a small change in $y$ is associated with a large change in $x$, the slope is large.

**12.** For a straight line, if a large change in $y$ is associated with a small change in $x$, the line is steep.

**13.** The slope of a curved line is not constant.

## Graphing Relationships Among More Than Two Variables

**14.** *Ceteris paribus* means "other things change."

**15.** Relationships between three variables can be displayed on a two-dimensional graph.

# Multiple-Choice

## Graphing Data

1. A point with a negative *x-coordinate* must be
   a. below the horizontal axis.
   b. above the horizontal axis.
   c. to the left of the vertical axis.
   d. to the right of the vertical axis.
   e. below the vertical axis.

2. A point's position on a graph is best described by its
   a. slope.
   b. coordinates.
   c. origin.
   d. causation.
   e. correlation.

3. Which of the following statements is *false*?
   a. The intersection of the *x-axis* and *y-axis* is the origin.
   b. Breaks in a graph's axes can be misleading.
   c. Breaks in a graph's axes can highlight a relationship.
   d. A causal relationship must imply a correlation.
   e. A correlation must imply a causal relationship

## Graphs Used in Economic Models

4. From the data in Table A1, it appears that
   a. *x* and *y* have a negative relationship.
   b. *x* and *y* have a positive relationship.
   c. there is no relationship between *x* and *y*.
   d. there is first a negative and then a positive relationship between *x* and *y*.
   e. there is first a positive and then a negative relationship between *x* and *y*.

| TABLE A1 | | |
|---|---|---|
| Year | x | y |
| 2004 | 6.2 | 143 |
| 2005 | 5.7 | 156 |
| 2006 | 5.3 | 162 |

**5.** If variables *x* and *y* move up and down together, they are said to be
   **a.** positively related.
   **b.** negatively related.
   **c.** conversely related.
   **d.** unrelated.
   **e.** trendy.

## The Slope of a Relationship

**7.** In Fig. A4 the relationship between *x* and *y* as *x* increases is
   **a.** positive with slope decreasing.
   **b.** negative with slope decreasing.
   **c.** negative with slope increasing.
   **d.** positive with slope increasing.
   **e.** positive with slope first increasing then decreasing.

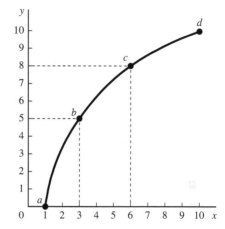

▲ **FIGURE A4**

**6.** The relationship between two variables that move in opposite directions is shown graphically by a line that is
   **a.** positively sloped.
   **b.** relatively steep.
   **c.** relatively flat.
   **d.** negatively sloped.
   **e.** curved.

**8.** What is the slope across the arc between *b* and *c* in Fig. A4?
   **a.** 1/2
   **b.** 2/3
   **c.** 1
   **d.** 2
   **e.** 3

**9.** In Fig. A4, consider the slopes of arc *ab* and arc *bc*. The slope at point *b* is difficult to determine exactly, but it must be

**a.** greater than 5/2.

**b.** about 5/2.

**c.** between 5/2 and 1.

**d.** about 1.

**e.** less than 1.

**10.** In Table A2, suppose that *w* is the independent variable measured along the horizontal axis. The slope of the line relating *w* and *u* is

**a.** positive with a decreasing slope.

**b.** negative with a decreasing slope.

**c.** positive with an increasing slope.

**d.** negative with a constant slope.

**e.** positive with a constant slope.

| TABLE A2 | | | | |
|---|---|---|---|---|
| *w* | 2 | 4 | 6 | 8 | 10 |
| *u* | 15 | 12 | 9 | 6 | 3 |

**11.** Refer to Table A2. Suppose that *w* is the independent variable measured along the horizontal axis. The slope of the line relating *w* and *u* is

**a.** +3.

**b.** −3.

**c.** −2/3.

**d.** +3/2.

**e.** −3/2.

**12.** In Fig. A5, if household income increases by $1,000, household expenditure will

**a.** increase by $1,333.

**b.** decrease by $1,333.

**c.** remain unchanged.

**d.** increase by $1,000.

**e.** increase by $750.

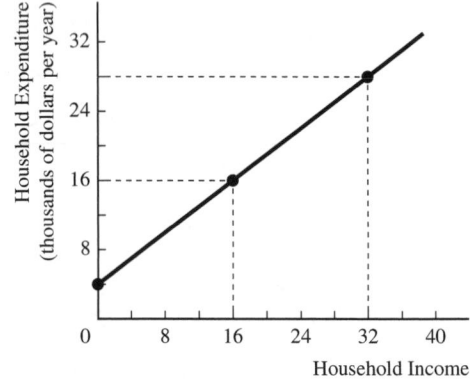

▲ **FIGURE A5**

**13.** In Fig. A5, if household income is zero, household expenditure is

   **a.** 0.

   **b.** −$4,000.

   **c.** $4,000.

   **d.** $8,000.

   **e.** impossible to determine from the graph.

**14.** In Fig. A5, if household expenditure is $28,000, household income is

   **a.** $36,000.

   **b.** $32,000.

   **c.** $28,000.

   **d.** $25,000.

   **e.** none of the above.

**15.** At all points along a straight line, slope is

   **a.** positive.

   **b.** negative.

   **c.** constant.

   **d.** zero.

   **e.** none of the above.

**16.** What is the slope of the line in Fig. A6?

   **a.** 2

   **b.** $1/2$

   **c.** 3

   **d.** $1/3$

   **e.** −3

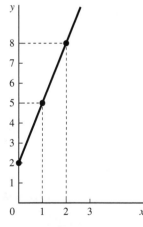

▲ **FIGURE A6**

**17.** If the line in Fig. A6 were to continue down to the $x$-axis, what would the value of $x$ be when $y$ is zero?

  **a.** 0
  **b.** 2
  **c.** 2/3
  **d.** −2/3
  **e.** −3/2

**18.** If the equation of a straight line is $y = 6 + 3x$, the slope is
  **a.** −3 and the $y$-intercept is 6.
  **b.** −3 and the $y$-intercept is −2.
  **c.** 3 and the $y$-intercept is 6.
  **d.** 3 and the $y$-intercept is −2.
  **e.** 3 and the $y$-intercept is −6.

**19.** If the equation of a straight line is $y = 8 - 2x$, then the slope is
  **a.** −2 and the $x$-intercept is −4.
  **b.** −2 and the $x$-intercept is 4.
  **c.** −2 and the $x$-intercept is 8.
  **d.** 2 and the $x$-intercept is −4.
  **e.** 2 and the $x$-intercept is 4.

## Graphing Relationships Among More Than Two Variables

**20.** To graph a relationship among more than two variables, what kind of assumption is necessary?
  **a.** normative
  **b.** positive
  **c.** linear
  **d.** independence of variables
  **e.** *ceteris paribus*

**21.** Given the data in Table A3, holding income constant, the graph relating the price of strawberries (vertical axis) to the purchases of strawberries (horizontal axis)

   **a.** is a vertical line.

   **b.** is a horizontal line.

   **c.** is a positively sloped line.

   **d.** is a negatively sloped line.

   **e.** reaches a minimum.

| TABLE A3 | | |
|---|---|---|
| Weekly Family Income ($) | Price per Box of Strawberries ($) | Number of Boxes Purchased per Week |
| 300 | $1.00 | 5 |
| 300 | $1.25 | 3 |
| 300 | $1.50 | 2 |
| 400 | $1.00 | 7 |
| 400 | $1.25 | 5 |
| 400 | $1.50 | 4 |

**22.** Given the data in Table A3, suppose family income decreases from $400 to $300 per week. Then the graph relating the price of strawberries (vertical axis) to the purchases of strawberries (horizontal axis) will

   **a.** become negatively sloped.

   **b.** become positively sloped.

   **c.** shift rightward.

   **d.** shift leftward.

   **e.** no longer exist.

**23.** Given the data in Table A3, holding price constant, the graph relating family income (vertical axis) to the purchases of strawberries (horizontal axis) is a

   **a.** vertical line.

   **b.** horizontal line.

   **c.** positively sloped line.

   **d.** negatively sloped line.

   **e.** positively or negatively sloped line, depending on the price that is held constant.

**24.** In Fig. A7, $x$ is

    **a.** positively related to $y$ and negatively related to $z$.

    **b.** positively related to both $y$ and $z$.

    **c.** negatively related to $y$ and positively related to $z$.

    **d.** negatively related to both $y$ and $z$.

    **e.** greater than $z$.

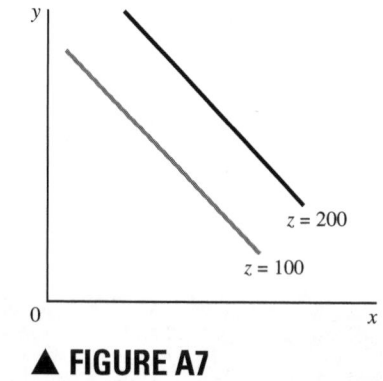

▲ **FIGURE A7**

**25.** In Fig. A7, a decrease in the value of $z$ will cause, *ceteris paribus*,

    **a.** a decrease in the value of $x$.

    **b.** an increase in the value of $x$.

    **c.** an increase in the value of $y$.

    **d.** no change in the value of $y$.

    **e.** no change in the value of $x$.

## Short Answer Problems

**1.** On the grid on the next page, draw a graph of variables $x$ and $y$ that illustrates each of the following relationships:

    **a.** $x$ and $y$ move up and down together.

    **b.** $x$ and $y$ move in opposite directions.

    **c.** as $x$ increases $y$ reaches a maximum.

    **d.** as $x$ increases $y$ reaches a minimum.

    **e.** $x$ and $y$ move in opposite directions, but as $x$ increases $y$ decreases by larger and larger increments for each unit increase in $x$.

    **f.** $y$ is unrelated to the value of $x$.

    **g.** $x$ is unrelated to the value of $y$.

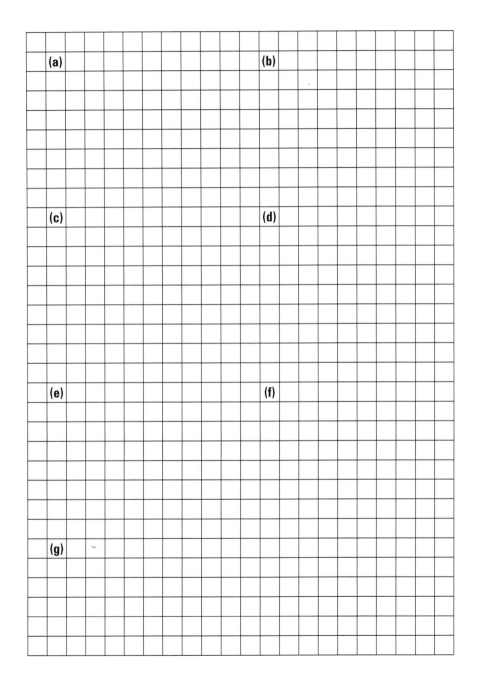

(a)

(b)

(c)

(d)

(e)

(f)

(g)

**2.** What does it mean to say that the slope of a line is $-2/3$?

**3.** Compute the slopes of the lines in Fig. A8(a) and (b).

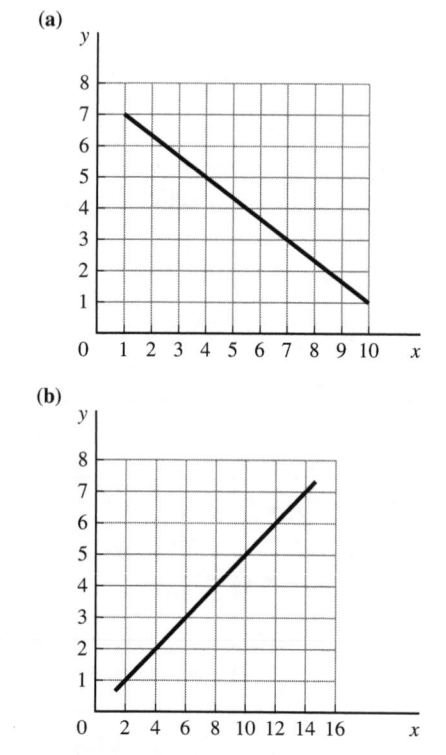

▲ **FIGURE A8**

**4.** On the grid, draw each of the following:

   **a.** a straight line with slope $-10$ and passing through the point (2, 80).

   **b.** a straight line with slope 2 and passing through the point (6, 10).

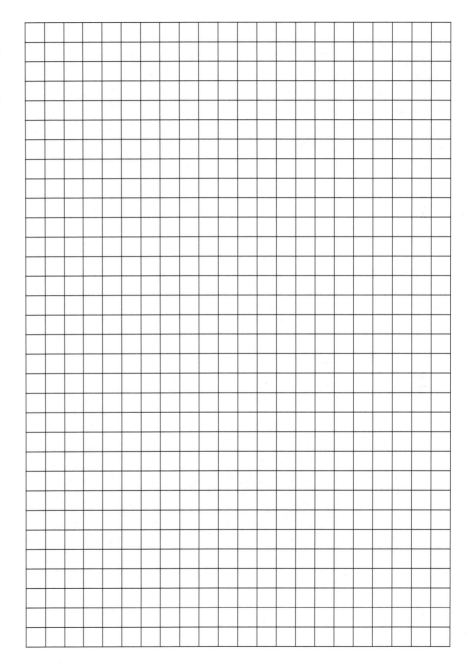

**5.** The equation for a straight line is $y = 4 - 2x$.

   **a.** Calculate the $y$-intercept, the $x$-intercept, and the slope.

**b.** On the grid, draw the graph of the line.

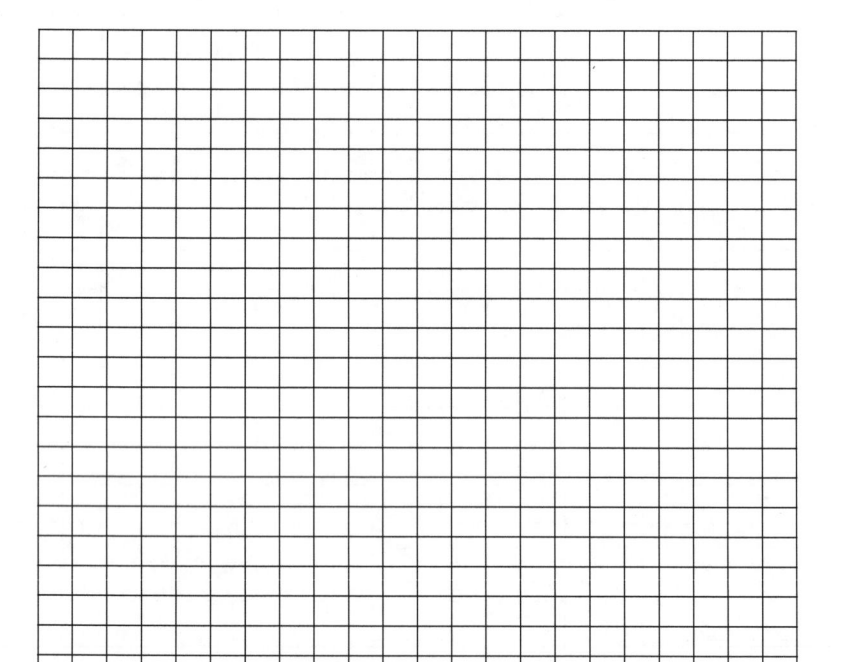

**6.** Explain two ways to measure the slope of a curved line.

**7.** Use the graph in Fig. A9 to compute the slope

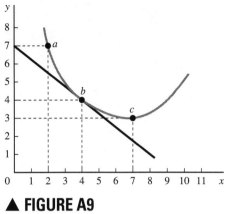

▲ **FIGURE A9**

**a.** across the arc between points $a$ and $b$.

**b.** at point $b$.

**c.** at point *c*, and explain your answer.

**8.** In Table A4, *x* represents the number of umbrellas sold per month, *y* represents the price of an umbrella, and *z* represents the average number of rainy days per month.

| TABLE A4 | | |
| --- | --- | --- |
| **Umbrellas Sold per Month (*x*)** | **Price per Umbrella (*y*)** | **Average Number of Rainy Days per Month (*z*)** |
| 120 | $10 | 4 |
| 140 | $10 | 5 |
| 160 | $10 | 6 |
| 100 | $12 | 4 |
| 120 | $12 | 5 |
| 140 | $12 | 6 |
| 80 | $14 | 4 |
| 100 | $14 | 5 |
| 120 | $14 | 6 |

**a.** Using the grid below, on the same diagram, graph the relationship between $x$ (horizontal axis) and $y$ (vertical axis) when $z = 4$, when $z = 5$, and when $z = 6$.

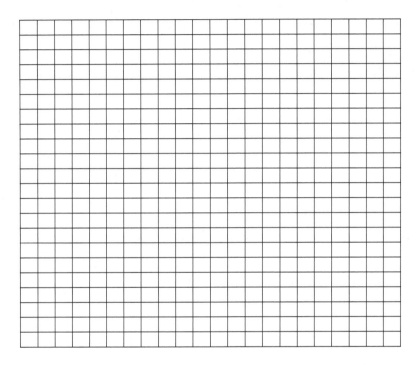

**b.** On average, it rains six days per month. This implies a certain average relationship between monthly umbrella sales and umbrella price. Suppose that the "greenhouse effect" reduces the average monthly rainfall to four days per month. What happens to the graph of the relationship between umbrella sales and umbrella prices?

**c.** Using the grid below, graph the relationship between $x$ (horizontal axis) and $z$ (vertical axis) when $y = \$10$ and when $y = \$12$. Is the relationship between $x$ and $z$ positive or negative?

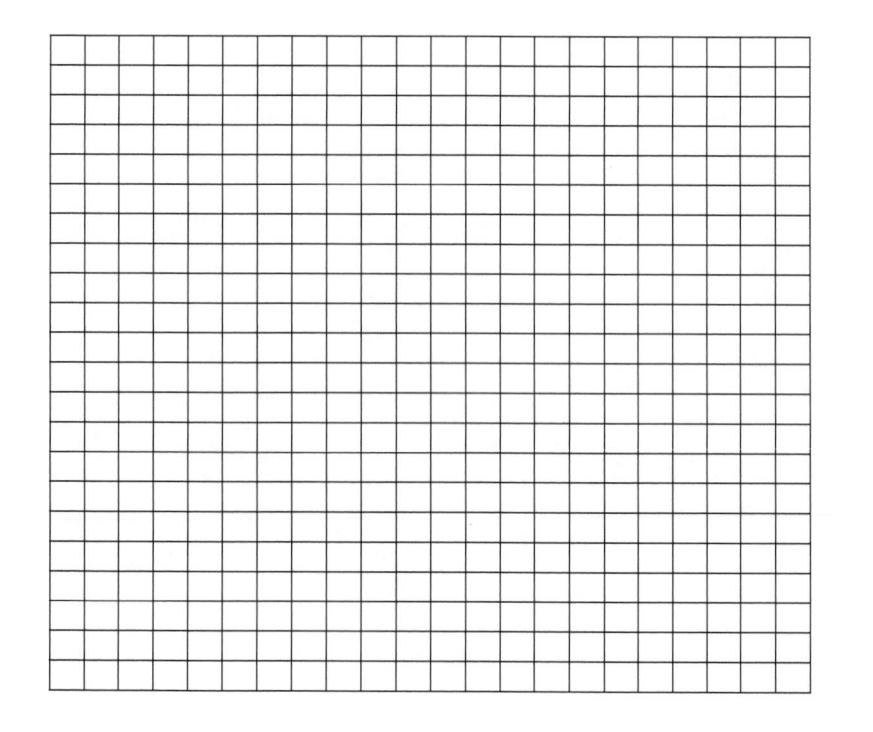

**d.** Using the grid below, graph the relationship between $y$ (horizontal axis) and $z$ (vertical axis) when $x = 120$ and when $x = 140$. Is the relationship between $y$ and $z$ positive or negative?

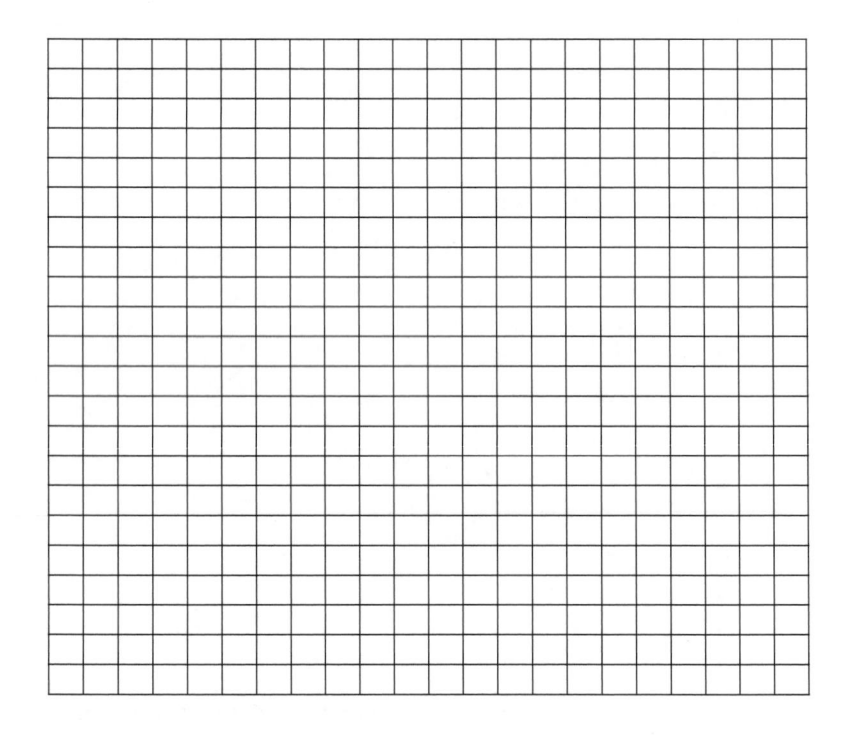

# Answers

## True/False and Explain

1. **T** Can exaggerate or hide relationships. (13–16)
2. **F** Breaks in the axes may be misleading, or may bring information into clearer view. (13–16)
3. **F** $x$ and $y$ are correlated, but correlation does not guarantee causation. (13–16)
4. **T** Upward-sloping curves/lines have positive slopes. (16–19)
5. **F** A graph of unrelated variables may be vertical or horizontal. (16–19)
6. **T** Arc $ab$ would have negative slope, arc $bc$ positive slope. (16–19)
7. **F** Value of $y$ is minimum at point $b$. (16–19)
8. **T** Curve becomes steeper, meaning $\Delta y$ is increasing faster than $\Delta x$, so slope is increasing. (20–22)
9. **T** At $b$, tangent has slope $= 0$, since $\Delta y = 0$ along the horizontal line through $b$. (20–22)
10. **F** Slope $= (\Delta$ variable on vertical $(y)$ axis$)/(\Delta$ variable on horizontal $(x)$ axis$)$. (20–22)
11. **F** Large slope means large $\Delta y$ associated with small $\Delta x$. (20–22)
12. **T** The steep line has a large slope, meaning large $\Delta y$ is associated with small $\Delta x$. (20–22)
13. **T** Slope of a straight line is constant. (20–22)
14. **F** "Other things remain the same." Only variables being studied are allowed to change. (22–23)
15. **T** A *ceteris paribus* assumption holds one variable constant, allowing the other two variables to be plotted in two dimensions. (22–23)

## Multiple-Choice

1. **c** Where $x$ values are less than 0. Depending on *y-coordinate*, may be above or below the horizontal axis. (13–16)
2. **b** Combination of *x-coordinate* and *y-coordinate*. (13–16)
3. **e** A high correlation may be a coincidence. (13–16)
4. **a** Higher values $x$ (6.2) associated with lower values $y$ (143). (16–19)
5. **a** Definition. (16–19)
6. **d** Graph may be steep, flat, or curved, but must have a negative slope. (16–19)
7. **a** Slope of arc $ab = +2.5$. Slope of arc $bc = +1$. (20–22)
8. **c** $\Delta y = 3(8 - 5)$; $\Delta x = 3(6 - 3)$. (20–22)
9. **c** $5/2$ is slope of $ab$, while 1 is slope of $bc$. (20–22)
10. **d** As $w$ increases, $u$ decreases. $\Delta u/\Delta w$ is constant. (20–22)
11. **e** Between any two points, $\Delta u = 3$, $\Delta w = -2$. (20–22)
12. **e** Slope $(\Delta y/\Delta x) = 3/4$. If $\Delta x$ ($\Delta$ household income) $= \$1,000$, then $\Delta y$ ($\Delta$ household expenditure) $= \$750 = $ ¾ of $\$1,000$. (20–22)

13. **c** Where the line intersects the household expenditure (*y*) axis. (20–22)

14. **b** From $28,000 on vertical (expenditure) axis, move across to line, then down to $32,000 on horizontal (income) axis. (20–22)

15. **c** Along straight line, the slope may or may not be **a**, **b**, or **d**. (20–22)

16. **c** Between any two points, $\Delta y = 3$ and $\Delta x = 1$. (20–22)

ct 17. **d** Equation of line is $y = 2 + 3x$. Solve for *x*-intercept (set $y = 0$). (20–22, 24–25)

18. **c** Use formula $y = a + bx$. Slope $= b$, *y*-intercept $= a$. (20–22, 24–25)

19. **b** Use formula $y = a + bx$. Slope $= b$, *x*-intercept $= -a/b$. (20–22, 24–25)

20. **e** Must hold constant other variables to isolate relationship between two variables. (22–23)

21. **d** Look either at data in the top 3 rows (income = 300) or data in bottom 3 rows (income = 400). Higher price is associated with lower purchases. (22–23)

ct 22. **d** At each price, fewer boxes will be purchased. (22–23)

ct 23. **c** For $P = 1$, two points on line are (5 boxes, $300) and (7 boxes, $400). Same relationship for other prices. (22–23)

24. **c** Increased *y* causes decreased *x* holding *z* constant. Increased *z* causes increased *x* holding *y* constant. (22–23)

ct 25. **a** Decreased *z* causes decreased *x* holding *y* constant. Decreased *z* causes decreased *y* holding *x* constant. (22–23)

## Short Answer Problems

1. Figures A10(a) through (g) illustrate the desired graphs.

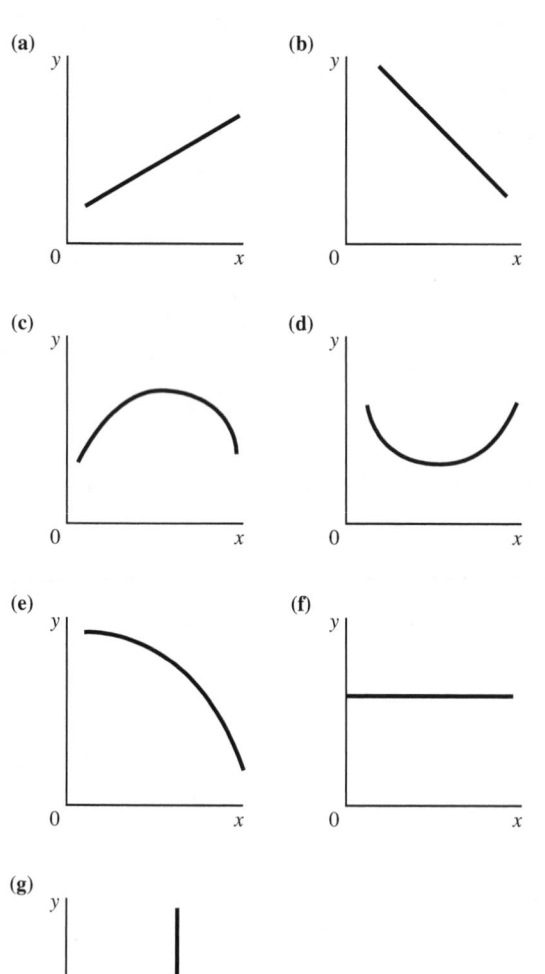

▲ **FIGURE A10**

**2.** The negative sign in the slope of $-2/3$ means that there is a negative relationship between the two variables. The value of $2/3$ means that when the variable measured on the vertical axis decreases by 2 units (the rise or $\Delta y$), the variable measured on the horizontal axis increases by 3 units (the run or $\Delta x$).

**3.** To find the slope, pick any two points on a line and compute $\Delta y/\Delta x$. The slope of the line in Fig. A8(a) is $-2/3$, and the slope of the line in Fig. A8(b) is $1/2$.

ⓒ **4. a.** The requested straight line is graphed in Fig. A11(a). First plot the point $(2, 80)$. Then pick a second point whose $y$-coordinate decreases by 10 for every 1 unit increase in the $x$-coordinate, for example, $(5, 50)$. The slope between the two points is $-30/3 = -10$.

  **b.** The requested straight line is graphed in Fig. A11(b). First plot the point $(6, 10)$. Then pick a second point whose $y$-coordinate decreases by 2 for every 1 unit decrease in the $x$-coordinate, for example, $(5, 8)$. The slope between the two points is $-2/-1 = 2$.

(a)

(b)
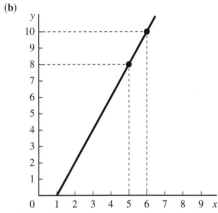

▲ **FIGURE A11**

**5. a.** To find the $y$-intercept, set $x = 0$.

$$y = 4 - 2(0)$$
$$y = 4$$

To find the $x$-intercept, set $y = 0$.

$$0 = 4 - 2x$$
$$x = 2$$

The slope of the line is $-2$, the value of the "$b$" coefficient on $x$.

**b.** The graph of the line is shown in Fig. A12.

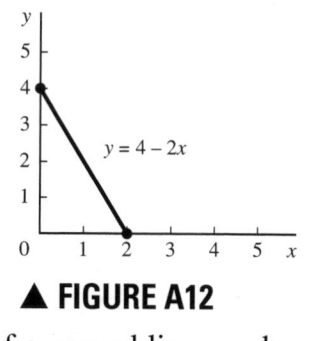

▲ **FIGURE A12**

**6.** The slope of a curved line can be measured at a point or across an arc. The slope at a point is measured by calculating the slope of the straight line that is tangent to (just touches) the curved line at the point. The slope across an arc is measured by calculating the slope of the straight line that forms the arc.

**7. a.** The slope across the arc between points *a* and *b* is $-3/2$.

**b.** The slope at point *b* is $-3/4$.

**c.** The slope at point *c* is zero because it is a minimum point. Nearby a minimum point the slope changes from negative to positive and must pass through zero, or no slope, to do so.

**8. a.** The relationships between *x* and *y* for $z = 4$, 5, and 6 are graphed in Fig. A13(a).

**b.** If the average monthly rainfall drops from 6 days to 4 days, the curve representing the relationship between umbrella sales and umbrella prices will shift from the curve labelled $z = 6$ to $z = 4$.

**c.** The relationships between *x* and *z* when *y* is $10 and when *y* is $12 are graphed in Fig. A13(b). The relationship between *x* and *z* is positive.

**d.** The relationships between *y* and *z* when $x = 120$ and when $x = 140$ are graphed in Fig. A13(c). The relationship between *y* and *z* is positive.

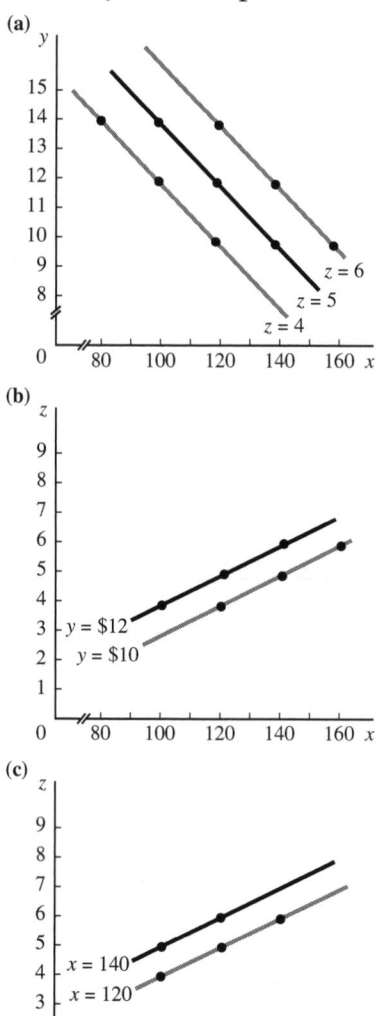

▲ **FIGURE A13**

# 2 The Economic Problem

## Key Concepts

### Production Possibilities and Opportunity Cost

The production possibility frontier (*PPF*)

- is the boundary between unattainable and attainable production possibilities.
- shows maximum combinations of outputs (goods and services) that can be produced with given resources and technology.

*PPF* characteristics:

- points on *PPF* represent **production efficiency**—outputs produced at the lowest possible cost.
- points inside *PPF* are inefficient—attainable, but not maximum combinations of outputs; they represent unused or misallocated resources.
- points on *PPF* are preferred to points inside *PPF*.
- points outside *PPF* are unattainable.
- choosing among efficient points on *PPF* involves an **opportunity cost** (highest-valued opportunity foregone) and a *tradeoff*.

*PPF*s are generally bowed outward (concave), reflecting increasing opportunity costs as more of a good is produced.

- *PPF* is bowed outward because resources are not equally productive in all activities (non-homogeneous). Resources most suitable for a given activity are the first to be used.

- Outward-bowed shape of *PPF* represents increasing opportunity cost—opportunity cost of good increases as its quantity produced increases.
- In moving between two points on *PPF* more of good *X* can be obtained only by producing less of good *Y*. Opportunity cost on *PPF* of additional *X* is amount of *Y* forgone.
- There is no opportunity cost in moving from point inside *PPF* to point on *PPF*.

## Using Resources Efficiently

To choose among points on *PPF*, compare

- **marginal cost**—the opportunity cost of producing one more unit of a good.

  - marginal cost curve slopes upwards because of *increasing opportunity cost*.

- **marginal benefit**—the benefit (measured in willingness to forgo other goods) from consuming one more unit of a good. Depends on **preferences**—likes, dislikes, and intensity of feelings.

  - **marginal benefit curve** slopes downwards because of *decreasing marginal benefit*.

We choose a point on *PPF* of **allocative efficiency** where

- outputs are produced at lowest possible cost, and in quantities providing greatest possible benefit
- marginal benefit = marginal cost.

## Economic Growth

**Economic growth** is the expansion of production possibilities—an outward shift of *PPF*.

- *PPF* shifts from changes in resources or technology.
- **Capital accumulation** and **technological change** shift *PPF* outward—economic growth.

- Opportunity cost of increased goods and services in future (economic growth through capital accumulation and technological progress) is decreased consumption today.

# Gains from Trade

Production increases if people *specialize* in the activity in which they have a comparative advantage.

- Person has **comparative advantage** in producing a good if she can produce at a lower opportunity cost than anyone else.
- When each person specializes in producing a good at which she has comparative advantage and exchanges for other goods, there are gains from trade.
- Specialization and exchange allow consumption (not production) at points outside *PPF*.
- Person has **absolute advantage** in producing a good if, using the same quantity of resources, she can produce more than anyone else.
  - Absolute advantage is irrelevant for specialization and gains from trade.
  - Even a person with an absolute advantage in producing all goods gains by specializing in an activity in which she has a comparative advantage and trading.

# Economic Coordination

Gains from trade and specialization require coordination. Decentralized coordination through markets depends on the social institutions of

- **firms**—hire and organize factors of production to produce and sell goods and services. Firms coordinate much economic activity, but the efficient size of a firm is limited.
- **markets**—coordinating buying and selling decisions through price adjustments.
- **property rights**—governing ownership, use, and disposal of resources, goods, and services.
- **money**—any generally acceptable means of payment; makes trading more efficient.

# Helpful Hints

1. This chapter reviews the absolutely critical concept of opportunity cost—the best alternative forgone—that was introduced in Chapter 1. Opportunity cost is a *ratio*. A helpful formula for opportunity cost, which works well in solving problems, especially problems that involve moving up or down a production possibility frontier (*PPF*), is:

$$\text{Opportunity Cost} = \frac{\text{Give Up}}{\text{Get}}$$

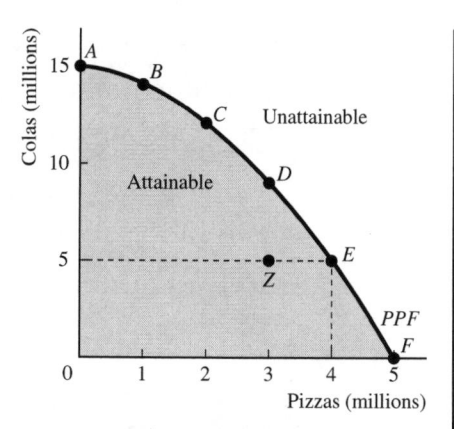

▲ **FIGURE 1 Production Possibilities Frontier**

Opportunity cost equals the quantity of goods you must give up divided by the quantity of goods you will get. This formula applies to all *PPF*s, whether they are linear or bowed out. To illustrate, look again at the bowed-out *PPF* as illustrated in Fig. 1:

First, consider an example of moving down the *PPF*. In moving from *C* to *D*, what is the opportunity cost of an additional pizza? This economy must give up 3 colas (12 – 9) to get 1 pizza (3 – 2). Substituting into the formula, the opportunity cost is:

$$\frac{3 \text{ colas}}{1 \text{ pizza}} = 3 \text{ colas per pizza}$$

Next, consider an example of moving up the *PPF*. In moving from *D* to *C*, what is the opportunity cost of an additional cola? We must give up 1 pizza (3 – 2) to get 3 colas (12 – 9). Substituting into the formula, the opportunity cost is:

$$\frac{1 \text{ pizza}}{3 \text{ colas}} = \frac{1}{3} \text{ pizza per colas}$$

Opportunity cost is always measured in the units of the forgone good.

**2.** Opportunity cost can also be related to the slope of the *PPF*. As we move down between any two points on the *PPF*, the opportunity cost of an additional unit of the good on the horizontal axis is:

$$|\text{slope of } PPF|$$

The slope of the *PPF* is negative, but economists like to describe opportunity cost in terms of a positive quantity of forgone goods. Therefore, we must use the absolute value of the slope to calculate the desired positive number.

As we move up between any two points on the *PPF*, the opportunity cost of an additional unit of the good on the vertical axis is:

$$\left|\frac{1}{\text{slope of } PPF}\right|$$

This is the *inverse* relation we saw between possibilities *C* and *D*. The opportunity cost of an additional pizza (on the horizontal axis) between *C* and *D* is 3 colas. The opportunity cost of an additional cola (on the vertical axis) between *D* and *C* is 1/3 pizza.

**3.** All points on a *PPF* achieve production efficiency in that they fully employ all resources. But how do we pick a point on the *PPF* and decide *what* combination of goods we want? The *PPF* provides information about resources and *costs*. But choosing what goods we want also requires information about *benefits*.

This choice, like all economic choices, is made at the margin. To decide what goods we want, compare the marginal cost (*MC*) and marginal benefit (*MB*) of different combinations. Marginal cost is the opportunity cost of producing one more unit. The marginal cost of producing more of any good increases as we move along the *PPF*. Marginal benefit is the benefit received from consuming one more unit. Marginal benefit decreases as we consume more of any good.

If the marginal cost of a good exceeds the marginal benefit, we decrease production of the good. If the marginal benefit exceeds the marginal cost, we increase production. When marginal cost equals marginal benefit for every good, we have chosen the goods that we value most highly. The decision rule of *MB* = *MC* yields an *efficient* allocation of resources.

4. The colas and pizza production possibility frontier assumes that resources are *not* equally productive in all activities. Resources with such differences are also called nonhomogeneous resources. As a result of this assumption, opportunity cost increases as we increase the production of either good. In moving from possibility *C* to *D*, the opportunity cost per unit of pizza is 3 colas. But in increasing pizza production from *D* to *E*, the opportunity cost per unit of pizza increases to 4 colas. In producing the first 1 (million) pizzas, we use the resources best suited to pizza production. As we increase pizza production, however, we must use resources that are less well suited to pizza production—hence increasing opportunity cost. A parallel argument accounts for the increasing opportunity cost of increasing cola production.

It is also possible to construct an even simpler model of a *PPF* that assumes resources are equally productive in all activities, or homogeneous resources. As a result of this assumption, opportunity cost is constant as we increase production of either good. Constant opportunity cost means that the *PPF* will be a straight line (rather than bowed out). As you will see in some of the following exercises, such a simple model is useful for illustrating the principle of comparative advantage, without having to deal with the complications of increasing opportunity cost.

5. This chapter gives us our first chance to develop and use economic models. It is useful to think about the nature of these models in the context of the general discussion of models in Chapter 1. For example, one model in this chapter is a representation of the production possibilities in the two-person and two-good world of Liz and Joe. The model abstracts greatly from the complexity of the real world in which there are billions of people and numerous different kinds of goods and services. The model allows us to explain a number of phenomena that we observe in the world such as specialization and exchange.

The production possibilities model also has some implications or predictions. For example, countries that devote a larger proportion of their resources to capital accumulation will have more rapidly expanding production possibilities. The model can be subjected to "test" by comparing these predictions to the facts we observe in the real world.

# Self-Test

## True/False and Explain

### Production Possibilities and Opportunity Cost

Refer to the production possibility frontier (*PPF*) in Fig. 2 for Questions **1** to **4**.

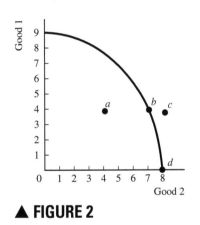

▲ **FIGURE 2**

**1.** Point *a* is not attainable.

**2.** The opportunity cost of increasing the production of good 2 from 7 to 8 units is 4 units of good 1.

**3.** Point *c* is not attainable.

**4.** In moving from point *b* to point *d*, the opportunity cost of increasing the production of good 2 equals the absolute value of the slope of the *PPF* between *b* and *d*.

**7.** The principle of decreasing marginal benefit states that the more we have of a good, the *less* we are willing to pay for an additional unit of it.

## Using Resources Efficiently

**5.** The marginal cost of the 4th pizza is the cost of producing all 4 pizzas.

**8.** All points on a *PPF* represent both production efficiency and allocative efficiency.

## Economic Growth

**6.** The marginal benefit of good *X* is the amount of good *Y* a person is willing to forgo to obtain one more unit of *X*.

**9.** Economic growth, by shifting out the *PPF*, eliminates the problem of scarcity.

**10.** In a model where capital resources can grow, points on the *PPF* that have more consumption goods yield faster growth.

**13.** Nadim definitely has a comparative advantage in producing skateboards if he can produce more than Elle.

## Gains from Trade

**11.** With specialization and trade, a country can produce at a point outside its *PPF*.

## Economic Coordination

**14.** The incentives for specialization and exchange do not depend on property rights but only on differing opportunity costs.

**12.** Canada has no incentive to trade with a cheap-labour country like Mexico.

**15.** Price adjustments coordinate decisions in goods markets but not in factor markets.

# Multiple-Choice

## Production Possibilities and Opportunity Cost

1. If Harold can increase production of good *X* without decreasing the production of any other good, he
   a. is producing on his *PPF*.
   b. is producing outside his *PPF*.
   c. is producing inside his *PPF*.
   d. must have a linear *PPF*.
   e. must prefer good *X* to any other good.

2. The bowed-out (concave) shape of a *PPF*
   a. is due to the equal usefulness of resources in all activities.
   b. is due to capital accumulation.
   c. is due to technological change.
   d. reflects the existence of increasing opportunity cost.
   e. reflects the existence of decreasing opportunity cost.

3. The economy is at point *b* on the *PPF* in Fig. 3. The opportunity cost of producing one more unit of *X* is
   a. 1 unit of *Y*.
   b. 20 units of *Y*.
   c. 1 unit of *X*.
   d. 8 units of *X*.
   e. 20 units of *X*.

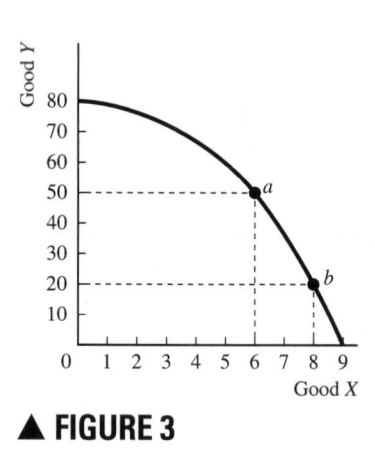

▲ **FIGURE 3**

**4.** Refer to the *PPF* in Fig. 3. Which of the following statements is *false*?

    **a.** Resources are not equally productive in all activities.

    **b.** Points inside the frontier represent unemployed resources.

    **c.** Starting at point *a*, an increase in the production of good *Y* will shift the frontier out.

    **d.** The opportunity cost of producing good *Y* increases as production of *Y* increases.

    **e.** Shifts in preferences for good *X* or good *Y* will not shift the frontier.

**5.** Refer to Fig. 4, which shows the *PPF* for an economy without discrimination operating at maximum efficiency. If discrimination against women workers is currently occurring in this economy, the elimination of discrimination would result in a(n)

    **a.** movement from *a* to *b*.

    **b.** movement from *b* to *c*.

    **c.** movement from *a* to *c*.

    **d.** outward shift of the *PPF*.

    **e.** inward shift of the *PPF*.

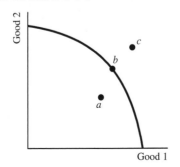

▲ **FIGURE 4**

Suppose a society produces only two goods—hockey sticks and maple leaves. Three alternative combinations on its *PPF* are given in Table 1. Use the information in Table 1 to answer Questions **6** and **7**.

| TABLE 1 Production Possibilities | | |
| --- | --- | --- |
| Possibility | Units of Hockey Sticks | Units of Maple Leaves |
| *a* | 3 | 0 |
| *b* | 2 | 3 |
| *c* | 0 | 9 |

**6.** In moving from combination *c* to combination *b*, the opportunity cost of producing one additional hockey stick is

    **a.** 2 maple leaves.

    **b.** 1/2 a maple leaf.

    **c.** 6 maple leaves.

    **d.** 1/6 a maple leaf.

    **e.** 3 maple leaves.

7. According to this *PPF*

    a. resources are equally productive in all activities.

    b. a combination of 3 hockey sticks and 9 maple leaves is attainable.

    c. a combination of 3 hockey sticks and 9 maple leaves would not employ all resources.

    d. the opportunity cost of producing hockey sticks increases as more hockey sticks are produced.

    e. the opportunity cost of producing hockey sticks decreases as more hockey sticks are produced.

## Using Resources Efficiently

8. The marginal benefit curve for a good

    a. shows the benefit a firm receives from producing one more unit.

    b. shows the amount a consumer is willing to pay for one more unit.

    c. is upward sloping.

    d. is bowed out.

    e. is none of the above.

9. With increasing production of food, its marginal benefit

    a. increases and marginal cost increases.

    b. increases and marginal cost decreases.

    c. decreases and marginal cost increases.

    d. decreases and marginal cost decreases.

    e. decreases and marginal cost is constant.

10. Suppose the *PPF* for skirts and pants is a straight line. As the production of skirts increases, the marginal benefit of skirts

    a. increases and marginal cost is constant.

    b. is constant and marginal cost increases.

    c. decreases and marginal cost decreases.

    d. decreases and marginal cost increases.

    e. decreases and marginal cost is constant.

**11.** With allocative efficiency, for each good produced, marginal
- **a.** benefit equals marginal cost.
- **b.** benefit is at its maximum.
- **c.** benefit exceeds marginal cost by as much as possible.
- **d.** cost exceeds marginal benefit by as much as possible.
- **e.** cost is at its minimum.

## Economic Growth

**12.** The *PPF* for wine and wool will shift if there is a change in
- **a.** the price of resources.
- **b.** the unemployment rate.
- **c.** the quantity of resources.
- **d.** preferences for wine and wool.
- **e.** all of the above.

**13.** A movement *along* a given *PPF* will result from
- **a.** technological change.
- **b.** change in the stock of capital.
- **c.** change in the labour force.
- **d.** all of the above.
- **e.** none of the above.

**14.** The opportunity cost of pushing the *PPF* outward is
- **a.** capital accumulation.
- **b.** technological change.
- **c.** reduced current consumption.
- **d.** the gain in future consumption.
- **e.** all of the above.

**15.** In general, the higher the proportion of resources devoted to technological research in an economy, the
  **a.** greater will be current consumption.
  **b.** faster the *PPF* will shift outward.
  **c.** faster the *PPF* will shift inward.
  **d.** closer it will come to having a comparative advantage in the production of all goods.
  **e.** more bowed out the shape of the *PPF* will be.

**16.** Refer to the *PPF* in Fig. 5. A politician who argues that "if our children are to be better off, we must invest now for the future" is recommending a current point like
  **a.** *a.*
  **b.** *b.*
  **c.** *c.*
  **d.** *d.*
  **e.** *e.*

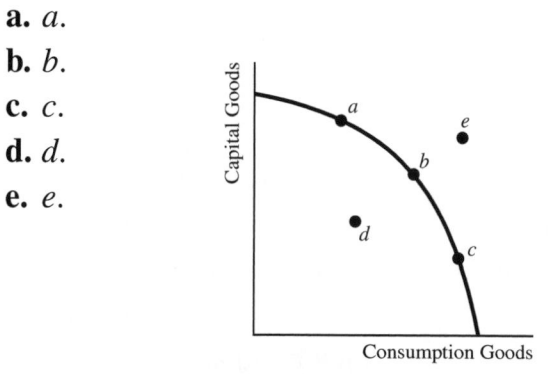

▲ **FIGURE 5**

**17.** Refer to the *PPF* in Fig. 5. The statement that "unemployment is a terrible waste of human resources" refers to a point like
  **a.** *a.*
  **b.** *b.*
  **c.** *c.*
  **d.** *d.*
  **e.** *e.*

## Gains from Trade

In an 8-hour day, Andy can produce either 24 loaves of bread or 8 kilograms of butter. In an 8-hour day, Rolfe can produce either 8 loaves of bread or 8 kilograms of butter. Use this information to answer Questions **18** and **19**.

**18.** Which of the following statements is *true*?
  **a.** Andy has an absolute advantage in butter production.
  **b.** Rolfe has an absolute advantage in butter production.
  **c.** Andy has an absolute advantage in bread production.
  **d.** Andy has a comparative advantage in butter production.
  **e.** Rolfe has a comparative advantage in bread production.

**19.** Andy and Rolfe

  **a.** can gain from exchange if Andy specializes in butter production and Rolfe specializes in bread production.

  **b.** can gain from exchange if Andy specializes in bread production and Rolfe specializes in butter production.

  **c.** cannot gain from exchange.

  **d.** can exchange, but only Rolfe will gain.

  **e.** can exchange, but only Andy will gain.

**20.** Mexico and Canada produce both oil and apples using labour only. A barrel of oil is produced with 4 hours of labour in Mexico and 8 hours of labour in Canada. A bushel of apples is produced with 8 hours of labour in Mexico and 12 hours of labour in Canada. Canada has

  **a.** an absolute advantage in oil production.

  **b.** an absolute advantage in apple production.

  **c.** a comparative advantage in oil production.

  **d.** a comparative advantage in apple production.

  **e.** none of the above.

**21.** In Portugal, the opportunity cost of a bale of wool is 3 bottles of wine. In England, the opportunity cost of 1 bottle of wine is 3 bales of wool. Given this information,

  **a.** England has an absolute advantage in wine production.

  **b.** England has an absolute advantage in wool production.

  **c.** Portugal has a comparative advantage in wine production.

  **d.** Portugal has a comparative advantage in wool production.

  **e.** no trade will occur.

**22.** To gain from comparative advantage, countries must not only trade, they must also

  **a.** save.

  **b.** invest.

  **c.** engage in research and development.

  **d.** engage in capital accumulation.

  **e.** specialize.

**23.** It takes Mom 30 minutes to cook dinner. In the same time she can iron 6 of your shirts. Dad takes 1 hour to cook dinner and 30 minutes to iron a single shirt. In this situation
  **a.** Dad has an absolute advantage in cooking dinner.
  **b.** Dad has an absolute advantage in ironing shirts.
  **c.** Mom should not cook dinner, as her opportunity cost is 6 shirts.
  **d.** there are no gains from trade.
  **e.** Mom should cook dinner, even though the opportunity cost is 12 shirts.

## Economic Coordination

**24.** Trade is organized using the social institutions of
  **a.** firms.
  **b.** property rights.
  **c.** money.
  **d.** markets.
  **e.** all of the above.

**25.** Markets
  1. enable buyers and sellers to get information.
  2. are defined by economists as geographical locations where trade occurs.
  3. coordinate buying and selling decisions through price adjustments.
  **a.** 1 only
  **b.** 3 only
  **c.** 1 and 3 only
  **d.** 2 and 3 only
  **e.** 1, 2, and 3

# Short Answer Problems

**1.** Why is a *PPF* negatively sloped? Why is it bowed out?

**2.** Suppose that an economy has the *PPF* shown in Table 2.

| Possibility | Maximum Units of Butter per Week | Maximum Units of Guns per Week |
|:---:|:---:|:---:|
| *a* | 200 | 0 |
| *b* | 180 | 60 |
| *c* | 160 | 100 |
| *d* | 100 | 160 |
| *e* | 40 | 200 |
| *f* | 0 | 220 |

**TABLE 2  Production Possibilities**

**a.** On the grid, plot these possibilities, label the points, and draw the *PPF*. (Put guns on the *x*-axis.)

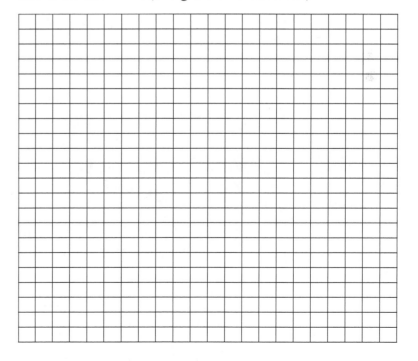

**b.** If the economy moves from possibility *c* to possibility *d*, the opportunity cost *per unit of guns* will be how many units of butter?

**d.** In general terms, what happens to the opportunity cost of guns as the output of guns increases?

**c.** If the economy moves from possibility *d* to possibility *e*, the opportunity cost *per unit of guns* will be how many units of butter?

**e.** In general terms, what happens to the opportunity cost of butter as the output of butter increases? What do the results in parts **d** and **e** imply about resources?

**f.** If (instead of the possibilities given) the *PPF* were a straight line joining points *a* and *f*, what would that imply about opportunity costs and resources?

**g.** Given the original *PPF* you have plotted, is a combination of 140 units of butter and 130 units of guns per week attainable? Would you regard this combination as an efficient one? Explain.

**h.** Given the original *PPF*, is a combination of 70 units of butter and 170 units of guns per week attainable? Does this combination achieve productive efficiency? Explain.

**3.** If the following events occurred (each is a separate event, unaccompanied by any other event), what would happen to the *PPF* in Short Answer Problem **2**?

**a.** A new, easily exploited energy source is discovered.

**b.** A large number of skilled workers immigrate into the country.

**c.** The output of butter increases.

**d.** A new invention increases output per person in the butter industry but not in the guns industry.

**e.** A new law is passed compelling workers, who could previously work as long as they wanted, to retire at age 60.

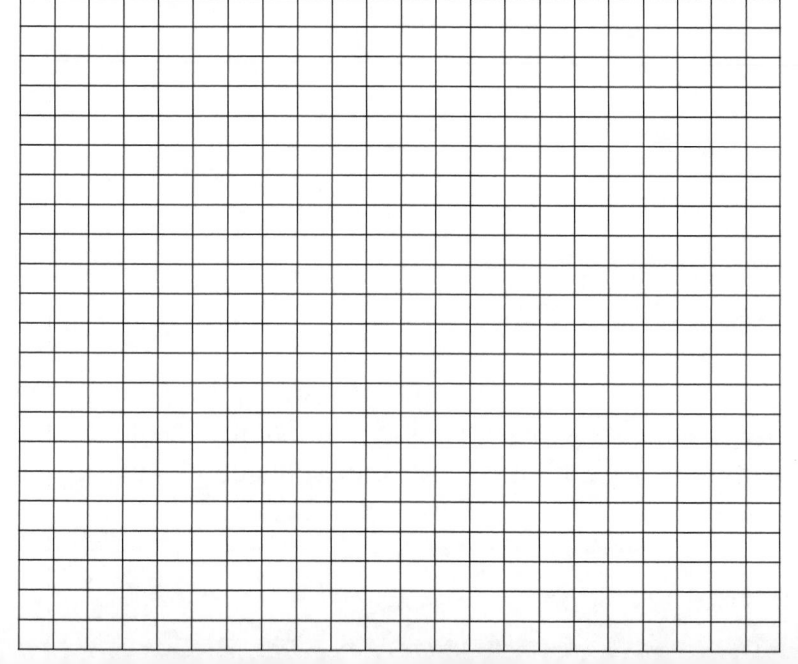

**4.** The Borg produce only two goods—cubes and transwarp coils—and want to decide where on their *PPF* to operate. Table 3 shows the marginal benefit and marginal cost of cubes, measured in the number of transwarp coils per cube.

| TABLE 3 | | |
|---|---|---|
| Borg Cubes | Marginal Benefit | Marginal Cost |
| 1 | 12 | 3 |
| 2 | 10 | 4 |
| 3 | 8 | 5 |
| 4 | 6 | 6 |
| 5 | 4 | 7 |
| 6 | 2 | 8 |

**a.** If the Borg are efficient (and they are!), what quantity of cubes will they produce?

**b.** If the Borg were to produce one more cube than your answer in **a**, why would that choice be inefficient?

**5.** Suppose the country of Quark has historically devoted 10 percent of its resources to the production of new capital goods. On the grid on the next page, use *PPF* diagrams to compare the consequences (costs and benefits) of each of the following:

**a.** Quark continues to devote 10 percent of its resources to the production of capital goods.

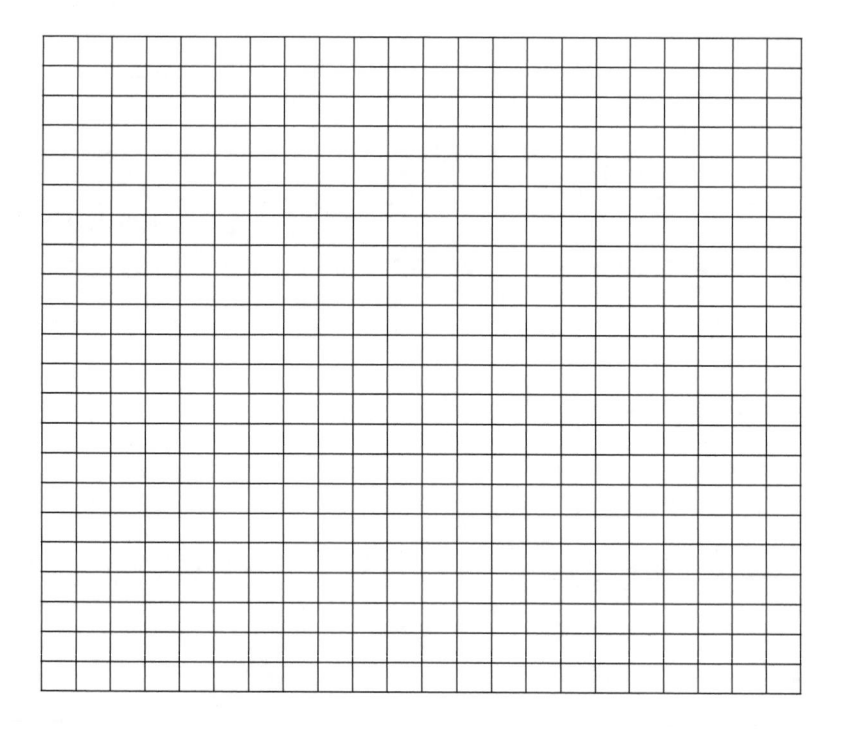

**b.** Quark begins now to permanently devote 20 percent of its resources to the production of capital goods.

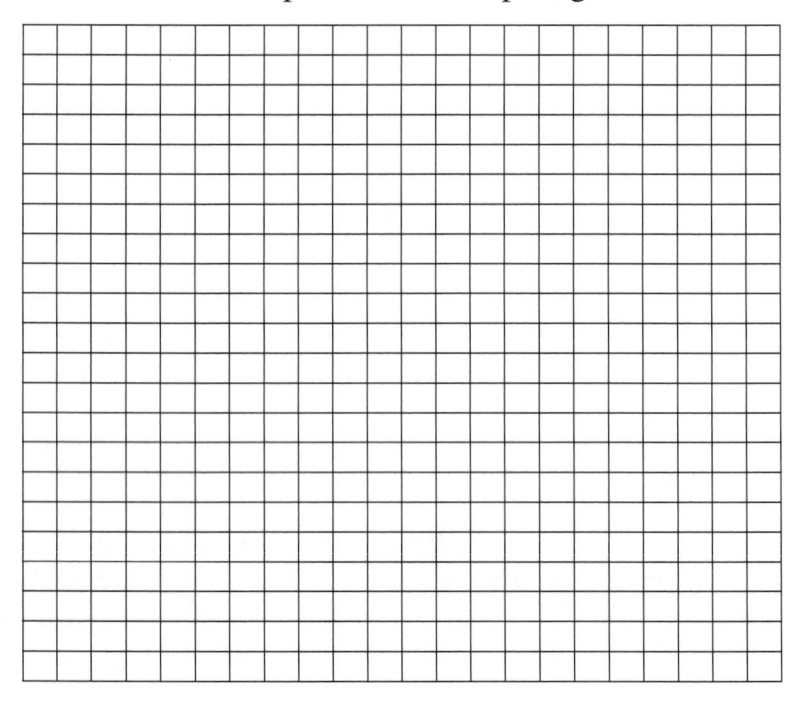

**6.** Lawyers earn $200 per hour while secretaries earn $15 per hour. Use the concepts of absolute and comparative advantage to explain why a lawyer who is a better typist than her secretary will still specialize in doing only legal work and will trade with the secretary for typing services.

**7.** France and Germany each produce both wine and beer, using a single, homogeneous input—labour. Their production possibilities are:

- France has 100 units of labour and can produce a maximum of 200 bottles of wine or 400 bottles of beer.
- Germany has 50 units of labour and can produce a maximum of 250 bottles of wine or 200 bottles of beer.

**a.** Complete Table 4.

| **TABLE 4** | | | | |
|---|---|---|---|---|
| | **Bottles Produced by I Unit of Labour** | | **Opportunity Cost of I Additional Bottle** | |
| | **Wine** | **Beer** | **Wine** | **Beer** |
| France | | | | |
| Germany | | | | |

Use the information in part **a** to answer the following questions.

**b.** Which country has an absolute advantage in wine production?

**c.** Which country has an absolute advantage in beer production?

**d.** Which country has a comparative advantage in wine production?

**e.** Which country has a comparative advantage in beer production?

**f.** If trade is allowed, describe what specialization, if any, will occur.

ⓒ **8.** Tova and Ron are the only two remaining inhabitants of the planet Melmac. They spend their 30-hour days producing widgets and woggles, the only two goods needed for happiness on Melmac. It takes Tova 1 hour to produce a widget and 2 hours to produce a woggle, while Ron takes 3 hours to produce a widget and 3 hours to produce a woggle.

**a.** For a 30-hour day, draw on the grid an individual *PPF* for Tova, then for Ron.

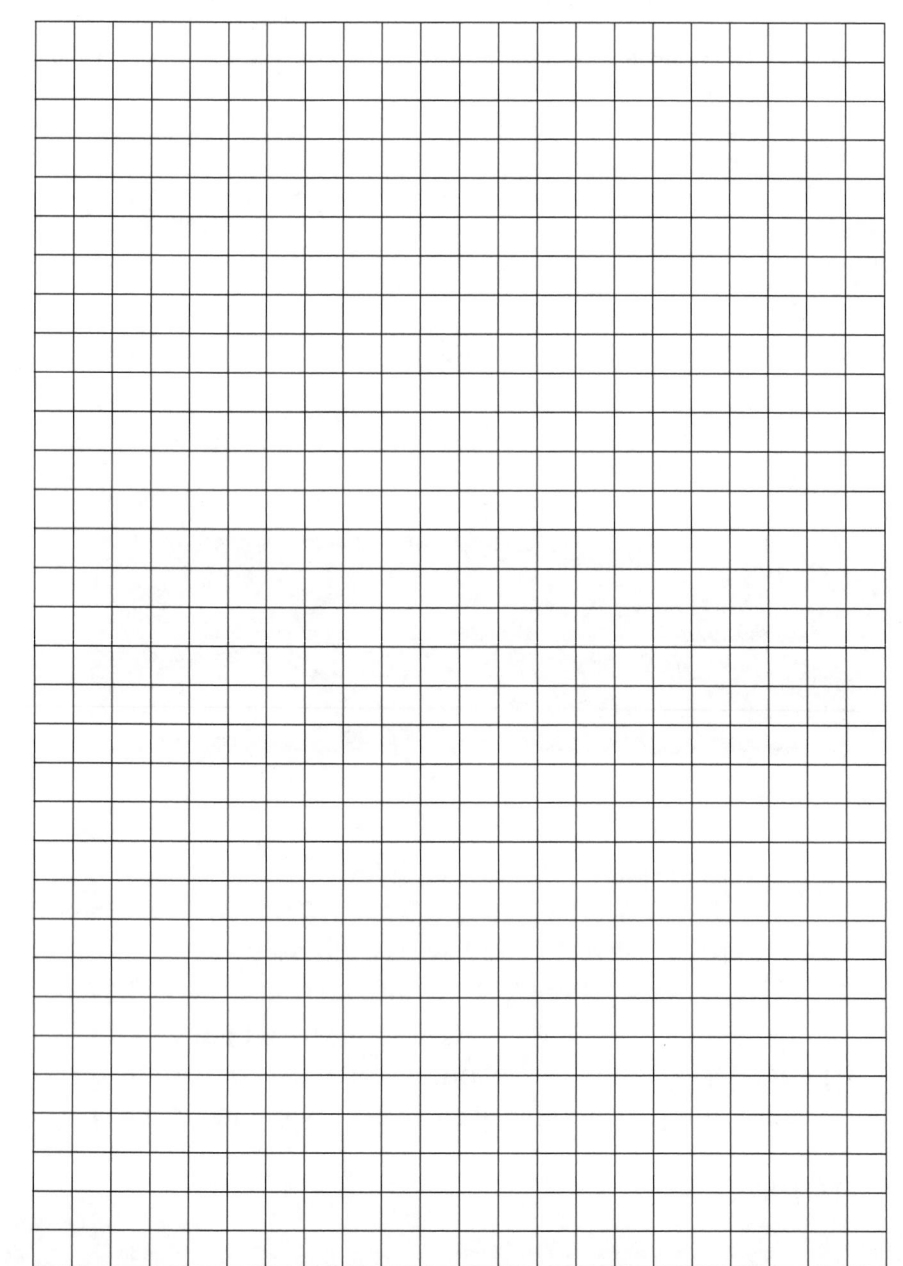

**b.** What does the shape of the *PPF*s tell us about opportunity costs? about resources?

**c.** Assume initially that Tova and Ron are each self-sufficient. Define self-sufficiency. Explain what the individual consumption possibilities are for Tova, then for Ron.

**d.** Who has an absolute advantage in the production of widgets? of woggles?

**e.** Who has a comparative advantage in the production of widgets? of woggles?

**f.** Suppose Tova and Ron each specialize in producing only the good in which she or he has a comparative advantage (one spends 30 hours producing widgets, the other spends 30 hours producing woggles). What will be the total production of widgets and woggles?

**g.** Suppose Tova and Ron exchange 7 widgets for 5 woggles. On your *PPF* diagrams, plot the new point of Tova's consumption, then of Ron's consumption. Explain how these points illustrate the gains from trade.

# Answers

## True/False and Explain

1. **F** Attainable but not an efficient point. (30–32)

2. **T** Moving from *b* to *d*, production good 1 decreases by 4 units. (30–32)

3. **T** Outside *PPF.* (30–32)

4. **T** See Helpful Hint **2**. (30–32)

5. **F** Marginal cost is the *additional* cost of producing the 4th pizza alone. (33–35)

6. **T** Marginal benefit is also the amount a person is willing to pay for one more unit, but payment in money ultimately represents an opportunity cost in goods forgone. (33–35)

7. **T** The more we have of a good, the smaller is the marginal benefit and hence the willingness to pay for it. (33–35)

8. **F** All points represent productive efficiency (efficient use of resources). But allocative efficiency only occurs at the single point (combination of goods) that we prefer above all others (where *MB* = *MC*). (33–35)

9. **F** Cost of growth is forgone current consumption. (36–37)

10. **F** Points with more capital goods yield faster growth. (36–37)

11. **F** Can *consume* at a point outside the *PPF*. (38–40)

12. **F** Mutually beneficial trade depends on comparative advantage, not absolute advantage. (38–40)

13. **F** Nadim has absolute advantage in skateboard production, but without information about opportunity costs, we don't know if he has comparative advantage. (38–40)

14. **F** Property rights are a prerequisite for specialization and exchange. (41–43)

15. **F** Price adjustments coordinate buying and selling decisions in all markets. (41–43)

## Multiple-Choice

1. **c** For 0 opportunity cost, there must be unemployed resources. (30–32)

2. **d** **a** would be true if *un*equal resources; **b** and **c** shift the *PPF*. (30–32)

3. **b** To increase quantity *X* to 9, must decrease quantity *Y* from 20 to 0. (30–32)

4. **c** Increased production of *Y* moves up *along* the *PPF*. (30–32)

5. **a** Discrimination causes underemployment of resources. Women are not allowed to produce up to their full abilities. (30–32)

6. **e** Give up 6 maple leaves to get 2 hockey sticks: 6/2 = 3 maple leaves per hockey stick. (30–32)

7. **a** Constant opportunity cost means resources are equally productive for producing all goods—see Helpful Hint **4**. (30–32)

8. **b** Benefits apply to consumers; the curve is downward sloping. (33–35)

9. **c** Principles of diminishing marginal benefit and increasing marginal cost. (33–35)

10. **e** Diminishing marginal benefit, but a linear *PPF* means constant opportunity and marginal costs. (33–35)

11. **a** Whenever *MB* ≠ *MC*, efficiency improves by real-locating resources to produce more goods with high marginal benefits, causing a decrease in their marginal benefit and increase in marginal cost. (33–35)

12. **c** Only changes in resources or technology shift the *PPF*. (36–37)

13. **e** **a**, **b**, and **c** all shift the *PPF*. (36–37)

14. **c** **a** and **b** cause an outward shift of the *PPF*, not opportunity cost; **d** is an effect of an outward shift in the *PPF*. (36–37)

15. **b** Technological change shifts *PPF* outward at the cost of current consumption. (36–37)

16. **a** Producing more capital goods now, shifts the *PPF* outward in the future. (36–37)

17. **d** Points inside the *PPF* represent unemployed resources, whether labour, capital, or land. (36–37)

18. **c** Andy produces 3 loaves bread per hour; Rolfe produces 1 loaf per hour—see Helpful Hint **5**. (38–40)

19. **b** Andy has comparative advantage (lower opportunity cost) in bread, Rolfe has comparative advantage in butter production. (38–40)

20. **d** Opportunity cost of oil in bushels of apples—Canada 2/3, Mexico 1/2. Opportunity cost of apples in barrels of oil—Canada 3/2, Mexico 2. (38–40)

21. **c** Opportunity cost of wine in bales of wool—Portugal 1/3, England 3. Opportunity cost of wool in bottles of wine—Portugal 3, England 1/3. (38–40)

22. **e** Gains from trade require specialization based on comparative advantage. **a–d** may increase productivity and absolute advantage, but not necessarily comparative advantage. (38–40)

23. **c** Dad has a comparative advantage cooking. (38–40)

24. **e** All 4 institutions are required for gains from trade and specialization through decentralized coordination. (41–43)

25. **c** 2 is the ordinary meaning of markets, not the economist's definition. (41–43)

## Short Answer Problems

1. The negative slope of the *PPF* reflects opportunity cost: in order to have more of one good, some of the other must be forgone. It is bowed out because the existence of resources not equally productive in all activities creates increasing opportunity cost as we increase the production of either good.

2. **a.** The graph of the *PPF* is given in Fig. 6.

▲ **FIGURE 6**

**b.** In moving from $c$ to $d$, in order to gain 60 units of guns, we must give up $160 - 100 = 60$ units of butter. The opportunity cost per unit of guns is

$$\frac{60 \text{ units butter}}{60 \text{ units guns}} = 1 \text{ unit butter per unit of guns}$$

**c.** In moving from $d$ to $e$, in order to gain 40 units of guns, we must give up $100 - 40 = 60$ units of butter. The opportunity cost per unit of guns is

$$\frac{60 \text{ units butter}}{40 \text{ units guns}} = 1.5 \text{ unit butter per unit of guns}$$

**d.** The opportunity cost of producing more guns increases as the output of guns increases.

**e.** Likewise, the opportunity cost of producing more butter increases as the output of butter increases. Increasing opportunity costs imply that resources are not equally productive in gun and butter production; that is, they are nonhomogeneous.

**f.** Opportunity costs would always be constant, regardless of the output of guns or butter. The opportunity cost per unit of guns would be

$$200/220 = 10/11 \text{ units of butter}$$

The opportunity cost per unit of butter would be

$$220/200 = 1.1 \text{ units of guns}$$

Constant opportunity costs imply that resources are equally productive in gun and butter production; that is, they are homogeneous.

**g.** This combination is outside the *PPF* and therefore is not attainable. Since the economy cannot produce this combination, the question of efficiency is irrelevant.

**h.** This combination is inside the *PPF* and is attainable. It is inefficient because the economy could produce more of either or both goods without producing less of anything else. Therefore some resources are not fully utilized.

**3. a.** Assuming that both goods require energy for their production, the entire *PPF* shifts out to the northeast as in Fig. 7(a).

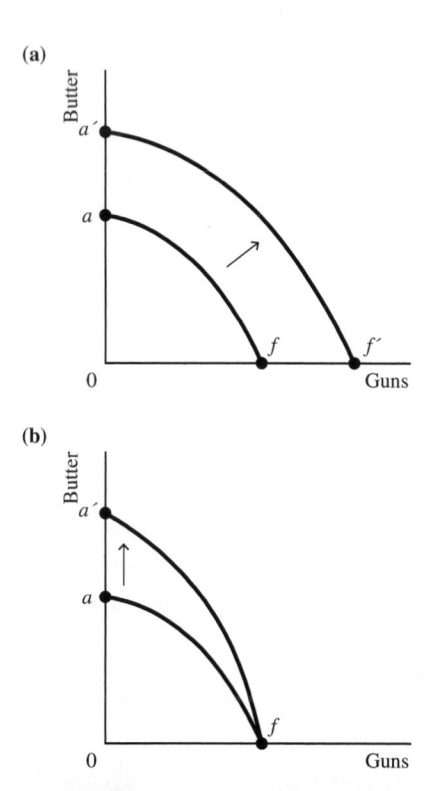

▲ **FIGURE 7**

**b.** Assuming that both goods use skilled labour in their production, the entire *PPF* shifts out to the northeast.

**c.** The *PPF* does not shift. An increase in the output of butter implies a movement along the *PPF* to the left, not a shift of the *PPF* itself.

**d.** The new invention implies that for every level of output of guns, the economy can now produce more butter. The *PPF* swings to the right, but remains anchored at point *f* as in Fig. 7(b).

**e.** The entire *PPF* shifts in toward the origin.

**4. a.** At the efficient quantity of output, marginal benefit = marginal cost. The Borg will produce 4 cubes (*MB* = *MC* = 4 transwarp coils/cube).

**b.** At 5 cubes, marginal benefit = 4 and marginal cost = 7. Since *MC* > *MB*, the Borg could better use their resources by shifting production out of cubes and into transwarp coils.

**5. a.** The situation for Quark is depicted in Fig. 8. Suppose Quark starts on *PPF*₁. If it continues to devote only

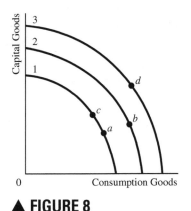

▲ **FIGURE 8**

10 percent of its resources to the production of new capital goods, it is choosing to produce at a point like *a*. This will shift the *PPF* out in the next period, but only to the curve labelled 2 (where, presumably, Quark will choose to produce at point *b*).

**b.** Starting from the same initial *PPF*, if Quark now decides to increase the resources devoted to the production of new capital to 20 percent, it will be choosing to produce at a point like *c*. In this case, next period's *PPF* will shift further—to curve 3, and a point like *d*, for example.

Thus in comparing points *a* and *c*, we find the following costs and benefits: point *a* has the benefit of greater present consumption but at a cost of lower future consumption; point *c* has the cost of lower present consumption, but with the benefit of greater future consumption.

**6.** The lawyer has an absolute advantage in producing both legal and typing services relative to the secretary. Nevertheless, she has a comparative advantage in legal services, and the secretary has a comparative advantage in typing. To demonstrate these comparative advantages, we can construct Table 5 of opportunity costs.

| TABLE 5 | | |
| --- | --- | --- |
| | **Opportunity Cost of I Additional Hour ($)** | |
| | **Legal Services** | **Typing** |
| Lawyer | 200 | 200 |
| Secretary | >200 | 15 |

Consider first the lawyer's opportunity costs. The lawyer's best forgone alternative to providing 1 hour of legal services is the $200 she could earn by providing another hour of legal services. If she provides 1 hour of typing, she is also forgoing $200 (1 hour) of legal services. What would the secretary have to forgo to provide 1 hour of legal services? He would have to spend 3 years in law school, forgoing 3 years of income in addition to the tuition he must pay. His opportunity cost is a very large number, certainly greater than $200. If he provides 1 hour of typing, his best forgone alternative is the $15 he could have earned at another secretarial job.

Thus Table 5 shows that the lawyer has a lower opportunity cost (comparative advantage) of providing legal services, and the secretary has a lower opportunity cost (comparative advantage) of providing typing services. It is on the basis of comparative advantage (not absolute advantage) that trade will take place from which both parties gain.

**7. a.** The completed table is shown here as Table 4 Solution.

**TABLE 4  Solution**

| | Bottles Produced by I Unit of Labour | | Opportunity Cost of I Additional Bottle | |
|---|---|---|---|---|
| | Wine | Beer | Wine | Beer |
| France | 2 | 4 | 2.0 beer | 0.50 wine |
| Germany | 5 | 4 | 0.8 beer | 1.25 wine |

**b.** Germany, which can produce more wine (5 bottles) per unit of input, has an absolute advantage in wine production.

**c.** Neither country has an absolute advantage in beer production, since beer output (4 bottles) per unit of input is the same for both countries.

**d.** Germany, with the lower opportunity cost (0.8 beer), has a comparative advantage in wine production.

**e.** France, with the lower opportunity cost (0.5 wine), has a comparative advantage in beer production.

**f.** The incentive for trade depends only on differences in comparative advantage. Germany will specialize in wine production and France will specialize in beer production.

ⓒ **8. a.** The individual *PPF*s for Tova and Ron are given by Fig. 9(a) and (b), respectively.

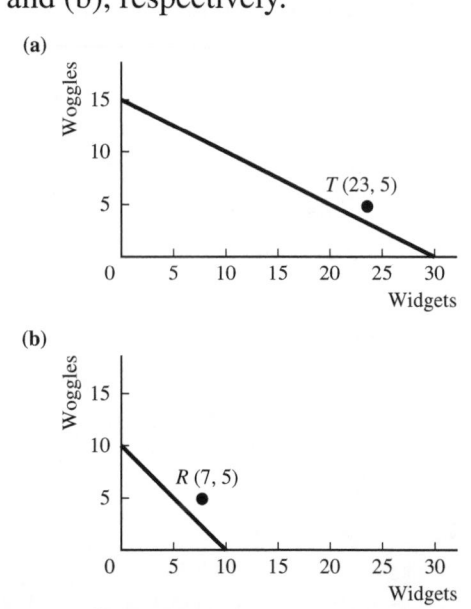

**FIGURE 9**

**b.** The linear shape of the *PPF*s tells us that opportunity costs are constant along each frontier and that resources are equally productive in all activities, or are homogeneous.

These linear *PPF*s with constant opportunity costs abstract from the complexity of the real world. The world generally has increasing opportunity costs, but that fact is not essential for understanding the gains from trade, which is the objective of this problem. Making the model more complex by including increasing opportunity costs would not change our results, but it would make it more difficult to see them.

**c.** Individuals are self-sufficient if they consume only what they produce. This means there is no trade. Without trade, Tova's (maximum) consumption possibilities are exactly the same as her production possibilities—points along her *PPF*. Ron's (maximum) consumption possibilities are likewise the points along his *PPF*.

**d.** Tova has an absolute advantage in the production of both widgets and woggles. Her absolute advantage can be defined either in terms of greater output per unit of inputs or fewer inputs per unit of output. A comparison of the *PPF*s in Fig. 9 shows that, for given inputs of 30 hours, Tova produces a greater output of widgets than Ron (30 versus 10) and a greater output of woggles than Ron (15 versus 10). The statement of the problem tells us equivalently that, per unit of output, Tova uses fewer inputs than Ron for both widgets (1 hour versus 3 hours) and woggles (2 hours versus 3 hours). Since Tova has greater productivity than Ron in the production of all goods (widgets and woggles), we say that overall she has an absolute advantage.

**e.** Tova has a comparative advantage in the production of widgets, since she can produce them at lower opportunity cost than Ron (1/2 woggle versus 1 woggle). On the other hand, Ron has a comparative advantage in the production of woggles, since he can produce them at a lower opportunity cost than Tova (1 widget versus 2 widgets).

**f.** Tova will produce widgets and Ron will produce woggles, yielding a total production between them of 30 widgets and 10 woggles.

**g.** After the exchange, Tova will have 23 widgets and 5 woggles (point *T*). Ron will have 7 widgets and 5 woggles (point *R*). These new post-trade consumption possibility points lie outside Tova's and Ron's respective pre-trade consumption (and production) possibilities. Hence trade has yielded gains that allow the traders to improve their consumption possibilities beyond those available with self-sufficiency.

# 3 Demand and Supply

## Key Concepts

### Markets and Prices

**Competitive market**—many buyers and sellers so no one can influence prices.
  **Relative price** of a good is

- its *opportunity cost*—the other goods that must be forgone to buy it.
- ratio of its **money price** to the money price of another good.
- determined by demand and supply.

### Demand

The **quantity demanded** of a good is the amount consumers plan to buy during a given time period at a particular price. The **law of demand** states: "Other things remaining the same, the higher the price of a good, the smaller is the quantity demanded." Higher price reduces quantity demanded for two reasons:

- *substitution effect*—with an increase in the relative price of a good, people buy less of it and more of substitutes for the good.
- *income effect*—with an increase in the relative price of a good and unchanged incomes, people have less money to spend on all goods, including the good whose price increased.

The **demand curve** represents the inverse relationship between quantity demanded and price, *ceteris paribus*. The demand curve also is a willingness-and-ability-to-pay curve, which measures marginal benefit.

- A change in price causes movement along the demand curve. This is called a **change in the quantity demanded**. The higher the price of a good, the lower the quantity demanded.
- A shift of the demand curve is called a **change in demand**. The demand curve shifts from changes in

  - prices of related goods.
  - expected future prices.
  - income.
  - expected future income and credit.
  - population.
  - preferences.

- Increase in demand—demand curve shifts rightward.
- Decrease in demand—demand curve shifts leftward.
- For an increase in

  - price of a **substitute**—demand shifts rightward.
  - price of a **complement**—demand shifts leftward.
  - expected future prices—demand shifts rightward.
  - income (**normal good**)—demand shifts rightward.
  - income (**inferior good**)—demand shifts leftward.
  - expected future income or credit (**normal good**)—demand shifts rightward.
  - expected future income or credit (**inferior good**)—demand shifts leftward
  - population—demand shifts rightward.
  - preferences—demand shifts rightward.

# Supply

The **quantity supplied** of a good is the amount producers plan to sell during a given time period at a particular price. The **law of supply** states: "Other things remaining the same, the higher the price of a good, the greater is the quantity supplied." Higher price increases quantity supplied because marginal cost increases with increasing quantities. Price must rise for producers to be willing to increase production and incur higher marginal cost.

The **supply curve** represents the positive relationship between quantity supplied and price, *ceteris paribus*. The supply curve is also a minimum-supply-price curve, showing the lowest price at which a producer is willing to sell another unit.

- A change in price causes movement along the supply curve. This is called a **change in the quantity supplied**. The higher the price of a good, the greater the quantity supplied.
- A shift of the supply curve is called a **change in supply**. The supply curve shifts from changes in
  - prices of factors of production.
  - prices of related goods produced.
  - expected future prices.
  - number of suppliers.
  - technology.
  - state of nature.
- Increase in supply—supply curve shifts rightward.
- Decrease in supply—supply curve shifts leftward.
- For an increase in
  - prices of factors of production—supply shifts leftward.
  - price of a *substitute in production*—supply shifts leftward.
  - price of a *complement in production*—supply shifts rightward.
  - expected future prices—supply shifts leftward.

- number of suppliers—supply shifts rightward.
- technology—supply shifts rightward.
- state of nature—supply shifts rightward.

## Market Equilibrium

The **equilibrium price** is where the demand and supply curves intersect—where quantity demanded equals quantity supplied.

- Above the equilibrium price, there is a surplus (quantity supplied > quantity demanded), and price will fall.
- Below the equilibrium price, there is a shortage (quantity demanded > quantity supplied), and price will rise.
- Only in equilibrium is there no tendency for the price to change. The **equilibrium quantity** is the quantity bought and sold at the equilibrium price.

## Predicting Changes in Price and Quantity

For a single change *either* in demand *or* in supply, *ceteris paribus,* when

- demand increases, $P$ rises and $Q$ increases.
- demand decreases, $P$ falls and $Q$ decreases.
- supply increases, $P$ falls and $Q$ increases.
- supply decreases, $P$ rises and $Q$ decreases.

When there is a simultaneous change *both* in demand *and* supply, we can determine the effect on either price or quantity. But without information about the relative size of the shifts of the demand and supply curves, the effect on the other variable is ambiguous. *Ceteris paribus,* when

- both demand and supply increase, $P$ may rise/fall/remain constant and $Q$ increases.
- both demand and supply decrease, $P$ may rise/fall/remain constant and $Q$ decreases.
- demand increases and supply decreases, $P$ rises and $Q$ may rise/fall/remain constant.
- demand decreases and supply increases, $P$ falls and $Q$ may rise/fall/remain constant.

# Helpful Hints

1. When you are first learning about demand and supply, think of specific examples to help you understand how to use the concepts. For example, in analysing complementary goods, think about hamburgers and french fries; in analysing substitute goods, think of hamburgers and hot dogs. This will reduce the "abstractness" of the economic theory and make concepts easier to remember.

2. The statement "Price is determined by demand and supply" is a shorthand way of saying that price is determined by all of the factors affecting demand (prices of related goods, expected future prices, income, expected future income and credit, population, preferences) and all of the factors affecting supply (prices of factors of production, prices of related goods produced, expected future prices, number of suppliers, technology, state of nature). The benefit of using demand and supply curves is that they allow us to systematically sort out the influences on price of each of these separate factors. Changes in the factors affecting demand shift the demand curve and move us up or down the given supply curve. Changes in the factors affecting supply shift the supply curve and move us up or down the given demand curve.

   Any demand and supply problem requires you to sort out these influences carefully. In so doing, *always draw a graph,* even if it is just a small graph in the margin of a true/false or multiple-choice problem. Graphs are a very efficient way to "see" what happens. As you become comfortable with graphs, you will find them to be effective and powerful tools for systematically organizing your thinking.

   Do not make the common mistake of thinking that a problem is so easy that you can do it in your head, without drawing a graph. This mistake will cost you dearly on examinations. Also, when you do draw a graph, be sure to label the axes. As the course progresses, you will encounter many graphs with different variables on the axes. It is easy to become confused if you do not develop the habit of labelling the axes.

3. Another common mistake among students is failing to *distinguish* correctly between *a shift in a curve* and *a movement along a curve.* This distinction applies both to demand and to supply curves. Many questions in the Self-Test are designed to test your understanding of this distinction, and you can be sure that your instructor will test you

heavily on this. The distinction between "shifts in" versus "movements along" a curve is crucial for systematic thinking about the factors influencing demand and supply, and for understanding the determination of equilibrium price and quantity.

Consider the example of the demand curve. The quantity of a good demanded depends on its own price, the prices of related goods, expected future prices, income, expected future income and credit, population, and preferences. The term "demand" refers to the relationship between the price of a good and the quantity demanded, holding constant all of the other factors on which the quantity demanded depends. This demand relationship is represented graphically by the demand curve. Thus, the effect of a change in price on quantity demanded is already reflected in the slope of the demand curve; the effect of a change in the price of the good itself is given by a movement along the demand curve. This is referred to as a **change in quantity demanded**.

On the other hand, if one of the other factors affecting the quantity demanded changes, the demand curve itself will shift; the quantity demanded *at each price* will change. This shift of the demand curve is referred to as a **change in demand**. The critical thing to remember is that a change in the price of a good will not shift the demand curve; it will only cause a movement along the demand curve. Similarly, it is just as important to distinguish between shifts in the supply curve and movements along the supply curve.

To confirm your understanding, consider the effect (draw a graph!) of an increase in household income on the market for energy bars. First note that an increase in income affects the demand for energy bars and not supply. Next we want to determine whether the increase in income causes a shift in the demand curve or a movement along the demand curve. Will the increase in income increase the quantity of energy bars demanded even if the price of energy bars does not change? Since the answer to this question is yes, we know that the demand curve will shift rightward. Note further that the increase in the demand for energy bars will cause the equilibrium price to rise. This price increase will be indicated by a movement along the supply curve (an increase in the quantity supplied) and will not shift the supply curve itself.

*Remember:* It is shifts in demand and supply curves that cause the market price to change, not changes in the price that cause demand and supply curves to shift.

Notes:

4. When analysing the shifts of demand and supply curves in related markets (for substitute goods like beer and wine), it often seems as though the feedback effects from one market to the other can go on endlessly. To avoid confusion, stick to the rule that each curve (demand and supply) for a given market can shift a maximum of *once*. (See Short Answer Problems **4** and **6** for further explanation and examples.)

5. The relationships between price and quantity demanded and supplied can be represented in three equivalent forms: demand and supply schedules, curves, and equations. Text Chapter 3 illustrates schedules and curves, but demand and supply equations are also powerful tools of economic analysis. The Mathematical Note to Chapter 3 (pages 76–77) provides the general form of these equations. The purpose of this Helpful Hint and the next is to further explain the equations and how they can be used to determine the equilibrium values of price and quantity.

Fig. 1 presents a simple demand and supply example in three equivalent forms: (a) schedules, (b) curves, and (c) equations. The demand and supply schedules in (a) are in the same format as used in the text. The price-quantity combinations from the schedules are plotted on the graph in (b), yielding linear demand and supply curves. What is new about this example is the representation of those curves by the equations in (c).

If you recall (Chapter 1 Appendix) the formula for the equation of a straight line ($y = a + bx$), you can see that the demand equation is the

(a) **Demand and Supply Schedules**

| Price ($) | $Q_D$ | $Q_S$ | Shortage (−)/ Surplus (+) |
|---|---|---|---|
| 1 | 4 | 0 | −4 |
| 2 | 3 | 1 | −2 |
| 3 | 2 | 2 | 0 |
| 4 | 1 | 3 | +2 |
| 5 | 0 | 4 | +4 |

(b) **Demand and Supply Curves**

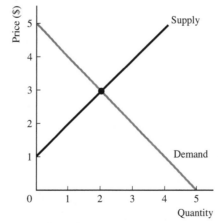

(c) **Demand and Supply Equations**

Demand: $P = 5 - 1Q_D$

Supply:  $P = 1 + 1Q_S$

▲ **FIGURE 1**

equation of a straight line. Instead of $y$, $P$ is the dependent variable on the vertical axis, and instead of $x$, $Q_D$ is the independent variable on the horizontal axis. The intercept on the vertical axis $a$ is $+5$, and the slope $b$ is $-1$. The supply equation is also linear and graphed in the same way, but with $Q_S$ as the independent variable. The supply curve intercept on the vertical axis is $+1$, and the slope is $+1$. The negative slope of the demand curve reflects the law of demand, and the positive slope of the supply curve reflects the law of supply.

You can demonstrate the equivalence of the demand schedule, curve, and equation by substituting various values of $Q_D$ from the schedule into the demand equation, and calculating the associated prices. These combinations of quantity demanded and price are the coordinates $(Q_D, P)$ of the points on the demand curve. You can similarly demonstrate the equivalence of the supply schedule, curve, and equation.

The demand and supply equations are very useful for calculating the equilibrium values of price and quantity. As the schedules and curves both show, two things are true in equilibrium: (1) the price is the same for consumers (the highest price they are willing to pay for the last unit) and producers (the lowest price they are willing to accept for the last unit) and (2) the quantity demanded equals the quantity supplied, so that there are no surpluses or shortages. In terms of the demand and supply equations, this means that, *in equilibrium,*

(1) the price in both equations is the same. We will denote the equilibrium price as $P^*$.

(2) $Q_D = Q_S =$ the equilibrium quantity bought and sold. We will denote the equilibrium quantity as $Q^*$.

In equilibrium, the equations become

$$\text{Demand: } P^* = 5 - 1Q^*$$
$$\text{Supply: } \ P^* = 1 + 1Q^*$$

These equilibrium equations constitute a simple set of simultaneous equations. Since there are two equations (demand and supply) and two unknowns ($P^*$ and $Q^*$), we can solve for the unknowns.

Begin the solution by setting demand equal to supply:

$$5 - 1Q^* = 1 + 1Q^*$$

Collecting like terms, we find

$$4 = 2Q^*$$

$$2 = Q^*$$

Once we have $Q^*$ (equilibrium quantity), we can solve for the equilibrium price using either the demand or the supply equations. Look first at demand:

$$P^* = 5 - 1Q^*$$

$$P^* = 5 - 1(2)$$

$$P^* = 5 - 2$$

$$P^* = 3$$

Alternatively, substituting $Q^*$ into the supply equation yields the same result:

$$P^* = 1 + 1Q^*$$

$$P^* = 1 + 1(2)$$

$$P^* = 1 + 2$$

$$P^* = 3$$

Once you have solved for $Q^*$, the fact that substituting it into either the demand or the supply equation yields the correct $P^*$ provides a valuable check on your calculations. If you make a mistake in your calculations, when you substitute $Q^*$ into the demand and supply equations, you will get two different prices. If that happens, you know to recheck your calculations. If you get the same price when you substitute $Q^*$ into the demand and supply equations, you know your calculations are correct.

6. Economists have developed the convention of graphing quantity as the independent variable (on the horizontal $x$-axis) and price as the dependent variable (on the vertical $y$-axis), and the foregoing equations reflect this. Despite this convention, economists

actually consider real-world prices to be the independent variables and quantities the dependent variables. In that case, the equations would take the form

$$\text{Demand: } Q_D = \phantom{-}5 - 1P$$

$$\text{Supply: } Q_S = -1 + 1P$$

You can solve these equations for yourself to see that they yield exactly the same values for $P^*$ and $Q^*$. (*Hint:* First solve for $P^*$ and then for $Q^*$.) Whichever form of the equations your instructor may use, the technique for solving the equations will be similar and the results identical.

# Self-Test
## True/False and Explain

### Markets and Prices

1. In a competitive market, every single buyer and seller influences price.

2. The relative price of a good is the other goods that must be forgone to buy it.

3. A good's relative price can fall even when its money price rises.

### Demand

4. The law of demand tells us that as the price of a good rises, demand decreases.

5. The demand curve is a willingness-and-ability-to-pay curve that measures marginal cost.

6. Hamburgers and fries are complements. If Burger Bar reduces the price of fries, the demand for hamburgers increases.

7. A decrease in income always shifts the demand curve leftward.

### Supply

8. A supply curve shows the maximum price at which the last unit will be supplied.

**9.** If *A* and *B* are substitutes, an increase in the price of *A* always shifts the supply curve of *B* leftward.

**10.** When a cow is slaughtered for beef, its hide becomes available to make leather. Thus beef and leather are substitutes in production.

**11.** If the price of beef rises, there will be an increase in both the supply of leather and the quantity of beef supplied.

## Market Equilibrium

**12.** When the actual price is above the equilibrium price, a shortage occurs.

## Predicting Changes in Price and Quantity

**13.** If the expected future price of a good increases, there will always be an increase in equilibrium price and a decrease in equilibrium quantity.

**14.** Suppose new firms enter the steel market. *Ceteris paribus*, the equilibrium price of steel will always fall and the quantity will rise.

**15.** Suppose the demand for PCs increases while the cost of producing them decreases. The equilibrium quantity of PCs will rise and the price will always fall.

# Multiple-Choice

## Markets and Prices

**1.** A relative price is
- **a.** the ratio of one price to another.
- **b.** an opportunity cost.
- **c.** a quantity of a "basket" of goods and services forgone.
- **d.** determined by demand and supply.
- **e.** all of the above.

## Demand

**2.** If an increase in the price of good *A* causes the demand curve for good *B* to shift leftward,
- **a.** *A* and *B* are substitutes in consumption.
- **b.** *A* and *B* are complements in consumption.
- **c.** *A* and *B* are complements in production.
- **d.** *B* is an inferior good.
- **e.** *B* is a normal good.

**3.** Which of the following could *not* cause an increase in demand for a commodity?
- **a.** an increase in income
- **b.** a decrease in income
- **c.** a decrease in the price of a substitute
- **d.** a decrease in the price of a complement
- **e.** an increase in preferences for the commodity

**4.** Some sales managers are talking shop. Which of the following quotations refers to a movement along the demand curve?
- **a.** "Since our competitors raised their prices our sales have doubled."
- **b.** "It has been an unusually mild winter; our sales of wool scarves are down from last year."
- **c.** "We decided to cut our prices, and the increase in our sales has been remarkable."
- **d.** "The Green movement has sparked an increase in our sales of biodegradable products."
- **e.** None of the above.

**5.** If Hamburger Helper is an inferior good, then, *ceteris paribus,* a decrease in income will cause

   **a.** a leftward shift of the demand curve for Hamburger Helper.

   **b.** a rightward shift of the demand curve for Hamburger Helper.

   **c.** a movement up along the demand curve for Hamburger Helper.

   **d.** a movement down along the demand curve for Hamburger Helper.

   **e.** none of the above.

**6.** A decrease in quantity demanded is represented by a

   **a.** rightward shift of the supply curve.

   **b.** rightward shift of the demand curve.

   **c.** leftward shift of the demand curve.

   **d.** movement upward and to the left along the demand curve.

   **e.** movement downward and to the right along the demand curve.

**7.** Which of the following "other things" are *not* held constant along a demand curve?

   **a.** income

   **b.** prices of related goods

   **c.** the price of the good itself

   **d.** preferences

   **e.** all of the above

## Supply

**8.** The fact that a decline in the price of a good causes producers to reduce the quantity of the good supplied illustrates

   **a.** the law of supply.

   **b.** the law of demand.

   **c.** a change in supply.

   **d.** the nature of an inferior good.

   **e.** technological improvement.

**9.** A shift of the supply curve for rutabagas will be caused by

**a.** a change in preferences for rutabagas.

**b.** a change in the price of a related good that is a substitute in consumption for rutabagas.

**c.** a change in income.

**d.** a change in the price of rutabagas.

**e.** none of the above.

**10.** If a factor of production can be used to produce either good $A$ or good $B$, then $A$ and $B$ are

**a.** substitutes in production.

**b.** complements in production.

**c.** substitutes in consumption.

**d.** complements in consumption.

**e.** normal goods.

**11.** Which of the following will shift the supply curve for good $X$ leftward?

**a.** a decrease in the wages of workers employed to produce $X$

**b.** an increase in the cost of machinery used to produce $X$

**c.** a technological improvement in the production of $X$

**d.** a situation where quantity demanded exceeds quantity supplied

**e.** all of the above

**12.** Some producers are chatting over a beer. Which of the following quotations refers to a movement along the supply curve?

**a.** "Wage increases have forced us to raise our prices."

**b.** "Our new, sophisticated equipment will enable us to undercut our competitors."

**c.** "Raw material prices have skyrocketed; we will have to pass this on to our customers."

**d.** "We anticipate a big increase in demand. Our product price should rise, so we are planning for an increase in output."

**e.** "New competitors in the industry are causing prices to fall."

**13.** If an increase in the price of good *A* causes the supply curve for good *B* to shift rightward,

    **a.** *A* and *B* are substitutes in consumption.

    **b.** *A* and *B* are complements in consumption.

    **c.** *A* and *B* are substitutes in production.

    **d.** *A* and *B* are complements in production.

    **e.** *A* is a factor of production for making *B*.

## Market Equilibrium

**14.** If the market for Twinkies is in equilibrium,

    **a.** Twinkies must be a normal good.

    **b.** producers would like to sell more at the current price.

    **c.** consumers would like to buy more at the current price.

    **d.** there will be a surplus.

    **e.** equilibrium quantity equals quantity demanded.

**15.** The price of a good will tend to fall if

    **a.** there is a surplus at the current price.

    **b.** the current price is above equilibrium.

    **c.** the quantity supplied exceeds the quantity demanded at the current price.

    **d.** all of the above are true.

    **e.** none of the above is true.

**16.** A surplus can be eliminated by

    **a.** increasing supply.

    **b.** government raising the price.

    **c.** decreasing the quantity demanded.

    **d.** allowing the price to fall.

    **e.** allowing the quantity bought and sold to fall.

**17.** A shortage is the amount by which quantity
   **a.** demanded exceeds quantity supplied.
   **b.** supplied exceeds quantity demanded.
   **c.** demanded increases when the price rises.
   **d.** demanded exceeds the equilibrium quantity.
   **e.** supplied exceeds the equilibrium quantity.

## Predicting Changes in Price and Quantity

**18.** Which of the following will definitely cause an increase in the equilibrium price?
   **a.** an increase in both demand and supply
   **b.** a decrease in both demand and supply
   **c.** an increase in demand combined with a decrease in supply
   **d.** a decrease in demand combined with an increase in supply
   **e.** none of the above

**19.** Coffee is a normal good. A decrease in income will
   **a.** increase the price of coffee and increase the quantity demanded of coffee.
   **b.** increase the price of coffee and increase the quantity supplied of coffee.
   **c.** decrease the price of coffee and decrease the quantity demanded of coffee.
   **d.** decrease the price of coffee and decrease the quantity supplied of coffee.
   **e.** cause none of the above.

**20.** An increase in the price of Pepsi (a substitute for coffee) will
   **a.** increase the price of coffee and increase the quantity demanded of coffee.
   **b.** increase the price of coffee and increase the quantity supplied of coffee.
   **c.** decrease the price of coffee and decrease the quantity demanded of coffee.
   **d.** decrease the price of coffee and decrease the quantity supplied of coffee.
   **e.** cause none of the above.

**21.** A technological improvement lowers the cost of producing coffee. At the same time, preferences for coffee decrease. The *equilibrium quantity* of coffee will

  **a.** rise.

  **b.** fall.

  **c.** remain the same.

  **d.** rise or fall depending on whether the price of coffee falls or rises.

  **e.** rise or fall depending on the relative shifts of demand and supply curves.

**22.** Since 1980, there has been a dramatic increase in the number of working mothers. On the basis of this information alone, we can predict that the market for child-care services has experienced a(n)

  **a.** increase in demand.

  **b.** decrease in demand.

  **c.** increase in quantity demanded.

  **d.** decrease in quantity supplied.

  **e.** increase in supply.

**23.** If $A$ and $B$ are complementary goods (in consumption) and the cost of a factor of production used in the production of $A$ decreases, the price of

  **a.** both $A$ and $B$ will rise.

  **b.** both $A$ and $B$ will fall.

  **c.** $A$ will fall and the price of $B$ will rise.

  **d.** $A$ will rise and the price of $B$ will fall.

  **e.** $A$ will fall and the price of $B$ will remain unchanged.

**24.** The demand curve for knobs is $P = 75 - 6Q_D$ and the supply curve for knobs is $P = 35 + 2Q_S$. What is the equilibrium price of a knob?

  **a.** $5

  **b.** $10

  **c.** $40

  **d.** $45

  **e.** none of the above

**25.** The demand curve for tribbles is $P = 300 - 6Q_D$. The supply curve for tribbles is $P = 20 + 8Q_S$. If the price of a tribble was set at $120, the tribble market would experience

**a.** equilibrium.

**b.** excess demand causing a rise in price.

**c.** excess demand causing a fall in price.

**d.** excess supply causing a rise in price.

**e.** excess supply causing a fall in price.

# Short Answer Problems

ⓒ **1.** A tax on crude oil would raise the cost of the primary resource used in the production of gasoline. A proponent of such a tax has claimed that it will not raise the price of gasoline using the following argument: While the price of gasoline may rise initially, that price increase will cause the demand for gasoline to decrease, which will push the price back down. What is wrong with this argument?

**2.** Brussels sprouts and carrots are substitutes in consumption and, since they can both be grown on the same type of land, substitutes in production too. Suppose there is an increase in the demand for brussels sprouts. On the grid, trace the effects on price and quantity traded in both the brussels sprout and the carrot market. (Keep in mind Helpful Hint **4.**)

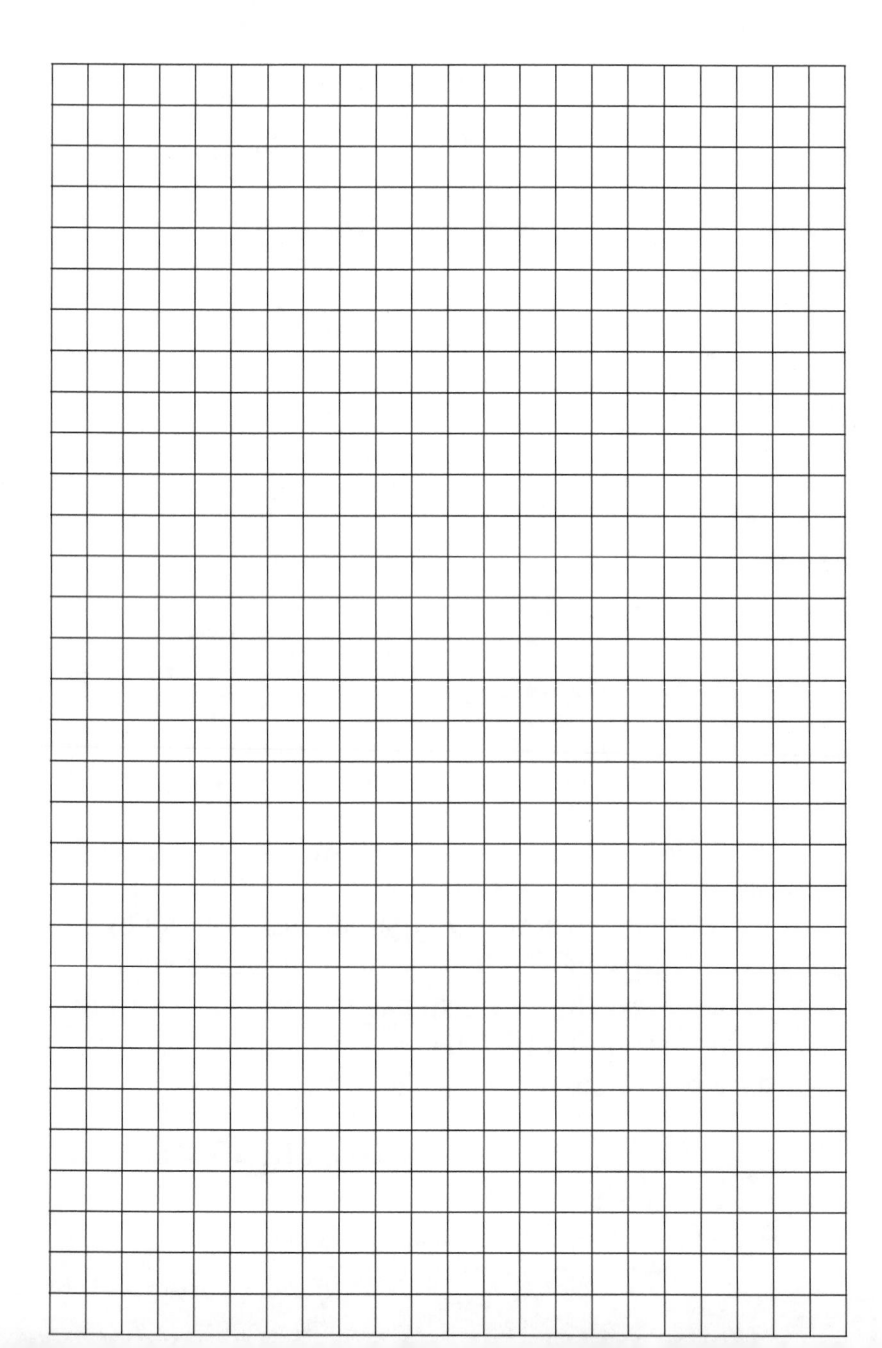

**3.** The information given in Table 1 is about the behaviour of buyers and sellers of fish at the market on a particular Saturday.

| TABLE 1 Demand and Supply Schedules for Fish | | |
|---|---|---|
| Price (per fish) | Quantity Demanded | Quantity Supplied |
| $0.50 | 280 | 40 |
| $1.00 | 260 | 135 |
| $1.50 | 225 | 225 |
| $2.00 | 170 | 265 |
| $2.50 | 105 | 290 |
| $3.00 | 60 | 310 |
| $3.50 | 35 | 320 |

**a.** On the grid, draw the demand curve and the supply curve. Be sure to label the axes. What is the equilibrium price?

**b.** We will make the usual *ceteris paribus* assumptions about the demand curve so that it does not shift. List six factors that we are assuming do not change.

**c.** We will also hold the supply curve constant by assuming that six factors do not change. List them.

**d.** Explain briefly what would happen if the price was initially set at $3.

**e.** Explain briefly what would happen if the price was initially set at $1.

**f.** Explain briefly what would happen if the price was initially set at $1.50.

**4.** A newspaper reported, "Despite a bumper crop of cherries this year, the price drop for cherries won't be as much as expected because of short supplies of plums and peaches."

   **a.** On the grid, use a demand and supply graph for the cherry market to explain the effect of the bumper crop alone.

   **b.** On the same graph, explain the impact on the cherry market of the short supplies of plums and peaches.

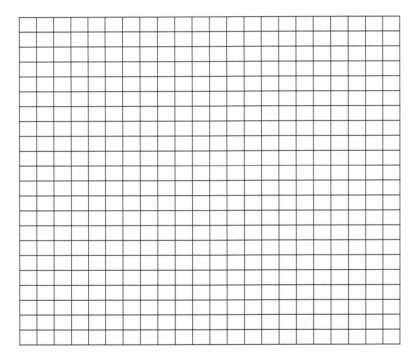

**5.** The market for wine in Canada is initially in equilibrium with supply and demand curves of the usual shape. Beer is a close substitute for wine; cheese and wine are complements. On the grid on the next page, use demand and supply diagrams to analyse the effect of each of the following (separate) events on the equilibrium price and quantity in the Canadian wine market. Assume that all of the *ceteris paribus* assumptions continue to hold except for the event listed. For both equilibrium price and quantity you should indicate in each case whether the variable rises, falls, remains the same, or moves ambiguously (may rise or fall).

**a.** The income of consumers falls (wine is a normal good).

**b.** Early frost (state of nature) destroys a large part of the world grape crop.

**c.** A new churning invention reduces the cost of producing cheese.

**d.** A new fermentation technique is invented that reduces the cost of producing wine.

**e.** A new government study is published that links wine drinking and increased heart disease.

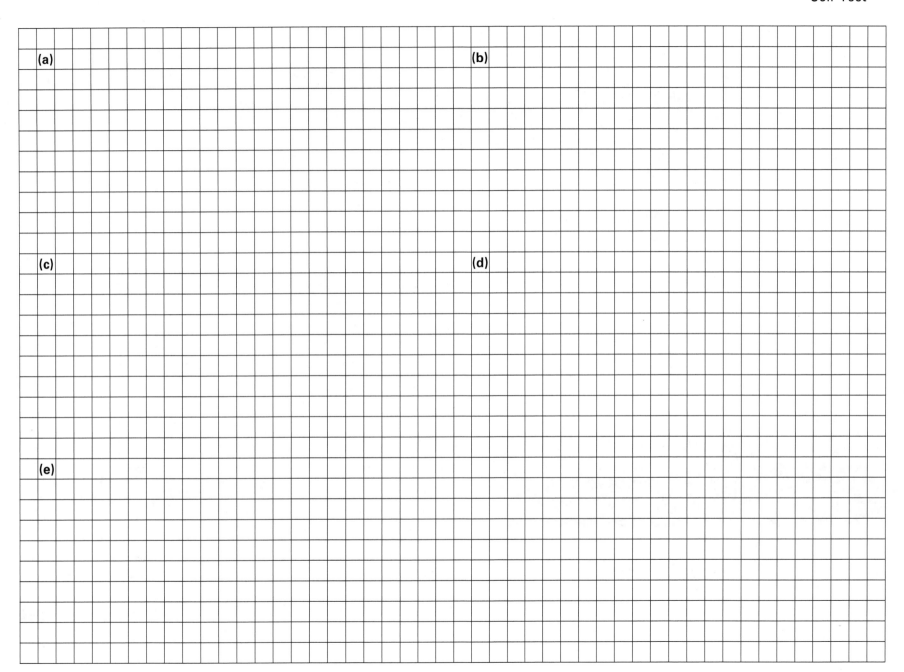

(a)

(b)

(c)

(d)

(e)

**f.** Costs of producing both beer and wine increase dramatically.

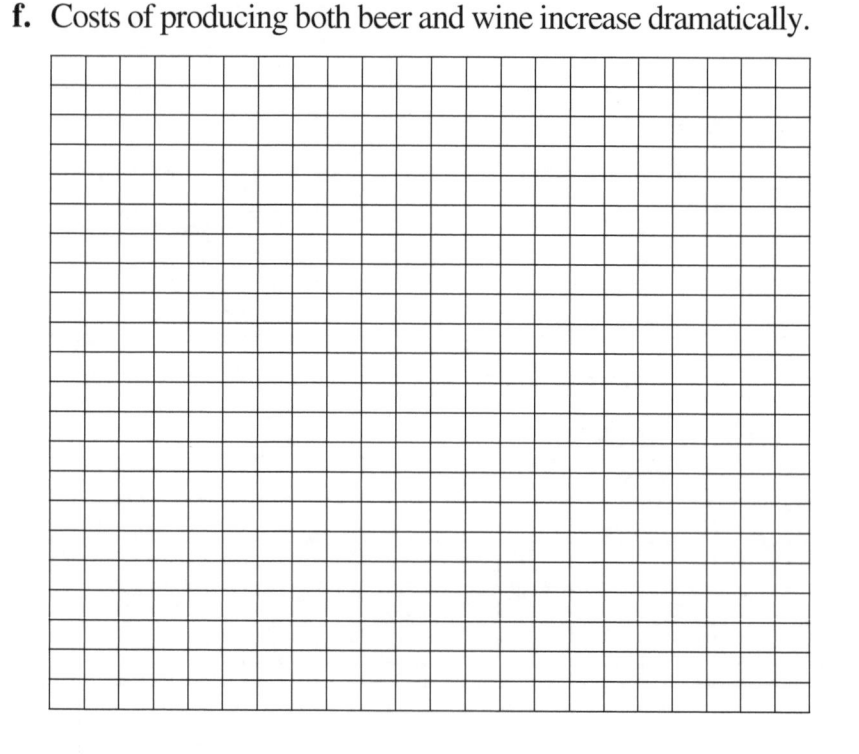

**6.** Table 2 lists the demand and supply schedules for cases of grape jam.

| TABLE 2  Demand and Supply Schedules for Grape Jam Per Week | | |
|---|---|---|
| Price (per case) | Quantity Demanded (cases) | Quantity Supplied (cases) |
| $70 | 20 | 140 |
| $60 | 60 | 120 |
| $50 | 100 | 100 |
| $40 | 140 | 80 |
| $30 | 180 | 60 |

**a.** On the graph in Fig. 2, draw the demand and supply curves for grape jam. Be sure to properly label the axes. Label the demand and supply curves $D_0$ and $S_0$ respectively.

▲ **FIGURE 2**

**b.** What are the equilibrium price and quantity in the grape jam market? On your diagram, label the equilibrium point *a*.

**c.** Is there a surplus or shortage at a price of $40? How much?

**d.** The demand and supply schedules can also be represented by the following demand and supply equations:

Demand: $P = 75 - 0.25Q_D$

Supply:   $P = 0.5Q_S$

Use these equations to solve for the equilibrium quantity ($Q^*$); equilibrium price ($P^*$). (*Hint:* Your answers should be the same as those in **6b**.)

**e.** Suppose the population grows sufficiently that the demand for grape jam increases by 60 cases per week at every price.

    **i.** In the space below, construct a table (price, quantity demanded) of the new demand schedule.

    **ii.** Draw the new demand curve on your original graph and label it $D_1$.

    **iii.** Label the new equilibrium point $b$. What are the new equilibrium price and quantity?

    **iv.** What is the new demand equation? (*Hints:* What is the new slope? What is the new price-axis intercept?)

**7.** The demand equation for dweedles is

$$P = 8 - 1Q_D$$

The supply equation for dweedles is

$$P = 2 + 1Q_S$$

where $P$ is the price of a dweedle in dollars, $Q_D$ is the quantity of dweedles demanded, and $Q_S$ is the quantity of dweedles supplied. The dweedle market is initially in equilibrium and income is $300.

**a.** What is the equilibrium quantity ($Q^*$) of dweedles?

**c.** As a result of an increase in income to $500, the demand curve for dweedles shifts (the supply curve remains the same). The new demand equation is

$$P = 4 - 1Q_D$$

Use this information to calculate the new equilibrium quantity of dweedles; calculate the new equilibrium price of a dweedle.

**b.** What is the equilibrium price ($P^*$) of a dweedle?

**d.** On the graph in Fig. 3, draw and label: (1) the supply curve, (2) the initial demand curve, (3) the new demand curve.

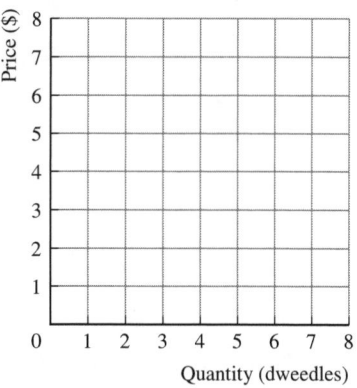

**▲ FIGURE 3**

**e.** Are dweedles a normal or inferior good? How do you know?

**a.** If the price of flubits was set at $56, calculate the exact surplus or shortage of flubits.

**8.** The demand equation for flubits is

$$P = 80 - 2Q_D$$

The supply equation for flubits is

$$P = 50 + 1Q_S$$

where $P$ is the price of a flubit in dollars, $Q_D$ is the quantity of flubits demanded, and $Q_S$ is the quantity of flubits supplied. Assume that there are no changes in *ceteris paribus* assumptions.

**b.** Explain the adjustment process that will bring the situation above to equilibrium.

**d.** What is the equilibrium price ($P^*$) of a flubit?

**c.** What is the equilibrium quantity ($Q^*$) of flubits?

**e.** Now assume that as a result of technological advances, the supply curve for flubits shifts (the demand curve remains the same). The new supply equation is

$$P = 20 + 1Q_S$$

Use this information to calculate the new equilibrium quantity of flubits; calculate the new equilibrium price of a flubit.

# Answers

## True/False and Explain

1. **F** No single buyer or seller influences price. (55–56)

2. **T** Relative price is an opportunity cost. (55–56)

ⓒⓣ 3. **T** If money prices of other goods rise even more, a good's relative price falls. If the price of gum rises from $1 to $2, but the price of coffee rises from $1 to $4, the opportunity cost of a pack of gum falls from 1 to 0.5 coffee forgone. (55–56)

4. **F** As price rises, *quantity demanded* decreases. (57–61)

5. **F** Measures marginal benefit. (57–61)

6. **T** Combined meal of hamburger and fries is now cheaper. (57–61)

ⓒⓣ 7. **F** Leftward shift for normal good, rightward shift for inferior good. (57–61)

8. **F** Supply curve shows minimum price at which last unit supplied. (62–65)

ⓒⓣ 9. **F** True if *A* and *B* are substitutes in production, but false if they are substitutes in consumption. (62–65)

ⓒⓣ 10. **F** Beef and leather are complements in production because they are produced together of necessity. (62–65)

11. **T** For complements in production, a higher price for one good causes increased quantity supplied and increase in supply of the other good. (62–65)

12. **F** At *P* > equilibrium *P*, there is surplus (quantity supplied > quantity demanded). (66–67)

ⓒⓣ 13. **F** Higher expected future prices cause a rightward shift in demand and leftward shift in supply. Price rises, but Δ quantity depends on relative magnitude of shifts. (68–65)

14. **T** Increased number of firms causes rightward shift in supply, leading to a fall in price and increased quantity. (68–75)

15. **F** Quantity will increase but Δ price depends on the relative magnitude of the shifts in demand and supply. (68–75)

## Multiple-Choice

1. **e** Definitions. (55–56)

2. **b** For example, higher-priced fries cause decreased demand for hamburgers. (57–61)

ⓒⓣ 3. **c** Both income answers could be correct if the commodity were normal (**a**) or inferior (**b**). (57–61)

4. **c** The other answers describe shifts of the demand curve. (57–61)

5. **b** Changes in income shift the demand curve rather than causing movement along the demand curve. (57–61)

6. **d** Decreased quantity demanded is movement up along the demand curve. Could also be caused by a leftward shift in supply. (57–61)

ⓒⓣ 7. **c** "Other things" shift the demand curve. Only price can change along a fixed demand curve. (57–61)

**8. a** Question describes movement down along the supply curve. (62–65)

**9. e** Answers **a**, **b**, and **c** shift demand, while **d** causes movement along the supply curve. (62–65)

**10. a** Definition of a substitute in production. (62–65)

**11. b** Higher-priced factors of production shifts supply leftward. (62–65)

**12. d** The other answers describe shifts of the supply curve. (62–65)

**13. d** Definition of complements in production. Price changes of related goods in consumption shift demand. (62–65)

**14. e** At equilibrium price, plans producers and consumers match; quantity demanded = quantity supplied. (66–67)

**15. d** All answers describe price above the equilibrium price. (66–67)

**16. d** Other answers make surplus (excess quantity supplied) larger. (66–67)

**17. a** Shortage is horizontal distance between the demand and supply curves at a price below the equilibrium price. (66–67)

**18. c** Answers **a** and **b** have an indeterminate effect on price, while **d** causes a lower price. (68–75)

**19. d** Demand shifts leftward. (68–75)

**20. b** Demand shifts rightward. (68–75)

**21. e** Supply shifts rightward, demand shifts leftward, price definitely falls. (68–75)

**22. a** More working mothers increases preferences for child care, causing increased demand for child-care services. (68–75)

**23. c** Supply $A$ shifts rightward causing lower-priced $A$. This increases demand for $B$, causing higher-priced $B$. (68–75)

**24. d** See Helpful Hint **5**. Set demand equal to supply, solve for $Q^* = 5$. Substitute $Q^* = 5$ into either demand or supply equation to solve for $P^*$. (68–77)

**25. b** At $P = \$120$, $Q_D = 30$, and $Q_S = 12.5$. There is excess demand so price will rise. (68–77)

## Short Answer Problems

**1.** This argument confuses a movement along an unchanging demand curve with a shift in the demand curve. The proper analysis is as follows. The increase in the price of oil (the primary factor of production in the production of gasoline) will shift the supply curve of gasoline leftward. This will cause the equilibrium price of gasoline to increase and thus the quantity demanded of gasoline will decrease. Demand itself will not decrease—that is, the demand curve will not shift. The decrease in supply causes a movement along an unchanged demand curve.

**2.** The answer to this question requires us to trace through the effects on the two graphs in Fig. 4: (a) for the brussels sprout market and (b) for the carrot market. The sequence of effects occurs in order of the numbers on the graphs.

Look first at the market for brussels sprouts. The increase in demand shifts the demand curve rightward from $D_0$ to $D_1$ (1), and the price of brussels sprouts rises. This price rise has two effects (2) on the carrot market. Since brussels sprouts and carrots are substitutes in consumption, the demand curve for carrots shifts rightward from $D_0$

**(a) Brussels Sprout Market**

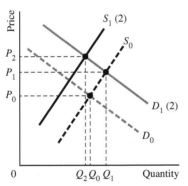

**(b) Carrot Market**

**▲ FIGURE 4**

to $D_1$. And, since brussels sprouts and carrots are substitutes in production, the supply curve of carrots shifts leftward from $S_0$ to $S_1$. Both of these shifts in the carrot market raise the price of carrots, causing feedback effects on the brussels sprout market. But remember the rule (Helpful Hint **4**) that each curve (demand and supply) for a given market can shift a maximum of *once*. Since the demand curve for brussels sprouts has already shifted, we can only shift the supply curve from $S_0$ to $S_1$ (3) because of the substitutes in production relationship. Each curve in each mar-

ket has now shifted once and the analysis must stop. We can predict that the net effects are increases in the equilibrium prices of both brussels sprouts and carrots, and indeterminate changes in the equilibrium quantities in both markets.

**3. a.** The demand and supply curves are shown in Fig. 5. The equilibrium price is $1.50 per fish.

**▲ FIGURE 5**

**b.** Prices of related goods; expected future prices; income; expected future income and credit; population; preferences.

**c.** Prices of productive resources; prices of related goods produced; expected future prices; number of suppliers; technology; state of nature.

**d.** At a price of $3, quantity supplied (310) exceeds quantity demanded (60). Fish sellers find themselves with surplus fish. Rather than be stuck with unsold fish (which yields no revenue), some sellers cut their price in an attempt to increase the quantity of fish demanded. Competition forces other sellers to follow suit, and the price falls until it reaches the equilibrium price of $1.50, while quantity demanded increases until it reaches the equilibrium quantity of 225 units.

**e.** At a price of $1, the quantity demanded (260) exceeds the quantity supplied (135)—there is a shortage. Unrequited fish buyers bid up the price in an attempt to get the "scarce" fish. Prices continue to be bid up as long as there is excess demand, so the quantity supplied increases in response to higher prices. Price and quantity supplied both rise until they reach the equilibrium price ($1.50) and quantity (225 units).

**f.** At a price of $1.50, the quantity supplied exactly equals the quantity demanded (225). There is no excess demand (shortage) or excess supply (surplus), and therefore no tendency for the price or quantity to change.

**4. a.** The demand and supply curves for the cherry market are shown in Fig. 6.

**Cherry Market**

▲ **FIGURE 6**

Suppose $D_0$ and $S_0$ represent the demand and supply curves for cherries last year. This year's bumper crop

increases supply to $S_1$. Other things being equal, the price of cherries would fall from $P_0$ to $P_1$.

**b.** But other things are not equal. Short supplies of plums and peaches (their supply curves have shifted leftward) drive up their prices. The increase in the prices of plums and peaches, which are substitutes in consumption for cherries, increases the demand for cherries to $D_1$. The net result is that the price of cherries only falls to $P_2$ instead of all the way to $P_1$.

**5.** The demand and supply diagrams for parts **a** to **e** are shown in Fig. 7.

**(a)**

↓ Price
↓ Quantity

**(b)**

↑ Price
↓ Quantity

**FIGURE 7**

**(c)**

**(d)**

**(e)**

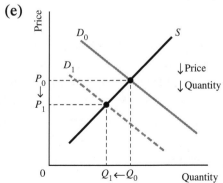

▲ **FIGURE 7 (Continued)**

**f.** Questions like this require the examination of two separate but related markets—the beer and wine markets. Since this kind of question often causes confusion for students, Fig. 8 gives a more detailed explanation of the answer.

**(a) Beer Market**

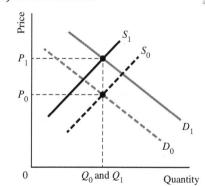

**(b) Wine Market**

▲ **FIGURE 8**

Look first at the beer market. The increase in the cost of beer production shifts the supply curve of beer leftward from $S_0$ to $S_1$. The resulting rise in the price of beer affects the wine market since beer and wine are substitutes (in consumption).

Turning to the wine market, there are two shifts to examine. The increase in beer prices causes the demand for wine to shift rightward from $D_0$ to $D_1$. The increase in the cost of wine production shifts the supply curve of wine leftward from $S_0$ to $S_1$. This is the end of the analysis, since the question only asks about the wine market. The final result is a rise in the equilibrium price of wine and an ambiguous change in the quantity of wine. Although the diagram shows $Q_1 = Q_0$, $Q_1$ may be $\geq$ or $\leq Q_0$.

Many students rightfully ask, "But doesn't the rise in wine prices then shift the demand curve for beer rightward, causing a rise in beer prices and an additional increase in the demand for wine?" This question, which is correct in principle, is about the dynamics of adjustment, and these graphs are only capable of analysing once-over shifts of demand or supply. We could shift the demand for beer rightward, but the resulting rise in beer prices would lead us to shift the demand for wine a *second time*. In practice, stick to the rule that each curve (demand and supply) for a given market can shift a maximum of *once*.

**6. a.** The demand and supply curves for grape jam are shown in Fig. 2 Solution.

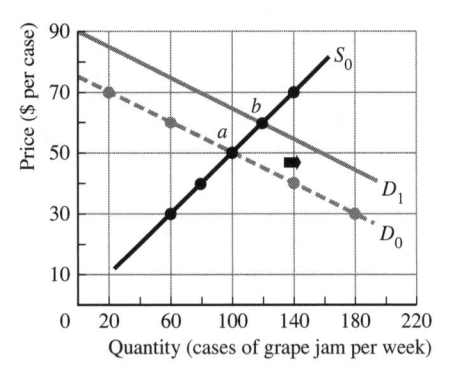

▲ **FIGURE 2  Solution**

**b.** The equilibrium is given at the intersection of the demand and supply curves (labelled point $a$). The equilibrium price is $50 per case and the equilibrium quantity is 100 cases per week.

**c.** At a price of $40 there is a shortage of 60 cases per week.

**d.** In equilibrium, the equations become:

$$\text{Demand: } P^* = 75 - 0.25Q^*$$
$$\text{Supply: } P^* = 0.5Q^*$$

To solve for $Q^*$, set demand equal to supply:

$$75 - 0.25Q^* = 0.5Q^*$$
$$75 = 0.75Q^*$$
$$100 = Q^*.$$

To solve for $P^*$, we can substitute $Q^*$ into either the demand or supply equations. Look at demand first:

$$P^* = 75 - 0.25Q^*$$
$$P^* = 75 - 0.25(100)$$
$$P^* = 75 - 25$$
$$P^* = 50$$

Alternatively, substituting $Q^*$ into the supply equation yields the same result:

$$P^* = 0.5Q^*$$
$$P^* = 0.5(100)$$
$$P^* = 50$$

**e. i.** Table 3 also contains the (unchanged) quantity supplied, for reference purposes.

**TABLE 3  New Demand and Unchanged Supply Schedules for Grape Jam Per Week**

| Price (per case) | Quantity Demanded (cases) | Quantity Supplied (cases) |
|---|---|---|
| $70 | 80 | 140 |
| $60 | 120 | 120 |
| $50 | 160 | 100 |
| $40 | 200 | 80 |
| $30 | 240 | 60 |

**ii.** The graph of the new demand curve, $D_1$, is shown in Fig. 2 Solution.

**iii.** The new equilibrium price is $60 per case and the quantity is 120 cases of grape jam per week.

**iv.** The new demand equation is $P = 90 - 0.25Q_D$. Notice that the slope of the new demand equation is the same as the slope of the original demand equation. An increase in demand of 60 cases at every price results in a rightward *parallel* shift of the demand curve. Since the two curves are parallel, they have the same slope. The figure of 90 is the price-axis intercept of the new demand curve, which you can see on your graph. *Remember:* The demand equation is the equation of a straight line ($y = a + bx$)—in this case, $a = 90$.

If you want additional practice in the use of demand and supply equations for calculating equilibrium values of price and quantity, you can use the new demand curve equation together with the supply curve equation to calculate the answers you found in **e iii**.

**7.** In equilibrium, the equations become

$$\text{Demand: } P^* = 8 - 1Q^*$$
$$\text{Supply: } P^* = 2 + 1Q^*$$

**a.** To solve for $Q^*$, set demand equal to supply:

$$8 - 1Q^* = 2 + 1Q^*$$
$$6 = 2Q^*$$
$$3 = Q^*$$

**b.** To solve for $P^*$, we can substitute $Q^*$ into either the demand or supply equations. Look first at demand:

$$P^* = 8 - 1Q^*$$
$$P^* = 8 - 1(3)$$
$$P^* = 8 - 3$$
$$P^* = 5$$

Alternatively, substituting $Q^*$ into the supply equation yields the same result:

$$P^* = 2 + 1Q^*$$
$$P^* = 2 + 1(3)$$
$$P^* = 2 + 3$$
$$P^* = 5$$

**c.** In equilibrium, the equations are

$$\text{Demand: } P^* = 4 - 1Q^*$$
$$\text{Supply: } P^* = 2 + 1Q^*$$

To solve for $Q^*$, set demand equal to supply:

$$4 - 1Q^* = 2 + 1Q^*$$
$$2 = 2Q^*$$
$$1 = Q^*$$

To solve for $P^*$, we can substitute $Q^*$ into either the demand or supply equations. Look first at demand:

$$P^* = 4 - 1Q^*$$
$$P^* = 4 - 1(1)$$
$$P^* = 4 - 1$$
$$P^* = 3$$

Alternatively, substituting $Q^*$ into the supply equation yields the same result:

$$P^* = 2 + 1Q^*$$
$$P^* = 2 + 1(1)$$
$$P^* = 2 + 1$$
$$P^* = 3$$

**d.** The supply curve, initial demand curve, and new demand curve for dweedles are shown in Fig. 3 Solution.

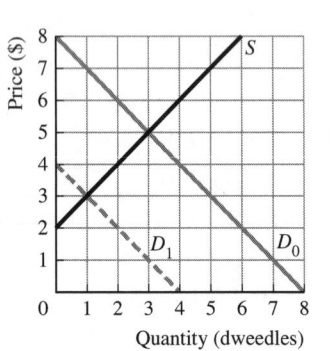

▲ **FIGURE 3** Solution

**e.** Dweedles are an inferior good. An increase in income (from \$300 to \$500) caused a decrease in demand—the demand curve for dweedles shifted leftward.

**8. a.** Substitute the price of \$56 into the demand and supply equations to calculate the quantities demanded and supplied at that price. This is the mathematical equivalent of what you do on a graph when you identify a price on the vertical axis, move your eye across to the demand (or supply) curve, and then move your eye down to read the quantity on the horizontal axis.

Substituting into the demand equation, we find

$$P = 80 - 2Q_D$$
$$56 = 80 - 2Q_D$$
$$2Q_D = 24$$
$$Q_D = 12.$$

Substituting into the supply equation,

$$P = 50 + 1Q_S$$
$$56 = 50 + 1Q_S$$
$$6 = Q_S$$

Quantity demanded exceeds quantity supplied by 6 $(12 - 6)$, so there is a shortage of 6 flubits.

**b.** A shortage means the price was set below the equilibrium price. Competition between consumers for the limited number of flubits will bid up the price and increase the quantity supplied until we reach the equilibrium price and quantity.

**c.** In equilibrium, the equations are

$$\text{Demand: } P^* = 80 - 2Q^*$$
$$\text{Supply: } P^* = 50 + 1Q^*$$

To solve for $Q^*$, set demand equal to supply:

$$80 - 2Q^* = 50 + 1Q^*$$
$$30 = 3Q^*$$
$$10 = Q^*$$

**d.** To solve for $P^*$, substitute $Q^*$ into the demand equation:

$$P^* = 80 - 2Q^*$$
$$P^* = 80 - 2(10)$$
$$P^* = 80 - 20$$
$$P^* = 60$$

You can check this answer yourself by substituting $Q^*$ into the supply equation.

**e.** The new equilibrium equations are

$$\text{Demand: } P^* = 80 - 2Q^*$$
$$\text{Supply: } P^* = 20 + 1Q^*$$

To solve for $Q^*$, set demand equal to supply:

$$80 - 2Q^* = 20 + 1Q^*$$
$$60 = 3Q^*$$
$$20 = Q^*$$

To solve for $P^*$, substitute $Q^*$ into the supply equations:

$$P^* = 20 + 1Q^*$$
$$P^* = 20 + 1(20)$$
$$P^* = 20 + 20$$
$$P^* = 40$$

You can check this answer yourself by substituting $Q^*$ into the demand equation.

# 4 Elasticity

## Key Concepts
### Price Elasticity of Demand

**Price elasticity of demand** ($\eta$) measures responsiveness of quantity demanded to change in price.

- $\eta$ is a units-free measure of responsiveness.

$$\eta = \left| \frac{\% \Delta \text{ quantity demanded}}{\% \Delta \text{ price}} \right| = \left| \frac{\Delta Q / Q_{ave}}{\Delta P / P_{ave}} \right|$$

- Elasticity is *not* equal to slope. Moving down along a linear demand curve, slope ($\Delta P / \Delta Q$) is constant, but elasticity decreases as $P_{ave}$ falls and $Q_{ave}$ increases.

  - *When*          *Demand Is*
    $\eta = \infty$          **perfectly elastic** (horizontal)
    $1 < \eta < \infty$     **elastic**
    $\eta = 1$              **unit elastic**
    $0 < \eta < 1$          **inelastic**
    $\eta = 0$              **perfectly inelastic** (vertical)

Elasticity and **total revenue** ($P \times Q$)—the **total revenue test**:

- *When Demand Is*          *Price Cut Causes*
  elastic ($\eta > 1$)          increased total revenue
  unit elastic ($\eta = 1$)          no change total revenue
  inelastic ($\eta < 1$)          decreased total revenue

Elasticity of demand depends on

- *closeness of substitutes*—closer substitutes for a good yield higher elasticity.

  - Goods that are defined more narrowly have higher elasticity.
  - Necessities generally have poor substitutes and inelastic demands.
  - Luxuries generally have many substitutes and elastic demands.

- *proportion of income spent on good*—the greater proportion of income spent on a good yields higher elasticity.

- *time elapsed since price change*—longer time lapse yields higher elasticity.

  - Short-run demand describes responsiveness to a change in price *before* there is sufficient time for all substitutions to be made.
  - Long-run demand describes responsiveness to a change in price *after* there is sufficient time for all substitutions to be made.
  - Short-run demand is usually less elastic than long-run demand.

## More Elasticities of Demand

**Cross elasticity of demand** ($\eta_x$) measures the *responsiveness* of quantity demanded of good $A$ to a change in price of good $B$.

- $\eta_x = \dfrac{\% \Delta \text{ quantity demanded good } A}{\% \Delta \text{ price good } B}$

- $\eta_x > 0$     Goods are substitutes.

- $\eta_x = 0$    Goods are independent.
- $\eta_x < 0$    Goods are complements.

**Income elasticity of demand** ($\eta_y$) measures *responsiveness* of demand to a change in income.

- $\eta_y = \dfrac{\% \Delta \text{ quantity demanded}}{\% \Delta \text{ income}}$

- *When*                     *Demand Is*
  $\eta_y > 1$               income elastic (normal good)
  $0 < \eta_y < 1$          income inelastic (normal good)
  $\eta_y < 0$               negative income elasticity (inferior good)

# Elasticity of Supply

**Elasticity of supply** ($\eta_s$) measures *responsiveness* of quantity supplied to change in price.

- $\eta_s = \dfrac{\% \Delta \text{ quantity supplied}}{\% \Delta \text{ income}}$

- *When*                     *Supply Is*
  $\eta_s = \infty$          perfectly elastic (horizontal)
  $1 < \eta_s < \infty$     elastic
  $\eta_s = 1$               unit elastic
  $0 < \eta_s < 1$          inelastic
  $\eta_s = 0$               perfectly inelastic (vertical)

Elasticity of supply depends on

- *resources substitution possibilities*—the more common the productive resources used, the higher $\eta_s$.

- *time frame for supply decision*—the longer the time elapsed, from momentary to short-run to long-run supply, the higher $\eta_s$.

  - Momentary supply describes responsiveness of quantity supplied immediately following a price change.
  - Short-run supply describes responsiveness of quantity supplied to a price change when *some* technologically possible adjustments to production have been made.
  - Long-run supply describes responsiveness of quantity supplied to a price change when *all* technologically possible adjustments to production have been made.

# Helpful Hints

1. There are many elasticity formulas in this chapter, but they are all based on the same simple, intuitive principle—*responsiveness*. All of the demand and supply elasticity formulas measure the *responsiveness* (sensitivity) *of quantity* (demanded or supplied) to changes in something else. Thus percentage change in quantity is always in the numerator of the relevant formula. As you come to understand how quantity responds to changes in price, income, and prices of related goods, you will be able to work out each elasticity formula, even if you have temporarily forgotten it.

2. The complete formula for calculating the price elasticity of demand between two points on the demand curve is

$$\eta = \frac{\% \Delta \text{ quantity demanded}}{\% \Delta \text{ price}}$$

$$= \left| \left( \frac{\Delta Q}{Q_{ave}} \bigg/ \frac{\Delta P}{P_{ave}} \right) \right|$$

   The law of demand assures us that price and quantity demanded always move in opposite directions along any demand curve. Thus without the absolute value sign, the formula for the price elasticity of demand would yield a negative number. Because our main interest is in the *magnitude* of the response in quantity demanded to a change in price, for simplicity's sake we take the absolute value to guarantee a positive number. Whenever you see the often-used shorthand term "*elasticity* of demand," remember that it means the absolute value of the *price* elasticity of demand.

3. Elasticity is *not* the same as slope (although they are related). Along a straight-line demand curve the slope is constant, but the elasticity varies from infinity to zero as we move down the demand curve. To see why, look at the formula below, which is just a rearrangement of the elasticity formula in Helpful Hint **2**.

$$\eta = \left| \left( \frac{\Delta Q}{\Delta P} \times \frac{P_{ave}}{Q_{ave}} \right) \right|$$

The term in the first parentheses is simply the inverse of the slope. Since the slope is constant everywhere along a straight-line demand curve, so is the inverse of the slope. Consider, however, what happens to the term in the second parentheses as we move down the demand curve. At the "top" of the demand curve, $P_{ave}$ is very large and $Q_{ave}$ is very small, so the term in the second parentheses is large. As we move down the demand curve, $P_{ave}$ becomes smaller and $Q_{ave}$ becomes larger, so the term in the second parentheses falls in value. The net result is that the absolute value of the price elasticity of demand falls as we move down the demand curve.

4. One of the most practical and important uses of the concept of price elasticity of demand is that it allows us to predict the effect on total revenue of a change in price. A fall in price will increase total revenue if demand is elastic, leave total revenue unchanged if demand is unit elastic, and decrease total revenue if demand is inelastic. Because price and quantity demanded always move in opposite directions along a demand curve, a fall in price will cause an increase in quantity demanded. Since total revenue equals price times quantity, the fall in price will tend to decrease total revenue, while the increase in quantity demanded will increase total revenue. The net effect depends on which of these individual effects is larger.

   The concept of price elasticity of demand conveniently summarizes the net effect. For example, if demand is elastic, the percentage change in quantity demanded is greater than the percentage change in price. Hence, with a fall in price, the quantity effect dominates and total revenue will increase. If, however, demand is inelastic, the percentage change in quantity demanded is less than the percentage change in price. Hence, with a fall in price, the price effect dominates and total revenue will decrease.

5. Two other important elasticity concepts are the income elasticity of demand and the cross elasticity of demand.

   Income elasticity of demand:

   $$\eta_y = \frac{\% \,\Delta \text{ quantity demanded}}{\% \,\Delta \text{ income}}$$

$$= \left(\frac{\Delta Q}{Q_{ave}}\right) \Big/ \left(\frac{\Delta Y}{Y_{ave}}\right)$$

Cross elasticity of demand:

$$\eta_x = \frac{\% \, \Delta \text{ quantity demanded good } A}{\% \, \Delta \text{ price good } B}$$

$$= \left(\frac{\Delta Q^A}{Q^A_{ave}}\right) \Big/ \left(\frac{\Delta P^B}{P^B_{ave}}\right)$$

Notice that these two elasticity formulas do *not* have absolute value signs and can take on either positive or negative values. While these formulas measure responsiveness, both the magnitude *and the direction* of the response are important. In the case of income elasticity of demand, the response of quantity demanded to an increase in income will be positive for a normal good and negative for an inferior good. In the case of cross elasticity of demand, the response of the quantity demanded of good *A* to an increase in the price of good *B* will be positive if the goods are substitutes and negative if the goods are complements.

In calculating an income elasticity or a cross elasticity, be alert to the fact that the *price of the good in the numerator* of the formula *is assumed constant*. Income elasticity measures the quantity response to a change in income, *ceteris paribus*. Cross elasticity measures the quantity response of good *A* to a change in the price of good *B*, *ceteris paribus*. This means that we cannot simply read numerical values for calculating these elasticities from the equilibrium positions of a set of demand and supply curves. For example, when income increases, demand shifts rightward (for a normal good), and the new equilibrium quantity will also have a higher equilibrium price. To calculate income elasticity correctly, we compare the income and quantity demanded of the initial equilibrium with the new income and quantity demanded. To obtain the correct new quantity demanded, we must use the new demand curve, but must calculate the quantity demanded that would have prevailed at the *initial*, unchanged price. (See Short Answer Problems **7** and **8** for examples.)

# Self-Test

## True/False and Explain

### Price Elasticity of Demand

1. The price elasticity of demand measures how responsive prices are to changes in demand.

2. Price elasticity of demand is constant along a linear demand curve.

3. If a decrease in supply causes total revenue to increase, demand must be inelastic.

4. If a 9 percent increase in price leads to a 5 percent decrease in quantity demanded, total revenue has decreased.

5. If you like Pepsi cola and Coca-Cola about the same, your demand for Pepsi is likely to be elastic.

6. The more narrowly we define a good, the more elastic its demand.

7. If your expenditures on toothpaste are a small proportion of your total income, your demand for toothpaste is likely to be inelastic.

8. The demand for gasoline is likely to become more inelastic with the passage of time after a price increase.

## More Elasticities of Demand

**9.** An inferior good has a negative cross elasticity of demand.

**10.** If a 10 percent increase in the price of widgets causes a 6 percent increase in the quantity of woozles demanded, then widgets and woozles must be complements.

**11.** We would expect a negative cross elasticity of demand between hamburgers and hamburger buns.

## Elasticity of Supply

**12.** Elasticity of supply equals the change in quantity supplied divided by the change in price.

**13.** A horizontal supply curve is perfectly elastic.

**14.** Goods produced with rare resources have a low elasticity of supply.

**15.** Supply is generally more inelastic in the long run than in the short run.

# Multiple-Choice

## Price Elasticity of Demand

**1.** There are two points on the demand curve for volleyballs, as shown in Table 1.

| TABLE 1 | |
|---|---|
| **Price per Volleyball** | **Quantity Demanded** |
| $19 | 55 |
| $21 | 45 |

What is the elasticity of demand between these two points?
   **a.** 2.5
   **b.** 2.0
   **c.** 0.5
   **d.** 0.4
   **e.** None of the above.

**2.** If the price elasticity of demand is 2, a 1 percent decrease in price will
   **a.** double the quantity demanded.
   **b.** reduce the quantity demanded by half.
   **c.** increase the quantity demanded by 2 percent.
   **d.** reduce the quantity demanded by 2 percent.
   **e.** increase the quantity demanded by 0.5 percent.

**3.** If price elasticity of demand is zero, then as the price falls
   **a.** total revenue does not change.
   **b.** quantity demanded does not change.
   **c.** quantity demanded falls to zero.
   **d.** total revenue increases from zero.
   **e.** none of the above occurs.

**4.** A perfectly vertical demand curve has a price elasticity of
   **a.** zero.
   **b.** greater than zero but less than one.
   **c.** one.
   **d.** greater than one.
   **e.** infinity.

**5.** A union leader who claims that "higher wages increase living standards without causing unemployment" believes that the demand for labour is

**a.** income elastic.

**b.** income inelastic.

**c.** perfectly elastic.

**d.** perfectly inelastic.

**e.** unit elastic.

**6.** Business people talk about price elasticity of demand without using the actual term. Which of the following statements reflects elastic demand for a product?

**a.** "A price cut won't help me. It won't increase sales, and I'll just get less money for each unit that I was selling before."

**b.** "I don't think a price cut will make any difference to my bottom line. What I may gain from selling more I would lose on the lower price."

**c.** "My customers are real bargain hunters. Since I set my prices just a few cents below my competitors', customers have flocked to the store and sales are booming."

**d.** "With the recent economic recovery, people have more income to spend and sales are booming, even at the same prices as before."

**e.** None of the above.

**7.** A technological breakthrough lowers the cost of photocopiers. If the demand for photocopiers is price inelastic, we predict that photocopier sales will

**a.** fall and total revenue will rise.

**b.** fall and total revenue will fall.

**c.** rise and total revenue will rise.

**d.** rise and total revenue will fall.

**e.** rise but changes in total revenue will depend on elasticity of supply.

**8.** A decrease in tuition fees will decrease the university's total revenue if the price elasticity of demand for university education is

**a.** negative.

**b.** greater than zero but less than one.

**c.** equal to one.

**d.** greater than one.

**e.** less than the price elasticity of supply.

9. If the demand for orange juice is price elastic, a severe frost that destroys large quantities of oranges will likely
   a. reduce the equilibrium price of juice, but increase total consumer spending on it.
   b. reduce the equilibrium quantity of juice as well as total consumer spending on it.
   c. reduce both the equilibrium quantity and the price of juice.
   d. increase the equilibrium price of juice as well as total consumer spending on it.
   e. increase the equilibrium price of juice, but leave total consumer spending on it constant.

㉢ 10. If a 4 percent rise in the price of peanut butter causes total revenue to fall by 8 percent, demand for peanut butter
   a. is elastic.
   b. is inelastic.
   c. is unit elastic.
   d. has an elasticity of 1/2.
   e. has an elasticity of 2.

11. Tina and Brian work for the same recording company. Tina claims that they would be better off by increasing the price of their CDs while Brian claims that they would be better off by decreasing the price. We can conclude that
   a. Tina thinks the demand for CDs has price elasticity of zero, and Brian thinks price elasticity equals one.
   b. Tina thinks the demand for CDs has price elasticity equal to one, and Brian thinks price elasticity equals zero.
   c. Tina thinks the demand for CDs is price elastic, and Brian thinks it is price inelastic.
   d. Tina thinks the demand for CDs is price inelastic, and Brian thinks it is price elastic.
   e. Tina and Brian should stick to singing and forget about economics.

**@ 12.** Given the relationship shown in Fig. 1 between total revenue from the sale of a good and the quantity of the good sold,

   **a.** this is an inferior good.

   **b.** this is a normal good.

   **c.** the elasticity of demand is zero.

   **d.** the elasticity of demand is infinity.

   **e.** the elasticity of demand is one.

**▲ FIGURE 1**

**13.** If the Jets decrease ticket prices and find that total revenue does not change, the price elasticity of demand for tickets is

   **a.** zero.

   **b.** greater than zero, but less than one.

   **c.** equal to one.

   **d.** greater than one.

   **e.** inferior.

**14.** The fact that butter has margarine as a close substitute in consumption

   **a.** makes the supply of butter more elastic.

   **b.** makes the supply of butter less elastic.

   **c.** makes the demand for butter more elastic.

   **d.** makes the demand for butter less elastic.

   **e.** does not affect butter's elasticity of supply or demand.

**15.** A given percentage increase in the price of a good is likely to cause a larger percentage decline in quantity demanded

   **a.** the shorter the passage of time.

   **b.** the larger the proportion of income spent on it.

   **c.** the harder it is to obtain good substitutes.

   **d.** all of the above.

   **e.** none of the above.

## More Elasticities of Demand

**16.** A negative value for
   **a.** price elasticity of supply implies an upward-sloping supply curve.
   **b.** cross elasticity of demand implies complementary goods.
   **c.** price elasticity of demand implies an inferior good.
   **d.** income elasticity of demand implies a normal good.
   **e.** income elasticity of demand implies an error in your calculation.

**17.** The cross elasticity of the demand for white tennis balls with respect to the price of yellow tennis balls is probably
   **a.** negative and high.
   **b.** negative and low.
   **c.** positive and high.
   **d.** positive and low.
   **e.** zero.

**18.** If a 10 percent increase in income causes a 5 percent increase in quantity demanded (at a constant price), what is the income elasticity of demand?
   **a.** 0.5
   **b.** − 0.5
   **c.** 2.0
   **d.** −2.0
   **e.** None of the above.

**19.** Luxury goods tend to have income elasticities of demand that are
   **a.** greater than one.
   **b.** greater than zero but less than one.
   **c.** positive.
   **d.** negative.
   **e.** first positive and then negative as income increases.

ⓒⓣ **20.** If a 4 percent decrease in income (at a constant price) causes a 2 percent decrease in the consumption of dweedles,

    **a.** the income elasticity of demand for dweedles is negative.

    **b.** dweedles are a necessity and a normal good.

    **c.** dweedles are a luxury and a normal good.

    **d.** dweedles are an inferior good.

    **e.** **a** and **d** are true.

## Elasticity of Supply

**21.** When price goes from $1.50 to $2.50, quantity supplied increases from 9,000 to 11,000 units. What is the price elasticity of supply?

    **a.** 0.4

    **b.** 0.8

    **c.** 2.5

    **d.** 4.0

    **e.** None of the above.

**22.** Preferences for brussels sprouts increase. The price of brussels sprouts will not change if the price elasticity of

    **a.** demand is 0.

    **b.** demand is 1.

    **c.** supply is 0.

    **d.** supply is 1.

    **e.** supply is infinity.

**23.** A sudden end-of-summer heat wave increases the demand for air conditioners and catches suppliers with no reserve inventories. The momentary supply curve for air conditioners is

    **a.** perfectly elastic.

    **b.** perfectly inelastic.

    **c.** elastic.

    **d.** upward sloping.

    **e.** horizontal.

**24.** The long-run supply curve is likely to be

    **a.** more elastic than momentary supply, but less elastic than short-run supply.

    **b.** less elastic than momentary supply, but more elastic than short-run supply.

    **c.** less elastic than both momentary and short-run supply curves.

    **d.** more elastic than both momentary and short-run supply curves.

    **e.** vertical.

**25.** Long-run elasticity of supply of a good is greater than short-run elasticity of supply because

    **a.** more substitutes in consumption for the good can be found.

    **b.** more complements in consumption for the good can be found.

    **c.** more technological ways of adjusting supply can be exploited.

    **d.** income rises with more elapsed time.

    **e.** the long-run supply curve is steeper.

# Short Answer Problems

**1.** Why does supply tend to be more elastic in the long run?

**2.** In Fig. 2, which demand curve ($D_A$ or $D_B$) is more elastic in the price range $P_1$ to $P_2$? Explain why in the space provided in the right column. (*Hint:* Use the formula for price elasticity of demand.)

▲ **FIGURE 2**

**3.** Consider the demand curve in Fig. 3(a). A portion of the demand curve is also described by the demand schedule in Table 2 on the next page.

▲ **FIGURE 3**

(b)

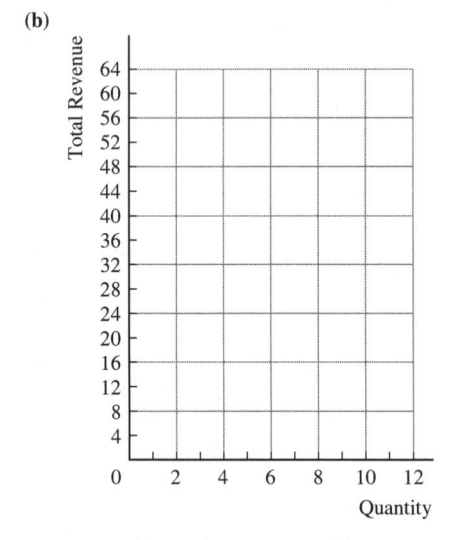

▲ **FIGURE 3 (Continued)**

shape of the total revenue curve as quantity increases (price decreases).

| TABLE 2 | | |
|---|---|---|
| **Price ($)** | **Quantity Demanded** | **Total Revenue** |
| 22 | 0 | |
| 20 | 1 | |
| 18 | 2 | |
| 16 | 3 | |
| 14 | 4 | |
| 12 | 5 | |
| 10 | 6 | |
| 8 | 7 | |
| 6 | 8 | |

Fill in the numbers for total revenue in the last column of Table 2, and graph your results on Fig. 3(b). Describe the

4. Using the same information for the demand curve in Short Answer Problem **3**:

   **a.** Complete the second and third columns of Table 3 on the next page: η (the price elasticity of demand) and $\Delta TR$ (the change in total revenue) as the price falls from the higher price to the lower price. Describe the relationship between elasticity and change in total revenue as price falls (moving down the demand curve).

## TABLE 3

| Δ P($) | η | Δ TR($) | η′ | Δ TR′($) |
|--------|---|---------|-----|----------|
| 16 – 14 | | | | |
| 14 – 12 | | | | |
| 12 – 10 | | | | |
| 10 – 8 | | | | |
| 8 – 6 | | | | |

**c.** Using the price range between $16 and $14, explain why $D'$ is more inelastic than $D$.

**b.** Suppose income increases from $10,000 to $14,000, causing an increase in demand: at every price, quantity demanded increases by 2 units. Draw the new demand curve on Fig. 3(a) and label it $D'$. Use this new demand curve to complete the last two columns of Table 3 for $η'$ (the new price elasticity of demand) and $ΔTR'$ (the new change in total revenue).

**d.** Calculate the income elasticity of demand, assuming the price remains constant at $12. Is this a normal or inferior good? Explain why you could have answered the question even without calculating the income elasticity of demand.

**a.** Calculate the price elasticity of demand for woozles between $Q_D = 4$ and $Q_D = 6$.

**b.** Initially, the woozle market is in equilibrium with $P* = 52$ and $Q* = 4$. Then, the supply curve shifts (the demand curve remains constant) yielding a new equilibrium price of $P* = 48$.

Using all of the relevant information above, show *two separate methods* for determining whether total

ⓒ **5.** The demand equation for woozles is $P = 60 - 2Q_D$. The supply equation for woozles is $P = 32 + 5Q_S$, where $P$ is the price of a woozle in dollars, $Q_D$ is the quantity of woozles demanded, and $Q_S$ is the quantity of woozles supplied.

revenue increases, decreases, or remains constant in moving from the initial equilibrium to the new equilibrium.

**6.** Suppose Jean loses his present job and his monthly income falls from \$10,000 to \$6,000, while his monthly purchases of grits increase from 200 to 400.

**a.** Calculate his income elasticity of demand for grits.

**b.** Are grits a normal or inferior good? Explain why.

**7.** The demand equation for tribbles is $P = 50 - 1Q_D$. The supply equation for tribbles is $P = 20 + 0.5Q_S$, where $P$ is the price of a tribble in dollars, $Q_D$ is the quantity of tribbles demanded, and $Q_S$ is the quantity of tribbles supplied. The tribble market is initially in equilibrium, and income is \$180.

**a.** What is the equilibrium quantity ($Q^*$) of tribbles?

**b.** What is the equilibrium price ($P^*$) of a tribble?

**c.** As a result of a decrease in income to $120, the demand curve for tribbles shifts (the supply curve remains the same). The new demand equation is:

$$P = 110 - 1Q_D$$

Use this information to calculate the new equilibrium quantity of tribbles; calculate the new equilibrium price of a tribble.

**d.** Calculate the income elasticity of demand for tribbles. Are tribbles a normal or inferior good? (*Hint*: In your calculation be sure to (1) use the information about the *initial* equilibrium conditions [price, quantity, and income] and (2) keep in mind that price is assumed *constant* in calculating income elasticity; only income and quantity change.)

**8.** Table 4 gives the demand schedules for good $A$ when the price of good $B$ ($P_B$) is $8 and $12. Complete the last column of the table by computing the cross elasticity of demand between goods $A$ and $B$ for each of the three prices of $A$. Are $A$ and $B$ complements or substitutes?

**TABLE 4 Demand Schedules for Good $A$**

| $P_A$ | $P_B = \$8$<br>$Q_A$ | $P_B = \$12$<br>$Q'_A$ | $\eta_x$ |
|---|---|---|---|
| $8 | 2,000 | 4,000 | |
| $7 | 4,000 | 6,000 | |
| $6 | 6,000 | 8,000 | |

# Answers

## True/False and Explain

1. **F** It measures the responsiveness of quantity demanded to $\Delta P$. (84–90)

2. **F** Slope is constant; $\eta$ falls as we move down the demand curve. (84–90)

3. **T** Decreased $S$ causes increased $P$ and increased total revenue, so demand is inelastic. (84–90)

4. **F** (% increase $P$) > (% decrease $Q$), so total revenue ($P \times Q$) increases. (84–90)

5. **T** Colas are substitutes for you. (84–90)

6. **T** With narrower definition, there are more substitutes. (84–90)

7. **T** Lower proportion of income spent on good, more inelastic is demand. (84–90)

8. **F** Elasticity increases with elapsed time. (84–90)

9. **F** An inferior good has negative income elasticity; the cross elasticity sign depends on whether substitute or complement. (91–93)

10. **F** $\eta_x$ is positive so goods are substitutes. (91–93)

11. **T** $\eta_x$ is negative for complements. (91–93)

12. **F** $\eta_s$ equals *percentage* change in quantity supplied divided by *percentage* change in price. (94–97)

13. **T** $\eta_s$ = infinity. (94–97)

14. **T** $\eta_s$ < 1. (94–97)

15. **F** Supply is more elastic in the long run. (94–97)

## Multiple-Choice

1. **b** |(−10/50)/(2/20)| = 2. (84–90)

2. **c** $\eta = |(\% \Delta Q_D)/(\% \Delta P)| = |(1/5)/(1/10)| = 2$. $Q_D$ and $P$ are always inversely related on the demand curve. (84–90)

3. **b** Demand curve is vertical, so lower $P$ does not $\Delta$ quantity demanded. (84–90)

4. **a** Definition. (84–90)

5. **d** Labour demand curve would be vertical. (84–90)

6. **c** Small fall in $P$ causes large increase in quantity demanded. **a** inelastic, **b** unit elastic, **d** on income elasticity. (84–90)

7. **d** Rightward shift in supply causes increased quantity sold and lower $P$; with inelastic demand causes decreased total revenue. (84–90)

8. **b** Lower $P$ causes decreased total revenue when $\eta < 1$. $\eta$ is never negative. (84–90)

9. **b** Decreased $S$ causes decreased $Q_D$ and higher $P$. Since $\eta > 1$, higher $P$ causes decreased expenditure. (84–90)

10. **a** If higher $P$ causes decreased total revenue, $\eta$ must be > 1. Must know (%$\Delta Q_D$) to precisely calculate $\eta$. (84–90)

11. **d** Better off means increased total revenue. By definition of relation between higher $P$, $\eta$, and total revenue. (84–90)

ⓒ **12. e** Note total revenue ($TR$) on $y$-axis. Since $TR$ is constant as increased $Q$ (and presumably lower $P$), $\eta = 1$. **a, b** depend on $\eta_y$. (84–90)

**13. c** Total revenue test. (84–90)

**14. c** Closer substitutes yield higher elasticity of demand. (84–90)

**15. b** $\eta$ increases with increased proportion of income spent on a good. $\eta$ increases when longer time passage and easier to obtain substitutes. (84–90)

**16. b** $\eta_s$ and $\eta$ are never negative. $\eta_y$ is negative for an inferior good. (91–93)

**17. c** Close substitutes, so $\eta_x$ is positive and very elastic (high). (91–93)

**18. a** $\eta_y = (\% \Delta Q_D)/(\% \Delta \text{ income}) = 5/10 = 0.5$. (91–93)

**19. a** See answer to **20** below. **c** is correct, but **a** is the best answer. (91–93)

ⓒ **20. b** $\eta_y > 0$ so it is a normal good. Necessities tend to have $\eta_y < 1$, while luxuries tend to have $\eta_y > 1$. (91–93)

**21. a** $\eta_s = (\% \Delta Q_S)/(\% \Delta P) = (2,000/10,000)/(1/2) = 0.4$. (94–97)

**22. e** Increased $D$ causes no $\Delta P$ if the supply curve is horizontal ($\eta_s = $ infinity). (94–97)

**23. b** Definition. (94–97)

**24. d** Definition. Momentary supply curve is the most vertical. (94–97)

**25. c** Definition. **a, b, d** affect demand, not supply. Long-run supply curve is flatter than short-run. (94–97)

## Short Answer Problems

1. Supply is more elastic in the long run, because the passage of time allows producers to find better (more efficient) ways of producing that are not available in the short run. The responsiveness of production to an increase in price will increase as firms have time to discover and implement new technologies or to increase the scale of operation.

2. $D_A$ is more elastic than $D_B$. To see why, look at the formula for price elasticity of demand:

$$\eta = \left| \frac{\% \Delta \text{ quantity demaded}}{\% \Delta \text{ price}} \right|$$

The percentage change in price is the same for the two demand curves. But the percentage change in quantity is greater for $D_A$. At $P_1$, the initial quantity demanded is the same for both demand curves ($Q_1$). With the fall in price to $P_2$, the increase in quantity demanded is greater for $D_A$ (to $Q_{2A}$) than for $D_B$ (to $Q_{2B}$). Therefore $D_A$ is more elastic than $D_B$. See Fig. 2 Solution.

▲ **FIGURE 2  Solution**

**3.** The numbers for total revenue are shown in Table 2 Solution. The total revenue curve is shown in Fig. 3(b) Solution. The total revenue curve first increases (at a diminishing rate—its slope is decreasing as we move up the curve), then reaches a maximum between $Q = 5$ and $Q = 6$, then decreases. We will encounter this pattern of changing total revenue again in studying monopoly in Chapter 13.

| TABLE 2 Solution | | |
|---|---|---|
| **Price ($)** | **Quantity Demanded** | **Total Revenue** |
| 22 | 0 | 0 |
| 20 | 1 | 20 |
| 18 | 2 | 36 |
| 16 | 3 | 48 |
| 14 | 4 | 56 |
| 12 | 5 | 60 |
| 10 | 6 | 60 |
| 8 | 7 | 56 |
| 6 | 8 | 48 |

▲ **FIGURE 3(b) Solution**

**4. a.** The completed columns are shown in Table 3 Solution. The second and third columns of the table show that as price falls, total revenue increases when demand is elastic; total revenue remains constant when demand is unit elastic; total revenue falls when demand is inelastic.

| TABLE 3 Solution | | | | |
|---|---|---|---|---|
| **$\Delta P$($)** | **$\eta$** | **$\Delta TR$($)** | **$\eta'$** | **$\Delta TR'$ ($)** |
| 16 − 14 | 2.14 | +8 | 1.36 | +4 |
| 14 − 12 | 1.44 | +4 | 1.00 | 0 |
| 12 − 10 | 1.00 | 0 | 0.73 | −4 |
| 10 − 8 | 0.69 | −4 | 0.53 | −8 |
| 8 − 6 | 0.47 | −8 | 0.37 | −12 |

**b.** The new demand curve is labelled $D'$ in Fig. 3(a) Solution. The last two columns of the table have been completed on the basis of the new demand curve.

▲ **FIGURE 3(a)  Solution**

**c.** Since they are parallel, $D'$ and $D$ have exactly the same slope. Thus we know that for a given change in price, the change in quantity demanded will be the same for the two curves. However, elasticity is determined by *percentage* changes, and the percentage change in quantity demanded is different for the two curves, although the percentage change in price will be the same. For a given percentage change in price, the percentage change in quantity demanded will always be less for $D'$. For example, as the price falls from \$16 to \$14 (a 13 percent change), the quantity demanded increases from 5 to 6 units along $D'$, but from 3 to 4 units along $D$. The percentage change in quantity demanded is only 18 percent along $D'$ and 29 percent along $D$. Since the percentage change in price is the same for both curves, $D'$ is more inelastic than $D$.

**d.** Income increases from \$10,000 to \$14,000. At a constant price of \$12, the increase in income, which shifts out the demand curve to $D'$, increases the quantity consumers will demand from 5 units to 7 units. Substituting these numbers into the formula for the income elasticity of demand yields

$$\eta_y = \left(\frac{\Delta Q}{Q_{ave}}\right)\bigg/\left(\frac{\Delta Y}{Y_{ave}}\right)$$

$$= \left(\frac{2}{6}\right)\bigg/\left(\frac{4{,}000}{12{,}000}\right) = +1$$

The income elasticity of demand is a positive number, since both $\Delta Q$ and $\Delta Y$ are positive. Therefore this is a normal good. We already knew that from the information in part **b**, which stated that the demand curve shifted rightward with an increase in income. If this were an inferior good, the increase in income would have shifted the demand curve leftward and the income elasticity of demand would have been negative.

© **5. a.** In order to calculate price elasticity of demand, we need to know two points (each point a combination of price and quantity demanded) on the demand curve. We are given only the quantity demanded coordinate of each point. By substituting $Q_D = 4$ and $Q_D = 6$ into the demand equation, we can solve for the two price coordinates:

At $Q_D = 4$; $P = 60 - 2(4) = 52$
At $Q_D = 6$; $P = 60 - 2(6) = 48$

These price and quantity demanded coordinates can now be substituted into the formula for the price elasticity of demand:

$$\eta = \left| \left( \frac{\Delta Q}{Q_{ave}} \right) \middle/ \left( \frac{\Delta P}{P_{ave}} \right) \right|$$

$$= \left| \left( \frac{-2}{5} \right) \middle/ \left( \frac{4}{50} \right) \right| = 5$$

**b.** One method is simply to compare total revenue ($P \times Q$) at each equilibrium:

- Initial equilibrium:

Total revenue $= (P \times Q) = (52 \times 4) = 208$.

- New equilibrium:

If $P^* = 48$, $Q^*$ can be calculated by substituting $P^*$ into the demand equation:

$$48 = 60 - 2Q^*$$
$$2Q^* = 12$$
$$Q^* = 6$$

So total revenue $= (P \times Q) = (48 \times 6) = 288$. In moving from the initial to the new equilibrium, total revenue has increased.

A second method is to use the information from part **a** on the price elasticity of demand. We know that between $Q_D = 4$ and $Q_D = 6$ on the demand curve, demand is elastic. These two points correspond to the initial equilibrium and, after the shift of the supply curve, the new equilibrium. Since demand here is elastic, we know that the fall in price from $P = 52$ to $P = 48$ will increase total revenue.

**6. a.** Using the formula for income elasticity of demand:

$$\eta_y = \left( \frac{\Delta Q}{Q_{ave}} \right) \middle/ \left( \frac{\Delta Y}{Y_{ave}} \right)$$

$$= \left( \frac{200 - 400}{\frac{1}{2}(200 + 400)} \right) \middle/ \left( \frac{10,000 - 6,000}{\frac{1}{2}(10,000 + 6,000)} \right)$$

$$= \left( \frac{-200}{300} \right) \middle/ \left( \frac{4,000}{8,000} \right) = -\frac{4}{3}$$

**b.** Grits are an inferior good because the income elasticity of demand is negative.

**7. a.** The initial equilibrium quantity ($Q^*$) of tribbles is 20. (Refer to *FlexText Workbook* Chapter 3 if you need help in solving demand and supply equations.)

**b.** The initial equilibrium price ($P^*$) of a tribble is $30. (Refer to *FlexText Workbook* Chapter 3 if you need help in solving demand and supply equations.)

**c.** The new equilibrium quantity of tribbles is 60. The new equilibrium price of a tribble is $50.

**d.** At the initial income of $180 and price of $30, the quantity of tribbles demanded is 20. In order to find the new quantity demanded at income of $120, we have to use the new demand equation. But since *price* is assumed constant in calculating income elasticity, we have to substitute $P = 30$ into the new demand equation to get the appropriate new quantity. It would be *incorrect* to use the new equilibrium quantity, because that quantity corresponds to a *different price* ($50).

$$P = 110 - 1Q_D$$
$$30 = 110 - 1Q_D$$
$$Q_D = 80$$

We now have appropriate information about the initial quantity demanded (20) and income ($180), and about the new quantity demanded (80) and income ($120). Substituting this information into the formula for income elasticity of demand yields

$$\eta_y = \left(\frac{\Delta Q}{Q_{ave}}\right)\Big/\left(\frac{\Delta Y}{Y_{ave}}\right)$$

$$= \left(\frac{-60}{50}\right)\Big/\left(\frac{60}{150}\right) = -3$$

Since the income elasticity of demand for tribbles is negative, tribbles are an inferior good.

8. The cross elasticities of demand between *A* and *B* are in Table 4 Solution. Since the cross elasticities are positive, we know that *A* and *B* are substitutes.

| TABLE 4 Solution Demand Schedules For Good *A* | | | |
|---|---|---|---|
| $P_A$ | $P_B = \$8$ $Q_A$ | $P_B = \$12$ $Q'_A$ | $\eta_x$ |
| $8 | 2,000 | 4,000 | 1.67 |
| $7 | 4,000 | 6,000 | 1.00 |
| $6 | 6,000 | 8,000 | 0.71 |

# 5 Efficiency and Equity

## Key Concepts

### Resource Allocation Methods

Alternative methods for allocating scarce resources are market price (resources go to those most willing and able to pay); **command system** (by order of authority); majority rule; contest; first-come, first-served; lottery; personal characteristics; force.

### Benefit, Cost, and Surplus

**Value** is what consumers are willing to pay; price is what consumers actually pay.

- Demand curve is a marginal benefit curve.

  - Marginal benefit = value = maximum willing to pay for an additional unit.

Individual demand and market demand:

- *individual demand*—relationship between quantity demanded and price for a single individual.
- *market demand*—sum of individual demands; relationship between total quantity demanded and price.
- *market demand curve*—horizontal sum of individual demand curves.

  - Market demand curve is the economy's marginal social benefit (*MSB*) curve.

- **Consumer surplus** is the marginal benefit of a good minus its price, summed over the quantity bought. It is the triangular area under the demand curve, but above the market price.

Opportunity cost is what producers pay; price is what producers receive.

- Supply curve is a marginal cost curve.

  - Marginal cost = minimum producers must receive to produce an additional unit.

Individual supply and market supply:

- *individual supply*—relationship between quantity supplied and price for a single producer.
- *market supply*—sum of individual supplies; relationship between total quantity supplied and price.
- *market supply curve*—horizontal sum of individual supply curves.

  - Market supply curve is the economy's marginal social cost (*MSC*) curve.

- **Producer surplus** is the price of a good minus its marginal cost, summed over the quantity sold. It is the triangular area below the market price, but above the supply curve.

## Is the Competitive Market Efficient?

In competitive equilibrium

- marginal social benefit = marginal social cost.
- resource allocation is efficient.
- *total surplus* (consumer surplus + producer surplus) is maximized.

**Market failure**—when markets deliver inefficient outcomes (from underproduction or overproduction); is measured by **deadweight loss**—decrease in total surplus below efficient levels.

Sources of market failure:

- price and quantity regulations, taxes, subsidies (Chapter 6).
- *externalities*—the cost or benefit affecting others besides the buyers and sellers of a good (Chapter 16).

- Competitive markets overproduce goods and services that have external costs.
- Competitive markets underproduce goods and services that have external benefits.
- *public goods*—consumed simultaneously by all, even if they don't pay for it (Chapter 17).
  - Competitive markets produce less than the efficient quantity of public goods because of the free-rider problem.
- *monopolies*—firms that restrict output and raise price, creating deadweight loss (Chapter 13).
- high **transactions costs**—opportunity costs of making trades in a market—lead to underproduction.

## Is the Competitive Market Fair?

Ideas about fairness divide into two approaches:

- Fair results—there should be equality of incomes.
  - **Utilitarianism**—result should be the "greatest happiness for the greatest number." Requires income transfers from rich to poor.
  - Income transfers create the "**big tradeoff**" between efficiency and fairness. Transfers use scarce resources and weaken incentives, so a more equally shared pie results in a smaller pie.
  - Modified utilitarianism—after incorporating costs of income transfers, result should make the poorest person as well off as possible.
- Fair rules—people in similar situations should be treated similarly.
  - **Symmetry principle.**
  - Equality of opportunity.
  - Requires property rights and voluntary exchange.

# Helpful Hints

1. This chapter provides important tools for analysing economic policies. Policy analysis involves judgments of efficiency and fairness (or equity). The concepts of consumer and producer surplus allow us to evaluate efficiency—efficient outcomes maximize total surplus—the sum of consumer and producer surplus. Efficiency is a positive concept. The outcomes of different policies can be measured and compared objectively (at least in principle) to see which is more efficient.

   Fairness is another important aspect of any economic policy. Fairness is a normative concept, depending on value judgments about which reasonable people can differ. But policymakers must make decisions, and it is helpful to be explicit about what ideas of fairness are used to judge policy. The two main normative ideas developed in this chapter are fair results and fair rules.

2. There are two ways to interpret or "read" a demand curve—as a demand curve and as a marginal benefit curve. Both readings are correct, but each provides slightly different information.

   The first reading starts with price. For a given price, the demand curve tells us the quantity demanded. Pick a price on the vertical axis. To find quantity demanded, we go "over" to the demand curve and "down" to the quantity axis. This is the standard demand curve of Chapter 3.

   The second reading starts with quantity. For a given quantity, the demand curve tells us the maximum price people are willing to pay. Pick a quantity on the horizontal axis. To find the maximum price people are willing to pay, we go "up" to the demand curve and "over" to the price axis. This is a reading of the demand curve as a marginal benefit curve. For a given quantity, the marginal benefit curve tells us the value (equals the maximum price people are willing to pay) of that unit of the good.

   We read a demand curve "over and down." But we read a marginal benefit curve "up and over." Each reading is helpful, depending on the problem you are trying to solve or the issue you are trying to analyse. If you get stuck with a demand or marginal benefit curve problem, you may not be using the most suitable reading. Try reading the curve both ways and see which one is most helpful.

3. As with the demand curve, there are two ways to interpret or "read" a supply curve—as a supply curve and as a marginal cost curve. Both readings are correct, but each provides slightly different information.

   The first reading starts with price. For a given price, the supply curve tells us the quantity supplied. Pick a price on the vertical axis. To find quantity supplied, we go "over" to the supply curve and "down" to the quantity axis. This is the standard supply curve of Chapter 3.

   The second reading starts with quantity. For a given quantity, the supply curve tells us the minimum price producers are willing to accept. Pick a quantity on the horizontal axis. To find the minimum price producers are willing to accept, we go "up" to the supply curve and "over" to the price axis. This is a reading of the supply curve as a marginal cost curve. For a given quantity, the marginal cost curve tells us the opportunity cost of producing that unit of the good.

   Thus we read a supply curve "over and down," while we read a marginal cost curve "up and over." Each reading is helpful, depending on the problem you are trying to solve or the issue you are trying to analyse. If you get stuck with a supply or marginal cost curve problem, you may not be using the most suitable reading. Try reading the curve both ways and see which one is most helpful.

4. The market demand curve is a marginal social benefit curve and the market supply curve is a marginal social cost curve *as long as there are no external benefits or costs.* Once you think of demand and supply curves as marginal social benefit and cost curves, the concepts of consumer surplus and producer surplus follow directly. Consumer surplus is the difference between the maximum amount people are willing to pay and the price actually paid. At any price, consumer surplus for the market is the area below the demand (marginal social benefit) curve but above the horizontal line at market price. Producer surplus is the difference between the minimum amount producers are willing to accept and the price actually received. At any price, producer

surplus for the market is the area above the supply (marginal social cost) curve but below the horizontal line at market price.

5. An efficient allocation of resources occurs at the quantity of output that maximizes total surplus (consumer surplus + producer surplus). Total surplus is maximized at the quantity where marginal social benefit ($MSB$) equals marginal social cost ($MSC$). To see why the $MSB = MSC$ condition signals maximum efficiency, consider outputs less than and greater than the efficient quantity of output.

   If output is less than the efficient quantity (to the left), $MSB$ is greater than $MSC$. Resources are creating more value ($MSB$) than they cost ($MSC$). By shifting more resources into production of this good and out of production of other goods where $MSB$ is only equal to or less than $MSC$, total surplus will increase.

   Similarly, if output is greater than the efficient quantity (to the right), $MSC$ is greater than $MSB$. Resources cost more ($MSC$) than the value ($MSB$) that they are creating. By shifting more resources out of production of this good and into production of other goods where $MSB$ is at least equal to or greater than $MSC$, total surplus will increase.

   Only at the output where $MSB = MSC$ is total surplus at a maximum, and no reallocation of resources can increase the sum of consumer surplus and producer surplus.

6. Fairness is a normative issue. But note that the tradeoff between economic efficiency and fairness (the "big tradeoff") is a positive issue. Income transfers to achieve fairness norms have real impacts on economic output due to administrative costs and incentive effects. The loss of output and reduced efficiency can be measured. Even though fairness has a cost, policymakers may still come to the conclusion that improved fairness or equity is worth the loss in efficiency. That is the normative issue.

# Self-Test

## True/False and Explain

### Resource Allocation Methods

**1.** A command system can work well to allocate resources when it is easy to monitor activities.

### Benefit, Cost, and Surplus

**2.** The value of a good is its consumer benefit.

**3.** The market demand curve is the horizontal sum of all individual demand curves.

**4.** The market demand curve is formed by adding the willingness to pay for each individual at each price.

**5.** Consumer surplus is the marginal benefit of a good minus the price paid for it.

**6.** Consumer surplus equals the area above the demand curve, but below market price.

**7.** The market supply curve is the vertical sum of the individual firm supply curves.

**8.** The opportunity cost of producing a given quantity of a good is the area under the supply curve.

**9.** Producer surplus is the marginal cost of producing a good minus its price.

## Is the Competitive Market Efficient?

**10.** Adam Smith's "invisible hand" suggests that competitive markets send resources to their highest-valued use.

**11.** Markets always use resources efficiently.

**12.** Deadweight loss is a loss to consumers and a gain to producers.

## Is the Competitive Market Fair?

**13.** Utilitarianism is an example of a fair results idea.

**14.** If we think of the total income of a society as a pie, a more equally shared pie results in a larger pie.

**15.** In economic life, the symmetry principle translates into equality of outcomes.

# Multiple-Choice

## Resource Allocation Methods

1. An efficient method to allocate resources when the efforts of the participants are hard to monitor and reward directly is a
   a. command system.
   b. lottery.
   c. contest.
   d. first-come, first-served rule.
   e. market price.

## Benefit, Cost, and Surplus

2. The maximum price a consumer is willing to pay for a good is known as the
   a. consumer surplus.
   b. value of a good.
   c. relative price of a good.
   d. money price of a good.
   e. marginal cost of a good.

3. Market demand is the
   a. sum of the prices that each individual is willing to pay for each quantity demanded.
   b. sum of the quantities demanded by each individual at each price.
   c. sum of the consumer surplus of each individual.
   d. difference between the maximum amount each individual is willing to pay for a good and the market price.
   e. difference between the market price and the maximum amount each individual is willing to pay for a good.

4. Consumer surplus is the
   a. difference between the maximum price consumers are willing to pay and the minimum price producers are willing to accept.
   b. difference between the marginal benefit of a good and the price paid for the good.
   c. total value to consumers of a good.
   d. area under the demand curve.
   e. total amount paid for the good.

**5.** Consider the demand curve in Fig. 1. What is the value of the first unit of the good?

   **a.** $10

   **b.** $9

   **c.** $8

   **d.** $5

   **e.** $4

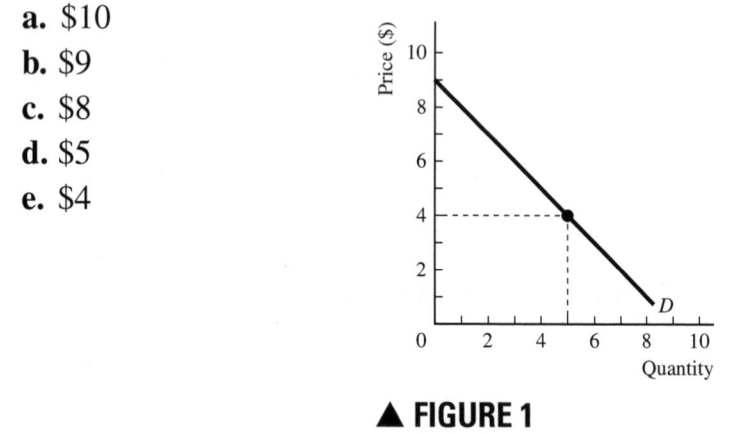

▲ **FIGURE 1**

**6.** Consider the demand curve in Fig. 1. If the price of the good is $4, what is the total consumer surplus?

   **a.** $32.50

   **b.** $25.00

   **c.** $20.00

   **d.** $12.50

   **e.** none of the above

**7.** The marginal cost of a service is

   **a.** the opportunity cost of the first unit produced.

   **b.** the maximum price producers must receive to induce them to supply an additional unit of the service.

   **c.** the value of all alternatives forgone.

   **d.** increasing with increased output.

   **e.** decreasing with increased output.

**8.** A supply curve is

   **a.** a marginal cost curve.

   **b.** a minimum supply-price curve.

   **c.** an opportunity cost of production curve.

   **d.** all of the above.

   **e.** none of the above.

**9.** Producer surplus is the
  **a.** difference between the maximum price consumers are willing to pay and the minimum price producers are willing to accept.
  **b.** difference between producers' revenues and opportunity costs of production.
  **c.** opportunity cost of production.
  **d.** area under the supply curve.
  **e.** total amount paid for the good.

**10.** Consider the demand and supply curves in Fig. 2. Which area in the diagram indicates the opportunity cost of production?
  **a.** *abc*
  **b.** *aec*
  **c.** *ebc*
  **d.** 0*bcd*
  **e.** 0*ecd*

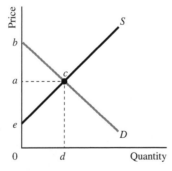

▲ **FIGURE 2**

**11.** Consider the demand and supply curves in Fig. 2. Which area in the diagram indicates producer surplus?
  **a.** *abc*
  **b.** *aec*
  **c.** *ebc*
  **d.** 0*bcd*
  **e.** 0*ecd*

## Is the Competitive Market Efficient?

**12.** At current output, the marginal benefit of Furbys is greater than marginal cost. To achieve an efficient allocation,
  1 Furby output must increase.
  2 Furby output must decrease.
  3 the marginal benefit of Furbys will rise.
  4 the marginal cost of Furbys will fall.
  **a.** 1 and 3
  **b.** 1 and 4
  **c.** 2 and 3
  **d.** 2 and 4
  **e.** 1 only

**13.** If production is not at an efficient level, which of the following *must* be true?

   **a.** Marginal benefit exceeds marginal cost.

   **b.** Marginal cost exceeds marginal benefit.

   **c.** Production will increase.

   **d.** Production will decrease.

   **e.** None of the above.

**14.** In competitive equilibrium, which of the following statements is *false*?

   **a.** Marginal social benefit equals marginal social cost.

   **b.** Willingness to pay equals opportunity cost.

   **c.** The sum of consumer surplus and producer surplus is maximized.

   **d.** Deadweight loss is maximized.

   **e.** Resources are used efficiently to produce goods and services that people value most highly.

**15.** If resources are allocated efficiently,

   **a.** consumer surplus exceeds producer surplus.

   **b.** producer surplus exceeds consumer surplus.

   **c.** the sum of consumer surplus and producer surplus is maximized.

   **d.** marginal social benefit is maximized.

   **e.** marginal social cost is minimized.

**16.** Markets may not achieve an efficient allocation of resources when there are

   **a.** public goods.

   **b.** external benefits.

   **c.** monopolies.

   **d.** subsidies.

   **e.** all of the above.

**17.** The overproduction of a good means that
   **a.** deadweight loss has been eliminated.
   **b.** the sum of consumer surplus and producer surplus is greater than the sum for an efficient allocation.
   **c.** marginal social cost exceeds marginal social benefit.
   **d.** marginal social benefit exceeds marginal social cost.
   **e.** this is a public good.

**19.** Consider the demand and supply curves in Fig. 3. Which area in the diagram indicates the deadweight loss from underproduction?
   **a.** *eacf*
   **b.** *acd*
   **c.** *abd*
   **d.** *bcd*
   **e.** *kaci*

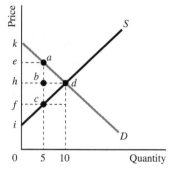

▲ **FIGURE 3**

**18.** Deadweight loss is
   **a.** borne entirely by consumers.
   **b.** gained by producers.
   **c.** the social loss from inefficiency.
   **d.** not a problem with overproduction.
   **e.** all of the above.

**20.** Consider the demand and supply curves in Fig. 3. Which area in the diagram indicates the loss in consumer surplus from underproduction?
   **a.** *eacf*
   **b.** *acd*
   **c.** *abd*
   **d.** *bcd*
   **e.** *kaci*

## Is the Competitive Market Fair?

**21.** Which of the following applies to the *results* principle of fairness?

   **a.** symmetry principle

   **b.** equality of opportunity

   **c.** the big tradeoff

   **d.** protection of private property

   **e.** purely voluntary exchange

**22.** A principle of fairness that emphasizes equality of opportunity is

   **a.** fair results.

   **b.** fair rules.

   **c.** fair incomes.

   **d.** utilitarianism.

   **e.** modified utilitarianism.

**23.** According to the "big tradeoff,"

   **a.** income transfers reduce efficiency.

   **b.** efficiency requires income transfers.

   **c.** a more equally shared pie results in a larger pie.

   **d.** property rights and voluntary exchange ensure equality of opportunity.

   **e.** income transfers should make the poorest person as well off as possible.

**24.** According to Rawls' modified utilitarianism, income should be redistributed until

   **a.** incomes are equal.

   **b.** opportunities are equal.

   **c.** the poorest person is as well off as possible.

   **d.** the poorest person is as well off as possible, after incorporating the costs of income transfers.

   **e.** the big tradeoff is eliminated.

**25.** Economists tend to

   **a.** agree about efficiency and about fairness.

   **b.** agree about efficiency but disagree about fairness.

   **c.** disagree about efficiency but agree about fairness.

   **d.** be more agreeable than philosophers about fairness.

   **e.** be more disagreeable than philosophers about fairness.

# Short Answer Problems

**1.** Table 1 gives the demand schedules for broccoli for three individuals: Tom, Jana, and Ted.

| TABLE 1  Individual Demand For Broccoli | | | |
|---|---|---|---|
| | Quantity Demanded (kilograms per week) | | |
| Price ($ per kilogram) | Tom | Jana | Ted |
| 0.50 | 10 | 4 | 10 |
| 0.75 | 9 | 2 | 7 |
| 1.00 | 8 | 0 | 4 |
| 1.25 | 7 | 0 | 1 |

   **a.** Calculate the market demand schedule.

**b.** Using the grid below, on a single graph draw the individual demand curves for Tom, Jana, and Ted, as well as the market demand curve.

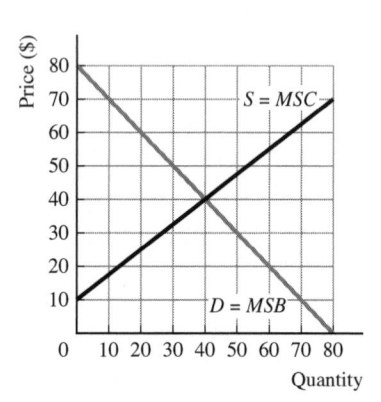

▲ **FIGURE 4  The Champagne Market**

**2. a.** If the price of a bottle of champagne is $60, what is the quantity demanded? the quantity supplied?

**b.** At the price of $60, is there a shortage or a surplus of champagne? Explain the forces that will move the market toward equilibrium.

Fig. 4 shows the market for champagne. Note that the demand curve is also a marginal social benefit curve, and the supply curve is also a marginal social cost curve. Use this information to answer Questions **2–5**.

**c.** If the quantity sold of champagne is 20 bottles, what is the marginal social benefit of the 20th bottle to consumers? the marginal social cost to producers?

**d.** At the quantity of 20 bottles, what is the relationship between the value of the 20th bottle of champagne and the value of the resources forgone to make it? Explain the forces that will move the market toward an efficient allocation of resources.

**3.** Suppose the champagne market in Fig. 4 on page 170 is in equilibrium.

**a.** Calculate the consumer surplus.

**c.** What is the sum of consumer surplus and producer surplus?

**d.** What is the condition for economic efficiency?

**b.** Calculate the producer surplus.

**4.** Suppose now that that there is underproduction in the champagne market in Fig. 4 and output is restricted to 20 bottles.

**a.** List three kinds of obstacles to efficiency that might cause underproduction.

**b.** Calculate the deadweight loss.

**c.** What is the sum of consumer surplus and producer surplus?

**d.** How does the sum compare to the sum in Short Answer Problem **3c**? Is the output of 20 bottles efficient?

**5.** Suppose instead that there is overproduction in the champagne market and output increases to 60 bottles.

**a.** List one kind of obstacle to efficiency that might cause overproduction.

**b.** Calculate the deadweight loss.

**c.** What is the sum of consumer surplus and producer surplus?

**d.** How does the sum compare to the sum in Short Answer Problem **3c**? Is the output of 60 bottles efficient?

ⓒ **6.** There appears to be a contradiction between the Chapter 1 claim that the basic economic problem is scarcity and the Chapter 5 claim that there can be a problem of "overproduction." When the basic problem is that there is too little to meet our wants, how can there be too much of a good?

**7.** Ideas about fairness divide into two groups—fair results and fair rules.

   **a.** What is the basic principle of fair-results ideas? What is the basic principle of fair-rules ideas?

   **b.** What is utilitarianism? Explain why it is a fair-results or fair-rules idea.

©t **8.** Suppose two political parties are vying for your vote in an upcoming election. The "Rights" advocate a more privatized health-care system, where the market sets the price for medical services and individuals pay more of their own bills. The "Lefts" advocate more government subsidies in health care, which would extend free coverage to preventative dental care and prescription drugs.

    **a.** As an intelligent and economically informed citizen, use the concepts of efficiency and fairness (equity) to evaluate the likely pros and cons of each party's policy.

    **b.** Which policy would you likely support? What does this say about your personal valuation of efficiency versus equity?

# Answers

## True/False and Explain

1. **T** Works badly when there are many, difficult-to-monitor activities. (106–107)

2. **F** Value = $MB$. (108–111)

3. **T** Definition. (108–111)

4. **F** Adding the quantities demanded by each individual at each price. (108–111)

5. **T** Definition. (108–111)

6. **F** The area under the demand curve, but above the market price. (108–111)

7. **F** Horizontal sum of individual firm supply curves. (108–111)

8. **T** That area sums the opportunity cost of production for each unit of good produced. (108–111)

9. **F** Price of a good minus its marginal cost of production. (108–111)

10. **T** Competitive markets are "led by an invisible hand" to promote efficient resource use, which benefits all. (112–115)

11. **F** Not when there are obstacles to efficiency like price and quantity regulations, externalities, monopoly, high transaction costs. (112–115)

12. **F** Social loss borne by entire society. (112–115)

13. **T** For utilitarianism, only equality of results is fair, bringing "the greatest happiness for the greatest number." (116–119)

14. **F** A more equally shared pie results in a smaller pie because of the "big tradeoff" between efficiency and fairness. (116–119)

15. **F** The symmetry principle—treat others as you would like to be treated—translates into equality of *opportunity*. (116–119)

## Multiple-Choice

1. **c** Only a few end up with a big prize, but many work harder trying to win. (106–107)

2. **b** Value = marginal benefit. (108–111)

3. **b** See text discussion. (108–111)

4. **b** Definition. Area under the demand curve but above the market price. (108–111)

5. **c** From $Q = 1$, go up to demand curve to read over to maximum price willing to pay. (108–111)

6. **d** Area of triangle ($1/2ba$) below demand and above $P = 4$. (108–111)

7. **d** Principle of increasing marginal cost; $MC$ = value of *best* alternative forgone. (108–111)

8. **d** All definitions of supply curve. (108–111)

9. **b** Definition. Area below the market price but above the supply curve. (108–111)

10. **e** Area below the supply curve. (108–111)

**11. b** Area below the market price but above the supply curve. (108–111)

**12. e** With increasing $Q$, $MSB$ must fall and $MSC$ rise. (112–115)

**13. e** If production is below efficient level, **a** and **c** are true; if production is above efficient level, **b** and **d** are true. (112–115)

**14. d** No deadweight loss. All other answers are definitions of competitive equilibrium. (112–115)

**15. c** Definition where marginal benefit equals marginal cost. No other necessary relation between consumer and producer surplus. (112–115)

**16. e** All change quantity produced above (**d**) or below (**a, b, c**) efficient quantity. (112–115)

**17. c** Production beyond efficient level creates deadweight loss, reducing total surplus. (112–115)

**18. c** Borne by consumers and producers when there is underproduction or overproduction. (112–115)

**19. b** Decrease in consumer and producer surplus compared to efficient quantity (10) of production. (112–115)

**20. c** Area subtracted from consumer surplus at efficient quantity (10) of production (*hkd*). (112–115)

**21. c** Other answers apply to *rules* principle of fairness. (116–119)

**22. b** Other answers apply to *results* principle of fairness. (116–119)

**23. a** Tradeoff between equity (which requires income transfers) and efficiency. (116–119)

**24. d** Rawls' idea incorporates the effects of the big trade-off in trying to redistribute income more equally, but not totally equally. (116–119)

**25. b** Efficiency is a positive issue; fairness is a normative issue. (116–119)

## Short Answer Problems

**1. a.** The market demand schedule is obtained by adding the quantities demanded by Tom, Jana, and Ted at each price (see Table 2).

| TABLE 2 Market Demand Schedule For Broccoli | |
|---|---|
| Price ($ per kilogram) | Quantity Demanded (kilograms per week) |
| 0.50 | 24 |
| 0.75 | 18 |
| 1.00 | 12 |
| 1.25 | 8 |

**b.** Fig. 5 illustrates the individual demand curves for Tom, Jana, and Ted as well as the market demand curve.

▲ **FIGURE 5**

**2. a.** Quantity demanded is 20 bottles; quantity supplied is approximately 67 bottles. We find these quantities by starting with the price of $60 and reading "over" to each curve and "down" to the quantity.

**b.** There is a surplus because quantity supplied exceeds quantity demanded. Producers have excess supplies, so they will cut prices rather than be stuck with unsold goods. Quantity demanded will increase as price falls, until we end up at the equilibrium price of $40/bottle and the equilibrium quantity of 40 bottles.

**c.** Marginal social benefit is $60; marginal social cost is $25. We find these values by starting with the quantity of 20 bottles and reading "up" to each curve and "over" to the marginal social benefit and cost (measured in prices).

**d.** The 20th bottle of champagne is valued by consumers at $60, but uses only $25 worth of resources to make. With marginal social benefit exceeding marginal social cost, consumers would happily pay more than $25 for an additional bottle of champagne and will bid up the price. Producers will increase the quantity supplied until the market reaches the equilibrium price of $40/bottle and the equilibrium quantity of 40 bottles. Producers increase champagne output by transferring resources from other uses. Resources, which were being used elsewhere to create value just equal to their cost, are now being used more efficiently in that they create more value in champagne production than their cost.

**3. a.** Consumer surplus is the triangular area under the demand curve but above the horizontal line at the market price of $40. The formula for the area of a triangle is 1/2(base)(altitude), so consumer surplus = 1/2(40)(40) = 800.

**b.** Producer surplus is the triangular area above the supply curve but below the horizontal line at the market price of $40. Producer surplus = 1/2(40)(30) = 600.

**c.** The sum of consumer and producer surplus is 800 + 600 = 1,400.

**d.** Economic efficiency occurs when the sum of consumer surplus and producer surplus is maximized. Is this specific outcome efficient? We can't be sure if 1,400 is a maximum until we compare other situations in the champagne market.

**4. a.** Price and quantity regulations, taxes, external benefits, public goods, monopoly, and high transactions costs all might cause output to be restricted.

**b.** Deadweight loss is the decrease in consumer surplus and producer surplus that results from an inefficient level of production. It is equal to the triangular area between the demand and supply curves from quantity = 20 to quantity = 40. Deadweight loss = 1/2(35)(20) = 350.

**c.** The new sum of consumer and producer surplus is the original amount of 1,400 minus the deadweight loss: 1,400 − 350 = 1,050.

**d.** The sum of consumer and producer surplus (1,050) is less than the equilibrium sum in Short Answer Problem **3c** at an output of 40 bottles. Since an efficient output maximizes the sum of consumer and producer surplus, the output of 20 bottles is not efficient.

**5. a.** Subsidies to producers or external costs can cause overproduction.

**b.** Deadweight loss is equal to the triangular area between the demand and supply curves from quantity = 40 to quantity = 60. Deadweight loss = 1/2(35)(20) = 350. (It is just a coincidence that this deadweight loss from overproduction happens to be equal to the deadweight loss from underproduction. In general these losses are not necessarily equal.)

**c.** The new sum of consumer and producer surplus is the original amount of 1,400 minus the deadweight loss: 1,400 − 350 = 1,050.

**d.** The sum of consumer and producer surplus (1,050) is less than the equilibrium sum in Short Answer Problem **3c** at an output of 40 bottles. Since an efficient output maximizes the sum of consumer and producer surplus, the output of 60 bottles is not efficient.

ⓒⓣ **6.** Because wants *in general* exceed the resources available to satisfy them, we cannot have everything we want and must make choices. This basic problem leads to economizing behaviour—choosing the best or optimal use of available resources. But *specific* wants can be satisfied. Each of us has relatively limited wants, for example, for salt, for heat in our houses during the winter, or for nail clippers. If these or other goods are produced beyond the point where the marginal benefit equals the marginal cost, there is a problem of overproduction.

Overproduction is a problem because the resources could be *better used* to produce different goods that could meet still-unsatisfied wants. The money invested in excessive salt production could be diverted to health research to find a cure for cancer, or to schools to allow more demands for education to be satisfied. Because wants *in general* are unlimited, producing too much of a good to satisfy a *specific* want actually prevents us from making optimal use of available resources. So the ideas of scarcity and overproduction are not contradictory. In fact, overproduction of a *specific* good is a problem precisely because there is a problem of scarcity in satisfying wants *in general*.

**7. a.** Fair-results ideas are based on the principle that results are most important, and that the fairest economic result is equal incomes for all. Fair-rules ideas are based on the symmetry principle—that people in similar situations should be treated similarly. This principle translates into equality of opportunity in economic life.

**b.** Utilitarianism is based on the principle that the fairest system is one in which incomes are equal. Utilitarians argue that transferring income from the rich to the poor will result in "the greatest happiness for the greatest number," since the marginal benefit of an additional dollar to the poor person is greater than the benefit to the rich person. Only at equal incomes for all is total social benefit at a maximum. Since utilitarianism focuses on equal incomes or results, it is a fair-results idea.

ⓒⓣ **8. a.** The "Rights" market-oriented health-care policy likely is more efficient. It requires less government administration and would probably allow lower taxes because less is being spent by government and more by private individuals. With lower taxes, incentives to work might increase, and the size of the economic pie might be larger.

With lower government subsidies, the price of health care to individuals will rise. Health care may become unaffordable to some members of society, so the "Rights" policy may be less fair from a "fair results" perspective. From a "fair rules" perspective, the "Rights" policy is fair as long as everyone faces the same opportunities.

The "Lefts" subsidized health-care policy likely is less efficient, because it would require subsidies to health-care providers and require more government administration and higher taxes to pay for the policy. With higher taxes, incentives to work might decrease, and the size of the economic pie might be smaller. On the other hand, with a healthier population, productivity might increase because fewer work days would be lost to illness. So the net effect on efficiency is unclear.

More health-care services will become available to a greater number of people, so the "Lefts" policy may be fairer from a fair-results perspective. From a fair-rules perspective, the "Lefts" policy may be less fair if, to pay for the policy, individuals with higher incomes are taxed more than those with lower incomes.

b. There is obviously no single correct answer to this question. The important thing is to think explicitly about your personal valuation of efficiency versus equity, and which idea of fairness appeals most to you.

# 6 Government Actions in Markets

## Key Concepts

### A Housing Market with a Rent Ceiling

In a government-regulated housing market

- a **rent ceiling** (a **price ceiling** applied to rents) makes it illegal to raise rents.
- housing stocks are lower than in an unregulated market both in the short and long run; no incentive to economize on space or build new housing.
- shortages cause excess demand and
    - **search activity** (time spent looking for someone with whom to do business).
    - **black markets** (illegal markets where prices exceed ceilings).

Unregulated markets allocate housing resources efficiently, while rent ceilings create inefficiencies (deadweight loss) without necessarily improving fairness.

### A Labour Market with a Minimum Wage

A **minimum wage** (a **price floor** applied to wages) makes it illegal to hire labour below a specified wage.

- Minimum wages create excess supply of labour (unemployment) and lower the quantity of labour demanded and hired.

- Unemployed workers willing to work at a lower wage spend more time searching for work.
- Minimum wage benefits those who keep jobs, but makes the unemployed worse off.

## Taxes

A tax on sellers shifts the supply curve up by a vertical distance equal to the amount of the tax. A tax on buyers shifts the demand curve down by a vertical distance equal to the amount of the tax. Results are the same.

**Tax incidence**—division of the burden of a tax between buyers and sellers—depends on elasticities of supply and demand.

*Supply elasticity and tax division:*

- Perfectly inelastic supply—sellers pay all.
- More inelastic supply—sellers pay more.
- More elastic supply—buyers pay more.
- Perfectly elastic supply—buyers pay all.

*Demand elasticity and tax division:*

- Perfectly inelastic demand—buyers pay all.
- More inelastic demand—buyers pay more.
- More elastic demand—sellers pay more.
- Perfectly elastic demand—sellers pay all.

Taxes decrease the quantity produced and consumed, creating deadweight loss.
 Fairness of taxes can be evaluated by

- *benefits principle*—fairness is people paying taxes equal to benefits they receive from government services
- *ability-to-pay principle*—fairness is people paying taxes according to their ability to pay (rich pay more than poor)

# Production Quotas and Subsidies

Government can take actions in markets for farm products by setting

- **production quotas** (quantity restrictions on production), which increase market price, decrease $Q$ grown, and create inefficient underproduction.
- **subsidies** (payments by governments to producers), which increase supply, decrease market price (but farmers receive market price plus subsidy), and create inefficient overproduction.

# Markets for Illegal Goods

Penalizing dealers for selling illegal goods increases the cost of selling goods and decreases supply. Penalizing buyers for consuming illegal goods decreases willingness to pay and decreases demand.

- When (sellers' penalties > buyers' penalties), $Q$ decreases, $P$ rises.
- When (sellers' penalties < buyers' penalties), $Q$ decreases, $P$ falls.
- Taxing (decriminalized) goods can achieve the same consumption levels as prohibition.

# Helpful Hints

1. In the real world, governments often regulate markets using price constraints, so it is important to study the effects of such regulation. Another benefit of studying government regulation is to understand how markets work when, by contrast, the government does *not* affect the normal operation of markets.

   Whenever something disturbs an equilibrium in an unregulated (free) market, the desires of buyers and sellers are brought back into balance by price movements. If prices are controlled by government regulation, however, the price mechanism can no longer serve this purpose. Thus *balance* must be restored in some other way. In the case of price ceilings, black markets are likely to arise. If black markets cannot develop because of strict enforcement of price ceilings, demanders will be forced to bear the costs of increased search activity, waiting in line, or something else.

2. This chapter discusses government price constraints in three markets: rental housing, labour, and farm products. The basic principles, however, can be generalized to other markets.

   In any market with a legal price ceiling set below the market-clearing price, we will observe excess quantity demanded, because price cannot increase to eliminate it. As a consequence, the marginal benefit of the last unit of the good available will exceed the controlled price. Demanders are willing to engage in costly activities up to the marginal benefit of that last unit (search activity, waiting lines, and black market activity) to obtain the good.

   Furthermore, if price is allowed to increase in response to a decrease in supply or an increase in demand, there are incentive effects for suppliers to produce more and demanders to purchase less (movements along the supply and demand curves). Indeed, it is the response to these incentives that restores equilibrium in markets with freely adjusting prices. If the price cannot adjust, these price-induced incentive effects do not have a chance to operate. In the case of rent ceilings, the inability of rents (price) to rise means that (1) there is no inducement to use the current stock of housing more intensively in the short run, and (2) there is no incentive to construct new housing in the long run. Similarly, the effects on any market in which a minimum price (price floor) is set above the market-clearing (equilibrium) price will be similar to those discussed in the text for the labour market under minimum wage or price floors in agricultural markets.

**3.** The division of the burden of a tax is called tax incidence. Who pays a sales tax imposed on producers depends on the elasticities of demand and supply. The general principles of tax incidence are

- more inelastic demand—consumers pay more.
- more elastic demand—producers pay more.
- more inelastic supply—producers pay more.
- more elastic supply—consumers pay more.

# Self-Test
## True/False and Explain

### A Housing Market with a Rent Ceiling

**1.** In an unregulated housing market, higher rents increase the short-run quantity of housing supplied.

**2.** When rents in an unregulated housing market rise due to a decrease in supply, people who are unable to pay the higher rents will not get housing.

**3.** If a rent ceiling exceeds people's willingness to pay, search activity and black markets will increase.

### A Labour Market with a Minimum Wage

**4.** In an unregulated labour market, a decrease in the demand for labour causes the wage rate to rise.

**5.** An increase in the minimum wage will reduce the number of workers employed.

**6.** Most economists believe that raising the minimum wage has no effect on unemployment.

**7.** Minimum wage laws increase the amount of time people spend searching for work.

### Taxes

**8.** The more elastic demand is for a product, the larger the fraction of a sales tax paid by consumers.

**9.** A sales tax always creates deadweight loss.

**10.** The deadweight loss from a sales tax equals the tax revenue collected by government.

## Production Quotas and Subsidies

**11.** Farm subsidies like those in Canada are a major source of tension between rich and developing nations.

**12.** A production quota creates inefficiency through overproduction.

**13.** A subsidy paid to producers shifts the demand curve for a good rightward.

## Markets for Illegal Goods

**14.** The statement "If we legalize and tax drugs, tax revenues could be used to finance more drug education programs" is normative.

**15.** If penalties are imposed on both sellers and buyers in a market for prohibited goods, the price may rise, fall, or remain constant, while the quantity bought always decreases.

# Multiple-Choice

## A Housing Market with a Rent Ceiling

1. The short-run supply curve for rental housing is positively sloped because
   a. the supply of housing is fixed in the short run.
   b. the current stock of buildings will be used more intensively as rents rise.
   c. the cost of constructing new buildings increases as the number of buildings increases.
   d. the cost of constructing a new buildings is about the same regardless of the number of buildings in existence.
   e. new buildings will be constructed as rents rise.

2. Rent ceilings imposed by governments
   a. keep rental prices below the unregulated market price.
   b. keep rental prices above the unregulated market price.
   c. keep rental prices equal to the unregulated market price.
   d. increase the stock of rental housing.
   e. increase the intensity of use of the current stock of rental housing.

3. A price ceiling set below the equilibrium price will result in
   a. excess supply.
   b. excess demand.
   c. the equilibrium price.
   d. an increase in supply.
   e. a decrease in demand.

4. Which of the following is *not* a likely outcome of rent ceilings?
   a. a black market for rent-controlled housing
   b. long waiting lists of potential renters of rent-controlled housing
   c. a short-run shortage of housing
   d. black market prices below the rent ceiling prices
   e. increased search activity for rent-controlled housing

## A Labour Market with a Minimum Wage

**5.** If the minimum wage is set at $2 per hour in Fig. 1, what is the level of unemployment in millions of hours?

  **a.** 50

  **b.** 40

  **c.** 20

  **d.** 10

  **e.** 0

▲ **FIGURE 1**

**6.** In Fig. 1, if the minimum wage is set at $6 per hour, what is the level of unemployment in millions of hours?

  **a.** 50

  **b.** 40

  **c.** 20

  **d.** 10

  **e.** 0

**7.** In Fig. 1, if the minimum wage is set at $6 per hour, what is the area of deadweight loss?

  **a.** *abd*

  **b.** *bcd*

  **c.** *cde*

  **d.** *ade*

  **e.** 0

## Taxes

**8.** Fig. 2 shows the market for frisbees before and after a sales tax is imposed. The sales tax on each frisbee is

  **a.** $0.40.

  **b.** $0.60.

  **c.** $1.00.

  **d.** $5.60.

  **e.** $6.60.

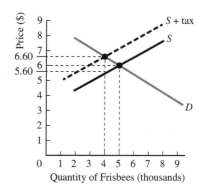

▲ **FIGURE 2**

**9.** Refer to Fig. 2. For each frisbee, the sellers' share of the tax is
   **a.** $0.40.
   **b.** $0.60.
   **c.** $1.00.
   **d.** $5.60.
   **e.** $6.60.

**10.** Refer to Fig. 2. For each frisbee, the buyers' share of the tax is
   **a.** $0.40.
   **b.** $0.60.
   **c.** $1.00.
   **d.** $5.60.
   **e.** $6.60.

**11.** Refer to Fig. 2. Government revenue from the tax is
   **a.** $4,000.
   **b.** $5,000.
   **c.** $22,400.
   **d.** $26,400.
   **e.** $30,000.

**12.** From Fig. 2 we can deduce that between 4,000 and 5,000 units, the demand for frisbees is
   **a.** inelastic.
   **b.** unit elastic.
   **c.** elastic.
   **d.** more elastic than the supply ($S$) of frisbees.
   **e.** soaring.

**13.** Refer to Fig. 2. Deadweight loss from the tax is
   **a.** $500.
   **b.** $1,000.
   **c.** $3,600.
   **d.** $4,000.
   **e.** $5,000.

**14.** A tax on buyers
   **a.** shifts the demand curve up by a vertical distance equal to the tax.
   **b.** shifts the supply curve up by a vertical distance equal to the tax.
   **c.** has the same effect on price and quantity as a tax on sellers.
   **d.** has a different effect on price and quantity as a tax on sellers.
   **e.** increases the price received by sellers.

**15.** If the price of a good is not affected by a sales tax,
   **a.** supply is perfectly elastic.
   **b.** demand is perfectly elastic.
   **c.** elasticity of supply is greater than elasticity of demand.
   **d.** elasticity of demand is greater than elasticity of supply.
   **e.** none of the above.

**16.** Which of the following statement(s) about taxes and fairness is/are *true*?
   **a.** The benefits principle of fairness is people paying taxes equal to the benefits they receive from government services
   **b.** For the ability-to-pay principle of fairness, the rich should pay more taxes than the poor.
   **c.** High fuel taxes to pay for highways are justified by the benefits principle.
   **d.** Tax cuts to the rich are unfair according to the ability-to-pay principle.
   **e.** All of the above are true.

## Production Quotas and Subsidies

**17.** A production quota set above the equilibrium quantity will cause

   **a.** a decrease in supply.

   **b.** a rise in price.

   **c.** inefficient underproduction.

   **d.** all of the above.

   **e.** none of the above.

**18.** Fig. 3 illustrates the short-run demand and supply curves in the wheat bran market. If the Wheat Marketing Board sets a quota of 50 million bushels, the market-clearing price of a bushel of wheat bran is

   **a.** $1.

   **b.** $3.

   **c.** $5.

   **d.** two scoops of raisins.

   **e.** none of the above.

▲ **FIGURE 3**

**19.** Refer to Fig. 3. With the quota of 50 million bushels, farmers have an incentive to

    **a.** decrease output because the market-clearing price is below cost of production.

    **b.** decrease output because there is a surplus at the market-clearing price.

    **c.** increase output because the market-clearing price is above cost of production.

    **d.** increase output because there is a shortage at the market-clearing price.

    **e.** stick to the quota.

**20.** Refer to Fig. 3. Suppose the marketing board develops a new kind of subsidy called a direct payment plan. Farmers are told, "We will guarantee you $5 per bushel, but everything you produce at this price must be sold on the market for whatever buyers will pay; then we will give you (at taxpayers' expense) the difference between the market price and $5 per bushel." How many bushels of wheat bran will be sold?

    **a.** 20 million

    **b.** 50 million

    **c.** 60 million

    **d.** 70 million

    **e.** none of the above

**21.** Refer to Fig. 3. The amount of taxpayers' money that the marketing board pays to farmers in Question **20** is

    **a.** zero.

    **b.** $70 million.

    **c.** $250 million.

    **d.** $280 million.

    **e.** $350 million.

**22.** European Union (EU) countries have been accumulating butter and cheese mountains and wine lakes. These surpluses are consistent with

    **a.** floor prices for agricultural products that are below market prices.

    **b.** floor prices for agricultural products that are above market prices.

    **c.** ceiling prices for agricultural products that are below market prices.

    **d.** ceiling prices for agricultural products that are above market prices.

    **e.** quotas for agricultural products.

**23.** An agricultural subsidy
  **a.** shifts the supply curve rightward.
  **b.** benefits consumers by lowering product prices.
  **c.** benefits farmers by raising the price they receive.
  **d.** imposes major costs on taxpayers.
  **e.** does all of the above.

## Markets for Illegal Goods

**24.** If enforcement is aimed at sellers of a prohibited good,
  **a.** price and quantity bought will decrease.
  **b.** price and quantity bought will increase.
  **c.** price will increase and quantity bought will decrease.
  **d.** price will decrease and quantity bought will increase.
  **e.** price change will be uncertain and quantity bought will decrease.

**25.** Which of the following statements about prohibited goods is *true*?
  **a.** Taxes are more effective in changing preferences than prohibition.
  **b.** Prohibition is more effective in generating revenue than an equivalent tax.
  **c.** Taxes and penalties cannot be set so as to yield equivalent outcomes.
  **d.** Taxes generate revenues, while prohibition generates more enforcement expenses.
  **e.** None of the above is true.

# Short Answer Problems

**1.** Suppose that the market for rental housing is initially in long-run equilibrium. Using the grid, draw a graph to answer the following:

   **a.** Explain how an unregulated market for rental housing would adjust if there is a sudden significant increase in demand. What will happen to rent and the quantity of units rented in the short run and in the long run? Be sure to discuss the effect on incentives (in both the short and the long run) as the market-determined price (rent) changes.

**b.** Now explain how the market would adjust to the increase in demand if rent ceilings are established at the level of the initial equilibrium rent. What has happened to supplier incentives in this case?

**2.** The demand for and supply of gasoline are given in Table 1.

| TABLE 1 | | |
| --- | --- | --- |
| Price ($ per litre) | Quantity Demanded (millions of litres per day) | Quantity Supplied (millions of litres per day) |
| 1.40 | 8 | 24 |
| 1.30 | 10 | 22 |
| 1.20 | 12 | 20 |
| 1.10 | 14 | 18 |
| 1.00 | 16 | 16 |
| 0.90 | 18 | 14 |

**a.** What are the equilibrium price and quantity of gasoline?

**b.** Suppose that the quantity of gasoline supplied suddenly declines by 8 million litres per day at every price. In the space below, construct a new table of price, quantity demanded, and quantity supplied, and using the grid, draw a graph of the demand curve and the initial and new supply curves. Assuming that the market for gasoline is unregulated, use either your table or your graph to find the new equilibrium price and quantity of gasoline.

**c.** How has the change in price affected the behaviour of demanders? the behaviour of suppliers?

**c.** What is the excess quantity of gasoline demanded?

**d.** For the last litre of gasoline sold, what is the marginal benefit? marginal cost?

**3.** Suppose that the government imposes a price ceiling of $1 per litre of gasoline at the same time as the decrease in supply reported in Short Answer Problem **2b**.

**a.** What is the quantity of gasoline demanded? quantity supplied?

**b.** What is the quantity of gasoline actually sold?

**e.** Is this an efficient outcome? Explain.

**4.** Governments tend to put high sales taxes (often called "sin" taxes) on liquor and cigarettes. Aside from moral and health reasons, why are these goods chosen as a source of tax revenue?

**5.** The Ministry of Treasury has been authorized to levy a $0.15 per unit excise (sales) tax on one of two goods—comic books or dog biscuits. As a summer student at the Ministry, you are given an assignment by the Director of Taxes, Dr. More. You must choose the good that meets two objectives: (1) it will yield the greatest tax revenue and (2) the major burden of the tax will fall on consumers. Ministry researchers have estimated the supply and demand curves (without the tax) for each market. The comic book market is shown in Fig. 4 below and the dog biscuit market in Fig. 5 on the next page. The following questions will help you complete your assignment.

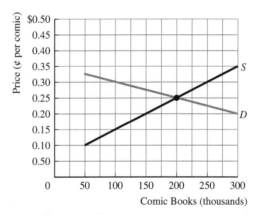

▲ **FIGURE 4  Comic Book Market**

**a.** For the comic book market, shift the appropriate curve to reflect the tax and draw it on Fig. 4 on the previous page. Label the curve either "S + *tax*" or "D + *tax*." Identify the new equilibrium price and quantity. Compare the total expenditure in the original and new equilibriums.

**c.** How much of the tax is paid by consumers? by producers?

**b.** Calculate the total tax revenue collected, and indicate it as an area on Fig. 4.

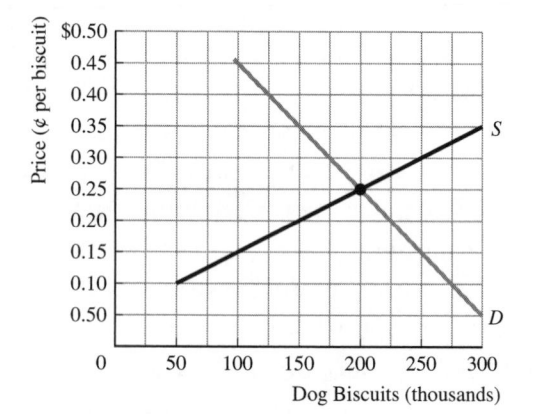

▲ **FIGURE 5  Dog Biscuit Market**

**d.** Now perform the same analysis on the dog biscuit market. Shift the appropriate curve to reflect the tax and draw it on Fig. 5 on the previous page. Label the curve either "*S + tax*" or "*D + tax*." Identify the new equilibrium price and quantity. Compare the total expenditure in the original and new equilibriums.

**f.** How much of the tax is paid by consumers? by producers?

**g.** What is your recommendation to Dr. More? Explain.

**e.** Using the space below, calculate the total tax revenue collected and indicate it as an area on Fig. 5.

℗ **6.** Dr. More was pleased with your excise tax recommendation in Short Answer Problem **5**, but you can't stop wondering about his comment, "Hmm, I thought you would do it the other way." If you haven't already figured out to what he was referring, the following questions will help.

    **a.** For the comic book market, calculate the elasticity of demand between the original and new equilibrium points. Is demand elastic or inelastic?

**b.** Perform the same calculation for the dog biscuit market. Is demand elastic or inelastic?

**c.** What do you know about demand elasticities that would have allowed you to complete your assignment "the other way" and predict which market would yield maximum tax revenue, and which market would place most of the tax burden on consumers?

**7.** After spending so much time on Dr. More's tax assignment in Short Answer Problems **5** and **6**, you realize you have one last chance to impress the boss. While your previous tax assignment had two important policy objectives—maximum tax revenue and appropriate tax burden—no one asked you about the relative efficiency loss of a tax on comic books versus dog biscuits. If the policy objective is to minimize deadweight loss, which good do you recommend be taxed?

8. Questions about the fairness of taxes are normative questions that depend on value judgments. If we arrange political parties in Canada on a spectrum from left (NDP) to right (Conservatives), which party is most likely to use the benefits principle to justify tax policy? Which party is most likely to use the ability-to-pay principle? Explain your answers.

# Answers

## True/False and Explain

1. **T** Higher rents create incentives to use current buildings more intensively. (128–130)

2. **T** At equilibrium rent, all who can afford housing get it, but not necessarily those who need housing. (128–130)

3. **F** Ceiling is above market price so search activity won't increase and black markets won't arise. (128–130)

4. **F** Leftward shift in demand causes the wage rate to fall. (131–133)

5. **T** Raising the minimum wage decreases the quantity of labour demanded. (131–133)

6. **F** Exceptions are economists Card and Krueger. (131–133)

7. **T** Compared to an unregulated market, increased job search by labour in excess supply at minimum wage. (131–133)

8. **F** More elastic demand means more substitutes available and consumers are better able to escape tax by not buying. (133–138)

ⓒⓣ 9. **F** Usually true; false if demand or supply is perfectly inelastic. (133–138)

10. **F** Tax revenue and deadweight loss come from lost surplus, but they are not equal. (133–138)

11. **T** See "Economics in Action." (141)

12. **F** Creates inefficiency through underproduction. (139–141)

13. **F** Shifts supply rightward. (139–141)

ⓒⓣ 14. **F** Positive statement; can be verified by observation. (142–143)

ⓒⓣ 15. **T** Effect on $P$ depends on the relative magnitude of penalties. (142–143)

## Multiple-Choice

1. **b** **c**, **d**, and **e** refer to long run. (128–130)

2. **a** Definition. **d** and **e** are the result of higher rent in an unregulated market. (128–130)

3. **b** Draw graph. No Δ *ceteris paribus* assumptions, so no shift in supply or demand. (128–130)

4. **d** Black market prices will be above ceiling. (128–130)

ⓒⓣ 5. **e** Floor below equilibrium $P$ doesn't prevent market from reaching equilibrium. (131–133)

6. **b** Quantity supplied (50) > quantity demanded (10). (131–133)

7. **d** Half of loss is consumer surplus, half is producer surplus. (131–133)

8. **c** Equals the vertical distance between the two supply curves. (133–138)

9. **a** Original $P$ = $6, new $P$ = $6.60. Sellers pay $1 tax and get $0.60 more from buyers, so sellers pay $0.40. (133–138)

10. **b** See previous answer. (133–138)

11. **a** $1 per frisbee × 4,000 units sold. (133–138)

**⊙ 12. c** Rise in $P$ ($6 to $6.60) decreases total revenue ($30,000 to $26,400). **d** is wrong: $\eta = 2.3$ and $\eta_s = 3.2$. (133–138)

**13. a** Area of triangle $(1/2ba)$ with base $= \$1$ ($6.60 − $5.60) and altitude $= 1,000$ (5,000 − 4,000). (133–138)

**14. c** Shifts demand curve down by vertical distance tax and decreases price received by sellers. (133–138)

**15. b a** would raise $P$ by full amount of tax. **c** and **d** affect $P$ but amounts uncertain. (133–138)

**16. e** The two principles are conflicting, but one can justify every statement. (133–138)

**17. e d** is true if quota is *below* equilibrium quantity. (139–141)

**18. c** Where vertical supply curve at 50 million bushels intersects demand. (139–141)

**⊙ 19. c** Farmers receiving $5 but willing to supply this quantity at (their cost of) $1. (139–141)

**⊙ 20. d** Quantity supplied at $P = \$5$. (139–141)

**⊙ 21. d** 70 million bushels sell for $1 per bushel. Taxpayers make up the difference of $4 per bushel × 70 million. (139–141)

**22. b** Floor above market $P$ creates excess supply. (139–141)

**23. e** Definition. (139–141)

**24. c** Supply shifts leftward as penalties are added to other costs. (142–143)

**25. d** Reverse taxes and prohibition to make **a** and **b** true. (142–143)

## Short Answer Problems

**1. a.** Fig. 6 on the next page corresponds to an unregulated market for rental housing. The initial demand, short-run supply, and long-run supply curves are $D_0$, $SS_0$, and $LS$. The market is initially in long-run equilibrium at point $a$ corresponding to rent $R_0$ and quantity of rental units $Q_0$. Demand then increases to $D_1$, creating excess quantity demanded of $Q_2 − Q_0$ at the initial rent. In the short run, in an unregulated market, rent rises to $R_1$ to clear the markets and the equilibrium quantity of housing rented is $Q_1$ (point $b$). As the rent rises, the quantity of rental housing supplied increases (movement from point $a$ to point $b$ along supply curve $SS_0$) as the existing stock of housing is used more intensively. The quantity of housing demanded decreases (movement from point $c$ to point $b$ along demand curve $D_1$). Together, these movements eliminate the excess quantity demanded. The higher rent also provides an incentive to construct new housing in the long run—the shift in the supply curve from $SS_0$ to $SS_1$. The new long-run equilibrium is at point $c$, with rent restored to its original level and the number of units rented equal to $Q_2$.

▲ **FIGURE 6**

**b.** We can also use Fig. 6 to discuss the behaviour of a market with a rent ceiling set at $R_0$. Start in the same long-run equilibrium at point $a$. Once again we observe an increase in demand from $D_0$ to $D_1$. In this case, however, the rent cannot rise to restore equilibrium. There will be no incentive to use the existing stock of housing more intensively in the short run or to construct new housing in the long run. The quantity of rental housing supplied will remain at $Q_0$. Since the last unit of rental housing is valued at $R_2$, but rent is fixed at $R_0$, demanders of rental housing will be willing to bear additional costs up to $R_2 - R_0$ (in the form of additional search activity or illegal payments) in order to obtain rental housing.

**2. a.** The equilibrium price of gasoline is $1 per litre, since at that price the quantity of gasoline demanded is equal to the quantity supplied (16 million litres per day). The equilibrium quantity of gasoline is 16 million litres per day.

**b.** The new table and graph are shown in Table 2 and Fig. 7.

| TABLE 2 | | |
| --- | --- | --- |
| **Price** | **Quantity Demanded (millions of litres per day)** | **Quantity Supplied (millions of litres per day)** |
| 1.40 | 8 | 16 |
| 1.30 | 10 | 14 |
| 1.20 | 12 | 12 |
| 1.10 | 14 | 10 |
| 1.00 | 16 | 8 |
| 0.90 | 18 | 6 |

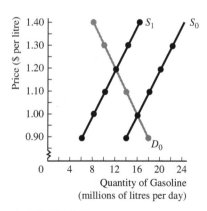

▲ **FIGURE 7**

The new equilibrium price is $1.20 per litre, since at that price the quantity of gasoline demanded equals the new quantity supplied (12 million litres per day).

The new equilibrium quantity is 12 million litres of gasoline per day.

**c.** The increase in price has caused the quantity of gasoline demanded to decrease by 4 million litres per day (from 16 to 12 million). Given the new supply curve $S_1$, the increase in price from \$1 to \$1.20 per litre increases the quantity of gasoline supplied by 4 million litres per day (from 8 to 12 million).

**3. a.** At the ceiling price of \$1, quantity demanded is 16 million litres per day, quantity supplied is 8 million litres per day.

**b.** The quantity of gasoline actually sold is 8 million litres per day. When, at a given price, quantity demanded and quantity supplied differ, whichever quantity is *less* determines the quantity actually sold.

**c.** The excess quantity of gasoline demanded is 8 million litres per day.

**d.** The marginal benefit of the 8-millionth litre per day of gasoline sold is \$1.40. You can obtain this answer from your graph by imagining a vertical line from the quantity 8 million litres up to where it intersects the demand curve at \$1.40. The demand curve is also a marginal benefit curve, showing the highest price consumers are willing to pay for each additional litre.

The marginal cost of the 8-millionth litre per day of gasoline sold is \$1. The imaginary vertical line from the quantity 8 million litres intersects the supply curve $S_1$ at \$1. The supply curve is also a marginal cost curve, showing the minimum producers must receive to produce an additional litre.

**e.** Since marginal benefit (\$1.40) > marginal cost (\$1), the outcome is *not* efficient. The sum of consumer and producer surplus could be increased by allowing the price to rise, which would shift more resources into production of this good and out of production of other goods where marginal benefit is only equal to or less than marginal cost.

**4.** Because alcohol and nicotine are addictive, the demands for liquor and cigarettes are relatively inelastic. When liquor and cigarette prices are increased by "sin" taxes, the percentage fall in quantity demanded is less than the percentage increase in price. Thus total revenue increases as does tax revenue. To raise a fixed amount of revenue, it takes a much smaller per-unit tax on goods with inelastic demand than on goods with elastic demand. Inelastic demand also means, *ceteris paribus*, that a greater portion of the tax is borne by consumers rather than producers.

**5. a.** See Fig. 4 Solution on the next page. In the comic book market, the supply curve shifts up vertically by an amount equal to the tax (\$0.15). The original equilibrium price is \$0.25 and quantity is 200,000. The new equilibrium price is \$0.30 and quantity is 100,000. Total expenditure has decreased, from \$50,000 (\$0.25 × 200,000) to \$30,000 (\$0.30 × 100,000).

**b.** Total tax revenue is \$0.15 per comic book × 100,000 units sold = \$15,000 and is indicated by the shaded area on Fig. 4 Solution.

**c.** As a result of the tax, the price to consumers has gone up by \$0.05 (from \$0.25 to \$0.30). Consumers' share of the tax burden is \$5,000 (\$0.05 × 100,000).

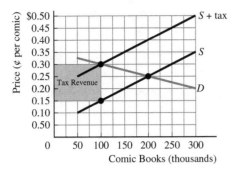

▲ **FIGURE 4 Solution Comic Book Market**

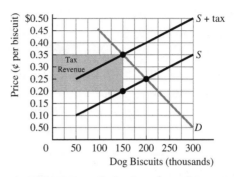

▲ **FIGURE 5 Solution Dog Biscuit Market**

Producers pay the $0.15 tax to government, but only get back $0.05 of it from consumers. Therefore, producers' share of the tax burden is $10,000 ($0.10 × 100,000).

**d.** See Fig. 5 Solution. In the dog biscuit market, the supply curve shifts up vertically by an amount equal to the tax ($0.15). The original equilibrium price is $0.25 and quantity is 200,000. The new equilibrium price is $0.35 and quantity is 150,000. Total expenditure has increased, from $50,000 ($0.25 × 200,000) to $52,500 ($0.35 × 150,000).

**e.** Total tax revenue is $0.15 per dog biscuit × 150,000 units sold = $22,500 and is indicated by the shaded area on Fig. 5 Solution.

**f.** As a result of the tax, the price to consumers has gone up by $0.10 (from $0.25 to $0.35). Consumers' share of the tax burden is $15,000 ($0.10 × 150,000). Producers pay the $0.15 tax to government, and get

back $0.10 of it from consumers. Therefore, producers' share of the tax burden is $7,500 ($0.05 × 150,000).

**g.** You confidently recommend to Dr. More that the Ministry tax dog biscuits. An excise tax on dog biscuits meets both objectives: (1) it will raise more tax revenue than a tax on comic books ($22,500 versus $15,000) and (2) it will put more of the tax burden on consumers. In the dog biscuit market, consumers will pay $15,000, which is 67 percent of the tax burden. In the comic book market, consumers will pay only $5,000, which is 33 percent of the tax burden.

**6.** You are kicking yourself because you forgot that there is a relationship between elasticity of demand and both (1) a change in total revenue for a (tax-induced) increase in price, and (2) whether consumers or producers bear more of the burden of a tax.

**a.** For the comic book market, the elasticity of demand ($\eta$) calculation is

$$\eta = \left| \left( \frac{\Delta Q}{Q_{ave}} \right) \Big/ \left( \frac{\Delta P}{P_{ave}} \right) \right|$$

$$= \left| \left( \frac{100 - 200}{150} \right) \Big/ \left( \frac{.30 - .25}{.275} \right) \right|$$

$$= \left| \left( \frac{-.667}{.182} \right) \right| = 3.67$$

Demand is elastic.

**b.** For the dog biscuit market, the elasticity of demand ($\eta$) calculation is

$$\eta = \left| \left( \frac{\Delta Q}{Q_{ave}} \right) \Big/ \left( \frac{\Delta P}{P_{ave}} \right) \right|$$

$$= \left| \left( \frac{150 - 200}{175} \right) \Big/ \left( \frac{.35 - .25}{.30} \right) \right|$$

$$= \left| \left( \frac{-.286}{.333} \right) \right| = 0.86$$

Demand is inelastic.

**c.** You forgot that an increase in price increases total expenditure when demand is inelastic, and decreases total expenditure when demand is elastic. Thus you could have used elasticity data to predict that expenditure would increase in the dog biscuit market. An increase in expenditure is not the same as an increase in tax revenue, but if more money is being spent, there is more to be spent on taxes. You also forgot that the more inelastic demand is, the more of a tax consumers pay.

If you had thought of the elasticity approach without prompting, good for you! Dr. More will be calling on you again for advice. If you didn't think of it, time to return to Drs. Parkin and Bade for a refresher.

7. Deadweight loss can be calculated from Fig. 4 Solution and Fig. 5 Solution. The loss is the area of the triangle bordered by the three black dots. For comic books, the triangle has a base of $0.15 and altitude of 100,000, so the area = $1/2ba$ = $1/2(\$0.15)(100,000)$ = $7,500.

For dog biscuits, the triangle has a base of $0.15 and altitude of 50,000, so the area = $1/2ba$ = $1/2(\$0.15)(100,000)$ = $3,750.

Once again, your recommendation is to tax dog biscuits. Dr. More is impressed—you are offered full-time employment!

8. Political parties on the right are most likely to use the benefits principle, arguing for a fair exchange value between what the government takes in taxes and gives back in benefits. The rich should not pay more than the poor unless the rich receive greater benefits. This is also consistent with the fair-rules view in Chapter 5.

Political parties on the left are most likely to use the ability-to-pay principle, arguing that because the rich can afford to pay more than the poor, they should shoulder the extra burden. This is consistent with the fair-outcomes view in Chapter 5. If the rich pay more taxes than the poor, after-tax outcomes will be more equal.

There is no right answer here. As a citizen, you must decide which principle of fairness appeals most to you.

# 7 Global Markets in Action

## Key Concepts

### How Global Markets Work

**Imports** are goods and services we buy from other countries; **exports** are what we sell to other countries.

*National comparative advantage* drives international trade—a country exports goods/services that it can produce at a lower opportunity cost than any other nation, and imports goods/services that other nations can produce at a lower opportunity cost.

- For import goods, world price < pre-trade domestic price.

  - Quantity demanded (= quantity bought) increases with international trade.

  - Quantity supplied decreases with international trade and is lower than quantity demanded.

  - At world price, Canadian imports = Canadian quantity demanded − Canadian quantity supplied.

- For export goods, world price > pre-trade domestic price.

  - Quantity supplied increases with international trade.

  - Quantity demanded (= quantity bought) decreases with international trade and is lower than quantity supplied.

- At world price, Canadian exports = Canadian quantity supplied − Canadian quantity demanded.

## Winners, Losers, and the Net Gain from Trade

Winners and losers from international trade can be identified through consumer and producer surpluses.

For imports

- *lower* price for imported goods leads to *more* consumption by consumers and *higher* consumer surplus (area under demand curve and above price)—consumers of imported goods *gain* from international trade.
- *lower* price for imported goods leads to *less* production by producers and *lower* producer surplus (area above supply curve and below price)—producers of import-competing goods *lose* from international trade.
- consumer surplus gain > producer surplus loss— there is a higher total surplus for society from imported goods.

For exports

- *higher* price for exported goods leads to *less* consumption by consumers and *lower* consumer surplus—consumers of exported goods *lose* from international trade.
- *higher* price for exported goods leads to *more* production by producers and *higher* producer surplus—producers of exported goods *gain* from international trade.

## International Trade Restrictions

Governments use four tools to influence international trade and protect domestic industries: tariffs, import quotas, other import barriers, and export subsidies.

**Tariffs** are taxes on imported goods, providing revenue for government, and benefiting import-competing industries.

- Higher domestic price = world price + tariff.
- Higher price means lower domestic quantity bought *and* higher domestic quantity produced—quantity imported shrinks.
- Government *gains* tariff revenue = tariff rate × quantity imported.
- Domestic producers *gain* producer surplus from higher price and higher production.
- Consumers *lose* consumer surplus from higher price and lower consumption.
- Society loses due to lower total surplus (= deadweight loss): Extra producer surplus + tariff revenue < lost consumer surplus.
- Tariffs have decreased due to **General Agreement on Tariffs and Trade** (**GAAT**) and other trade agreements.
- Recent attempts by the **World Trade Organization (WTO)** to lower barriers to trade in the **Doha Round** of trade talks has failed due to disputes between rich and developing nations.

**Import quotas** restrict import quantities, with quota licences distributed to importers.

- New supply curve = domestic supply curve + quota amount.
- Domestic price higher than world price—quantity demanded and bought falls, quantity supplied rises.
- Consumers lose consumer surplus from higher price.
- Domestic producers gain producer surplus from higher price.
- Importers gain profits from buying at world price and selling at higher domestic price.
- Society loses due to lower total surplus in a similar manner to effects of tariffs.

Other import barriers restrict supply of imports, increasing domestic price and domestic production.

- Examples include health, safety, and regulation barriers and voluntary export restraints (similar to a quota allocated to foreign exporters).

Export subsidies are payments from government to producers of exported goods.

- Export subsidies are illegal under international trade agreements, but agricultural subsidies to farmers increase domestic production, some of which is exported, creating deadweight loss.

## The Case Against Protection

Trade restrictions are used despite losses of gains from trade for two somewhat credible reasons—to protect **infant industries** as they mature and to prevent foreign companies from **dumping** products on world markets at prices less than cost.

A country may restrict trade for less credible reasons:

- to save the jobs lost from free trade
- to compete with cheap foreign labour
- to penalize lax environmental standards
- to prevent rich countries from exploiting developing countries

One new worry is **offshoring** (hiring foreign labour or buying goods/services from abroad), especially **offshore outsourcing** (hiring foreign labour to produce in other countries).

- Lower transportation and communications costs have increased offshoring.
- Benefits, costs, winners, and losers from offshoring are similar to those for free trade, with losers concentrated in the domestic services industry.

The biggest problem with protection is that it invites retaliation from other countries (trade wars). There are still trade restrictions because:

- tariff revenue is an attractive tax base for governments in developing countries.
- rent-seeking (lobbying) by groups/industries that suffer disproportionately under freer trade.

In Canada, employment insurance and interprovincial transfers provide some compensation for losses due to free trade, but in general losers are not compensated.

# Helpful Hints

1. This chapter demonstrates that a country gains from trading internationally, both from exporting and from importing.

   A country gains from exporting because the world price is higher than the domestic price. Producers gain surplus from selling inter-nationally at this higher price. Even though consumers lose some of their surplus (due to the higher price), the producers' gains more than outweigh this loss, so the country's total surplus is higher.

   Similarly, a country gains from importing because the world price is lower than the domestic price. Consumers gain surplus from buying at this lower price. Even though producers lose some of their surplus (due to the lower price), the consumers' gain more than outweighs this loss, and the country's total surplus is higher.

   Note that an importing country even gains from buying a good that is dumped at below-cost on the world market by another country. In essence, the dumping country is giving the importing country a subsidy!

2. Given the considerable gains from free trade, why then do countries have such a strong tendency to impose trade restrictions? The key is that while free trade creates benefits to the economy as a whole, there are both winners and losers. The winners gain more in total than the losers lose, but the losers tend to be concentrated in a few industries.

   Given this concentration, free trade will be resisted by some acting on the basis of rational self-interest. Even though the overwhelming majority will benefit while only a small minority are hurt, it is not surprising to see trade restrictions implemented. The cost of a given trade restriction to *each* of the majority will be individually quite small, while the benefit to *each* of the few will be individually large. Thus the minority will have a significant incentive to see that restriction takes place, while the majority will have little incentive to expend time and energy in resisting trade restriction.

3. To understand the source of pressures for trade restrictions, let's summarize the winners and losers from trade restrictions.

Under three forms of restrictions (tariffs, quotas, and voluntary export restraints) *consumers* lose, because the price of the imported good increases. *Domestic producers* of the imported good and their factors of production gain from all three, because the price of the imported good increases. *Foreign producers* and their factors of production lose under all three schemes, because their export sales decrease. Under quotas and voluntary export restraints, the *holders of import licences* gain from buying low and selling high (they may be foreign or domestic). *Government* gains tariff revenue under tariffs and, potentially, votes under other schemes.

Given this list, it is hardly surprising that the main supporters of trade restrictions are domestic producers and their factors of production.

# Self-Test
## True/False and Explain

### How Global Markets Work

**1.** When a Canadian citizen stays in a hotel in France, Canada is exporting a service.

**2.** Countries will export goods and services that they can produce at a lower opportunity cost than other countries.

**3.** For a country to export a good, the world price must be lower than the domestic price.

**4.** If Canada starts importing widgets, the price of widgets in Canada will fall and the quantity bought will increase.

### Winners, Losers, and the Net Gain from Trade

**5.** All parts of society gain from being able to export goods at a higher price than the domestic price.

**6.** Domestic producers gain from the introduction of imports.

**7.** Domestic consumers gain from the introduction of imports.

### International Trade Restrictions

**8.** When governments impose import quotas, they increase their country's gains from trade.

**9.** A tariff on a good will raise its domestic price and reduce the domestic quantity traded.

**13.** Since Mexican labour is paid so much less than Canadian labour, a free trade agreement guarantees Canada will lose jobs to Mexico.

**10.** An import quota will cause the domestic price of the imported good to decrease.

**14.** Elected governments are slow to reduce trade restrictions because there would be more domestic losers than winners.

**11.** The government revenue plus the increase in producer surplus offsets the losses in consumer surplus from a tariff.

**15.** A trade agreement that increases both imports and exports will decrease jobs domestically.

## The Case Against Protection

**12.** Japan is dumping steel if it sells steel in Japan at a lower price than it sells it in Canada.

# Multiple-Choice

## How Global Markets Work

**1.** Which of the following is a Canadian service export?

**a.** A Canadian buys dinner while travelling in Switzerland.

**b.** A Swiss buys dinner while travelling in Canada.

**c.** A Canadian buys a clock made in Switzerland.

**d.** A Swiss buys a computer made in Canada.

**e.** A Canadian buys a Canadian computer in Switzerland.

**2.** If Canada imports widgets, it must be the case that

**a.** Canada has a comparative advantage in widget production.

**b.** widgets are cheaper in Canada than the rest of the world.

**c.** the Canadian quantity supplied of widgets is greater than the Canadian quantity demanded for widgets at the world price.

**d.** the Canadian quantity supplied of widgets is less than the Canadian quantity demanded for widgets at the world price.

**e.** there is no tariff on widgets.

**3.** Table 1 shows Glazeland's doughnut market before international trade. Glazeland opens up to international trade. If the world price is $0.60, then Glazeland will produce ____ doughnuts and will ____ ____ doughnuts.

**a.** 2 million; import 3 million

**b.** 4 million; import 1 million

**c.** 4 million; export 1 million

**d.** 5 million; import 3 million

**e.** 5 million; export 3 million

| TABLE 1  Glazeland's Doughnut Market | | |
|---|---|---|
| Price (dollars per doughnut) | Glazeland's Supply (millions) | Glazeland's Demand (millions) |
| 0.20 | 1 | 10 |
| 0.30 | 2 | 8 |
| 0.40 | 3 | 6 |
| 0.50 | 4 | 4 |
| 0.60 | 5 | 2 |
| 0.70 | 6 | 0 |

**4.** Table 1 shows Glazeland's doughnut market before international trade. Glazeland opens up to international trade. If the world price is $0.40, then Glazeland will produce _____ doughnuts and will _____ _____ doughnuts.

   **a.** 3 million; import 3 million

   **b.** 3 million; export 3 million

   **c.** 4 million; import 1 million

   **d.** 4 million; export 1 million

   **e.** 6 million; export 3 million

**5.** If Canada starts exporting gadgets, then the domestic price of gadgets

   **a.** decreases, leading to a decline in production and imports fill the gap.

   **b.** decreases, leading to a decline in quantity demanded and the difference is exported.

   **c.** stays the same, but Canada increases production in response to the world demand.

   **d.** increases, quantity demanded declines, production increases and the difference is exported.

   **e.** increases, quantity demanded increases and the difference is imported.

## Winners, Losers, and the Net Gain from Trade

**6.** If the widget industry enters the world market, and the world price is higher than the domestic price, then the

   **a.** higher price will make consumers better off.

   **b.** higher price will make producers worse off.

   **c.** increased production will make consumers better off.

   **d.** decreased production will make producers worse off.

   **e.** amount of exports will be positive.

**7.** Fig. 1 shows a domestic import market. What is the area of *producer* surplus at the world price?

   **a.** ABICDFGH

   **b.** ABCF

   **c.** FGHJ

   **d.** FGJ

   **e.** J

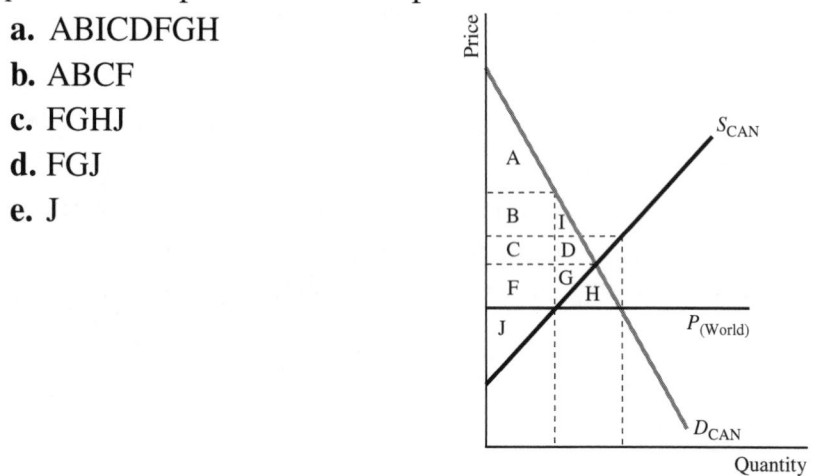

▲ **FIGURE 1**

**8.** Fig. 1 shows a domestic import market. What is the area of *consumer* surplus at the world price?

a. ABICDFGH

b. ABCF

c. FGHJ

d. FGJ

e. J

**9.** Fig. 1 shows a domestic import market. What is the area of *increase* in *total* surplus from moving from the domestic price to the world price?

a. H

b. J

c. FGH

d. IDG

e. ABICDFGH

**10.** Fig. 2 shows a domestic export market. What is the area of *producer* surplus at the world price?

a. ABI

b. ABICDE

c. CDEFGJ

d. FGJ

e. J

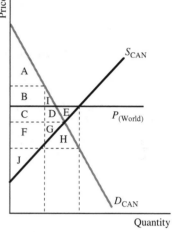

▲ **FIGURE 2**

**11.** Fig. 2 shows a domestic export market. What is the area of *consumer* surplus at the world price?

a. ABI

b. ABICD

c. ABCDFJ

d. FGJ

e. J

**12.** Fig. 2 shows a domestic export market. What is the area of *increase* in *total* surplus from moving from the domestic price to the world price?

a. CD

b. CDE

c. E

d. CDEFGJ

e. H

**14.** When a *voluntary export restraint* agreement is reached, the gap between the domestic import price and the export price is captured by

a. consumers in the importing country.

b. the domestic producers of the good.

c. the government of the importing country.

d. foreign exporters.

e. the domestic importers of the good.

## International Trade Restrictions

**13.** When an *import quota* is imposed, the gap between the domestic price and the export price is captured by

a. consumers in the importing country.

b. the domestic producers of the good.

c. the government of the importing country.

d. foreign exporters.

e. the importers of the good.

**15.** When a *tariff* is imposed, the gap between the domestic price and the export price is captured by

a. consumers in the importing country.

b. the domestic producers of the good.

c. the government of the importing country.

d. foreign exporters.

e. the domestic importers of the good.

**16.** Table 2 shows the Canadian supply of and demand for widgets. Widgets are available on the world market for $7. If the Canadian government imposes a tariff of $1, the domestic selling price will be _____ and quantity bought will be _____.

a. $6; 48 million

b. $7; 44 million

c. $8; 16 million

d. $8; 24 million

e. $8; 40 million

**17.** Table 2 shows the Canadian supply of and demand for widgets. Widgets are available on the world market for $7. If the Canadian government imposes a tariff of $1, how many widgets will Canada import?

a. 32 million

b. 24 million

c. 16 million

d. 24 million

e. 40 million

**TABLE 2  Canada's Market for Widgets**

| Price (dollars per widgets) | Canadian Supply (millions) | Canadian Demand (millions) |
|---|---|---|
| 5 | 12 | 52 |
| 6 | 16 | 48 |
| 7 | 20 | 44 |
| 8 | 24 | 40 |
| 9 | 28 | 36 |
| 10 | 32 | 32 |
| 12 | 36 | 28 |

**18.** Table 2 shows the Canadian supply of and demand for widgets. Widgets are available on the world market for $7. Canadian widget producers convince their government to protect the domestic industry from cheap imports. If the Canadian government sets an import quota of 8 million widgets, the resulting price of a widget in Canada will be _____ and domestic production will be _____.

a. $6; 40 million

b. $7; 36 million

c. $8; 32 million

d. $9; 28 million

e. $10; 32 million

**19.** A tariff on watches imported by Atlantis will cause Atlantis's domestic price of watches to
  **a.** decrease and imports to increase.
  **b.** increase and watch production in Atlantis to increase.
  **c.** increase and watch production in Atlantis to decrease.
  **d.** decrease and watch production in Atlantis to increase.
  **e.** decrease and watch production in Atlantis to decrease.

**20.** The introduction of a tariff will
  **a.** increase consumer surplus, decrease producer surplus, and decrease total surplus.
  **b.** increase consumer surplus, increase producer surplus, and decrease total surplus.
  **c.** decrease consumer surplus, decrease producer surplus, and decrease total surplus.
  **d.** decrease consumer surplus, increase producer surplus, and decrease total surplus.
  **e.** decrease consumer surplus, increase producer surplus, and increase total surplus.

## The Case Against Protection

**21.** Which of the following is *not* an argument for protectionism?
  **a.** to prevent dumping
  **b.** to save jobs in import-competing industries
  **c.** to gain a comparative advantage
  **d.** to allow infant industries to grow
  **e.** to prevent rich nations from exploiting poor nations

**22.** The biggest problem with protection is that
  **a.** it invites retaliation from trading partners.
  **b.** losers are not compensated.
  **c.** it worsens environmental standards.
  **d.** it can worsen national security.
  **e.** it lowers wages.

**23.** Why is international trade restricted?

    **a.** because government revenue is costly to collect via tariffs

    **b.** to get higher consumption possibilities

    **c.** to realize the gains from trade

    **d.** due to rent-seeking

    **e.** because free trade creates economic losses on average

**24.** The effects of offshoring from opening up call centres in India are similar to the effects from

    **a.** free trade.

    **b.** tariffs.

    **c.** import quotas.

    **d.** voluntary export restraints.

    **e.** export subsidies.

**25.** In Canada, when international trade hurts producers and reduces jobs in import-competing industries, the government response is to

    **a.** introduce tariffs.

    **b.** do absolutely nothing.

    **c.** fully compensate all losers.

    **d.** guarantee every job loser retraining.

    **e.** use employment insurance to help job losers with temporary relief.

# Short Answer Problems

1. It is often argued by union leaders that tariffs are needed to protect domestic jobs. In light of the explanation in the textbook, evaluate this argument.

2. In a recent case, the U.S. government investigated Chinese bra manufacturers for suspected "dumping" of bras in the United States. The U.S. Department of Trade determined that the cost of making a bra in China was equivalent to $12 per bra, although they were being sold in the United States for $11 each. They then imposed dumping duties (tariffs) on Chinese bras of $1 per bra.

   a. Define dumping, and explain whether this is a case of dumping.

   b. Dumping duties are put in place to protect the U.S. economy from the "unfair" low price of the dumped imports. Did the dumping duties on bras make the U.S. economy better off?

3. Consider a simple world in which there are two countries, Atlantis and Beltran, each producing and consuming gadgets. The Atlantean gadget market is shown in Table 3, and the Beltranian market is given in Table 4. Both countries use the dollar as their currency.

## TABLE 3  Atlantis's Market for Gadgets

| Price (dollars per gadgets) | Atlantean Supply (millions) | Atlantean Demand (millions) |
|---|---|---|
| 0 | 0 | 240 |
| 10 | 50 | 210 |
| 20 | 100 | 180 |
| 30 | 150 | 150 |
| 40 | 180 | 120 |
| 50 | 210 | 90 |
| 60 | 240 | 60 |
| 70 | 270 | 30 |
| 80 | 300 | 0 |

## TABLE 4  Beltran's Market for Gadgets

| Price (dollars per gadgets) | Beltranian Supply (millions) | Beltranian Demand (millions) |
|---|---|---|
| 0 | 0 | 200 |
| 10 | 25 | 190 |
| 20 | 50 | 180 |
| 30 | 75 | 170 |
| 40 | 100 | 160 |
| 50 | 120 | 150 |
| 60 | 140 | 140 |
| 70 | 160 | 130 |
| 80 | 180 | 120 |

**a.** Do the conditions exist for the two countries to trade in gadgets? Explain briefly.

**b.** If they do trade, who will be the exporter and who will be the importer?

**c.** Using the information in Tables 3 and 4 on the previous page, find the trading price of gadgets, and indicate how much will be exported from one country to another, and how much will be imported.

**4.** Suppose that Atlantis and Beltran engage in trade. (You should have been able to show in Short Answer Problem **3** that Atlantis will export gadgets to Beltran.) On the grid, graph the Atlantis market for gadgets, indicating the pre-trade equilibrium and the free trade equilibrium. Indicate the change in consumer surplus, change in producer surplus, and change in total surplus for Atlantis. Indicate the winners and losers in Atlantis from free trade.

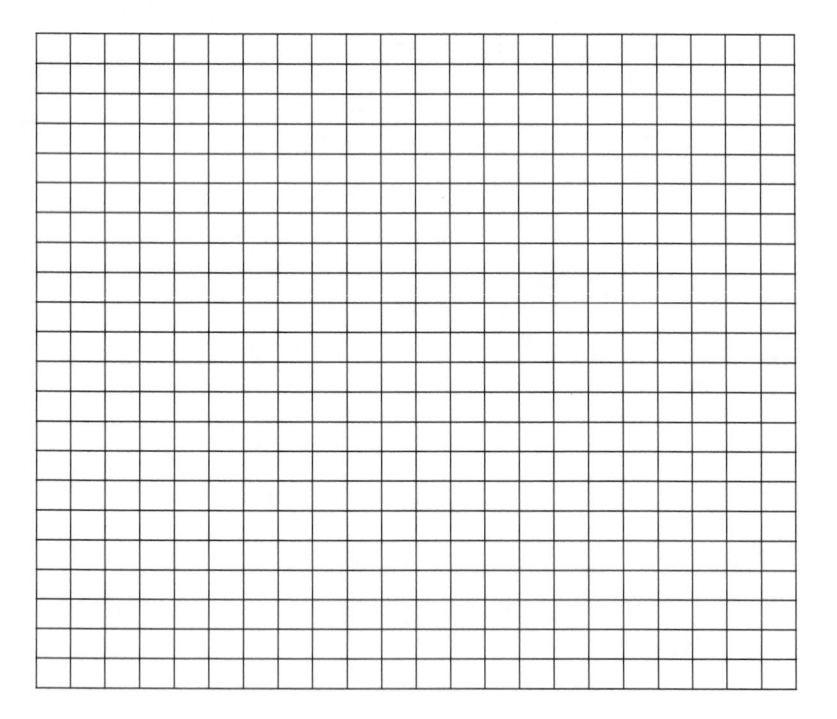

**5.** Suppose that Atlantis and Beltran engage in trade. (You should have been able to show in Short Answer Problem **3** that Atlantis will export gadgets to Beltran.) On the grid, graph the Beltran market for gadgets, indicating the pre-trade equilibrium and the free trade equilibrium. Indicate the change in consumer surplus, change in producer surplus, and change in total surplus for Beltran. Identify the winners and losers in Beltran from free trade.

**6.** Continue the analysis of Atlantis and Beltran trading gadgets. Suppose that the importing country (Beltran) introduces a tariff of $10. Show on your graph from Short Answer Problem **5** what this will do to the quantity demanded in Beltran, quantity produced, and amount imported. Indicate in words who will gain and who will lose from the tariff in Beltran. How much is the tariff revenue for Beltran?

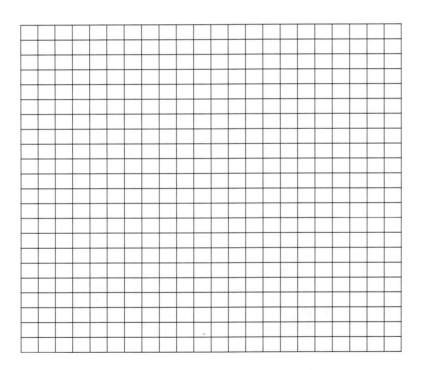

℅ **7.** Continue the analysis of Atlantis and Beltran trading gadgets. What will the impact of the tariff introduced by Beltran be on the quantity exported from Atlantis, and what will be the impact on the domestic price of gadgets, quantity produced, and quantity demanded in Atlantis? Indicate in words who will gain and who will lose from the tariff in Atlantis. (It is likely easier to work with Table 3 on page 227 than doing this graphically.)

**8.** Rich countries are often worried about the impact of off-shoring of services (such as call centres for computers or software) to developing countries like India. Suppose that Canada was to ban the use of offshoring for call centres. Explain in words who would gain and who would lose from this ban in Canada, and in India.

# Answers

## True/False and Explain

1. **F** Canada is importing (using) a service. (152)
2. **T** Definition of national comparative advantage. (152)
3. **F** Must be higher to generate profits. (154)
4. **T** (153)
5. **F** Consumers lose surplus from higher price. (156)
6. **F** Imports lower prices for import-competing producers, reducing producer surplus. (155)
7. **T** Imports lower prices for import-competing goods, increasing consumer surplus. (155)
8. **F** Trade restrictions reduce gains from trade. (157–159)
9. **T** Tariff raises price paid inside the country, which decreases quantity traded. (157–159)
10. **F** Quota decreases supply, increasing domestic price. (160)
11. **F** There is deadweight loss. (159)
12. **F** Dumping is selling in Canada at a lower price than in Japan. (163)
13. **F** Must also examine productivity of workers in each country, and Canadian workers are more productive. (164)
14. **F** Because losers' losses are individually much greater than winners' gains. (166)
15. **F** More imports will likely decrease jobs, but more exports will increase them—net outcome is not clear. (164)

## Multiple-Choice

1. **b** **a** and **c** are imports, **d** and **e** are exports of a *good*. (152)
2. **d** If we import, world price is lower and our supply is therefore too low compared to demand. Could still have a tariff. (153)
3. **e** Price = $0.60 implies supply of 5 million, but demand is only 2 million, so 3 million are exported. (153–154)
4. **a** Price = $0.40 implies supply of 3 million, but demand is 6 million, so 3 million are imported. (153–154)
5. **d** (154)
6. **e** Higher price and higher production increases producer surplus and lowers consumer surplus. (156)
7. **e** Area below price and above supply curve. (155)
8. **a** Area above price and below demand curve. (155)
9. **a** Gain in consumer surplus (FGH)—loss of producer surplus (FG). (155)
10. **c** Area below price and above supply curve. (156)
11. **a** Area above price and below demand curve. (156)
12. **c** Gain in producer surplus (CDE)—loss of consumer surplus (CD). (156)
13. **e** Under a quota, domestic government allocates the licences to import. (160)
14. **d** Because they have the right to export. (162)

**15. c** They collect tariff revenue = import price – world price. (157–159)

**16. e** New price is $1 + $7 = $8, so quantity bought (from demand curve) is 40 million. (157–159)

**17. c** Difference between quantity demanded and supplied at $8. (157–159)

**18. d** Equilibrium is price where quota of 8 million = import demand = quantity demanded – quantity supplied. (160–161)

**19. b** Tariff increases domestic price = export price + tariff, and domestic production increases in response. (157–159)

**20. d** (159)

**21. c** See text discussion. (163–167)

**22. a** See text discussion. (163–167)

**23. d** See text discussion. (163–167)

**24. a** Similar effect on domestic price of good, domestic production, imports, winners, and losers. (165)

**25. e** See text discussion. (166–167)

## Short Answer Problems

**1.** This argument has some truth to it. As the textbook shows on pages 157–158, the tariff will lead an increase in domestic production of the protected good, which will lead to an increase in jobs in that industry. However, the same tariff could trigger a trade war, which would reduce foreign purchases of goods, reducing exports and export production, and reducing jobs in the export industry. The net effect on jobs is unclear.

**2. a.** Dumping occurs when a foreign firm sells its exports at a lower price than the cost of production. Since the cost of production is higher than the export price, this is indeed a case of dumping.

**b.** The dumping duties are exactly like a tariff. The effect of a tariff is to increase the domestic price of bras, reduce domestic bra consumption (and reduce consumer surplus) and increase domestic bra production (and increase producer surplus), and lower U.S. total surplus. The U.S. economy is made worse off.

**3. a.** The pre-trade price of gadgets in Atlantis would be $30, while the pre-trade price in Beltran would be $60. If a trading price between $30 and $60 could come about, both sides would gain. Therefore, the appropriate conditions exist for trade.

**b.** The exporter would be Atlantis, with the lower price, and Beltran would be the importer with the higher price.

**c.** We can find the trading price ($40) in a variety of manners. We could combine the two supply schedules into a "world" supply schedule, and combine the two demand schedules into a "world" demand schedule, and find the equilibrium world price. Such a schedule is shown in Table 5, and world equilibrium occurs with a quantity of 280 million and price of $40.

We can also find the trading price ($40) by looking at Tables 3 and 4, and noting that at a price of $40, supply in Atlantis exceeds demand by 60 million, while supply in Beltran is short of demand by 60 million, indicating that sending 60 million from Atlantis to Beltran would create equilibrium. In summary, Atlantis exports 60 million gadgets and Beltran imports 60 million.

## TABLE 5 "World" Market for Gadgets

| Price (dollars per gadgets) | World Supply (millions) | World Demand (millions) |
|---|---|---|
| 0 | 0 | 440 |
| 10 | 75 | 400 |
| 20 | 150 | 360 |
| 30 | 225 | 320 |
| 40 | 280 | 280 |
| 50 | 330 | 240 |
| 60 | 380 | 200 |
| 70 | 430 | 160 |
| 80 | 480 | 120 |

4. Fig. 3 shows the Atlantean market. The initial pre-trade equilibrium occurs at a price of $30 and a quantity traded of 150 million. We have established the world price will be $40. At this price, Atlantis will demand only 120 million gadgets (read off the demand curve), and

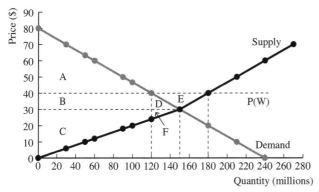

▲ **FIGURE 3  Atlantis's Market for Gadgets**

will produce 180 million gadgets (read off the supply curve), and will export the surplus of 60 million gadgets.

Table 6 summarizes the amounts of consumer surplus (the area above the price and below the demand curve), producer surplus (the area below the price and above the supply curve), and total surplus (consumer surplus + producer surplus) in the two situations, as well as the change in each from pre-trade to the trade equilibrium.

## TABLE 6  Atlantis's Gains and Losses from Free Trade

| | Pre-Trade | Free Trade | Change |
|---|---|---|---|
| CS | A + B + D | A | Loss of B + D |
| PS | C + F | B + C + D + E + F | Gain of B + D + E |
| TS | A + B + C + D + F | A + B + C + D + E + F | Gain of E |

Table 6 shows that consumers lose and producers win, with an overall gain for Atlantis.

5. Fig. 4 on the next page shows the Beltran market. The initial pre-trade equilibrium occurs at a price of $60 and a quantity traded of 140 million. We have established the world price will be $40. At this price, Beltran will demand 160 million gadgets (read off the demand curve), and will produce only 100 million gadgets (read off the supply curve), and will import the shortage of 60 million gadgets.

▲ **FIGURE 4  Beltran's Market for Gadgets**

Table 7 summarizes Beltran's amounts of consumer surplus (the area above the price and below the demand curve), producer surplus (the area below the price and above the supply curve), and total surplus (consumer surplus + producer surplus) in the two situations, as well as the change in each from pre-trade to the trade equilibrium.

| **TABLE 7  Beltran's Gains and Losses from Free Trade** | | | |
|---|---|---|---|
| | **Pre-Trade** | **Free Trade** | **Change** |
| CS | A | A + B + E | Gain of B + E |
| PS | B + C | C | Loss of B |
| TS | A + B + C | A + B + C + E | Gain of E |

Table 7 shows that consumers win and producers lose, with an overall gain for Beltran.

6. Fig. 5 shows the impact of the tariff on Beltran's market. The tariff adds $10 to the world price, leading to a domestic price of $50. At this price, demand is only 150 million gadgets, and supply increases to 120 million gadgets, leading to a decreased amount of imports at 30 million units.

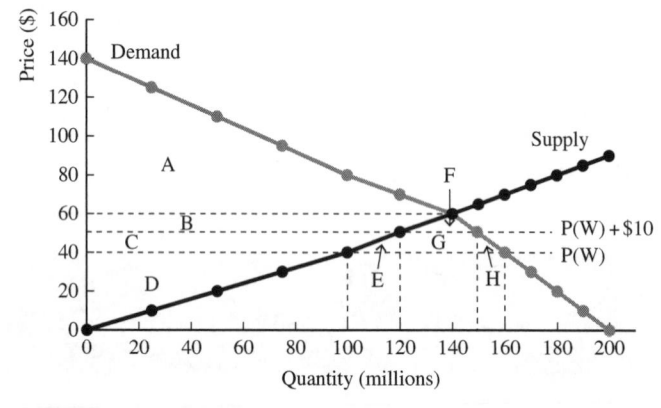

▲ **FIGURE 5  Impact of a Tariff on Beltran**

Table 8 summarizes the gains and losses from the introduction of the tariff. Consumers lose consumer surplus, producers gain producer surplus, the government gains tariff revenue ($10 × 30 million gadget imports), but overall total surplus is lower.

7. The answer to this question is complicated by the fact that we are attempting to use a simple model to answer a more complex question, so only an approximate answer is possible. Beltran is now importing only 30 million gadgets from Atlantis, instead of the previous 60 million units. Therefore, Atlantis will export only 30 million units. Looking at Table 3, we can see

## TABLE 8  Beltran's Gains and Losses from a Tariff of $10

|  | Free Trade | Post-Tariff | Change |
|---|---|---|---|
| CS | A + B + C + E + F + G + H | A + B + F | Loss of C + E + G + H |
| PS | D | C + D | Gain of C |
| Tariff Rev. | None | G | G |
| TS | A + B + C + D + E + F + G + H | A + B + C + D + F + G | Loss of E + H |

that this will occur at some price between $30 and $40 (we cannot exactly tell where without a mathematical model incorporating the tax, which is beyond the complexities of this model). Therefore, the impact of the Beltran tariff is to reduce the world price somewhat. Since the price received by Atlantean sellers will fall, they will lose some producer surplus. Since the price paid by Atlantean consumers will fall, they will gain some consumer surplus. The overall impact of the fall in world price for Atlantis will be a reduction in total surplus, which can be shown on Fig. 3 on page 233 (the area E gets smaller).

8. If a Canadian company "offshores" a call centre to India, it is essentially the same as the company importing a service from India. All the gains and losses to individuals and the overall economy are identical to the normal case of an import (p. 155 of the textbook). The company as an importer gains the less expensive service, which means lower costs and presumably more profits for the Canadian company (and potentially lower prices for its buyers). The losers are the potential sellers in Canada (people who operate or work in call centres), who lose their producer surplus. Overall, there is an increase in total surplus in Canada from being able to import the cheaper product.

Similarly, for India this is an export of a service (p. 156 of the textbook), and we can see that the Indian suppliers of the call centre services gain producer surplus, Indian consumers lose consumer surplus from the higher Indian price, and overall Indian total surplus is higher.

If the use of offshore call centres is banned, then all the gains and losses are reversed. The Canadian buyers of call centre services lose their consumer surplus (they face higher costs). The Canadian import-competing call centres gain back their lost producer surplus, but overall Canadian total surplus is lower. For India, the Indian suppliers lose producer surplus, the Indian consumers gain consumer surplus, and overall Indian total surplus is lower.

# 8 Utility and Demand

## Key Concepts

### Consumption Choices

Household consumption choices are determined by consumption possibilities and preferences.

A budget line marks the boundary between affordable (points on the line or inside) and unaffordable (outside the line) choices.

- Income and prices ($P$) of goods and services are given.

Preferences (likes and dislikes) are based on **utility**—benefit or satisfaction from consumption.

- **Total utility** ($TU$) is the total benefit from consumption of goods and services. Increased consumption increases total utility.
- **Marginal utility** ($MU$) is the $\Delta$ in total utility from a one-unit increase in quantity good consumed. $MU$ is positive, but due to **diminishing marginal utility**, decreases as consumption good increases.

### Utility-Maximizing Choices

Consumers strive for utility maximization—maximum attainable benefit.

- Given income and the prices of goods and services, **consumer equilibrium** occurs when the consumer allocates income in a way that maximizes total utility.

- Total utility is maximized when all income is spent and **marginal utility per dollar** spent is equal for all goods. For substitute goods movies ($M$) and pop ($P$), this occurs when

$$\frac{MU_M}{P_M} = \frac{MU_P}{P_P}$$

The power of marginal analysis for predicting economic choices stems from a simple rule—if the marginal gain from an action exceeds the marginal loss, take the action.

- The rule applied to the utility maximization example is—if the marginal utility per dollar spent on movies exceeds the marginal utility per dollar spent on pop, buy more movies and less pop.
- The marginal gain from more movies exceeds the marginal loss from less pop.

## Predictions of Marginal Utility Theory

*Ceteris paribus*, if $P_M$ falls, $Q_M$ consumed increases (movement down along the demand curve for movies); also causes a leftward shift in the demand curve for pop.

*Ceteris paribus*, if $P_P$ rises, $Q_P$ consumed decreases (movement up along the demand curve for pop); also causes a rightward shift in the demand curve for movies.

Movies and pop are normal goods. *Ceteris paribus*, increased income causes increased consumption of movies and pop (rightward shifts in both demand curves).

Marginal utility theory allows us to derive and predict the above results, which, in Chapter 3, were just *assumptions* about consumer demand.

Value is related to total utility or consumer surplus. Price is related to marginal utility. Distinction between total utility and marginal utility resolves the diamond–water paradox:

- Diamonds, though less useful (low *TU* and small consumer surplus) than water, have higher price (high *MU*).
- Water is more useful (high *TU* and large consumer surplus), but has lower price (low *MU*).

## New Ways of Explaining Consumer Choices

**Behavioural economics** studies how limits on the human brain's ability to compute and implement rational decisions influences economic behaviour. Limits include bounded rationality, bounded willpower, and bounded self-interest.

**Neuroeconomics** uses neuroscience to study the effects of economic events and choices inside the human brain.

Notes:

# Helpful Hints

1. Utility is a useful abstract concept for thinking clearly about consumer choice. The arbitrary units used to measure utility don't matter. All that marginal utility theory requires is that you can judge whether the additional satisfaction per dollar spent on good $X$ is greater or less than the additional satisfaction per dollar spent on $Y$. If it is greater, then you choose more $X$. How much greater is irrelevant for the decision.

2. The marginal utility per dollar spent on good $X$ can be written as $MU_X/P_X$, where $MU_X$ is the marginal utility of the last unit of $X$ consumed, and $P_X$ is the price of a unit of good $X$. The consumer equilibrium (utility-maximizing) condition for goods $X$ and $Y$ can be written

$$\frac{MU_X}{P_X} = \frac{MU_Y}{P_Y}$$

This implies that, in consumer equilibrium, the ratio of marginal utilities equals the ratio of prices of the two goods:

$$\frac{MU_X}{MU_Y} = \frac{P_X}{P_Y}$$

This result is often useful.

3. If you are not in consumer equilibrium, then the above equation is not satisfied. For example, consider spending all of your income on a consumption plan where

$$\frac{MU_X}{P_X} > \frac{MU_Y}{P_Y}$$

or, equivalently,

$$\frac{MU_X}{MU_Y} > \frac{P_X}{P_Y}$$

Since $P_X$ and $P_Y$ are given, this means that $MU_X$ is "too large" and $MU_Y$ is "too small." Total utility can be increased by consuming more $X$ (and thereby decreasing $MU_X$ due to the principle of diminishing marginal utility) and less $Y$ (and thereby increasing $MU_Y$ due to diminishing marginal utility).

# Self-Test

## True/False and Explain

### Consumption Choices

1. All points inside a consumer's budget line are unaffordable.

    *False* ✓

2. The principle of diminishing marginal utility means that as consumption of a good increases, total utility increases but at a decreasing rate.

    ~~False~~ True

### Utility-Maximizing Choice

3. A household is maximizing utility if the marginal utility per dollar spent is equal for all goods and all its income is spent.

    True ✓

4. If the marginal utilities from consuming two goods are not equal, the consumer cannot be in equilibrium.

    ~~True~~ False

5. If the marginal utility per dollar spent on good X exceeds the marginal utility per dollar spent on good Y, total utility will increase by increasing consumption of X and decreasing consumption of Y.

    True

6. If the marginal gain from an action exceeds the marginal loss, you should take the action.

    ~~False~~ True

### Predictions of Marginal Utility Theory

7. When the price of good X rises, the marginal utility from the consumption of X decreases.

    ~~True~~ False

8. When income decreases, the marginal utility derived from a good will always increase.

    False ✓

9. When the price of one good rises, demand decreases for goods that are substitutes.

False ✓

10. When income increases, the quantity demanded of all goods increases.

False ✓

11. In consumer equilibrium, price is proportional to total utility.

~~True~~ False

12. A demand curve describes the quantity demanded at each price when marginal utility is maximized.

~~True~~ False

13. If a shift in supply decreases the price of a good, consumer surplus increases.

True ✓

## New Ways of Explaining Consumer Choice

14. Neuroeconomics studies how limits on the human brain's ability to compute and implement rational decisions influences economic behaviour.

False — Behavioural ✓

15. All economists agree that it is important to explain what goes on inside people's heads.

False. ✓

9/15

# Multiple-Choice

## Consumption Choices

1. A household's consumption choices are determined by
   a. prices of goods and services.
   b. income.
   c. preferences.
   d. all of the above. ✓
   e. a and b only.

2. Total utility equals
   a. the sum of the marginal utilities of each unit consumed. ✓
   b. the area below the demand curve but above the market price.
   c. the slope of the marginal utility curve.
   d. the marginal utility of the last unit divided by price.
   e. the marginal utility of the last unit consumed multiplied by the total number of units consumed

3. Total utility is always
   a. greater than marginal utility.
   b. less than marginal utility.
   c. decreasing when marginal utility is decreasing.
   d. decreasing when marginal utility is increasing.
   e. increasing when marginal utility is positive. ✓

4. According to the principle of diminishing marginal utility, as consumption of a good increases, total utility
   a. decreases and then eventually increases.
   b. decreases at an increasing rate.
   c. decreases at a decreasing rate.
   d. increases at an increasing rate.
   e. increases at a decreasing rate. ✓

## Maximizing Utility

**5.** If a consumer is in equilibrium, ✓

    **a.** total utility is maximized given the consumer's income and the prices of goods.

    **b.** marginal utility is maximized given the consumer's income and the prices of goods.

    **c.** marginal utility per dollar spent is maximized given the consumer's income and the prices of goods.

    **d.** the marginal utility of each good will be equal.

    **e.** none of the above is true.

**6.** Suppose that Ally spends her entire income of $10 on law books and miniskirts. Law books cost $2 and miniskirts cost $4 (see Table 1). The marginal utility of each good is independent of the amount consumed of the other good.

| TABLE 1  Ally's Marginal Utility | | |
| --- | --- | --- |
| | $2 **Marginal Utility** $4 | |
| **Quantity** | **Law Books** | **Miniskirts** |
| 1 | 12 | 16  4 |
| 2 | 10 | 12  3 |
| 3 | 8 | 8  2 |
| 4 | 6 | 4  1 |

If Ally is maximizing her utility, how many miniskirts does she buy?

    **a.** 0

    **b.** 1

    **c.** 2

    **d.** 3

    **e.** 4

1 miniskirt

$(MU/P = 16/4)$

3 books

$(MU/P = 8/2)$

**7.** If potato chips were free, individuals would consume

    **a.** an infinite quantity of chips.

    **b.** the quantity of chips at which total utility from chips falls to zero.

    **c.** the quantity of chips at which marginal utility from chips falls to zero.

    **d.** zero chips, since this equates marginal utility and price.

    **e.** none of the above.

Maximizes Total Utility

→ fewer chips, MU still (+), TU increases

→ more chips, MU is (−), TU decreases

8. In consumer equilibrium, a consumer equates the
   a. total utility from each good.
   b. marginal utility from each good.
   c. total utility per dollar spent on each good.
   d. marginal utility per dollar spent on each good. ✓
   e. total income spent on each good with total utility from each good.

9. Samir consumes apples and bananas and is in consumer equilibrium. The marginal utility of the last apple is 10 and the marginal utility of the last banana is 5. If the price of an apple is $0.50, what is the price of a banana?
   a. $0.05
   b. $0.10
   c. $0.25 ✓
   d. $0.50
   e. $1.00

10. If Ms. Petersen is maximizing her utility in the consumption of goods A and B, which of the following statements must be *true*?
   a. $MU_A = MU_B$
   b. $\dfrac{MU_A}{P_A} = \dfrac{MU_B}{P_B}$ ✓
   c. $\dfrac{MU_A}{P_B} = \dfrac{MU_B}{P_A}$
   d. $TU_A = TU_B$
   e. $\dfrac{TU_A}{P_A} = \dfrac{TU_B}{P_B}$

11. Squid costs $2 per kilogram and octopus costs $1 per kilogram. Jacques buys only octopus and gets 10 units of utility from the last kilogram he buys. Assuming that Jacques has maximized his utility, his marginal utility, in units, from the first kilogram of squid must be
   a. more than 10.
   b. less than 10.
   c. more than 20.
   d. less than 20.
   e. zero.

Octopus $MU_o/P_o = 10$

squid $MU_s/2$ must $< 10$

so $MU_s$ must be $< 20$

**12.** If Soula is maximizing her utility and two goods have the same marginal utility, she will
   **a.** buy only one.
   **b.** buy equal quantities of both.
   **c.** be willing to pay the same price for each.
   **d.** get the same total utility from each.
   **e.** do none of the above.

*maximum condition of equal MU/P*

→ *no relation necessarily between*
*MU and quantity or TU*

**13.** Sergio is maximizing his utility in his consumption of beer and bubblegum. If the price of beer is greater than the price of bubblegum, then we know with *certainty* that
   **a.** Sergio buys more beer than bubblegum.
   **b.** Sergio buys more bubblegum than beer.
   **c.** the marginal utility of the last purchased beer is greater than the marginal utility of the last purchased bubblegum.
   **d.** the marginal utility of the last purchased bubblegum is greater than the marginal utility of the last purchased beer.
   **e.** the marginal utilities of the last purchased beer and bubblegum are equal.

*maximum condition of equal MU/P*

→ *no relation necessarily between*
*MU and quantity*

**14.** Suppose that Madonna spends her entire income of $6 on purple nail polish and leather outfits. Nail polish costs $1 per unit and outfits cost $2 per unit (see Table 2). The marginal utility of each good is independent of the amount consumed of the other good.

| TABLE 2  Madonna's Marginal Utility | | |
| --- | --- | --- |
| | $1  Marginal Utility  $2 | |
| Quantity | Nail Polish | Outfits |
| 1 | 8 | 16   *8* |
| 2 | 6 | 12   *6* |
| 3 | 4 | 10   *5* |
| 4 | 3 | 6   *3* |

If Madonna is maximizing her utility, what is her *total* utility?
   **a.** 19
   **b.** 28
   **c.** 38
   **d.** 42
   **e.** none of the above

*TU = 8 + 6 + 16 + 12*

*2 Nail Polish*
*2 outfits*

## Predictions of Marginal Utility Theory

**15.** Bikes and roller blades are substitutes. Marginal utility theory predicts that when the price of bikes increases due to a decrease in supply, the quantity demanded of bikes

  **a.** decreases and the demand curve for roller blades shifts rightward.

  **b.** decreases and the demand curve for roller blades shifts leftward.

  **c.** decreases and the demand curve for roller blades will not shift.

  **d.** increases and the demand curve for roller blades shifts rightward.

  **e.** increases and the demand curve for roller blades shifts leftward.

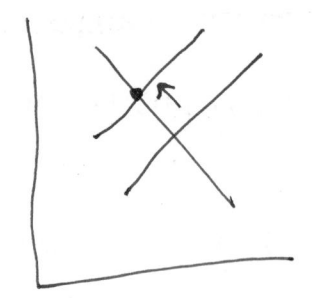

**16.** Which of the following is *not* a prediction of marginal utility theory?

  **a.** Other things remaining the same, the higher the price of a good, the lower the quantity demanded.

  **b.** Other things remaining the same, the higher the price of a good, the higher the consumption of substitutes for that good.

  **c.** Other things remaining the same, the lower the price of a good, the lower the consumption of substitutes for that good.

  **d.** the law of demand

  **e.** diminishing marginal utility

↳ assumptions

**17.** Chuck and Barry have identical preferences but Chuck has a much higher income. If each is maximizing his utility,

  **a.** they will have equal total utilities.

  **b.** Chuck will have lower total utility than Barry.

  **c.** Chuck will have lower marginal utility than Barry for each normal good consumed.

  **d.** Chuck will have higher marginal utility than Barry for each normal good consumed.

  **e.** they will have equal marginal utilities for each normal good consumed.

$2  $1

**18.** The relative prices of beer to back bacon are 2:1. If Bob's current consumption is at a level where $MU_{BEER}/MU_{BACKBACON}$ is 1:2, to achieve maximum utility Bob must

a. consume more beer and less back bacon.

**b.** not change his current consumption of beer and back bacon.

c. consume less beer and more back bacon.

d. increase the price of beer.

e. consume twice as much beer and one-half as much back bacon.

*equalize.*

To ~~increase~~ $MU/P$, both must increase

**19.** Broomhilda is initially maximizing her utility in her consumption of goods X and Y. The price of good X doubles, *ceteris paribus*. For Broomhilda to once again maximize her utility, her *quantity* of X consumed must

a. rise until the marginal utility of X has doubled.

b. fall to one-half its previous level.

**c.** fall until the marginal utility of X has doubled. ✓

d. fall until the marginal utility of X falls to one-half its previous level.

e. yield infinite bliss.

**20.** Beverly is currently in consumer equilibrium. An increase in her income will

a. increase her total utility.

**b.** decrease her total utility.

c. increase her marginal utility of all goods.

d. decrease her marginal utility of all goods.

e. increase her consumption of all goods.

*Inferror good, consumption may decrease and MU increase*

**21.** Bill and Ted consume 15 chocolate bars each at the current price. If Bill's demand curve is more elastic than Ted's demand curve,

a. Bill's willingness to pay for the 15th chocolate bar is greater than Ted's.

**b.** Ted's willingness to pay for the 15th chocolate bar is greater than Bill's.

c. Bill's consumer surplus is greater than Ted's.

d. Ted's consumer surplus is greater than Bill's.

e. Bill's consumer surplus equals Ted's.

*Ted has a steeper demand curve, greater willingness to pay.*

*at 15th unit, willingness is equal*

**22.** The high price of diamonds relative to the price of water reflects the fact that, at typical levels of consumption,
   **a.** the total utility of water is relatively low.
   **b.** the total utility of diamonds is relatively high.
   **c.** the marginal utility of water is relatively high.
   **d.** the marginal utility of diamonds is relatively low.
   **e.** none of the above is true. ✓

**23.** The principle of diminishing marginal utility means that the consumer surplus from the second slice of pizza is
   **a.** greater than that from the first.
   **b.** equal to that of the first
   **c.** less than that of the first. ✓
   **d.** equal to that of the first divided by 2.
   **e.** equal to that of the first multiplied by 2.

## New Ways of Explaining Consumer Choices

**24.** Which of the following barriers to rational choices are studied by behavioural economics?
   **a.** bounded rationality
   **b.** bounded willpower
   **c.** bounded self-interest
   **d.** the endowment effect
   **e.** all of the above ✓

**25.** Neuroeconomics studies all of the following concepts *except*
   **a.** the prefrontal cortex.
   **b.** the hippocampus.
   **c.** the hippopotamus. ✓
   **d.** dopamine.
   **e.** anxiety and fear.

15/25

## Short Answer Problems

1. Explain why the consumer equilibrium condition and the principle of diminishing marginal utility imply the law of demand.

2. Consider the following information for a consumer who is trying to allocate her income between goods $X$ and $Y$ so as to maximize utility. The price of $X$ is $2 and the price of $Y$ is $1 per unit. When all income is spent, the marginal utility of the last unit of $X$ is 20 and the marginal utility of the last unit of $Y$ is 16.

   **a.** Why is the consumer not in equilibrium?

**b.** To increase utility, which good should this consumer consume more of and which less of?

Use this condition for utility maximization to explain how the consumer will move to a new utility-maximizing equilibrium. Show the connection between your explanation and the change on the diagram.

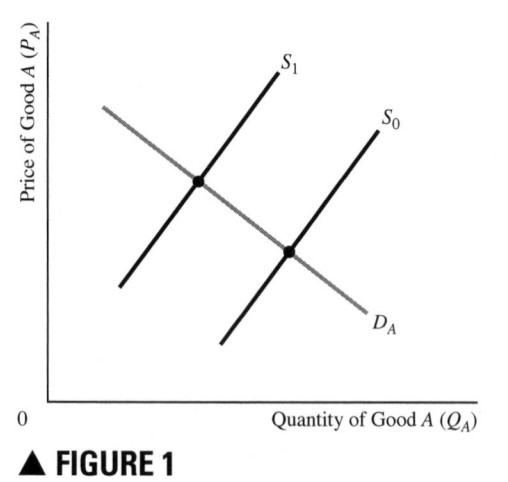

▲ **FIGURE 1**

**3.** A consumer is initially maximizing his utility in the consumption of goods $A$ and $B$ so that

$$\frac{MU_A}{P_A} = \frac{MU_B}{P_B}$$

The price of $A$ then rises as a result of the shift in supply shown in Fig. 1.

**4.** Tables 3 and 4 give Amy's utility from the consumption of popcorn and candy bars during a week.

### TABLE 3   Amy's Utility from Popcorn

| Bags of Popcorn | Total Utility | Marginal Utility |
|---|---|---|
| 1 | 20 | |
| 2 | 36 | |
| 3 | 50 | |
| 4 | | 12 |
| 5 | 72 | |
| 6 | 80 | |

### TABLE 4   Amy's Utility from Candy Bars

| Number of Candy Bars | Total Utility | Marginal Utility |
|---|---|---|
| 1 | 14 | |
| 2 | 26 | |
| 3 | | 10 |
| 4 | 44 | |
| 5 | 51 | |
| 6 | 57 | |

**a.** Complete the tables.

**b.** Suppose the price of a bag of popcorn is \$1 and the price of a candy bar is \$0.50. Given the information in Tables 3 and 4, complete Table 5 where *MU/P* means marginal utility divided by price, which is equivalent to marginal utility per dollar spent.

### TABLE 5   Amy's *MU/P*

| Bags of Popcorn | MU/P | Number of Candy Bars | MU/P |
|---|---|---|---|
| 1 | | 1 | |
| 2 | | 2 | |
| 3 | | 3 | |
| 4 | | 4 | |
| 5 | | 5 | |
| 6 | | 6 | |

**5.** Amy's weekly allowance is $4. Using your answers to Short Answer Problem **4**, answer the following if Amy spends her entire allowance on popcorn and candy bars.

**a.** How much popcorn and how many candy bars will Amy consume each week if she maximizes her utility?

**b.** Show that the utility-maximizing condition is satisfied.

**c.** What is total utility?

**d.** If, instead, Amy consumed 3 bags of popcorn and 2 candy bars, explain why she would not be maximizing her utility using figures both for total utility and for the terms $MU/P$.

**6.** Suppose that Amy's preferences remain as they were in Short Answer Problem **4**, but the price of a candy bar doubles to $1.

**a.** In the space below, construct a new table (similar to Table 5) of $MU/P$ for popcorn and candy bars.

**b.** Amy's allowance continues to be $4. After the price change, how much popcorn and how many candy bars will she consume each week?

**c.** Are popcorn and candy bars substitutes or complements for Amy? Why?

**d.** On the basis of the information you have obtained, use the grid to graph Amy's demand curve for candy bars.

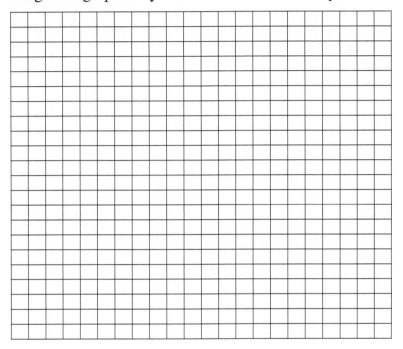

**e.** Suppose that both bags of popcorn and candy bars continue to sell for $1 each, but now Amy's allowance increases to $6 per week.

   **i.** How many candy bars and bags of popcorn will Amy choose to consume per week under the new situation?

   **ii.** Are popcorn and candy bars normal goods? Why or why not?

**7.** Suppose that Andre Agassi spends his entire income of $8 on razors and toy tennis rackets (see Table 6). The price of a razor is $2 and the price of a tennis racket is $4. The marginal utility of each good is independent of the amount consumed of the other good.

| TABLE 6 | Andre's Marginal Utility | |
|---|---|---|
| | **Marginal Utility** | |
| **Quantity** | **Razors** | **Rackets** |
| 1 | 20 | 36 |
| 2 | 18 | 32 |
| 3 | 16 | 20 |
| 4 | 8 | 16 |

**a.** If Andre is maximizing his utility, how many units of each good should he purchase?

**b.** If Andre's income rises to $24, how many units of each good should he purchase?

**c.** Using the information above, calculate Andre's income elasticity of demand for razors.

**8.** Suppose that Igor maximizes his utility by spending his entire income on bats and lizards (see Table 7). The marginal utility of each good is independent of the amount consumed of the other good.

**TABLE 7  Igor's Marginal Utility**

| | Marginal Utility | |
|---|---|---|
| Quantity | Bats | Lizards |
| 1 | 20 | 45 |
| 2 | 18 | 40 |
| 3 | 16 | 25 |
| 4 | 8 | 20 |

Igor's income is $16. The price of a bat is $2, and he buys 3 bats. If the marginal utility of the last lizard he buys is 40, calculate the price of a lizard using two separate methods.

# Answers

## True/False and Explain

1. **F** Points on and inside the budget line are affordable. (180–182)

2. **T** Because *MU* is positive but diminishing. (180–182)

3. **T** Rules for maximizing total utility. (183–186)

4. **F** Ratios of *MU/P* are crucial. If prices are unequal, marginal utilities are unequal in consumer equilibrium. (183–186)

ⓒⓣ 5. **T** Increased consumption of *X* causes decreased $MU_X$. Decreased consumption of *Y* causes increased $MU_Y$. Moves ratios *MU/P* toward equality and total utility maximization. (183–186)

6. **T** Rule for maximizing total utility. (183–186)

7. **F** Rising *P* causes decreased *Q* and increased *MU*. (187–193)

ⓒⓣ 8. **F** True for a normal good; may be false for an inferior good. (187–193)

9. **F** Demand increases for substitutes because now they are relatively cheaper. (187–193)

ⓒⓣ 10. **F** Quantity demanded increases for normal goods but decreases for inferior goods. (187–193)

11. **F** Price is proportional to marginal utility. (187–193)

12. **F** When *total* utility is maximized. (187–193)

13. **T** With a fall in price and increased quantity consumed, more units with willingness-to-pay > price. (187–193)

14. **F** This is the definition of behavioural economics. (194–195)

15. **F** Most economists do not agree on importance of new areas of economics. (194–195)

## Multiple-Choice

1. **d** Consumption possibilities (constraints) and preferences. (180–182)

2. **a** **b** is consumer surplus. For **c**, *MU* = slope of *TU* curve. **d** and **e** are nonsense. (180–182)

3. **e** *TU* is increasing when *MU* is positive, whether *MU* is decreasing or increasing. *TU* may be *MU*. (180–182)

ⓒⓣ 4. **e** Because marginal utility is positive but diminishing with increased consumption. (180–182)

5. **a** Consumers maximize *TU*. **c** and **d** are wrong because *MU/P* equal for *TU* maximization. (183–186)

6. **b** Buys 1 miniskirt (*MU/P* = 16/4) and 3 books (*MU/P* = 8/2). (183–186)

ⓒⓣ 7. **c** Maximizes *TU*. With fewer chips, *MU* is still positive, so *TU* could increase. With more, *MU* turns negative so *TU* would decrease. (183–186)

8. **d** Definition. *MU/P* is key to utility maximization. (183–186)

9. **c** Solve $10/0.5 = 5/P_{BANANA}$ for $P_{BANANA}$. (183–186)

10. **b** Definition. (183–186)

ⓒⓣ 11. **d** For octopus, $MU_O/P_O = 10$. For squid, $MU_S/2$ would need to be < 10, so $MU_S$ must be < 20. (183–186)

ⓒ **12. c** From maximum condition of equal $MU/P$. No necessary relation between $MU$ and quantity or $TU$. (183–186)

**13. c** From maximum condition of equal $MU/P$. No necessary relation between $MU$ and quantity. (183–186)

**14. d** Buys 2 polish and 2 outfits. $TU = 8 + 6 + 16 + 12$. (183–186)

**15. a** See text discussion. (187–193)

**16. e** Diminishing $MU$ is *assumption* of theory. (187–193)

**17. c** Chuck consumes greater quantities of each good, so $MU$ is lower. (187–193)

**18. c** To equalize $MU/P$ must increase $MU_{BEER}$ and decrease $MU_{BACKBACON}$. **d** is wrong because no control over prices. (187–193)

**19. c** From maximum condition of equal $MU/P$. No necessary relation between $MU$ and quantity consumed. (187–193)

ⓒ **20. a** For inferior goods, consumption may decrease and $MU$ increase. (187–193)

**21. d** Ted's steeper demand curve means greater willingness to pay for previous units. Willingness to pay for last unit is equal. (187–193)

**22. e** For diamonds: $TU$ is relatively low, $MU$ is relatively high. For water: $TU$ is relatively high, $MU$ is relatively low. (187–193)

**23. c** 2nd slice value is less than 1st because of diminishing marginal utility; consumer surplus is less. (187–193)

**24. e** All limits on rational choice. (194–195)

**25. c** See text discussion. (194–195)

## Short Answer Problems

**1.** Suppose we observe an individual in consumer equilibrium consuming $X_0$ units of good $X$ and $Y_0$ units of good $Y$, with the prices of $X$ and $Y$ given by $P_X$ and $P_Y$ respectively. This means that at consumption levels $X_0$ and $Y_0$, the marginal utility per dollar spent on $X$ equals the marginal utility per dollar spent on $Y$. Now let the price of $X$ increase to $P^1_X$. The marginal utility per dollar spent on $X$ declines and thus is now less than the marginal utility per dollar spent on $Y$. To restore equilibrium, our consumer must increase the marginal utility of $X$ and decrease the marginal utility of $Y$. From the principle of diminishing marginal utility we know that the only way to do this is to decrease the consumption of $X$ and increase the consumption of $Y$. This demonstrates the law of demand, since an increase in the price of $X$ has been shown to require a decrease in the consumption of $X$ to restore consumer equilibrium.

**2. a.** This consumer is not in equilibrium because the marginal utility per dollar spent is not the same for goods $X$ and $Y$. The marginal utility per dollar spent on $X$ is $MU_X/P_X = 20/2 = 10$, which is less than the marginal utility per dollar spent on $Y$: $MU_Y/P_Y = 16$.

**b.** To equate the marginal utilities per dollar spent (and thus increase utility), this consumer should increase consumption of $Y$ and decrease consumption of $X$. The principle of diminishing marginal utility implies that this will decrease the marginal utility of $Y$ and increase the marginal utility of $X$.

**3.** When the price of *A* rises, *ceteris paribus*,

$$\frac{MU_A}{P_A} < \frac{MU_B}{P_B}$$

The consumer is no longer in equilibrium. In order to restore the equality in the equilibrium condition, the consumer must change his consumption to make $MU_A$ rise and $MU_B$ fall. (The consumer cannot change the prices of *A* and *B*.) Since marginal utility diminishes with increases in quantity consumed, the consumer must decrease consumption of *A* and increase consumption of *B*. Decreased consumption of *A* moves the consumer up to the left on the demand curve, from the initial intersection of *D* and $S_0$ to the new intersection of *D* and $S_1$. In the new consumer equilibrium, equality will be restored in the equilibrium condition.

**4. a.** The tables are completed in Table 3 Solution and Table 4 Solution.

### TABLE 3  Solution Amy's Utility from Popcorn

| Bags of Popcorn | Total Utility | Marginal Utility |
|---|---|---|
| 1 | 20 | 20 |
| 2 | 36 | 16 |
| 3 | 50 | 14 |
| 4 | 62 | 12 |
| 5 | 72 | 10 |
| 6 | 80 | 8 |

### TABLE 4  Solution Amy's Utility from Candy Bars

| Number of Candy Bars | Total Utility | Marginal Utility |
|---|---|---|
| 1 | 14 | 14 |
| 2 | 26 | 12 |
| 3 | 36 | 10 |
| 4 | 44 | 8 |
| 5 | 51 | 7 |
| 6 | 57 | 6 |

**b.** The table is completed in Table 5 Solution.

### TABLE 5  Solution Amy's *MU/P*

| Bags of Popcorn | MU/P | Number of Candy Bars | MU/P |
|---|---|---|---|
| 1 | 20 | 1 | 28 |
| 2 | 16 | 2 | 24 |
| 3 | 14 | 3 | 20 |
| 4 | 12 | 4 | 16 |
| 5 | 10 | 5 | 14 |
| 6 | 8 | 6 | 12 |

**5. a.** 2 bags of popcorn and 4 candy bars.

**b.** The utility-maximizing condition is satisfied, since Amy spends all her income ($4), and the marginal utility per dollar spent is the same for popcorn and candy bars (16).

**c.** Total utility is the utility from the consumption of 2 bags of popcorn (36) plus the utility from the consumption of 4 candy bars (44) = 80.

**d.** If Amy consumed 3 bags of popcorn and 2 candy bars, total utility would be 76, which is less than 80, the total utility from the consumption of 2 bags of popcorn and 4 candy bars. For the combination of 3 bags of popcorn and 2 candy bars, $MU/P$ for popcorn is 14 while $MU/P$ for candy bars is 24. Since $MU/P$ is not the same for both goods, this combination does not meet the condition for utility maximization.

**6. a.** See Table 8.

| TABLE 8  Amy's *MU/P* | | | |
|---|---|---|---|
| Bags of Popcorn | *MU/P* | Number of Candy Bars | *MU/P* |
| 1 | 20 | 1 | 14 |
| 2 | 16 | 2 | 12 |
| 3 | 14 | 3 | 10 |
| 4 | 12 | 4 | 8 |
| 5 | 10 | 5 | 7 |
| 6 | 8 | 6 | 6 |

**b.** 3 bags of popcorn and 1 candy bar. Amy spends all of her income ($4), and the marginal utility per dollar spent is the same for popcorn and candy bars (14).

**c.** Popcorn and candy bars are substitutes for Amy, since an increase in the price of a candy bar causes an increase in the demand for popcorn.

**d.** Amy's demand curve for candy bars is given in Fig. 2. Two points on the demand curve have been identified: when the price of a candy bar is $1, one candy bar will be demanded, and when the price is $0.50, 4 candy bars will be demanded. The demand curve is a line through these two points.

▲ **FIGURE 2**

**e. i.** Now, Amy will choose to consume 4 bags of popcorn and 2 candy bars (instead of 3 bags of popcorn and 1 candy bar). Amy spends all of her income ($6) and the marginal utility per dollar spent is the same for popcorn and candy bars (12).

**ii.** Popcorn and candy bars are both normal goods for Amy, since the increase in income (allowance) leads to increases in the demand for both goods.

**7. a.** The utility-maximizing combination of goods is shown in Table 9.

**TABLE 9  Andre's *MU/P***

| Quantity | MU/P | |
| :---: | :---: | :---: |
| | Razors | Rackets |
| 1 | 10 | 9 |
| 2 | 9 | 8 |
| 3 | 8 | 5 |
| 4 | 4 | 4 |

Andre should purchase 2 razors and 1 racket. Andre spends all of his income ($8), and the marginal utility per dollar spent is the same for razors and rackets (9).

**b.** Andre should purchase 4 razors and 4 rackets. He spends all of his income ($24), and the marginal utility per dollar spent is the same for razors and rackets (4).

**c.** The income elasticity of demand ($\eta_y$) for razors is

$$\eta_y = \frac{\dfrac{\Delta Q}{Q_{ave}}}{\dfrac{\Delta Y}{Y_{ave}}} = \frac{\dfrac{4-2}{\frac{1}{2}(4+2)}}{\dfrac{24-8}{\frac{1}{2}(24+8)}} = \frac{\dfrac{2}{3}}{\dfrac{16}{16}} = \frac{2}{3}$$

**8.** There are two methods for calculating the price of a lizard. One method is based on the fact that Igor spends all of his income on bats and lizards. This means that

$$Y = P_B Q_B + P_L Q_L$$

where $Y$ = income, $P_B$ = the price of a bat, $Q_B$ = the quantity of bats purchased, $P_L$ = the price of a lizard, and $Q_L$ = the quantity of lizards purchased. We know $Y = 16$, $P_B = 2$, $Q_B = 3$, and if the marginal utility of the last lizard is 40, then $Q_L = 2$. Substituting these values, we can solve for $P_L$.

$$16 = 2(3) + P_L(2)$$
$$10 = P_L(2)$$
$$5 = P_L$$

The second method uses the condition for utility maximization:

$$\frac{MU_B}{P_B} = \frac{MU_L}{P_L}$$

We know that $MU_L = 40$, $P_B = 2$, and if Igor buys 3 bats $MU_B = 16$. Substituting these values, we can solve for $P_L$.

$$\frac{16}{2} = \frac{40}{P_L}$$
$$80 = 16P_L$$
$$5 = P_L$$

# 9 Possibilities, Preferences, and Choices

## Key Concepts

### Consumption Possibilities

A **budget line** shows limits to household consumption, given income, and prices of goods and services. Consider the example of movies (horizontal axis) and pop (vertical axis).

- The budget equation is

$$Q_P = \frac{Y}{P_P} - \frac{P_M}{P_P} Q_M$$

- The magnitude of the slope of the budget equation ($P_M/P_P$) equals the **relative price** of movies in terms of pop.
- Intercepts measure a household's **real income** in movies ($x$-intercept) and pop ($y$-intercept).
- Higher $P_M$ yields steeper budget line, fixed pop-intercept.
- Higher $P_P$ yields flatter budget line, fixed movie-intercept.
- Higher $Y$ yields rightward parallel shift budget line.

### Preferences and Indifference Curves

An **indifference curve** maps household preferences, joining combinations of goods giving equal satisfaction.

- Indifference curves generally slope downward and bow toward the origin (convex).
- Indifference curves farther from the origin represent higher levels of satisfaction.
- Indifference curves never intersect.
- **Marginal rate of substitution** (*MRS*) is the magnitude of the slope of an indifference curve—the rate at which household gives up good *y* (pop) for additional unit of good *x* (movies) and remains indifferent (remains on same indifference curve).
- **Diminishing marginal rate of substitution** is the tendency for *MRS* to diminish as we move down along an indifference curve. Accounts for bowed-toward-the-origin shape of indifference curves.
    - More substitutability between goods yields straighter indifference curves.
    - Less substitutability between goods yields more tightly curved indifference curves.

# Predicting Consumer Choices

Given income and prices of goods, a household allocates income to maximize satisfaction. Household chooses best affordable point, which is on the budget line and on the highest possible indifference curve. At the best affordable point,

- household spends all its income and achieves maximum possible satisfaction.
- budget line and indifference curve are tangent and have same slope—*MRS* equals the relative price.

   **Price effect** is $\Delta$ consumption resulting from $\Delta$ price of a good. Price effect = substitution effect + income effect.

- **Substitution effect**—$\Delta$ in consumption resulting from $\Delta$ in price accompanied by (hypothetical) $\Delta$ in income leaving household indifferent between initial and new situations. For normal and inferior goods, substitution effect of falling price is increased consumption.
- **Income effect**—$\Delta$ in consumption resulting from (hypothetically) restoring original income but keeping prices constant at new level. For normal goods, income effect of

(hypothetically) increased income is increased consumption. For inferior goods, (hypothetically) increased income yields decreased consumption.

- The downward-sloping demand curve is a consequence of the consumer choosing his best affordable combination of goods. The demand curve can be derived from the price effect— by tracing the best affordable quantity of a good as its price changes.

*For normal goods*, substitution and income effects work in the same direction, so falling price yields increased consumption.

*For inferior goods*, substitution and income effects work in opposite directions, but net effect of falling price usually yields (smaller) increased consumption.

# Helpful Hints

1. The consumer's basic problem is to do the best given her constraints. These constraints, which limit possible choices, depend on income and the prices of goods and are represented graphically by the budget line. Doing the best means finding the most preferred outcome consistent with those constraints. In this chapter, preferences are represented graphically by indifference curves.

   Graphically, the consumer problem is to find the highest indifference curve attainable given the budget line. To make graphical analysis easier, we examine choices between only two goods, but the same principles apply in the real world to many choices, including the choice between labour and leisure.

2. The budget equation for pop and movies on text page 205 is

$$Q_P = \frac{Y}{P_P} - \frac{P_M}{P_P} Q_M$$

   This is the type of straight-line equation ($y = a + bx$) that we discussed in the Chapter 1 appendix. The differences are that $Q_P$ is the dependent variable (instead of $y$) and $Q_M$ is the independent variable (instead of $x$). We can use the budget equation to graph the budget line by finding the $Q_P$-intercept (where the line intersects the vertical $Q_P$-axis), finding the $Q_M$-intercept (where the line intersects the horizontal $Q_M$-axis), and then connecting those two points with a straight line.

   To find the $Q_P$-intercept, set $Q_M = 0$.

$$Q_P = \frac{Y}{P_P} - \frac{P_M}{P_P}(0)$$

$$Q_P = \frac{Y}{P_P}$$

To find the $Q_M$-intercept, set $Q_P = 0$.

$$0 = \frac{Y}{P_P} - \frac{P_M}{P_P} Q_M$$

$$\frac{P_M}{P_P} Q_M = \frac{Y}{P_P}$$

$$Q_M = \frac{Y}{P_M}$$

The $Q_P$-intercept, $Q_P = Y/P_P$, is the consumer's real income in terms of pop. It tells us how much pop could be purchased if all income was spent on pop. The $Q_M$-intercept, $Q_M = Y/P_M$, is the consumer's real income in terms of movies. It tells us how many movies could be purchased if all income was spent on movies. These intercepts provide an easy method for drawing a budget line. Each of the two endpoints (the intercepts) is just income divided by the price of the good on that axis. Connecting those endpoints with a straight line yields the budget line.

The slope of the budget line provides additional information for the consumer's choice. The magnitude (absolute value) of the slope equals the relative price (or opportunity cost) of movies in terms of pop. In other words, the magnitude of the slope equals the number of units of pop it takes to buy one movie. More generally, the magnitude of the slope of the budget line ($P_X/P_Y$) equals the relative price (or opportunity cost) of the good on the horizontal $x$-axis in terms of the good on the vertical $y$-axis; or the number of units of vertical-axis goods it takes to buy one unit of the horizontal-axis good.

3. The marginal rate of substitution (*MRS*) is the rate at which a consumer gives up good $Y$ for an additional unit of good $X$ and still remains indifferent (on the same indifference curve). The *MRS* equals the magnitude of the slope of the indifference curve, $\Delta Q_Y / \Delta Q_X$.

Because indifference curves are bowed toward the origin (convex), the magnitude of the slope and hence the *MRS* diminishes as we move down an indifference curve. The diminishing *MRS* means that the consumer is willing to give up less of good $Y$ for each additional unit of good $X$. As the consumer moves down an indifference curve, she is coming to value good $Y$ more and value good $X$ less. This is easily explained by the principle of diminishing marginal utility, which underlies the following equation:

$$\frac{\text{Marginal rate}}{\text{of substitution}} = \frac{MU_X}{MU_Y}$$

At the top of the indifference curve, the consumer is consuming little $X$ and much $Y$, so the marginal utility of $X$ ($MU_X$) is high and the marginal utility of $Y$ ($MU_Y$) is low. Moving down the curve, as the quantity of $X$ consumed increases, $MU_X$ decreases; and as the quantity of $Y$ consumed decreases, $MU_Y$ increases. Thus the principle of diminishing marginal utility provides an intuitive understanding of why the *MRS* diminishes as we move down an indifference curve.

4. At the consumer's best affordable point, the budget line is just tangent to the highest-affordable indifference curve, so the magnitude of the slope of the budget line equals the magnitude of the slope of the indifference curve. Combining the information from Helpful Hint **2** (the magnitude of the slope of the budget line equals $P_X/P_Y$) and Helpful Hint **3** (the magnitude of the slope of the indifference curve equals $MU_X/MU_Y$) yields

$$\frac{P_X}{P_Y} = \frac{MU_X}{MU_Y}$$

Rearranging terms yields

$$\frac{MU_X}{P_X} = \frac{MU_Y}{P_Y}$$

This is the equation for utility maximization from Chapter 8. You can now see why the budget equation/indifference curve analysis of consumer choice developed in Chapter 9 complements the marginal utility analysis of Chapter 8.

5. Understanding the distinction between the income and substitution effects of a change in the price of a good is often challenging for students. Consider a decrease in the price of good $A$. This has two effects that will influence the consumption of $A$. First, the decrease in the price of $A$ will reduce the relative price of $A$, and second, it will increase

real income. The substitution effect is the answer to the question: How much would the consumption of $A$ change as a result of the relative price decline if we also (hypothetically) reduce income by enough to leave the consumer indifferent between the new and original situations? The income effect is the answer to the question: How much more would the consumption of $A$ change if we (hypothetically) restore the consumer's real income but leave relative prices at the new level?

# Self-Test

## True/False and Explain

### Consumption Possibilities

1. The graph of a budget line will be bowed toward the origin.

2. At any point on a budget line, all income is spent.

3. *Ceteris paribus*, an increase in the price of goods means that real income falls.

4. An increase in income causes a leftward parallel shift of the budget line.

### Preferences and Indifference Curves

5. We assume that more of any good is preferred to less of the good.

6. Higher indifference curves represent higher levels of income.

7. The principle of the diminishing marginal rate of substitution explains why indifference curves are bowed toward the origin.

8. Perfect substitutes will have L-shaped indifference curves.

**9.** The closer two goods are to perfect substitutes, the closer the marginal rate of substitution is to being constant.

**10.** If an indifference curve is steep, the marginal rate of substitution is low.

## Predicting Consumer Choices

**11.** At the best affordable consumption point of movies and pop, the marginal rate of substitution equals the ratio of the price of movies to the price of pop.

**12.** When the relative price of a good decreases, the income effect always leads to increased consumption of the good.

**13.** When the relative price of a good increases, the substitution effect always leads to decreased consumption of the good.

**14.** The law of demand can be derived from an indifference curve model by tracing the impact on quantity demanded of an increase in price.

**15.** When the price of an inferior good falls, the substitution effect increases consumption and the income effect decreases consumption.

# Multiple-Choice

## Consumption Possibilities

1. Which of the following statements best describes a consumer's budget line?
   a. the amount of each good a consumer can purchase
   b. the limits to a consumer's set of affordable consumption choices
   c. the desired level of consumption for the consumer
   d. the consumption choices made by a consumer
   e. the set of all affordable consumption choices

2. Real income is measured in
   a. monetary units.
   b. price units.
   c. units of satisfaction.
   d. units of indifference.
   e. units of goods.

3. Consider the budget line and indifference curve in Fig. 1. If the price of good $X$ is $2, what is the price of good $Y$?
   a. $0.37
   b. $0.67
   c. $1.50
   d. $2.67
   e. impossible to calculate without additional information

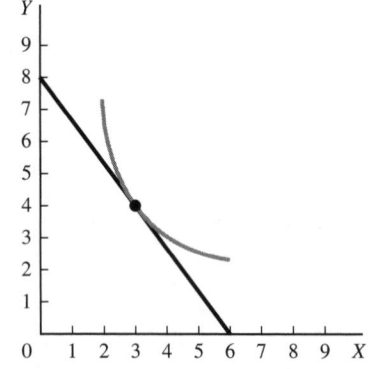

▲ FIGURE 1

4. The budget line depends on
   a. income only.
   b. prices only.
   c. income and prices.
   d. preferences only.
   e. preferences and prices.

**5.** Bill consumes apples and bananas. Suppose Bill's income doubles and the prices of apples and bananas also double. Bill's budget line will

**a.** shift left but not change slope.

**b.** remain unchanged.

**c.** shift right but not change slope.

**d.** shift right and become steeper.

**e.** shift right and become flatter.

**6.** The initial budget equation for pop and movies is $Q_P = 20 - 4Q_M$, and the price of pop ($P_P$) is \$5. If the price of pop falls to \$4, which of the following is the new budget equation?

**a.** $Q_P = 25 - 2Q_M$

**b.** $Q_P = 25 - 4Q_M$

**c.** $Q_P = 25 - 5Q_M$

**d.** $Q_P = 20 - 5Q_M$

**e.** none of the above

**7.** Zarina's income allows her to afford 3 tomatoes and no toothbrushes, or 2 toothbrushes and no tomatoes. The relative price of toothbrushes (price toothbrush/price tomato) is

**a.** 2/3.

**b.** 3/2.

**c.** 6/1.

**d.** 1/6.

**e.** impossible to calculate without additional information.

**8.** If the price of the good measured on the vertical axis increases, the budget line will

**a.** become steeper.

**b.** become flatter.

**c.** shift leftward but stay parallel to the original budget line.

**d.** shift rightward but stay parallel to the original budget line.

**e.** shift leftward and become steeper.

9. If income increases, the budget line will
   a. become steeper.
   b. become flatter.
   c. shift leftward but stay parallel to the original budget line.
   d. shift rightward but stay parallel to the original budget line.
   e. stay parallel but shift leftward or rightward depending on whether a good is normal or inferior.

10. The budget equation for pop ($P$) and movies ($M$) is $Q_P = 10 - 5Q_M$, with movies on the horizontal axis and pop on the vertical axis. The price of pop ($P_P$) is \$4. That means income ($Y$) is ___ and the price of movies ($P_M$) is ___.
    a. $Y = \$50$; $P_M = \$20$
    b. $Y = \$200$; $P_M = \$20$
    c. $Y = \$40$; $P_M = \$2$
    d. $Y = \$40$; $P_M = \$20$
    e. none of the above combinations

## Preferences and Indifference Curves

11. The shape of an indifference curve depends on
    a. the prices of goods.
    b. household income.
    c. the substitutability between goods for the household.
    d. the level of satisfaction for the household.
    e. all of the above.

12. In general, as a consumer moves down an indifference curve increasing consumption of good $X$ (measured on the horizontal axis),
    a. more of $Y$ must be given up for each additional unit of $X$.
    b. a constant amount of $Y$ must be given up for each additional unit of $X$.
    c. less of $Y$ must be given up for each additional unit of $X$.
    d. the relative price of $Y$ increases.
    e. the relative price of $Y$ decreases.

**13.** Which of the following statements is *false*?

   **a.** Indifference curves are negatively sloped.

   **b.** A preference map consists of a series of nonintersecting indifference curves.

   **c.** Indifference curves are bowed out from the origin.

   **d.** The marginal rate of substitution is the magnitude of the slope of an indifference curve.

   **e.** The marginal rate of substitution increases with movement up an indifference curve.

**14.** In moving down along an indifference curve, the marginal rate of substitution (*MRS*) for complements will

   **a.** increase faster than the *MRS* for substitutes.

   **b.** increase more slowly than the *MRS* for substitutes.

   **c.** be relatively constant.

   **d.** decrease faster than the *MRS* for substitutes.

   **e.** decrease more slowly than the *MRS* for substitutes.

**15.** If two goods are perfect substitutes, their

   **a.** indifference curves are positively sloped straight lines.

   **b.** indifference curves are negatively sloped straight lines.

   **c.** indifference curves are L-shaped.

   **d.** marginal rate of substitution is zero.

   **e.** marginal rate of substitution is infinity.

## Predicting Consumer Choices

**16.** When the price of an inferior good rises, the income effect

   **a.** is always larger than the substitution effect.

   **b.** decreases consumption of the good and the substitution effect increases consumption.

   **c.** and the substitution effect both increase consumption of the good.

   **d.** and the substitution effect both decrease consumption of the good.

   **e.** increases consumption of the good and the substitution effect decreases consumption.

**17.** Which of the following statement(s) about Fig. 2 is *true*?
   **a.** Point *s* is preferred to point *q*, but *s* is not affordable.
   **b.** Points *q* and *r* yield the same utility, but *q* is more affordable.
   **c.** Point *t* is preferred to point *q*, but *t* is not affordable.
   **d.** Points *q* and *s* cost the same, but *q* is preferred to *s*.
   **e.** All of the above statements are true.

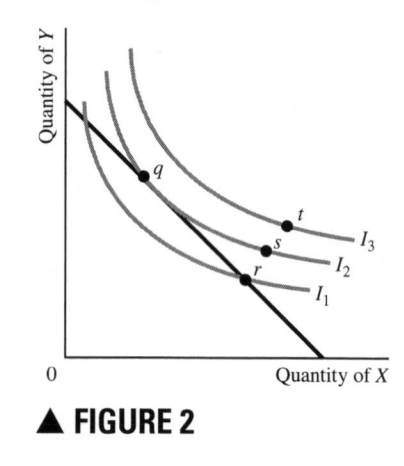

▲ **FIGURE 2**

**18.** For a rise in price, the substitution effect
   **a.** always increases consumption.
   **b.** increases consumption for normal goods only.
   **c.** decreases consumption for normal goods only.
   **d.** decreases consumption for inferior goods only.
   **e.** does none of the above.

**19.** The initial budget line labelled *RS* in Fig. 3 would shift to *RT* as a result of a(n)
   **a.** rise in the price of good *X*.
   **b.** fall in the price of good *X*.
   **c.** decrease in preferences for good *X*.
   **d.** rise in the price of good *Y*.
   **e.** increase in real income.

▲ **FIGURE 3**

**20.** When the initial budget line labelled *RS* in Fig. 3 shifts to *RT*, the substitution effect is illustrated by the move from point
  **a.** *a* to *b*.
  **b.** *a* to *c*.
  **c.** *a* to *d*.
  **d.** *b* to *d*.
  **e.** *d* to *c*.

**21.** When the initial budget line labelled *RS* in Fig. 3 shifts to *RT*, the income effect is illustrated by the move from point
  **a.** *a* to *b*.
  **b.** *a* to *c*.
  **c.** *a* to *d*.
  **d.** *b* to *c*.
  **e.** *b* to *d*.

**22.** If the price of good *X* (measured on the horizontal axis) falls, the substitution effect is represented by a movement to a
  **a.** higher indifference curve.
  **b.** lower indifference curve.
  **c.** steeper part of the same indifference curve.
  **d.** flatter part of the same indifference curve.
  **e.** flatter part of a higher indifference curve.

**23.** When Clark Gable took off his shirt in *It Happened One Night*, he was not wearing an undershirt. As a result, men's undershirt sales plummeted. *Ceteris paribus*, we can conclude that men's undershirt
  **a.** preferences changed when prices changed.
  **b.** preferences changed when income changed.
  **c.** choices changed when preferences changed.
  **d.** choices changed when prices changed.
  **e.** choices changed when income changed.

**24.** When the price of an inferior good falls, the

    1 income and substitution effects both move quantity demanded in the same direction.

    2 income and substitution effects move quantity demanded in opposite directions.

    3 income effect is usually larger than the substitution effect.

    4 substitution effect is usually larger than the income effect.

  **a.** 1 and 2

  **b.** 1 and 4

  **c.** 2 and 3

  **d.** 2 and 4

  **e.** none of the above

**25.** For a rise in price, the substitution effect

  **a.** increases consumption for normal goods only.

  **b.** always increases consumption.

  **c.** decreases consumption for normal goods only.

  **d.** decreases consumption for inferior goods only.

  **e.** does none of the above.

# Short Answer Problems

1. Explain why it is logically impossible for indifference curves to intersect each other by comparing points *a*, *b*, and *c* in Fig. 4.

▲ **FIGURE 4**

ⓒⓣ **2.** For normal goods,

- an increase in income causes an *increase in demand* (demand curve shifts to the right).

- the income effect (due to a decrease in price) causes an *increase in quantity demanded*.

Explain why these two statements are or are not contradictory. Be sure to define clearly any important concepts.

**3.** Jan and Dan both like bread and peanut butter and have the same income. Since they face the same prices, they have identical budget lines. Currently, Jan and Dan consume exactly the same quantities of bread and peanut butter; they have the same best affordable consumption point. Jan, however, views bread and peanut butter as close (though not perfect) substitutes, while Dan considers bread and peanut butter to be quite (but not perfectly) complementary.

**a.** Using the grid, on the same graph draw a budget line and representative indifference curves for Jan and Dan. (Measure the quantity of bread on the horizontal axis.)

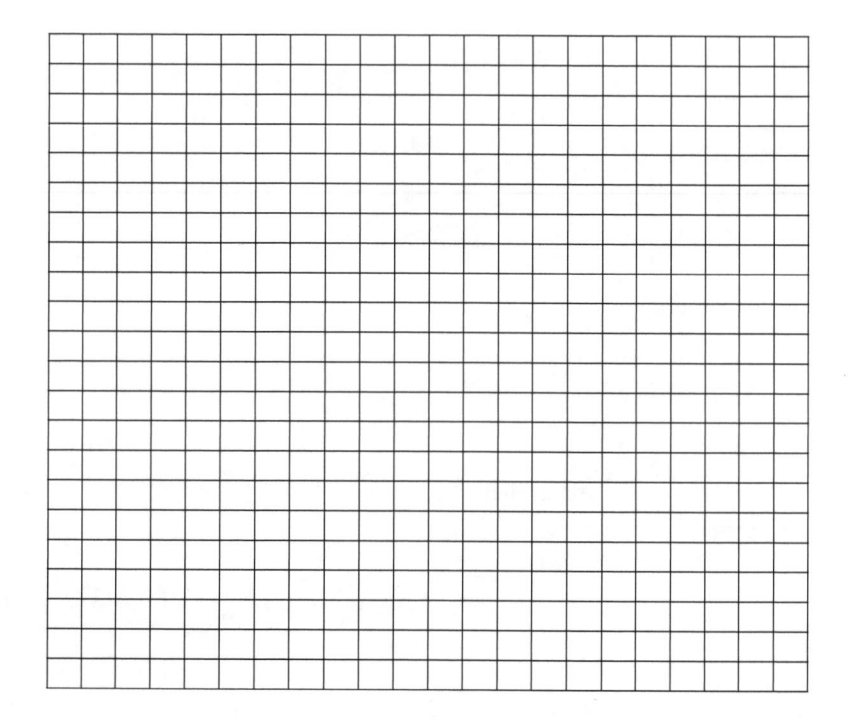

**b.** Now, suppose the price of bread declines. Graphically represent the substitution effects for Jan and Dan. For whom is the substitution effect greater?

⊕ **4.** Fig. 5 illustrates a consumer's indifference map for food and clothing.

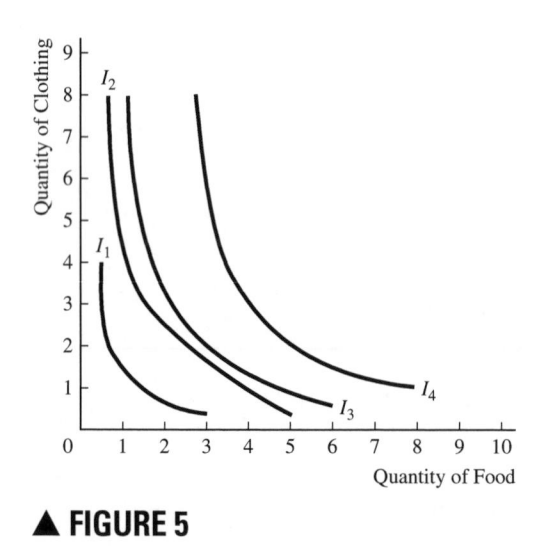

▲ **FIGURE 5**

**a. i.** Initially, the price of a unit of clothing is $P_C = \$1$ and the price of a unit of food is $P_F = \$1.50$. If income is $Y = \$9$, draw the consumer's budget line on Fig. 5 and label the best affordable point as point $a$. What is the quantity of food consumed?

**ii.** What is the equation of the budget line in terms of $P_C$, $P_F$, and $Y$? What is the equation of the budget line in numerical terms? Express the magnitude (absolute value) of the slope of the budget line as a ratio of $P_C$ and $P_F$.

**iii.** At point $a$, what is the value of the marginal rate of substitution (or equivalently, $MU_F/MU_C$)?

**iv.** Use your answers in parts **ii** and **iii** to derive the formula for utility maximization. Explain.

**b.** If $P_F$ increases to $3 per unit while income and $P_C$ remain unchanged, draw the new budget line and label the new best affordable point as point $b$. What is the new quantity of food consumed?

**c.** If $P_F$ increases again to $4.50 per unit while income and $P_C$ remain unchanged, draw the corresponding budget line and label the best affordable point as point $c$. What is the quantity of food consumed?

**d.** On the grid below, plot and draw the demand curve for food that corresponds to points *a*, *b*, and *c*. Be sure to clearly label the axes.

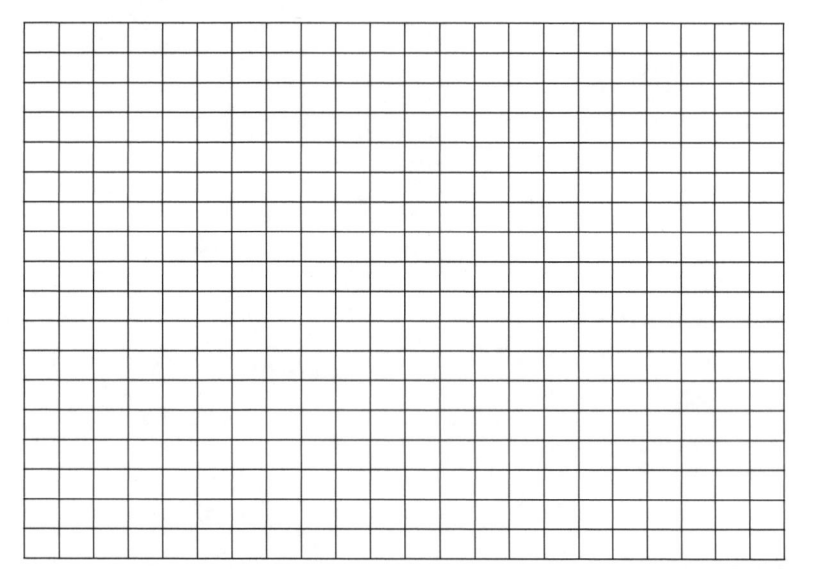

**e.** Suppose prices remain at their initial values ($P_C$ = $1, $P_F$ = $1.50) but income falls to $3. On Fig. 5 on page 280, draw the new budget line and label the best affordable point as point *z*. What is the quantity of food consumed? Is food a normal or inferior good? Explain. On your demand curve graph from part **d**, plot point *z* and roughly sketch a demand curve corresponding to the new income level.

**5.** Sharon, a fitness fanatic, plays squash and takes aerobics classes at her health club. Squash courts rent for $2 per hour and aerobics classes are $1 per hour. Sharon has decided to spend $12 per week for fitness activities. Fig. 6 illustrates several indifference curves for squash and aerobics on Sharon's preference map.

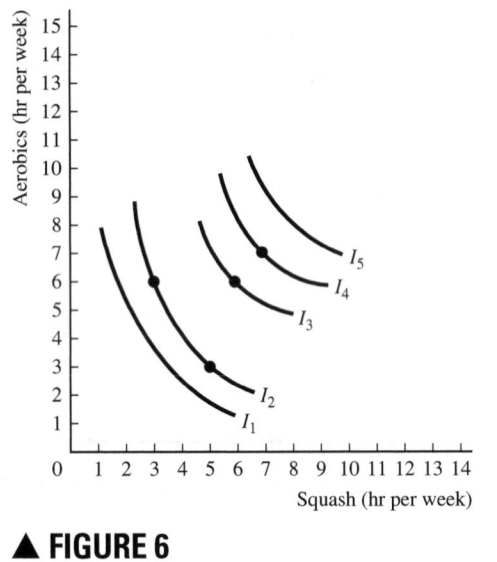

▲ **FIGURE 6**

**a.** How many hours of squash and aerobics will Sharon consume at her best affordable point?

**b.** Suppose that squash rentals fall to $1 per hour.
   **i.** How many hours of squash and aerobics will Sharon now consume? What is the increase in her hours of squash?

**ii.** Of the total increase in hours of squash, how many hours are due to the substitution effect of the price fall?

**iii.** Of the total increase in hours of squash, how many hours are due to the income effect of the price fall?

**c.** On the grid below, plot two points on Sharon's demand curve for squash and draw her straight-line demand curve.

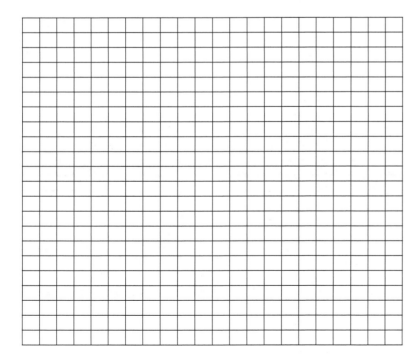

**d.** The price of squash continues to be $1 but Sharon's fitness budget increases to $14. How many hours of squash and aerobics will Sharon now consume?

Ⓒ **6.** Ms. Muffet consumes both curds and whey. The initial price of curds is $1 per unit, and the price of whey is $1.50 per unit. Ms. Muffet's initial income is $12.

**a.** What is the relative price of curds?

**b.** Derive Ms. Muffet's budget equation and graph her budget line on the grid on the next page. (Measure curds on the horizontal axis.)

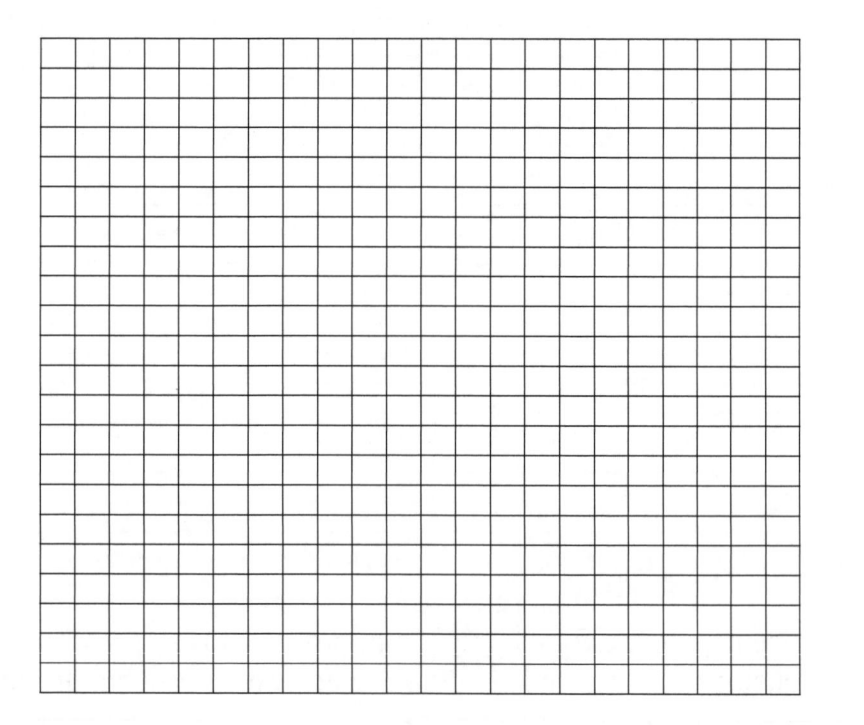

**d.** What is the marginal rate of substitution of curds for whey at this point?

**c.** On your graph, draw an indifference curve so that the best affordable point corresponds to 6 units of curds and 4 units of whey.

**e.** Show that any other point on the budget line is inferior.

**7.** Given the initial situation described in Short Answer Problem **6**, suppose Ms. Muffet's income now increases.

  **a.** On the grid below, illustrate graphically how the consumption of curds and whey are affected if both goods are normal. (Numerical answers are not necessary. Just show whether consumption increases or decreases.)

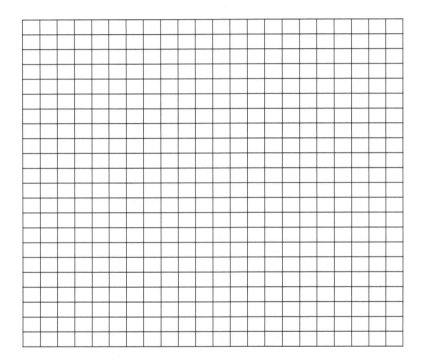

  **b.** On the grid below, draw a new graph showing the effect of an increase in Ms. Muffet's income if whey is an inferior good.

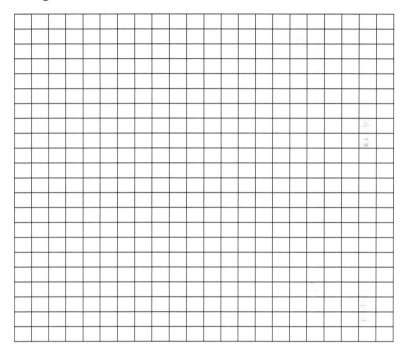

**8.** Return to the initial circumstances described in Short Answer Problem **6**. Now suppose the price of curds doubles to $2 a unit, while the price of whey remains at $1.50 per unit and income remains at $12.

**a.** On the grid below, draw the new budget line.

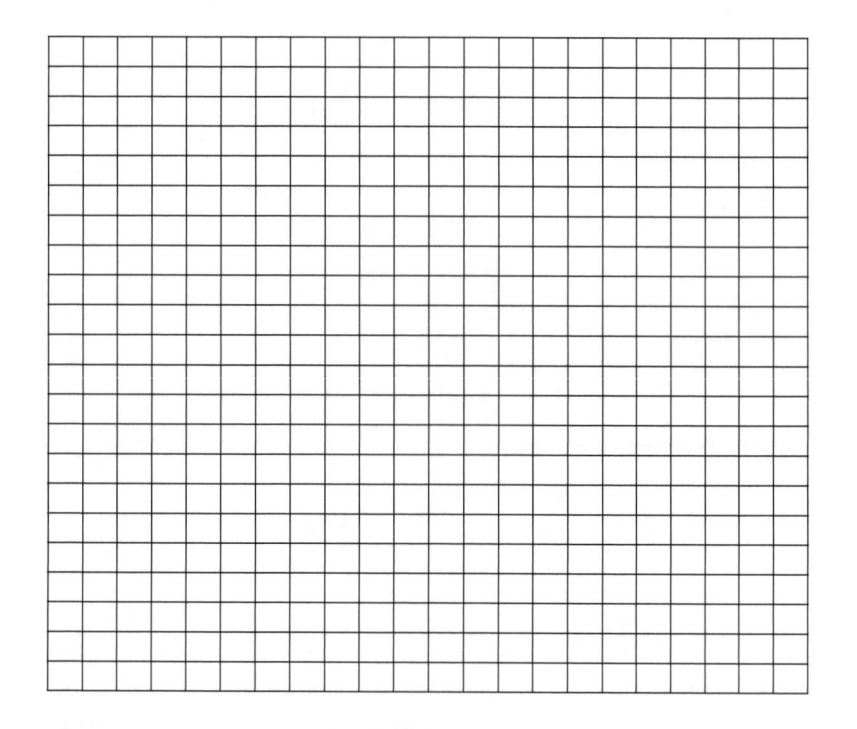

**b.** Why is the initial best affordable point (label it point $r$) no longer the best affordable point?

**c.** Using your graph, show the new best affordable point and label it $t$. What has happened to the consumption of curds?

**d.** Decompose the effect on the consumption of $X$ into the substitution effect and the income effect. On your graph, indicate the substitution effect as movement from point $r$ to point $s$ (which you must locate) and indicate the income effect as movement from point $s$ to point $t$.

# Answers

## True/False and Explain

1. **F** Budget lines are straight. Indifference curves are bowed toward origin. (204–205)
2. **T** Expenditure = income along budget line. (204–205)
3. **T** Real income = income/price goods. (205)
4. **F** Rightward parallel shift. (206)
5. **T** See text discussion. (207–208)
6. **F** Represent higher levels of satisfaction. (207–208)
7. **T** See text discussion. (208–209)
8. **F** True for perfect complements. (209–210)
9. **T** Constant *MRS* is a straight line. (209–210)
10. **F** *MRS* is high. (209–210)
⊕ 11. **T** Budget line is tangent to indifference curve. (210–211)
⊕ 12. **F** True for normal goods, false for inferior goods. (213–214)
13. **T** The substitution effect for normal and inferior goods always works in the same direction. (213–214)
14. **T** See text discussion. (211–212)
15. **T** Income effect decreases consumption—higher real income means household can afford to buy higher-quality (normal) goods instead. (213–214)

## Multiple-Choice

1. **b** **a** should be combinations of goods; **c** is about indifference curves; **d** is about the best affordable point; **e** includes the area inside the budget line. (204–205)
2. **e** Quantity of goods household can buy. (205)
3. **c** Income = $12 ($2 × 6 units X), so price Y = $12/8 units Y. (204–206)
4. **c** See text discussion. Indifference curves depend on preferences. (204–205)
5. **b** Numerators and denominators of both intercepts double, so intercepts do not change. (205–206)
⊕ 6. **c** From $Q_P = (Y/P_P) - (P_M/P_P)Q_M$. If $P_P = \$5$, then $Y = \$100$ and $P_M = \$20$. Then recalculate $Q_P$ equation for $P_P = \$4$. (205–206)
⊕ 7. **b** (3 × price tomato) = (2 × price toothbrush). Divide both sides by price tomato and by 2. (204–206)
8. **b** *y*-intercept shifts down, *x*-intercept unchanged. (205–206)
9. **d** Increased income does not change slope but increases *x*- and *y*-intercepts. (205–206)
10. **d** From $Q_P = (Y/P_P) - (P_M/P_P)Q_M$. If $P_P = \$4$, and $(Y/P_P) = 10$, then $Y = \$40$. If $(P_M/P_P) = 5$, then $P_M = \$20$. (205–206)
11. **c** Budget line depends on **a** and **b**. At any level of satisfaction, indifference curve could be any shape. (207–210)

**12. c** Due to diminishing *MRS*. **d** and **e** are wrong since relative price relates to the budget line, not the indifference curve. (207–210)

**13. c** Indifference curves bow in toward the origin. (207–210)

**14. d** *MRS* is always diminishing moving down the indifference curve. Complements have more tightly curved indifference curves. (209–210)

**15. b** With constant slope = 1. (209–210)

**16. e** Rising price reduces real income, increasing consumption for inferior good. (209–210)

**17. c** *t* is on a higher indifference curve, but outside the budget line. *s* and *q* yield the same utility so and are wrong. *q* is preferred to *r* so **b** is wrong. (210–211)

**18. e** For rising price, the substitution effect always decreases consumption for both normal and inferior goods. (213–214)

**19. a** With the same income, less *X* can be purchased. **c** relates to indifference curves. Increase in real income is a move from point *b* to *c*. (211–212)

**20. a** Budget line with new prices is tangent to the original indifference curve. (213–214)

**21. d** Hypothetically restore original income (reverse the increase in real income) but keep prices constant at new level. (213–214)

**22. d** New budget line is flatter and drawn tangent to the same indifference curve. (213–214)

**23. c** Gable's influence caused decreased preference for undershirts. Combined with unchanged prices and incomes, this caused decreased consumption. (210–214)

**24. d** See text discussion. (213–214)

**25. e** Always decreases consumption. (213–214)

## Short Answer Problems

1. The explanation takes the form of a proof by contradiction. Since points *a* and *b* are on the same indifference curve ($I_1$), the consumer is indifferent between them. Since points *a* and *c* are on the same indifference curve ($I_2$), the consumer is also indifferent between them. If the consumer is indifferent between *a* and *b* and between *a* and *c*, this implies an indifference between *b* and *c*. But indifference between points *b* and *c* is logically impossible, because we assume that more of any good is preferred to less of that good. Since point *c* has more of both good *X* and good *Y* than point *b*, the consumer cannot be indifferent between *b* and *c*. Indifference between *b* and *c* contradicts the assumption that more is preferred to less. Hence indifference curves cannot intersect.

2. These statements appear to be contradictory because an increase in income leads, in the first statement, to a shift of the demand curve but, in the second statement, to a movement along the demand curve. The reason the statements are *not* contradictory has to do with a crucial distinction between *nominal* income and *real* income.

   The first statement (an *increase* in income causes an increase in *demand* [demand curve shifts rightward]) describes how an increase in *nominal* income shifts the demand curve. *Nominal* income is measured in dollars.

The second statement (the income effect [due to a decrease in price] causes an increase in *quantity demanded*) describes how an increase in *real* income causes a movement along the stationary demand curve.

*Real* income is measured in purchasing power, or the quantities of goods that nominal income can buy. When the price of a good decreases, your *real* income goes up because you can now purchase more of that good with the same, unchanged, *nominal* income. Because *nominal* income is unchanged in the second statement, the demand curve does not shift. But because *real* income has increased, the decrease in price leads to an increase in *quantity demanded*.

**3. a.** Initially, Jan and Dan are at point $c$ on the budget line labelled *AB* in Fig. 7. Jan's indifference curve is $I_J$. Note that her indifference curve is close to a straight line, reflecting the fact that bread and peanut butter are close substitutes. On the other hand, since Dan considers bread and peanut butter to be complementary, his indifference curve, $I_D$, is more tightly curved.

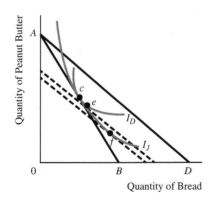

▲ **FIGURE 7**

**b.** If the price of bread declines, the budget line will become flatter, such as the line labelled *AD* in Fig. 7. In order to measure the substitution effect, find the point on the original indifference curve that has the same slope as the new budget line. Since Dan's indifference curve is more sharply curved, it becomes flatter quite rapidly as we move away from point $c$. Thus the substitution effect is quite small, from $c$ to point $e$. Since Jan's indifference curve is almost a straight line, the substitution effect must be much larger, from $c$ to point $f$.

**4.** The consumer's budget line is shown in Fig. 5 Solution.

▲ **FIGURE 5 Solution**

**a. i.** 4 units of food.

**ii.** The consumer's budget is given by

$$P_C Q_C + P_F Q_F = Y$$

To obtain the budget equation, follow the calculation procedure on text page 205. Divide by $P_C$ to obtain

$$Q_C + \frac{P_F}{P_C} Q_F = \frac{Y}{P_C}$$

Subtract $(P_F/P_C)Q_F$ from both sides to obtain

$$Q_C = \frac{Y}{P_C} - \frac{P_F}{P_C} Q_F$$

To obtain the budget equation in numerical terms, substitute in the values $P_C = \$1$, $P_F = \$1.50$, and $Y = \$9$.

$$Q_C = \frac{9}{1} - \frac{1.50}{1} Q_F$$

The magnitude (absolute value) of the slope of the budget line is 3/2, which is the ratio of $P_F/P_C$. Note that this price ratio cannot be read directly off the graph, since the axes measure quantities, not prices.

**iii.** The marginal rate of substitution at point $a$ is defined as the magnitude of the slope of the indifference curve at point $a$. Since the slope of the indifference curve at point $a$ is equal to the slope of the tangent at $a$, and since the budget line is tangent at $a$, the magnitude of the slope of the indifference curve is 3/2. This magnitude is equivalent to $MU_F/MU_C$.

**iv.** The magnitude of the slope of the budget line is $P_F/P_C$ and the magnitude of the slope of the indifference curve at $a$ is $MU_F/MU_C$. Since the two magnitudes are equal, $P_F/P_C = MU_F/MU_C$ or $MU_F/P_F = MU_C/P_C$.

**b.** See Fig. 5 Solution: 2 units of food.

**c.** See Fig. 5 Solution: 1 unit of food.

**d.** The demand curve for food is shown in Fig. 8.

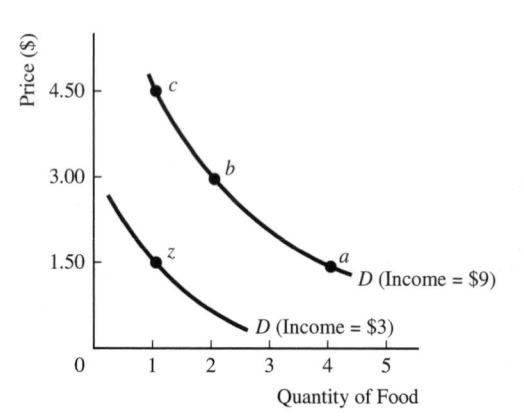

▲ **FIGURE 8**

**e.** See Fig. 5 Solution: 1 unit of food. Food is a normal good because a *decrease* in income (with prices constant) causes a decrease in food consumption (from 4 units to 1 unit). See Fig. 8 for the new demand curve (income = $3).

**5. a.** In order to find Sharon's best affordable point, draw the budget line in Fig. 6 Solution on the next page. The initial budget line is labelled *AB* and Sharon's best affordable point is point *c* on indifference curve $I_2$. Thus Sharon consumes 3 hours of squash and 6 hours of aerobics per week.

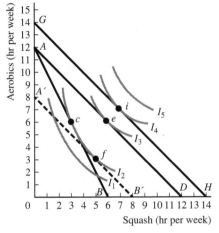

**▲ FIGURE 6  Solution**

**b.** If the price of squash falls to $1, the budget line becomes *AD*.

   **i.**  Now Sharon's best affordable point is point *e* on indifference curve $I_3$. This corresponds to 6 hours of squash and 6 hours of aerobics per week. Her squash consumption has increased by 3 hours.

   **ii.**  To measure the substitution effect, shift the new budget line leftward in parallel until it is tangent to indifference curve $I_2$, where Sharon was before the fall in the price of squash. In effect, budget line *A′B′* removes the increase in real income due to the price fall in order to isolate the substitution

effect of the price fall on Sharon's squash consumption. Point *f* is what Sharon would have consumed at the new prices if her income fell just enough to return her to her original indifference curve. The substitution effect of the fall in the price of squash is the movement from initial point *c* to point *f*, which is an increase in squash hours consumed of 2 (from 3 to 5 hours).

   **iii.**  To measure the income effect, shift the budget line *A′B′* rightward in parallel fashion until it is tangent to the indifference curve $I_3$, where Sharon was before we hypothetically reduced her real income. In effect, this shift isolates the income effect by restoring the increase in real income due to the price fall while keeping prices constant at their new values. The income effect of the fall in the price of squash is the movement from point *f* to point *e*, which is an increase in squash hours consumed of 1 (from 5 to 6 hours).

The results are summarized in Table 1.

**TABLE 1  Price Effect from Figure 6 Solution**

| Effect | Move from Point | Δ Hours Squash |
|---|---|---|
| Substitution effect | *c* to *f* | 2 |
| + Income effect | *f* to *e* | 1 |
| = Price effect | *c* to *e* | 3 |

**c.** In parts **a** and **b**, income spent on fitness was constant at $12 and the price of aerobics was constant at $1 per hour. When the price of squash was $2 per hour Sharon wanted to consume 3 hours of squash, and when the price of squash was $1 Sharon wanted to consume 6 hours of squash. This gives us two points on Sharon's demand curve for squash, which are labelled *a* and *b* in Fig. 9. Drawing a line passing through these points allows us to obtain her straight-line demand curve, labelled *D*.

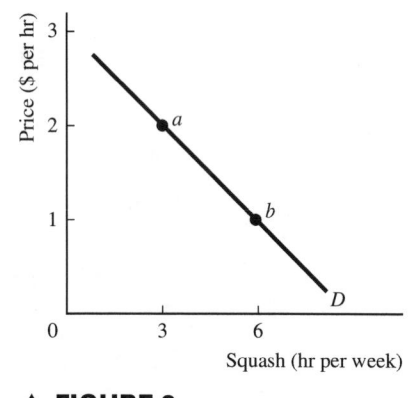

▲ **FIGURE 9**

**d.** When Sharon's fitness budget increases to $14, the budget line shifts right to the line labelled *GH* in Fig. 6 Solution. Sharon's best affordable point is now at *j*, which corresponds to 7 hours of squash and 7 hours of aerobics consumed per week.

ⓒ **6. a.** The relative price of curds is the price of curds divided by the price of whey:

$$\$1 / \$1.50 = 2/3$$

**b.** Let $P_C$ = the price of curds, $P_W$ = the price of whey, $Q_C$ = quantity of curds, $Q_W$ = quantity of whey, and $Y$ = income. The budget equation, in general form, is

$$Q_W = \frac{Y}{P_W} - \frac{P_C}{P_W} Q_C$$

Since $P_C = \$1$, $P_W = \$1.50$, and $Y = \$12$, Ms. Muffet's budget equation is specifically given by

$$Q_W = 8 - 2/3 Q_C$$

The graph of this budget equation, the budget line, is given by the line labelled *AB* in Fig. 10.

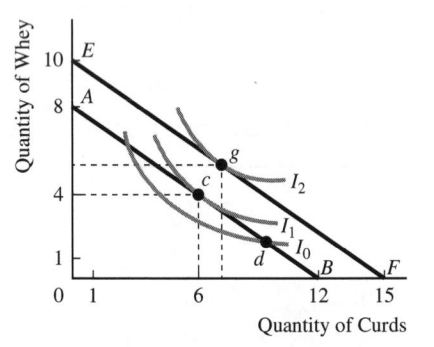

▲ **FIGURE 10  Curds & Whey Normal Goods**

**c.** If the best affordable point corresponds to 6 units of curds and 4 units of whey, then the relevant indifference curve must be tangent to (just touch) the budget line *AB* at *c*, which is indifference curve $I_1$.

**d.** The marginal rate of substitution is given by the magnitude of the slope of the indifference curve at point *c*. We do not know the slope of the indifference curve directly, but we can easily compute the slope of the budget line. Since, at point $c$, the indifference curve and the budget line have the same slope, we can obtain the marginal rate of substitution of curds for whey. Since the slope of the budget line is $-2/3$, the marginal rate of substitution is $2/3$. For example, Ms. Muffet is willing to give up 2 units of whey in order to receive 3 additional units of curds and still remain indifferent.

**e.** Since indifference curves cannot intersect each other and since indifference curve $I_1$ lies everywhere above the budget line (except at point $c$), we know that every other point on the budget line is on a lower indifference curve. For example, point $d$ lies on indifference curve $I_0$. Thus every other point on the budget line is inferior to point $c$.

**7. a.** An increase in income will cause a parallel rightward shift of the budget line, for example to $EF$ in Fig. 10 on the previous page. If both curds and whey are normal goods, Ms. Muffet will move to a point like $g$ at which the consumption of both goods has increased.

**b.** If whey is an inferior good, its consumption will fall as income rises. This is illustrated in Fig. 11. Once again the budget line shifts from $AB$ to $EF$, but Ms. Muffet's preferences are such that her new consumption point is a point like $g'$ where the consumption of whey has actually declined.

**8. a.** Ms. Muffet's initial budget line is $AB$ and the initial best affordable point is $r$ in Fig. 12. Note that point $r$ in Fig. 12 is the same as point $c$ in Fig. 10. The new budget line following an increase in the price of curds to \$2 (income remains at \$12) is $AH$.

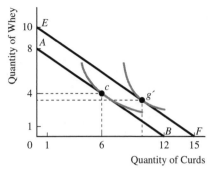

▲ **FIGURE 11  Whey as Inferior Good**

**b.** After the price increase, point $r$ is no longer the best affordable point, since it is no longer even affordable.

**c.** The new best affordable point (labelled $t$ in Fig. 12) indicates a decrease in the consumption of curds.

**d.** The substitution effect of the increase in the price of curds is indicated by the movement from $r$ to $s$ in Fig. 12. This gives the effect of the change in relative prices while keeping Ms. Muffet on the same indifference curve. The income effect is indicated by movement from $s$ to $t$.

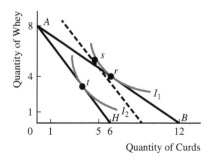

▲ **FIGURE 12**

# 10 Organizing Production

## Key Concepts

### The Firm and Its Economic Problem

A **firm** is an institution that hires and organizes factors of production to produce and sell goods and services. A firm's goal is profit maximization.

- Accounting costs = explicit costs + conventional depreciation
- Accounting profit = revenues − (explicit costs + conventional depreciation)

Opportunity costs of production consist of explicit costs (paid in money) and implicit costs (opportunities forgone but not paid in money). A firm's major implicit costs are

- **implicit rental rate**—the opportunity cost of using its own capital. Equals **economic depreciation** (change in market value of capital) + forgone interest.
- cost of owner's resources—(wage income forgone) + normal profit. **Normal profit** is the expected return to *entrepreneurial ability* and is part of a firm's opportunity costs of production. Normal profit is the average profit in the industry.

Economists' costs and profits:

- *opportunity costs* = explicit costs + implicit costs
- **economic profit** = revenues − (explicit costs + implicit costs)

- because normal profit is part of implicit costs, economic profit (when positive) is over and above normal profit.
- opportunity cost and economic profit are key to correctly predicting firm behaviour.

Limits to profit maximization are

- **technology** constraints—available resources and technology.
- information constraints—limited information and uncertainty about the firm's workforce, potential customers, and competitors.
- market constraints—limited demand for firm's output; marketing efforts of competitors.

## Technological and Economic Efficiency

**Technological efficiency**—using least inputs to produce given output.
**Economic efficiency**—least cost of producing given output.

## Information and Organization

Firms organize production by using

- **command systems** based on a managerial hierarchy.
- **incentive systems** to overcome problems of limited information and uncertainty.

With limited information, the **principal–agent problem** arises when *agents* (those employed by others) do not act in the best interests of the *principals* (employers of the agents).

- Strategies for coping with the principal–agent problem and inducing agents to act in the best interests of the principals include ownership, incentive pay, and long-term contracts.
- To cope with limited information and uncertainty, firms have devised different forms of business organization:

  - *sole proprietorship*—single owner with unlimited liability
  - *partnership*—two or more owners with unlimited liability.
  - *corporation*—owned by limited liability stockholders.

# Markets and the Competitive Environment

Types of market structure:

- **perfect competition**—many firms; identical products; easy entry of new firms.
- **monopolistic competition**—many firms; slightly differentiated products (**product differentiation**); easy entry.
- **oligopoly**—few firms; identical or differentiated products; some barriers to entry.
- **monopoly**—single firm; product with no close substitutes; high barriers to new entry.

Market structure of most industries lies between the extremes of perfect competition and monopoly.

- To evaluate competitiveness of a market, economists use two measures of industrial concentration:

    - **four-firm concentration ratio**—percentage of industry sales made by largest four firms.
    - **Herfindahl–Hirschman Index** (HHI)—sum of squared market shares of the 50 largest firms in the industry.

- High concentration ratios usually indicate low degree of competition.
- Problems with concentration ratios:

    - national, but many industries regional/global.
    - no indication of entry barriers and turnover.
    - firms operate in other industries.

# Produce or Outsource? Firms and Markets

Firms coordinate economic activity when they perform tasks more efficiently than markets. Firms often have advantages of

- lower **transactions costs**—costs arising from finding someone with whom to do business.

- **economies of scale**—lower unit cost of producing good as output rate increases.
- economies of scope—lower unit cost from producing a range of goods and services.
- economies of team production—individuals in the production process specializing in mutually supportive tasks.

# Helpful Hints

1. In this chapter, we again meet our old friend opportunity cost. Here we look at the costs firms face and examine the differences between *opportunity cost* measures used by economists and *accounting cost* measures. Opportunity cost, which is the relevant cost concept for economic decisions, includes *explicit* and *implicit costs*. Important examples of implicit costs include economic depreciation, the owner's forgone interest and forgone wages, and normal profits. Accounting cost includes only explicit out-of-pocket costs and conventional depreciation. These differences in cost measures between accountants and economists also lead to the following differences in profit measures:

**Economists**

Opportunity costs = Explicit costs + Implicit costs

Economic profit = Revenues − (Explicit costs + Implicit costs)

**Accountants**

Accounting costs = Explicit costs + Conventional depreciation

Accounting profit = Revenues − (Explicit costs + Conventional depreciation)

Implicit costs, which economists include but accountants exclude, are the key difference between economists' and accountants' measures of cost and profit. Accounting profit does *not* subtract normal profits or other implicit costs, so accounting profit is generally greater than economic profit.

Because normal profit is part of implicit costs, economic profit is profit over and above normal profit. If we think of normal profit as average profit, economic profit is *above-average* profit. Economic profit is a signal to firms that they are earning a greater return on investment than could be earned on average elsewhere in the economy.

Economic profit can also be negative if revenues are less than opportunity costs. As we will see in Chapter 12, such an *economic loss* is a signal to firms that they are earning a lower return on investment than could be earned on average elsewhere.

2. The difference between *technological efficiency* and *economic efficiency* is critical since economic decisions are made only on the basis of economic efficiency. Technological efficiency is an engineering concept and occurs when the firm produces a given output using the least inputs. There is no consideration of input costs. Economic efficiency occurs when the firm produces a given output at least cost. All technologically efficient production methods are not economically efficient. But all economically efficient methods are also technologically efficient. Competition favours firms that choose economically efficient production methods and penalizes firms that do not.

3. This chapter introduces four types of market structure—perfect competition, monopolistic competition, oligopoly, and monopoly. These market structures will not mean much to you now, but you will learn more about them in Chapters 12–15. Pay attention to the table on text page 240, which summarizes the characteristics of the different market structures and gives you a sense of how the structures differ. As you study each market structure in the following chapters, refer back to this table to put it in perspective.

# Self-Test
## True/False and Explain

### The Firm and Its Economic Problem

1. The goal of the firm is to maximize market share.

*False*

2. Normal profit is the expected return for supplying entrepreneurial ability.

*True*

3. Implicit costs include ~~economic~~ normal profit.

*False*

4. A firm's opportunity cost of using its own machine is lower than if it had rented the machine.

*False*

## Technological and Economic Efficiency

**5.** Economically efficient production methods use relatively less of higher-cost resources and relatively more of lower-cost resources.

~~False~~ True

achieves lowest - per unit cost

**6.** An economically efficient production process can become economically inefficient if the relative prices of inputs change.

True.

**7.** All economically efficient production methods are also technologically efficient.

~~False~~ True.

## Information and Organization

**8.** Giving corporate managers stock in their companies is a strategy for coping with a principal–agent problem.

True

Make manager incentive same as stakeholders

**9.** In a principal–agent relationship between the stockholders and managers of Scotiabank, the stockholders are agents and the managers are principals.

False

**10.** Owners of a corporation have limited liability.

↘ unlimited is
~~False~~ True. sole proprietorship

## Markets and the Competitive Environment

**11.** Product differentiation gives a monopolistically competitive firm some monopoly power.

True

**12.** A high concentration ratio always indicates a low degree of competition.

False

depends on geographical scope of market, barriers to entry and multiproduct firms

**13.** Concentration ratios measure barriers to entry in a market.

False

high concentration can have low barriers to entry

## Produce or Outsource? Firms and Markets

**14.** Outsourcing is an example of firm coordination of economic activity.

~~True~~ False

market coordination

**15.** Markets will coordinate economic activity in situations where there are economies of scale.

False

# Multiple-Choice

## The Firm and Its Economic Problem

1. Abdul operates his own business and pays himself a salary of $20,000 per year. He refused a job that pays $30,000 per year. What is the opportunity cost of Abdul's time in the business?
   a. $10,000
   b. $20,000
   c. $30,000 ✓
   d. $50,000
   e. zero

2. Economic profit is revenues minus
   a. explicit costs.
   b. implicit costs.
   c. opportunity costs. ✓
   d. accounting costs.
   e. (explicit costs + conventional depreciation).

3. The rate of interest is 10 percent per year. You invest $50,000 of your own money in a business and earn *accounting* profit of $20,000 after one year. *Ceteris paribus*, what is your *economic* profit?
   a. $20,000
   b. $15,000
   c. $5,000
   d. $2,000
   e. –$15,000

   Economic Profit = accounting profit – implicit costs

   = 20000 – (0.10 × 50000)

   = 20000 – 5000

4. In general,
   1  opportunity cost is greater than accounting cost.
   2  opportunity cost is less than accounting cost.
   3  economic profit is greater than accounting profit.
   4  economic profit is less than accounting profit.
   a. 1 only
   b. 1 and 3
   c. 1 and 4 ✓
   d. 2 and 3
   e. 2 and 4

**5.** A profit-maximizing firm is constrained by

   **a.** demand for its product.

   **b.** limited resources.

   **c.** available technology.

   **d.** limited information.

   **e.** all of the above. ✓

## Technological and Economic Efficiency

**6.** In Table 1, which method(s) of making a photon torpedo is/are technologically efficient?

   **a.** 1 only

   **b.** 2 only

   **c.** 3 only

   **d.** all of the methods

   **e.** 1 and 3 only

*no method has more of one input and the same for another input as compared to other methods*

| TABLE 1 | Three Methods of Making One Photon Torpedo | |
| --- | --- | --- |
| | **Quantities of Inputs** | |
| **Method** | **Labour** | **Capital** |
| 1 | 5 | 10 |
| 2 | 10 | 7 |
| 3 | 15 | 5 |

*$10          $20*

*250*
*240*
*250*

**7.** Refer to Table 1. If the price of labour is $10 per unit and the price of capital is $20 per unit, which method(s) is/are economically efficient?

   **a.** 1 only

   **b.** 2 only

   **c.** 3 only

   **d.** all of the methods

   **e.** 1 and 3 only

**8.** Which of the following statements is *true*?

   **a.** All technologically efficient methods are also economically efficient.

   **b.** All economically efficient methods are also technologically efficient. ✓

   **c.** Technological efficiency changes with changes in relative input prices.

   **d.** Technologically efficient firms will be more likely to survive than economically efficient firms.

   **e.** None of the above

9. The business people are still talking over coffee. Which of their statements below describes *economic* efficiency?

a. "The new production process we've installed uses less capital and labour than the old one."

b. "The new assembly line has higher capital costs, but the fall in workers' hours has lowered overall costs." *lowest cost*

c. "The costs per unit fell dramatically as we increased the length of our production runs."

d. "Despite the higher costs of negotiating the contracts, hiring the cleaning firm is much cheaper than using our own staff."

e. "The computer servicing people we hired work well as an integrated problem-solving group."

$125    $100

10. To produce a unit of output, Alphaworks uses 10 hours of labour and 5 kilos of material, Betaworks uses 5 hours of labour and 10 kilos of material, and Gammaworks uses 10 hours of labour and 10 kilos of material. If labour costs $10/hour and material costs $5/kilo, which firm(s) is/are economically efficient?

a. Alphaworks only

b. Betaworks only ✓

c. Gammaworks only

d. Alphaworks and Betaworks

e. Alphaworks and Gammaworks

## Information and Organization

11. Firms organize production using

a. command systems only.

b. incentive systems only.

c. command and incentive systems.

d. market systems only.

e. principal–agent systems only.

12. The possibility that an employee may not work hard is an example of the

a. limited liability problem.

b. principal–agent problem.

c. transactions cost problem.

d. technological efficiency problem.

e. partnership problem.

**13.** Firm strategies for coping with the principal–agent problem are
  **a.** ownership, incentive pay, and long-term contracts.
  **b.** proprietorship, partnership, and the corporation.
  **c.** economies of scale, scope, and team production.
  **d.** technology, information, and the market.
  **e.** none of the above.

**14.** A firm that has two or more owners with joint unlimited liability is
  **a.** a proprietorship.
  **b.** a partnership.
  **c.** a conglomerate.
  **d.** a corporation.
  **e.** none of the above.

**15.** What is a *disadvantage* of a corporation relative to a proprietorship or partnership?
  **a.** owners' unlimited liability
  **b.** profits are taxed twice as corporate profits and stockholders' dividends
  **c.** high cost of capital
  **d.** perpetual life
  **e.** none of the above

**16.** The majority of business revenues are accounted for by
  **a.** proprietorships.
  **b.** partnerships.
  **c.** corporations.
  **d.** cooperatives.
  **e.** not-for-profit organizations.

## Markets and the Competitive Environment

**17.** The most extreme *absence* of competition is
- **a.** perfect competition. → most
- **b.** monopolistic competition.
- **c.** product differentiation.
- **d.** oligopoly.
- **e.** monopoly.

→ least

**18.** A market structure where a small number of firms compete is
- **a.** perfect competition.
- **b.** monopolistic competition.
- **c.** product differentiation.
- **d.** oligopoly.
- **e.** monopoly.

**19.** Product differentiation is an important feature of the market structure of
- **a.** perfect competition.
- **b.** monopolistic competition.
- **c.** oligopoly.
- **d.** monopoly.
- **e.** all of the above.

→ many firms selling slightly differentiated products.

**20.** The four-firm concentration ratio measures the share of the largest four firms in total industry
- **a.** profits.
- **b.** sales.
- **c.** cost.
- **d.** capital.
- **e.** none of the above.

**21.** Which of the following statements is *false*? Concentration ratios

a. are national measures, but firms in some industries operate in regional markets.

b. are national measures, but firms in some industries operate in global markets.

c. tell us nothing about barriers to entry in the industry.

d. tell us nothing about how sales vary among firms in the industry.

e. have difficulty classifying multi-product firms by industry.

## Produce or Outsource? Firms and Markets

**22.** Which of the following statements is *false*?

a. Firms and markets are institutions for coordinating economic activity.

b. Firms organize productive resources to produce goods and services.

c. Firms sell goods and services.

d. Technologically efficient firms can eliminate scarcity.

e. Firms use command systems to organize production.

**23.** Firms coordinate economic activity more efficiently than markets when firms have

a. lower transactions costs.

b. economies of scale.

c. economies of scope.

d. economies of team production.

e. all of the above.

**24.** Economies of scale exist when

a. transactions costs are high.

b. transactions costs are low.

c. hiring additional inputs does not increase the price of inputs.

d. the cost of producing a unit of output falls as the output rate increases.

e. the firm is too large and too diversified.

**25.** A firm with lower unit cost from producing a wider range of goods and services has economies of

  **a.** transactions costs.

  **b.** scale.

  **c.** scope.

  **d.** team production.

  **e.** market coordination.

# Short Answer Problems

**1.** A year ago, Frank, the bricklayer, decided to start a business manufacturing doll furniture. Frank has two sisters; Angela is an accountant and Edith is an economist. (Both sisters are good with numbers, but Edith doesn't have enough personality to be an accountant.) Each of the sisters computes Frank's cost and profit for the first year using the following information:

1  Frank took no income from the firm. He has a standing offer to return to work as a bricklayer for $30,000 per year.

2  Frank rents his machinery for $9,000 a year.

3  Frank owns the garage in which he produces, but could rent it out at $3,000 per year.

4  To start the business, Frank used $10,000 of his own money and borrowed $30,000 at the market rate of interest of 10 percent per year.

5  Frank hires one employee at an annual salary of $20,000.

6  The cost of materials during the first year is $40,000.

7  Frank's entrepreneurial abilities are worth $14,000.

8  Frank's revenue for his first year is $100,000.

**a.** In the space below, set up a table indicating how Angela and Edith would compute Frank's cost. Ignore any depreciation. What is Frank's cost as computed by Angela? by Edith?

**2.** According to your roommate, it is always more economically efficient to produce wheat using some machinery than using only labour. Suppose that there are two technologically efficient methods of producing one tonne of wheat:

- Method 1 requires 20 machine hours plus 20 hours of labour.

- Method 2 requires 100 hours of labour.

Country *A* has a highly developed industrial economy, while country *B* is less developed. In country *A* the price of an hour of labour (the wage rate) is $8, while the wage rate in country *B* is $4. The price of a machine hour is $20 in both countries. Which method is economically efficient in country *A*? in country *B*? Explain.

**b.** What is Frank's profit (or loss) as computed by Angela? by Edith?

ⓒ **3.** Consider countries $A$ and $B$ described in Short Answer Problem **2**.

   **a.** What wage rate in country $B$ would make the two methods equally efficient in country $B$?

   **b.** What price of a machine hour would make the two methods equally efficient in country $A$?

ⓒ **4.** Explain why an economically efficient production method must be technologically efficient.

**5.** The standard tip in a restaurant is 15 percent. Restaurants could raise their prices 15 percent, set a no-tipping policy, and pay servers the extra 15 percent. Use principal–agent analysis to explain why most restaurants prefer tipping.

**6.** The annual sales for firms in the Canadian thingamabob industry are reported in Table 2.

### TABLE 2 Thingamabob Industry Sales

| Firm | Sales ($) |
|------|-----------|
| Things 'R' Us | 500 |
| ThingMart | 400 |
| The Thing Club | 350 |
| Thingmania | 250 |
| All other firms | 13,500 |

**a.** Calculate the four-firm concentration ratio for the thingamabob industry.

**b.** How competitive is the industry according to the ratio?

**7.** The U.S. yadayada industry consists of only five firms, whose markets shares are reported in Table 3.

### TABLE 3 Yadayada Industry Market Share

| Firm | Market Share (%) |
|------|------------------|
| Jerry's Yadayadas | 30 |
| Elaine's Yadayadas | 40 |
| George's Yadayadas | 20 |
| Kramer's Yadayadas | 5 |
| Neuman's Yadayadas | 5 |

**a.** Calculate the Herfindahl–Hirschman Index for the yadayada industry.

**b.** How competitive is the industry according to the index?

8. Considering the geographical scope of markets, how might a concentration ratio *understate* the degree of competitiveness in an industry? How might it *overstate* the degree of competitiveness?

# Answers

## True/False and Explain

1. **F** Maximize profit. (228–230)

2. **T** Definition. (228–230)

3. **F** Implicit costs include normal profit. (228–230)

4. **F** Opportunity cost is equal for ownership or rental. Explicit cost is lower for ownership. (228–230)

5. **T** That achieves lowest per-unit cost. (231–232)

6. **T** Technological efficiency does not change with price changes, but economic efficiency can. (231–232)

7. **T** But the reverse is false—technological efficiency does not guarantee economic efficiency. (231–232)

8. **T** Makes managers' (agents) incentives same as shareholders' (principals). (233–236)

9. **F** Stockholders' (principals) profits depend on job done by managers (agents). (233–236)

10. **T** Liability only for value of investment. Sole proprietorship has unlimited liability. (234–236)

11. **T** Firm is sole producer of differentiated version of a good. (237–241)

12. **F** Often true, but depends on geographical scope of market, barriers to entry, and multi-product firms. (237–241)

13. **F** Small town with 4 restaurants has high concentration ratio but low entry barriers. (237–241)

14. **F** Example of market coordination. (242–243)

15. **F** Firms more efficient if economies of scale. (242–243)

## Multiple-Choice

1. **c** Forgone income. (228–230)

2. **c** Definition. (228–230)

3. **b** Economic profit = accounting profit − implicit costs = $20,000 − (0.10 × $50,000). (228–230)

4. **c** See formulas in Helpful Hint **1**. (228–230)

5. **e** Technology, information, and market constraints. (228–230)

6. **d** No method has more of one input and the same amount of the other input, compared with the alternative method. (231–232)

7. **b** 2 costs $240 while 1 and 3 cost $250. (231–232)

8. **b** **c** is true for economic efficiency. Reverse of **d** is true. (231–232)

9. **b** Lowest cost. **c** describes economies of scale. **d** and **e** describe market coordination of production. (231–232)

10. **b** Costs are Alphaworks = $125, Betaworks = $100, Gammaworks = $150. (231–232)

11. **c** Principal–agent solutions are part of an incentive system. (233–236)

12. **b** See text discussion. (233–236)

13. **a** All create incentives for the agent to work in interests of the principal. **b** lists types of business organization, **c** lists advantages of firms over markets, **d** lists constraints on firms. (233–236)

14. **b** Definition. (234–236)

15. **b** (p. 235); **d** is an advantage, **a** and **c** are disadvantages of proprietorship and partnership. (233–236)

16. **c** See text graphic. (233–236)

17. **e** Monopoly is least competition, perfect competition is the most. (237–241)

18. **d** Definition. (237–241)

19. **b** Many firms producing slightly differentiated products. (237–241)

20. **b** Definition. (237–241)

21. **d** Concentration ratios measure sales by size of firm. (237–241)

22. **d** Scarcity can never be eliminated. (242–243)

23. **e** See text discussion. (242–243)

24. **d** See text discussion. (242–243)

25. **c** Definition. (242–243)

## Short Answer Problems

1. **a.** Table 4 gives the cost as computed by Angela and Edith. The item numbers correspond to the item numbers in the problem.

| TABLE 4 | | |
| --- | --- | --- |
| Item Number | Angela's Accounting Computation (accounting cost) | Edith's Economic Computation (opportunity cost) |
| 1. | $0 | $30,000 |
| 2. | 9,000 | 9,000 |
| 3. | 0 | 3,000 |
| 4. | 3,000 | 4,000 |
| 5. | 20,000 | 20,000 |
| 6. | 40,000 | 40,000 |
| 7. | 0 | $14,000 |
| Total Cost | $72,000 | $120,000 |

**b.** Revenue is $100,000. Angela's accounting computation of profit uses this formula:

$$\text{Accounting profit} = \text{Revenues} - \text{Explicit costs}$$
$$= \$100,000 - \$72,000$$
$$= \$28,000$$

Edith's economic computation of profit uses this formula:

$$\text{Economic profit} = \text{Revenues} - \text{Opportunity costs}$$
$$= \$100,000 - \$120,000$$
$$= -\$20,000 \text{ (an economic loss)}$$

**2.** Both production methods are technologically efficient. The economically efficient production method has the lower cost of producing a tonne of wheat. In country $A$, the price of an hour of labour is $8 and the price of a machine hour is $20. The cost of producing a tonne of wheat is $560 using method 1 and $800 using method 2. Therefore method 1 is economically efficient for country $A$.

The price of an hour of labour is $4 in country $B$, and thus it will face different costs of producing a tonne of wheat. Under method 1, the cost will be $480 but under method 2, which uses only labour, the cost will be $400. So method 2 is economically efficient for country $B$.

The reason for this difference is that economic efficiency means producing at lowest cost. If the relative prices of inputs are different in two countries, there will be differences in the relative costs of production using alternative methods. Therefore, your roommate is wrong.

**3. a.** If the wage rate in country $B$ were to increase to $5 an hour, then production of a tonne of wheat would be $500 under either method. How did we obtain this answer? Express the cost under method 1 ($C_1$) and the cost under method 2 ($C_2$) as follows:

$$C_1 = 20P_m + 20P_h$$
$$C_2 = 100P_h$$

where $P_m$ is the price of a machine hour and $P_h$ is the price of an hour of labour (the wage rate). We are given that $P_m = $20$ and asked to find the value of $P_h$ that

makes the two methods equally efficient; the value of $P_h$ that makes $C_1 = C_2$. Thus we solve the following equation for $P_h$:

$$20P_m + 20P_h = 100P_h$$
$$20(\$20) + 20P_h = 100P_h$$
$$\$400 = 80P_h$$
$$\$5 = P_h$$

**b.** If the price of a machine hour is $32, production of a tonne of wheat would be $800 under either method in country $A$. This question asks: Given the wage rate of $8 ($P_h$) in country $A$, what value of $P_m$ makes $C_1 = C_2$? Thus we solve the following equation for $P_m$:

$$20P_m + 20P_h = 100P_h$$
$$20P_m + 20(\$8) = 100(\$8)$$
$$20P_m = \$640$$
$$P_m = \$32$$

**4.** If a production method is economically efficient, then it is the least-cost method of producing a given level of output. Why does this imply that the method must also be technologically efficient—using the least inputs?

Try to imagine an economically efficient production method that is technologically *inefficient*. The method would *not* use the least inputs. No matter what the price of those inputs, there would always be a method that uses less inputs and therefore costs less. So a technologically inefficient method could *not* be economically efficient. Economic efficiency implies technological efficiency.

5. Restaurants face a classic principal–agent problem because servers may provide poor service to customers and drive away future business. Instead of having managers try to closely monitor each server, it is more efficient to delegate monitoring to customers. Customers tip on the basis of quality of service, creating an incentive for the server—the agent—to provide good service. This is exactly what the restaurant owner—the principal—wants.

6. **a.** The four-firm concentration ratio is the percentage of the value of sales accounted for by the four largest firms in an industry. For thingamabobs, sales of the four largest firms are $500 + 400 + 350 + 250 = 1,500$. Total industry sales are $1,500 + 13,500 = 15,000$. So the ratio is $1,500/15,000 = 10$ percent.

   **b.** Since a ratio of less than 40 percent indicates a competitive market, the thingamabob industry is very competitive.

7. **a.** The Herfindahl–Hirschman Index, for an industry of fewer than 50 firms, is the square of the percentage market share of each firm. For the yadayada industry, the index is

$$30^2 + 40^2 + 20^2 + 5^2 + 5^2 = 2,950$$

   **b.** Since an index of more than 1,800 indicates a concentrated market, the yadayada industry is very competitive.

8. Concentration ratios are calculated from a national geographical perspective. If the actual scope of the market is not national, the concentration ratio will likely misstate the degree of competitiveness in an industry. If the actual market is global, the concentration ratio will understate the degree of competitiveness. A firm may have a concentration ratio of 100 as the only producer in the nation, but may face a great deal of international competition. When the scope of the market is regional, the concentration ratio will overstate the degree of competitiveness. The concentration ratio includes firms elsewhere in the nation that are not real competitors in the region.

# 11 Output and Costs

## Key Concepts

### Decision Time Frames

A firm has two decision time frames:

- **Short run**—quantities of some resources are fixed; quantities of other resources are variable.

  - Fixed resources are called the firm's fixed *plant*—usually technology, buildings, capital, and management.
  - Variable resources—usually labour.
  - Short-run decisions are easily reversed.

- **Long run**—quantities of all resources are variable.

  - **Sunk cost**—*past* cost of buying a new plant. Firm's decisions depend only on short-run cost of changing labour input and long-run cost of changing plant. Sunk costs are irrelevant.
  - Long-run decisions are *not* easily reversed.

### Short-Run Technology Constraint

Short-run production is described by

- **total product** curve (*TP*)—maximum attainable output with fixed quantity of capital as the quantity of labour varies.

- **marginal product** curve (*MP*)—Δ*TP* resulting from a one-unit increase in variable input.
- **average product** curve (*AP*)—*TP* per unit of variable input.

As variable input increases, *MP* increases (increasing marginal returns), reaches maximum, and then decreases (**diminishing marginal returns**). When *MP* > *AP*, *AP* is increasing. When *MP* < *AP*, *AP* is decreasing. When *MP* = *AP*, maximum *AP*.

- **Law of diminishing returns**—with given quantity of fixed inputs, as firm uses more variable input, its *MP* eventually diminishes.

## Short-Run Cost

Short-run cost curves are determined by technology and prices of productive resources.

- **Total cost** (*TC*) = *TFC* + *TVC*

  - **Total fixed cost** (*TFC*)—cost of fixed inputs (including normal profit)
  - **Total variable cost** (*TVC*)—cost of variable inputs

- **Marginal cost** (*MC*)—Δ*TC* resulting from a one-unit increase in output
- **Average total cost** (*ATC*) = *AFC* + *AVC*

  - **Average fixed cost** (*AFC*)—total fixed cost per unit of output
  - **Average variable cost** (*AVC*)—total variable cost per unit of output
  - *AFC* curve decreases constantly as output increases.
  - *AVC*, *ATC*, and *MC* curves are U-shaped.
  - As output increases, *MC* decreases, reaches minimum, and then increases.
  - When *MC* < *ATC*, *ATC* decreases.
    When *MC* > *ATC*, *ATC* increases.
    When *MC* = *ATC*, minimum *ATC*.
    Same relation of *MC* and *AVC*.

# Long-Run Cost

*Long-run cost*—cost of production when all inputs (capital and labour) are adjusted to economically efficient quantities.

- *Production function*—relationship between maximum attainable output and quantities of all inputs—describes long-run costs.

**Long-run average cost curve** (*LRAC*)—a planning curve that tells the firm the plant size and quantity of labour to use at each output to minimize cost. Consists of the segments of different short-run *ATC* curves along which average total cost is lowest.

- In the long run, when all inputs increase by the same percentage, increases in output can show three different returns to scale:

  - **economies of scale** (increasing returns to scale)—percentage increase in firm's output > percentage increase in inputs. *LRAC* slopes downward.

  - **constant returns to scale**—percentage increase in firm's output = percentage increase in inputs. *LRAC* is horizontal.

  - **diseconomies of scale** (decreasing returns to scale)—percentage increase in firm's output < percentage increase in inputs. *LRAC* slopes upward.

- **Minimum efficient scale**—smallest quantity of output yielding minimum *LRAC*.

# Helpful Hints

1. Be sure to understand how economists use the terms *short run* and *long run*. These terms do *not* refer to calendar time. Think of them as planning horizons. The short run is a planning horizon short enough that while some resources are variable, at least one resource cannot be varied but is fixed. The long run refers to a planning horizon that is long enough that all resources can be varied.

2. This chapter introduces many new concepts and graphs and may at first appear overwhelming. Don't get lost among the trees and lose sight of the forest. There is a simple and fundamental relationship between product curves and cost curves.

   The chapter explains the short-run product curves and concepts of total product, marginal product, and average product. This is followed by the short-run cost function and concepts of total cost, marginal cost, average variable cost, and average total cost.

   But all of these seemingly separate concepts are related to the *law of diminishing returns*. The law states that as a firm uses more of a variable input, with a given quantity of fixed inputs, the marginal product of the variable input eventually diminishes. This law explains why the marginal product and average product curves eventually fall, and why the total product curve becomes flatter. When productivity falls, costs increase, and the law explains the eventual upward slope of the marginal cost curve. When marginal product falls, marginal cost increases.

   The marginal cost curve, in turn, explains the U-shape of the average variable cost and average total cost curves. When the marginal cost curve is below the average variable (or total) cost curve, the average variable (or total) cost curve is falling. When marginal cost is above the average variable (or total) cost curve, the average variable (or total) cost curve is rising. The marginal cost curve intersects the average variable (or total) cost curve at the minimum point on the average variable (or total) cost curve.

   Use the law of diminishing returns as the key to understanding the relationships between the many short-run concepts and graphs in the chapter. But all concepts and graphs are not equally important. Pay most attention to the unit-cost concepts and graphs—especially marginal cost, average variable cost, and average total cost—because these will be used the most in later chapters to analyse the behaviour of firms.

3. Be sure to thoroughly understand Fig. 1. It is the most important graph in the chapter and one of the most important graphs in all of microeconomics.

   The curves for average total cost (*ATC*), average fixed cost (*AFC*), and average variable cost (*AVC*) are derived by taking the values for *TC*, *TFC*, and *TVC* and dividing by quantity of output. Since these are average values for a fixed quantity of output, they are plotted directly above the corresponding units of output.

▲ **FIGURE 1**

On the other hand, marginal cost (*MC*) is the *change* in total cost (or equivalently, in total variable cost) resulting from a one-unit increase in output. It is plotted *midway* between the corresponding units of output. The *ATC*, *AVC*, and *MC* curves are crucially important. The *ATC* and *AVC* curves are both U-shaped. The *MC* curve is also U-shaped and intersects the *ATC* and *AVC* curves at their minimum points. The *MC* curve is below the *ATC* and *AVC* curves when *ATC* and *AVC* are falling, and above the *ATC* and *AVC* curves when they are rising. The less important *AFC* curve falls continuously as output increases.

4. You will probably draw a graph like the one in Fig. 1 at least a hundred times in this course. Here are some hints on drawing the graph quickly and easily:

   - Be sure to label the axes: quantity of output (*Q*) on the horizontal axis and average cost on the vertical axis.

   - Draw an upward-sloping marginal cost curve, as shown here in Fig. 2. The marginal cost curve can have a small downward-sloping section at first, but this is not important. Next, draw a shallow U-shaped

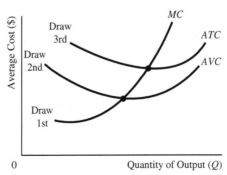

▲ **FIGURE 2**

curve that falls until it intersects the marginal cost curve, and then rises. Then pick a point further up the marginal cost curve. Draw another shallow U-shaped curve whose minimum point passes through your second point. Finally, label the curves.

Any time a test question (including those in the Self-Test) asks about these curves, *draw a graph* before you answer.

5. The later sections of the chapter explain long-run costs using a production function where both labour and capital inputs are variable. While diminishing returns is the key for understanding short-run costs, the concept of *returns to scale* is the key for understanding long-run costs. Returns to scale are the increase in output relative to the increase in inputs when all inputs are increased by the same percentage. Returns to scale can be increasing, constant, or decreasing, and correspond to the downward-sloping, horizontal, and upward-sloping sections of the long-run average cost curve.

# Self-Test

## True/False and Explain

### Decision Time Frames

1. All resources are fixed in the short run.

2. The firm's short-run decisions are easily reversed.

3. The firm's long-run decisions depend on sunk costs.

5. The law of diminishing returns implies that eventually the marginal product curve will be negatively sloped as the variable input increases.

6. Marginal product is measured by the slope of the total product curve.

7. The law of diminishing returns implies that we will not observe a range of increasing marginal returns.

### Short-Run Technology Constraint

4. Given a fixed quantity of capital, if 2 additional labourers produce 15 additional units of output, the marginal product of labour is 15 units of output.

8. If the marginal product of labour is greater than the average product of labour, average product is increasing.

## Short-Run Cost

**9.** Average variable cost reaches its minimum at the same level of output at which average product is a maximum.

**10.** If average variable cost is decreasing, then marginal cost must be decreasing.

**11.** The average total cost curve always intersects the minimum point of the marginal cost curve.

## Long-Run Cost

**12.** No part of any short-run average total cost curve can lie below the long-run average cost curve.

**13.** Economies of scale means that the long-run average cost curve is positively sloped.

**14.** If a firm can double its output by building a second plant identical to its first plant, there are constant returns to scale.

**15.** Minimum efficient scale occurs at the minimum point on the average total cost curve.

# Multiple-Choice

## Decision Time Frames

1. In economics, the short run is a time period in which
   **a.** one year or less elapses.
   **b.** all resources are variable.
   **c.** all resources are fixed.
   **d.** some resources are variable but some resources are fixed.
   **e.** all resources are variable but the technology is fixed.

2. Long-run decisions
   **a.** are not easily reversed.
   **b.** do not depend on sunk costs.
   **c.** involve changes in a firm's plant.
   **d.** can vary all resources of a firm.
   **e.** are all of the above.

## Short-Run Technology Constraint

3. The average product of labour is
   **a.** the slope of the total product curve.
   **b.** the slope of the marginal product curve.
   **c.** the increase in total product divided by the increase in labour employed.
   **d.** the total product divided by the quantity of labour employed.
   **e.** none of the above.

4. When the marginal product of labour is less than the average product of labour,
   **a.** the average product of labour is increasing.
   **b.** the marginal product of labour is increasing.
   **c.** the total product curve is negatively sloped.
   **d.** the firm is experiencing diminishing returns.
   **e.** none of the above is true.

**5.** Refer to Fig. 3 illustrating Swanky's short-run total product curve. Which of the following statements is *true*?

**a.** Points above the curve are attainable and inefficient.

**b.** Points below the curve are attainable and inefficient.

**c.** Points below the curve are unattainable and inefficient.

**d.** Points on the curve are unattainable and efficient.

**e.** Points on the curve all have equal marginal products.

▲ **FIGURE 3**

**6.** Refer to Fig. 3 illustrating Swanky's short-run total product curve. Marginal product reaches a maximum when you add which labourer?

**a.** 1st labourer

**b.** 2nd labourer

**c.** 3rd labourer

**d.** 4th labourer

**e.** 5th labourer

**7.** Which of the following statements by a restaurant owner refers to the law of diminishing returns?

**a.** "The higher the quality of the ingredients we use, the higher the cost of producing each meal."

**b.** "If we double the size of our premises and double everything else—kitchen staff, serving staff, equipment—we can increase the number of meals we serve, but not to double current levels."

**c.** "We can increase the number of meals we serve by just adding more kitchen staff, but each additional worker adds fewer meals than the previous worker because traffic in the kitchen will get worse."

**d.** "We can serve the same number of meals with fewer kitchen staff, but we would have to buy more labour-saving kitchen equipment."

**e.** "We can serve the same number of meals with less kitchen equipment, but we would have to hire more kitchen staff."

## Short-Run Cost

**8.** The vertical distance between the *TC* and *TVC* curves is
   **a.** decreasing as output increases.
   **b.** increasing as output increases.
   **c.** equal to *AFC*.
   **d.** equal to *TFC*.
   **e.** equal to *MC*.

**9.** Total cost is $20 at 4 units of output and $36 at 6 units of output. Between 4 and 6 units of output, marginal cost
   **a.** is less than average total cost.
   **b.** is equal to average total cost.
   **c.** is equal to average variable cost.
   **d.** is greater than average total cost.
   **e.** cannot be compared with any average cost without additional information.

**10.** Marginal cost is the amount that
   **a.** total cost increases when one more labourer is hired.
   **b.** fixed cost increases when one more labourer is hired.
   **c.** variable cost increases when one more labourer is hired.
   **d.** total cost increases when one more unit of output is produced.
   **e.** fixed cost increases when one more unit of output is produced.

**11.** A firm's fixed costs are $100. If total costs are $200 for one unit of output and $310 for two units, what is the marginal cost of the second unit?
   **a.** $100
   **b.** $110
   **c.** $200
   **d.** $210
   **e.** $310

**12.** If *ATC* is falling *MC* must be
   **a.** rising.
   **b.** falling.
   **c.** equal to *ATC*.
   **d.** above *ATC*.
   **e.** below *ATC*.

**13.** Which of the following does *not* cause decreasing *ATC*?
   **a.** decreasing marginal cost
   **b.** decreasing average variable cost
   **c.** decreasing average fixed cost
   **d.** increasing marginal product
   **e.** increasing returns to scale

**14.** The average variable cost curve will shift up if
   **a.** there is an increase in fixed costs.
   **b.** there is a technological advance.
   **c.** the price of a variable input decreases.
   **d.** the price of a variable input increases.
   **e.** the price of output increases.

**15.** The marginal cost (*MC*) curve intersects the
   **a.** *ATC*, *AVC*, and *AFC* curves at their minimum points.
   **b.** *ATC* and *AFC* curves at their minimum points.
   **c.** *AVC* and *AFC* curves at their minimum points.
   **d.** *ATC* and *AVC* curves at their minimum points.
   **e.** *TC* and *TVC* curves at their minimum points.

**16.** According to the law of diminishing returns,

    1  marginal productivity eventually rises.

    2  marginal productivity eventually falls.

    3  marginal cost eventually rises.

    4  marginal cost eventually falls.

  **a.** 1 and 3

  **b.** 1 and 4

  **c.** 2 and 3

  **d.** 2 and 4

  **e.** 4 only

**17.** Average variable cost is at a minimum at the same output where

  **a.** average product is at a maximum.

  **b.** average product is at a minimum.

  **c.** marginal product is at a maximum.

  **d.** marginal product is at a minimum.

  **e.** marginal cost is at a minimum.

**18.** A rise in the price of a fixed input will cause a firm's

  **a.** average variable cost curve to shift up.

  **b.** average total cost curve to shift up.

  **c.** average total cost curve to shift down.

  **d.** marginal cost curve to shift up.

  **e.** marginal cost curve to shift down.

**19.** A technological advance will shift

    1  $TP$, $AP$, and $MP$ curves up.

    2  $TP$, $AP$, and $MP$ curves down.

    3  $TC$, $ATC$, and $MC$ curves up.

    4  $TC$, $ATC$, and $MC$ curves down.

  **a.** 1 and 3

  **b.** 1 and 4

  **c.** 2 and 3

  **d.** 2 and 4

  **e.** none of the above

## Long-Run Cost

**20.** In the long run,
   **a.** only the plant size is fixed.
   **b.** all inputs are variable.
   **c.** all inputs are fixed.
   **d.** a firm must experience diseconomies of scale.
   **e.** none of the above is true.

**21.** The long-run average cost curve
   **a.** is a planning curve.
   **b.** identifies the cost-minimizing plant size and quantity of labour for each output level.
   **c.** is the relation between lowest attainable *ATC* and output when both plant size and labour are variable.
   **d.** consists of the segments of different short-run *ATC* curves along which average total cost is lowest.
   **e.** is all of the above.

**22.** Constant returns to scale means that as all inputs are increased,
   **a.** total output remains constant.
   **b.** average total cost remains constant.
   **c.** average total cost increases at the same rate as inputs.
   **d.** long-run average cost remains constant.
   **e.** long-run average cost rises at the same rate as inputs.

**23.** If all inputs are increased by 10 percent and output increases by less than 10 percent, it must be the case that
   **a.** average total cost is decreasing.
   **b.** average total cost is increasing.
   **c.** the *LRAC* curve is negatively sloped.
   **d.** there are economies of scale.
   **e.** there are diseconomies of scale.

**24.** Minimum efficient scale is the smallest quantity of output at which
  **a.** the *LRAC* curve reaches it lowest level.
  **b.** the *ATC* curve reaches its lowest level.
  **c.** the *AFC* curve reaches its lowest level.
  **d.** economies of scale begin.
  **e.** diminishing returns begin.

**25.** A firm will always want to increase its scale of plant if
  **a.** it persistently produces on the upward-sloping part of its short-run average total cost curve.
  **b.** it persistently produces on the downward-sloping part of its short-run average total cost curve.
  **c.** it is producing below minimum efficient scale.
  **d.** marginal cost is below average total cost.
  **e.** marginal cost is below average variable cost.

# Short Answer Problems

**1.** Why must the marginal cost curve intersect the average total cost curve at the minimum point of the average total cost curve?

**2.** Explain the connection, if any, between the U-shape of the average total cost curve and (a) fixed costs and (b) the law of eventually diminishing returns.

© **3.** Use the concepts of marginal and average to answer the following question. Suppose the worst student at Hubertville High School transfers to Histrionic High School. Is it possible that the average grade-point of the students at each school rises? Explain.

**4.** What is the difference, if any, between diminishing returns and diseconomies of scale?

**5.** For a given scale of plant, Table 1 gives the total monthly output of golf carts attainable using varying quantities of labour.

| **TABLE 1** | **Monthly Golf Cart Production** | | |
|---|---|---|---|
| Labourers (per month) | Output (units per month) | Marginal Product | Average Product |
| 0 | 0 | | |
| 1 | 1 | | |
| 2 | 3 | | |
| 3 | 6 | | |
| 4 | 12 | | |
| 5 | 17 | | |
| 6 | 20 | | |
| 7 | 22 | | |
| 8 | 23 | | |

**a.** Complete the table for the marginal product and average product of labour. (Note that marginal product should be entered *midway* between rows to emphasize that it is the result of *changing* inputs—moving from one row to the next. Average product corresponds to a fixed quantity of labour and should be entered on the appropriate row.)

**b.** On the grid below, label the axes and draw a graph of the total product curve (*TP*).

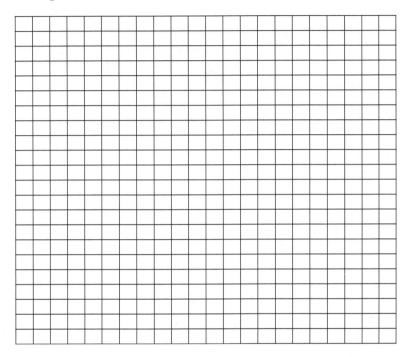

**c.** On the grid below, label the axes and draw a graph of both marginal product (*MP*) and average product (*AP*). (Marginal product should be plotted *midway* between the corresponding units of labour, while average product should be plotted directly above the corresponding units of labour.)

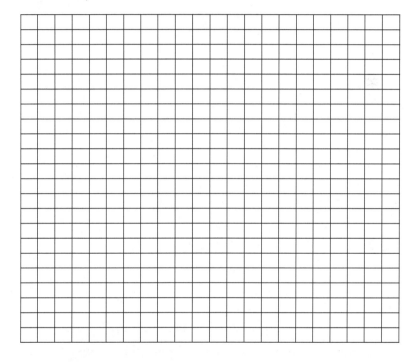

**6.** Now let's examine the short-run costs of golf cart production. The first two columns of Table 1 are reproduced in the first two columns of Table 2. The cost of 1 labourer (the only variable input) is $2,000 per month. Total fixed cost is $2,000 per month.

**a.** Given this information, complete Table 2 by computing total fixed cost (*TFC*), total variable cost (*TVC*), total cost (*TC*), marginal cost (*MC*), average fixed cost (*AFC*), average variable cost (*AVC*), and average total cost (*ATC*). Your completed table should include the marginal cost entered *midway* between the rows.

| TABLE 2 | Short-Run Costs (Monthly) | | | | | | | |
|---|---|---|---|---|---|---|---|---|
| **L** | **Q** | **TFC ($)** | **TVC ($)** | **TC ($)** | **MC ($)** | **AFC ($)** | **AVC ($)** | **ATC ($)** |
| 0 | 0 | 2,000 | | | | | | |
| 1 | 1 | | | | | | | |
| 2 | 3 | | | | | | | |
| 3 | 6 | | | | | | | |
| 4 | 12 | | | | | | | |
| 5 | 17 | | | | | | | |
| 6 | 20 | | | | | | | |
| 7 | 22 | | | | | | | |
| 8 | 23 | | | | | | | |

**b.** Using the grid below, on a single graph label the axes and draw the *TC*, *TVC*, and *TFC* curves.

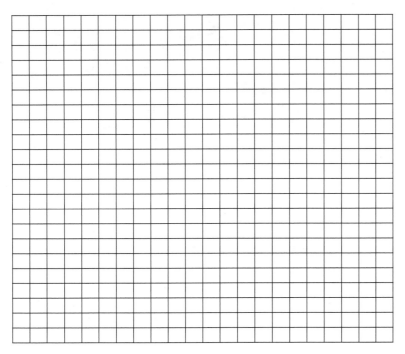

**c.** Using the grid below, on a single graph label the axes and draw the *MC*, *ATC*, *AVC*, and *AFC* curves. Be sure to plot *MC midway* between the corresponding units of output.

7. Now suppose that the price of a labourer increases to $2,500 per month. Construct a table in the space below for the new *MC* and *ATC* curves (output, *MC*, *ATC*) for golf cart production. On the grid in the next column, label the axes and draw a graph of the new *MC* and *ATC* curves. What is the effect of the increase in the price of the variable input on these curves?

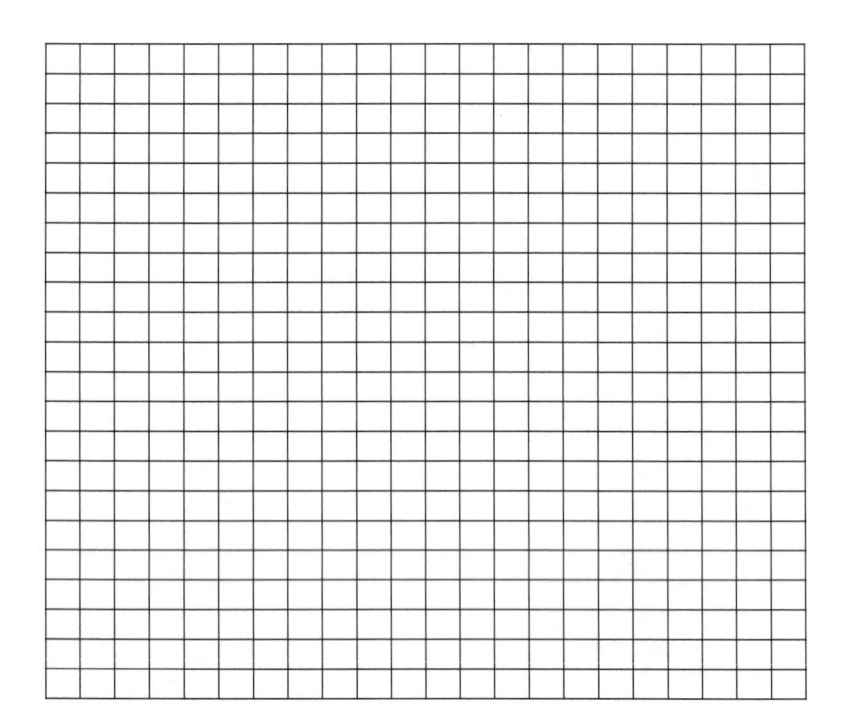

8. Return to the original price of labour of $2,000 per month. Now suppose that we double the quantity of fixed inputs so that total fixed costs also double to $4,000 per month. This increases the monthly output of golf carts for each quantity of labour as indicated in Table 3 on the next page.

| TABLE 3 | New Monthly Production of Golf Carts |
|---|---|
| **Labourers (per month)** | **Output (units per month)** |
| 0 | 0 |
| 1 | 1 |
| 2 | 4 |
| 3 | 10 |
| 4 | 19 |
| 5 | 26 |
| 6 | 31 |
| 7 | 34 |
| 8 | 36 |

**a.** Construct a table in the space below for the new *MC* and *ATC* curves (output, *MC*, *ATC*). On the grid in the next column, label the axes and draw a graph of the new *MC* and *ATC* curves.

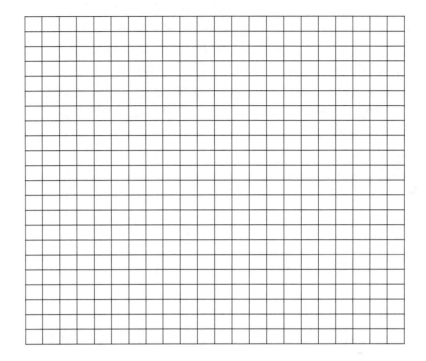

**b.** What is the effect on these curves (compared with the original *MC* and *ATC* curves in Short Answer Problem **6c**) of an increase in "plant size"? Are there economies of scale?

**c.** Draw the long-run average cost (*LRAC*) curve if these are the only two plant sizes available.

# Answers

## True/False and Explain

1. **F** Some resources fixed, some variable. (252)

2. **T** Firm can change output by changing quantity of labour hired. Long-run decisions are not easily reversed. (252)

3. **F** Sunk costs are past costs and are irrelevant to all firm decisions about the present or the future. (252)

4. **F** $\Delta TP/\Delta L = 15/2 = 7.5$. (253–256)

5. **T** $MP$ must eventually diminish with increasing $L$. (253–256)

6. **T** $\Delta TP/\Delta L$. (253–256)

7. **F** *Eventually* diminishing returns. $MP$ can initially increase. (253–256)

8. **T** See grade-point discussion for intuition. (253–256)

⊕ 9. **T** $AVC = TVC/Q = WL/Q = W/(Q/L) = W/AP$. (257–261)

⊕ 10. **F** $MC$ must be below $AVC$, but $MC$ may be increasing or decreasing. (257–261)

11. **F** $MC$ intersects at minimum $ATC$. (257–261)

12. **T** $LRAC$ consists of lowest-cost segments of all average total cost curves. (262–265)

13. **F** Negatively sloped; falling long-run average costs as output increases. (262–265)

14. **T** All inputs increase by 100 percent and output increases by 100 percent. (262–265)

15. **F** Smallest $Q$ at which $LRAC$ curve is at minimum. $ATC$ is short-run. (262–265)

## Multiple-Choice

1. **d** Definition. (252)

2. **e** From definition of long run. (252)

3. **d** Definition. (253–256)

⊕ 4. **d** When $MP < AP$, $MP$ is decreasing (diminishing returns), $AP$ is decreasing, and $TP$ is positively sloped. (253–256)

5. **b** Attainable but not maximum $TP$. (253–256)

6. **b** $MP =$ slope $TP$ curve $= 6$ for 2nd labourer. (253–256)

7. **c** $MP$ decreases as the restaurant uses more variable resource (labour). (253–256)

8. **d** $TC = TFC + TVC$. Distance is constant. (257–258)

⊕ 9. **d** $MC = 16/2 = 8$. $ATC$ is $5 at 4 units and $6 at 6 units. (258)

10. **d** Definition; **b** and **e** are wrong because fixed costs don't change; **a** and **c** are wrong because $MC$ can also decrease and may be affected by costs other than labour. (258)

11. **b** Fixed costs are irrelevant. $\Delta TC/\Delta Q = (\$310 - \$200)/(2 - 1)$. (257–258)

⊕ 12. **e** $MC$ could be increasing or decreasing below the $ATC$ when $ATC$ is decreasing. (258–261)

13. **e** Increasing returns to scale is a long-run concept; $ATC$ is a short-run concept. (258–261)

14. **d** **a** and **e** don't affect $AVC$; **b** and **c** shift $AVC$ down. (258–261)

**15. d** *AFC* always decreases, *TC* and *TVC* always increase. (257–259)

**16. c** Decreasing *MP* causes increasing *MC*. (258–261)

**17. a** *AVC* decreases as long as *AP* is increasing. (260)

**18. b** Won't affect *AVC* or *MC*. (260–261)

**19. b** Productivity increases, costs decrease. (260–261)

**20. b** Definition. All returns to scale are possible in the long run. (262–265)

**21. e** All definitions of the *LRAC*. (262–265)

**22. d** *LRAC* is horizontal. (262–265)

**23. e** Definition. Since all resources are variable, **a** and **b** are irrelevant. (262–265)

**24. a** Definition of a long-run concept; **b**, **c**, and **e** are short-run concepts; **d** would be correct if where economies of scale *end*. (262–265)

ⓒⓣ **25. a** Plant already too big in **b**; for **c**, sales may not justify a plant that big; **d** and **e** relate to short run. (262–265)

## Short Answer Problems

**1.** The average total cost curve is U-shaped, first falling and then rising as output increases. When average total cost is falling, marginal cost must be less than average total cost, and when average total cost is rising, marginal cost must be greater than average total cost. Therefore, the marginal cost curve must intersect the average total cost curve at its minimum point. In order for average total cost to fall, it must have been *pulled down* by a smaller increase in cost from the last unit of output. Therefore, marginal cost is lower than average total cost. Similarly, when average total cost is rising, it must be that it has been *pulled up* by a higher marginal cost. When average total cost is at its minimum, it is neither falling nor rising, so marginal cost cannot be lower or higher than average total cost. Therefore, marginal cost must be equal to average total cost.

**2.** The U-shape of the average total cost (*ATC*) curve arises from the opposing forces of (a) spreading fixed costs over a larger output and (b) the law of eventually diminishing returns.

As output increases, fixed costs are spread over a larger output so average fixed cost (*AFC*) falls. Initially, as output increases, the marginal productivity of the variable resource rises, causing average variable cost (*AVC*) to fall. Falling *AVC*, together with falling *AFC*, causes average total cost (*ATC*) to fall, contributing to the downward-sloping portion of *ATC*. Eventually, as output increases, diminishing returns set in, marginal productivity falls, and *AVC* rises. Eventually, *AVC* rises more quickly than *AFC* falls, contributing to the upward-sloping portion of the *ATC*.

ⓒⓣ **3.** Yes, it is possible that the average grade-point of the students at each school rises. Think of the transferring student as the *marginal* student. If his grade-point average, although the lowest at Hubertville High, is higher than the *average* grade-point at Histrionic High, then the results are: the *average* grade-point at Hubertville High rises with the elimination of the lowest grade-point, and the average grade-point at Histrionic High rises because the transferring (*marginal*) student's grade-point pulls up the *average* grade-point.

**4.** The law of diminishing returns states that as a firm uses more of a variable input, with a given quantity of fixed inputs, the marginal product of the variable input eventually diminishes. Diseconomies of scale occur when a firm increases all of its inputs by an equal percentage, and this results in a lower percentage increase in output. Diminishing (marginal) returns is a short-run concept since there must be a fixed input. Diseconomies of scale is a long-run concept since all inputs must be variable.

**5. a.** The completed Table 1 is shown here as Table 1 Solution.

**TABLE 1   Solution Monthly Golf Cart Production**

| Labourers (per month) | Output (units per month) | Marginal Product | Average Product |
|---|---|---|---|
| 0 | 0 | | 0 |
| | | ········· 1 | |
| 1 | 1 | | 1.00 |
| | | ········· 2 | |
| 2 | 3 | | 1.50 |
| | | ········· 3 | |
| 3 | 6 | | 2.00 |
| | | ········· 6 | |
| 4 | 12 | | 3.00 |
| | | ········· 5 | |
| 5 | 17 | | 3.40 |
| | | ········· 3 | |
| 6 | 20 | | 3.33 |
| | | ········· 2 | |
| 7 | 22 | | 3.14 |
| | | ········· 1 | |
| 8 | 23 | | 2.88 |

**b.** Fig. 4 gives the graph of the total product curve.

▲ **FIGURE 4**

**c.** Fig. 5 gives the graphs of marginal product and average product.

▲ **FIGURE 5**

**6. a.** Completed Table 2 is shown here as Table 2 Solution.

| TABLE 2 | | Solution Short-Run Costs (Monthly) | | | | | |
|---|---|---|---|---|---|---|---|
| L | Q | TFC ($) | TVC ($) | TC ($) | MC ($) | AFC ($) | AVC ($) | ATC ($) |
| 0 | 0 | 2,000 | 0 | 2,000 | | – | – | – |
| | | | | | 2,000 | | | |
| 1 | 1 | 2,000 | 2,000 | 4,000 | | 2,000 | 2,000 | 4,000 |
| | | | | | 1,000 | | | |
| 2 | 3 | 2,000 | 4,000 | 6,000 | | 667 | 1,333 | 2,000 |
| | | | | | 667 | | | |
| 3 | 6 | 2,000 | 6,000 | 8,000 | | 333 | 1,000 | 1,333 |
| | | | | | 333 | | | |
| 4 | 12 | 2,000 | 8,000 | 10,000 | | 167 | 667 | 833 |
| | | | | | 400 | | | |
| 5 | 17 | 2,000 | 10,000 | 12,000 | | 118 | 588 | 706 |
| | | | | | 667 | | | |
| 6 | 20 | 2,000 | 12,000 | 14,000 | | 100 | 600 | 700 |
| | | | | | 1,000 | | | |
| 7 | 22 | 2,000 | 14,000 | 16,000 | | 91 | 636 | 727 |
| | | | | | 2,000 | | | |
| 8 | 23 | 2,000 | 16,000 | 18,000 | | 87 | 696 | 783 |

**b.** The *TC*, *TVC*, and *TFC* curves are graphed in Fig. 6.

▲ **FIGURE 6**

**c.** The *MC*, *ATC*, *AVC*, and *AFC* curves are graphed in Fig. 7.

▲ **FIGURE 7**

**7.** The new *MC* and *ATC* curves (and the associated table) for golf cart production are given in Fig. 8. The original curves, $MC_0$ and $ATC_0$, are indicated for reference. The new curves are labelled $MC_1$ and $ATC_1$. Both curves have shifted up as a result of an increase in the price of labour.

▲ **FIGURE 8**

| Output | MC ($) | ATC ($) |
|--------|--------|---------|
| 0 |  | 0 |
|  | ·········· 2,500 |  |
| 1 |  | 4,500 |
|  | ·········· 1,250 |  |
| 3 |  | 2,333 |
|  | ·········· 833 |  |
| 6 |  | 1,583 |
|  | ·········· 417 |  |
| 12 |  | 1,000 |
|  | ·········· 500 |  |
| 17 |  | 853 |
|  | ·········· 833 |  |
| 20 |  | 850 |
|  | ·········· 1,250 |  |
| 22 |  | 886 |
|  | ·········· 2,500 |  |
| 23 |  | 957 |

| Output | MC ($) | ATC ($) |
|--------|--------|---------|
| 0 |  | 0 |
|  | ·········· 2,000 |  |
| 1 |  | 6,000 |
|  | ·········· 667 |  |
| 4 |  | 2,000 |
|  | ·········· 333 |  |
| 10 |  | 1,000 |
|  | ·········· 222 |  |
| 19 |  | 632 |
|  | ·········· 286 |  |
| 26 |  | 538 |
|  | ·········· 400 |  |
| 31 |  | 516 |
|  | ·········· 667 |  |
| 34 |  | 529 |

**8. a.** The new $MC$ and $ATC$ curves (and the associated table) are given in Fig. 9. The new curves are labelled $MC_2$ and $ATC_2$. The original curves, $MC_0$ and $ATC_0$, are indicated for reference.

▲ **FIGURE 9**

**b.** The curves have shifted (generally) down and to the right as a result of increasing the plant size. There are economies of scale (increasing returns to scale) up to the level of output at which $MC_2$ intersects $ATC_2$ (approximately 32 units).

**c.** The long-run average cost curve is indicated in Fig. 9 by the heavy line tracing out the lowest short-run average total cost of producing each level of output. In this example, that happens to correspond entirely to $ATC$.

# 12 Perfect Competition

## Key Concepts

### What Is Perfect Competition?

**Perfect competition** is a model of market structure where the force of *competition* is extreme and firms have no *market power*. Assumptions include many firms; identical products; many buyers; free entry; no advantages for existing firms over new firms; complete information.

Perfect competition can arise when

- industry demand is *large* relative to the minimum efficient scale of a firm (smallest quantity of output yielding minimum *LRAC*).
- products of each firm are identical.

In perfect competition,

- each firm is a **price taker**.
- each firm faces a perfectly elastic demand curve at the market price.

The firm maximizes economic profit.

- Economic profit = total revenue – total cost (total cost includes normal profit)
- Normal profit = expected return to entrepreneurial ability

- **Total revenue** ($TR$)—price ($P$) $\times$ quantity ($Q$)
  - Average revenue ($AR$)—$TR/Q$
  - Marginal revenue ($MR$)—$\Delta TR/\Delta Q$
  - In perfect competition, $AR = MR = P$

## The Firm's Output Decision

In the short run, the firm decides what quantity to produce or to shut down.

- Economic profit is maximized at the quantity where $MR = MC$:
  - If $MR > MC$, the firm increases $Q$ to increase economic profit.
  - If $MR < MC$, the firm decreases $Q$ to increase economic profit.
- For a firm incurring economic loss:
  - if $P > AVC$, firm will continue to produce.
  - if $P < AVC$, firm will temporarily shut down.
  - **shutdown point** is at minimum $AVC$.

The perfectly competitive firm's supply curve is its $MC$ curve above minimum $AVC$.

## Output, Price, and Profit in the Short Run

**Short-run industry supply curve** is the horizontal sum of individual firm's supply curves. In the short run, the number of firms and their plant size are fixed.

Equilibrium market price and quantity are determined by industry demand and supply curves.

- Three possible short-run profit-maximizing outcomes for firms:
  - $P\,(= AR = MR) > ATC$ yields economic profit.
  - $P\,(= AR = MR) = ATC$ yields zero economic profit (*break-even point* at minimum $ATC$; firm just earning normal profit).
  - $P\,(= AR = MR) < ATC$ yields economic loss (firm earning less than normal profit).

# Output, Price, and Profit in the Long Run

In the long run, the number of firms in the industry and the plant size of each firm can adjust. Economic profit/loss are signals for firms to enter/exit the industry and cause reallocation of resources.

- Economic profit attracts new entry, causing a rightward shift of industry supply, causing falling $P$ and the elimination of economic profit.
- Economic loss induces existing firms to exit, causing a leftward shift of industry supply, causing rising $P$ and the elimination of economic loss.

In long-run competitive equilibrium,

- $MR = P = MC$; firms maximize short-run profit.
- $P = $ minimum $ATC$; economic profit is zero; no incentive for firms to enter or exit industry.
- $P = $ minimum $LRAC$; optimum plant size; no incentive for firm to change plant size.

# Changing Tastes and Advancing Technology

For a permanent shift in demand,

- decreased demand causes falling $P$, economic loss and exit, decreased industry supply, causing rising $P$. In the long run, enough firms exit so remaining firms earn normal profit.
- increased demand causes rising $P$, economic profit and entry, increased industry supply, causing falling $P$. In the long run, enough firms enter so economic profit is eliminated and firms earn normal profit.

The change in long-run equilibrium price from a permanent shift in demand depends on

- **external economies**—factors beyond control of firm that lower costs as industry output increases.

- **external diseconomies**—factors beyond control of firm that raise costs as industry output increases.

The shape of the **long-run industry supply curve** depends on the existence of external economies or diseconomies. The long-run industry supply curve shows how industry quantity supplied varies as market price varies after all possible adjustments, including changes in plant size and number of firms. Shape may be

- horizontal for constant-cost industry.
- upward sloping for increasing cost industry with external diseconomies.
- downward sloping for decreasing cost industry with external economies.

New technology lowers costs, increases industry supply, causing falling $P$. New technology firms make economic profit and enter. Old technology firms incur economic loss and exit or switch to new technology. In the long run, all firms use new technology and earn zero economic profit (normal profit only).

## Competition and Efficiency

Resource use is efficient when the most highly valued goods are produced; when no one can become better off without someone else becoming worse off; when marginal benefit equals marginal costs. Requires

- consumers to be on their demand = marginal social benefit curves and to be getting the most value from their resources.
- firms to be on their supply = marginal social cost curves and to be technologically efficient and economically efficient (lowest possible $LRAC$).
- equilibrium to be where price = marginal social benefit = marginal social cost; maximum gains from trade (consumer surplus + producer surplus).

Perfect competition achieves efficient use of resources at the market equilibrium price and quantity if there are no external benefits and external costs (Ch. 5).

# Helpful Hints

1. Although perfectly competitive markets are rare in the real world, there are three important reasons to develop a thorough understanding of their behaviour.

    First, many markets closely approximate perfectly competitive markets. The analysis in this chapter gives direct and useful insights into the behaviour of these markets.

    Second, the theory of perfect competition allows us to isolate the effects of competitive forces that are at work in *all* markets, even in those that do not match the assumptions of perfect competition.

    Third, the perfectly competitive model serves as a useful benchmark for evaluating the relative efficiency of different market structures in subsequent chapters.

2. In the short run, a perfectly competitive firm cannot change the size of its plant—it has fixed inputs. The firm is also a price taker; it always sells at the market price, which it cannot influence. The only variable that the firm controls is its level of output. The short-run condition for profit maximization is to choose the level of output at which marginal revenue equals marginal cost. This is a general condition that, as we will see in subsequent chapters, applies to other market structures such as monopoly and monopolistic competition. Since for the perfectly competitive firm marginal revenue is equal to price, this profit-maximizing condition takes a particular form: choose the level of output at which price is equal to marginal cost ($P = MC$).

3. Many students have trouble understanding why a firm continues to operate at the break-even point, where economic profit is zero. The key to understanding lies in the definition of which costs are included in the average total cost curve. Recall from Chapter 10 that the economist defines a firm's total costs as *opportunity costs*, which include both explicit costs and *implicit costs*.

    Implicit costs include forgone interest, forgone rent, and forgone cost of the owner's resources. Owners supply their time, which could have been used to earn income elsewhere. Owners also supply entrepreneurial ability. Normal profit is the expected return to entrepreneurial ability and is part of a firm's implicit costs.

At the break-even point where total revenue equals total cost (or, equivalently, average revenue equals average total cost), the owners of the firm are still earning a return on their investment, time, and entrepreneurial ability, which is equal to the best return that they could earn elsewhere. That is the definition of opportunity cost—the best alternative forgone. As the phrase "normal profit" implies, this profit could normally be earned as a return to entrepreneurial ability, on average, in any other industry. At the break-even point, the firm is earning normal profit even though its economic profit (sometimes called "extra-normal" or "above-average" profit) is zero. In earning normal profit, the firm is earning just as much profit as it could anywhere else, and is therefore totally content to continue producing in this industry.

4. When the price of output falls below the break-even point, but is above the shutdown point, the firm will continue to produce even though it is incurring economic losses. In this price range, the firm is no longer earning normal profit and theoretically could earn more by switching to another industry. Nonetheless, the firm will continue to operate in the short run because switching has costs. In order to switch industries, the firm must shut down, which entails still paying its total fixed costs.

   As long as price is above the shutdown point (minimum average variable cost), a firm will decide to produce since it will be covering total variable cost and part of total fixed cost. Its loss will be less if it continues to produce at the output where $P = MC$ than if it shuts down.

   If price falls below the shutdown point, a firm that produces output will not only lose its total fixed costs, it will lose *additional* money on every unit of output produced, since average revenue is less than average variable cost. Thus, when price is less than average variable cost, the firm will choose to minimize its loss by shutting down.

5. In the long run, fixed costs disappear, and the firm can switch between industries and change plant size without cost. Economic profit serves as the signal for the movement or reallocation of firm resources until long-run equilibrium is achieved. Firms will move out of industries with negative economic profit (economic loss) and into industries with positive economic profit. Only when economic profit is zero will there be no tendency for firms to exit or enter industries.

The fact that there are no restrictions on entry into the industry is what assures that economic profit will be zero and that firms will be producing at the minimum of their long-run average cost curves in long-run equilibrium.

6. In long-run equilibrium, three conditions are satisfied for each firm in an industry:

   **i.** $MR = P = MC$. This implies that profits are maximized for each firm.

   **ii.** $P = ATC$. This implies that economic profit is zero and each firm is just earning normal profit.

   **iii.** $P = $ minimum $LRAC$. This implies that production takes place at the point of minimum long-run average cost.

# Self-Test

## True/False and Explain

### What Is Perfect Competition?

1. A firm in a perfectly competitive industry cannot influence price.

2. The industry demand curve in a perfectly competitive industry is horizontal.

3. The objective of firms in a competitive industry is to maximize revenue.

### The Firm's Output Decision

4. Firms will incur an economic loss in the long run but not the short run.

5. At prices below minimum average total cost, a firm will always shut down.

### Output, Price, and Profit in the Short Run

6. The supply curve of a perfectly competitive firm gives the quantities of output supplied at alternative prices as long as the firm earns economic profit.

## Output, Price, and Profit in the Long Run

**7.** In long-run equilibrium, each firm in a perfectly competitive industry will choose the plant size associated with minimum long-run average cost.

**8.** Suppose a perfectly competitive industry is in long-run equilibrium when there is a substantial increase in total fixed costs. All firms will now incur economic losses and some firms will go out of business.

**9.** Suppose a perfectly competitive industry is in long-run equilibrium when there is an increase in demand. As new firms start entering the industry, the output of each existing firm will increase.

## Changing Tastes and Advancing Technology

**10.** Suppose a perfectly competitive industry is in long-run equilibrium when there is a permanent increase in demand. In the short run, firms will earn an economic profit.

**11.** Suppose a perfectly competitive industry is in long-run equilibrium when there is a permanent decrease in demand. In the long run, firms will incur an economic loss.

**12.** In a perfectly competitive industry with external economies, the long-run industry supply curve is positively sloped.

## Competition and Efficiency

**13.** Resource use is efficient as long as marginal benefit is greater than marginal cost.

**14.** Resource use is efficient as long as consumer surplus equals producer surplus.

**15.** A perfectly competitive industry will achieve efficiency if there are no external costs or external benefits.

# Multiple-Choice

## What Is Perfect Competition?

1. Which of the following is *not* a characteristic of a perfectly competitive industry?
   a. downward-sloping industry demand curve
   b. perfectly elastic demand curve for each individual firm
   c. each firm decides its quantity of output
   d. slightly differentiated products
   e. many firms each supplying a small fraction of industry supply

2. For perfect competition to arise it is necessary that industry demand be
   a. inelastic.
   b. elastic.
   c. perfectly elastic.
   d. large relative to the minimum efficient scale of a firm.
   e. small relative to the minimum efficient scale of a firm.

3. If a firm faces a perfectly elastic demand for its product,
   a. it is not a price taker.
   b. it will want to lower its price to increase sales.
   c. it will want to raise its price to increase total revenue.
   d. its marginal revenue curve is equal to the price of the product.
   e. it will always earn zero economic profit.

## The Firm's Output Decision

4. In a perfectly competitive industry, the market price is $10. An individual firm is producing the output at which $MC = ATC = \$15$. $AVC$ at that output is $10. What should the firm do to maximize its short-run profits?
   a. shut down
   b. expand output
   c. contract output
   d. leave output unchanged
   e. insufficient information to answer

**5.** In which of the following situations will a perfectly competitive firm earn economic profit?
   **a.** $MR > AVC$
   **b.** $MR > ATC$
   **c.** $ATC > MC$
   **d.** $ATC > AR$
   **e.** $AR > AVC$

**6.** In the price range below minimum average variable cost, a perfectly competitive firm's supply curve is
   **a.** horizontal at the market price.
   **b.** vertical at zero output.
   **c.** the same as its marginal cost curve.
   **d.** the same as its average variable cost curve.
   **e.** none of the above.

**7.** A firm in a perfectly competitive industry is maximizing its short-run profits by producing 500 units of output. At 500 units of output, which of the following *must be false*?
   **a.** $MC < AVC$
   **b.** $MC < ATC$
   **c.** $MC > ATC$
   **d.** $AR < ATC$
   **e.** $AR > AVC$

**8.** If a profit-maximizing firm in perfect competition is earning economic profit, it must be producing a level of output where
   **a.** price is greater than marginal cost.
   **b.** price is greater than marginal revenue.
   **c.** marginal cost is greater than marginal revenue.
   **d.** marginal cost is greater than average total cost.
   **e.** average total cost is greater than marginal cost.

## Output, Price, and Profit in the Short Run

**9.** If a perfectly competitive firm in the short run is able to pay its variable costs and part, but not all, of its fixed costs, then it is operating in the range on its marginal cost curve that is anywhere
  **a.** above the break-even point.
  **b.** below the break-even point.
  **c.** above the shutdown point.
  **d.** below the shutdown point.
  **e.** between the shutdown and break-even points.

**10.** The short-run industry supply curve is
  **a.** the horizontal sum of the individual firms' supply curves.
  **b.** the vertical sum of the individual firms' supply curves.
  **c.** vertical at the total level of output being produced by all firms.
  **d.** horizontal at the current market price.
  **e.** none of the above.

**11.** The supply curve for an individual firm in a perfectly competitive industry is $P = 1 + 2Q_S$. If the industry consists of 100 identical firms, then what is industry supply when $P = 7$?
  **a.** 300
  **b.** 400
  **c.** 600
  **d.** 800
  **e.** none of the above

**12.** Refer to Fact 1. If the price of fiddleheads last month was $15 per bag, Franklin
  **a.** should have shut down because total revenue did not cover total variable cost.
  **b.** incurred an economic loss of $135.
  **c.** earned zero economic profit.
  **d.** earned economic profit of $50.
  **e.** earned economic profit of $100.

---

FACT I

Franklin is a fiddlehead farmer. He sold 10 bags of fiddleheads last month, with total fixed cost of $100 and total variable cost of $50.

---

**13.** Refer to Fact 1. If fiddlehead prices fell to $10 per bag while production and cost figures remained the same, Franklin would

**a.** shut down immediately.

**b.** break even because total revenues just cover total fixed costs.

**c.** be indifferent between producing and shutting down because his loss of $50 just covers total variable costs.

**d.** continue producing despite his loss of $50.

**e.** continue producing despite his loss of $100.

**14.** Refer to Fact 1. Suppose the price of fiddleheads is expected to stay at $10 per bag, and Franklin's production and cost figures are expected to stay the same. His total fixed cost consists entirely of rent on land, and his five-year lease on the land runs out at the end of the month. Should Franklin renew the lease?

**a.** Yes, because total revenue will still cover total fixed cost.

**b.** Yes, because total revenue will still cover total variable cost and a portion of total fixed cost.

**c.** No, because total revenue must cover all costs for resources to remain in fiddlehead farming in the long run.

**d.** No, because in the long run, zero economic profit is a signal to move resources out of fiddlehead farming.

**e.** There is insufficient information to answer.

## Output, Price, and Profit in the Long Run

**15.** The maximum loss for a firm in long-run equilibrium is

**a.** zero.

**b.** its total cost.

**c.** its total variable cost.

**d.** its average total cost.

**e.** none of the above.

**16.** For a perfectly competitive firm in long-run equilibrium, which of the following is *not* equal to price?

**a.** short-run average total cost

**b.** short-run average variable cost

**c.** short-run marginal cost

**d.** long-run average cost

**e.** average revenue

**17.** When economic profit is zero
  **a.** the product will not be produced in the short run.
  **b.** the product will not be produced in the long run.
  **c.** firms will leave the industry.
  **d.** revenues are not covering implicit costs.
  **e.** none of the above will occur.

## Changing Tastes and Advancing Technology

**18.** A perfectly competitive industry is in short-run equilibrium with price below average total cost. Which of the following is *not* a prediction of the long-run consequences of such a situation?
  **a.** Price will increase.
  **b.** The output of the industry will increase.
  **c.** Firms will leave the industry.
  **d.** The output of each remaining firm will increase.
  **e.** Economic profit will be zero.

**19.** Fig. 1 illustrates the cost curves for a perfectly competitive firm. The current market price is $11 and the firm has the plant size shown by $SRAC_1$. The firm's short-run equilibrium output is
  **a.** 7 units.
  **b.** 9 units.
  **c.** 10 units.
  **d.** 17 units.
  **e.** 18 units.

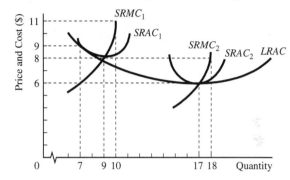

▲ **FIGURE 1**

**20.** Refer to Fig. 1. The current market price is $11 and the firm has the plant size shown by $SRAC_1$. In the long run, the firm will
  **a.** exit from the industry.
  **b.** keep its current plant size, and other firms will enter the industry.
  **c.** keep its current plant size, and other firms will exit from the industry.
  **d.** increase its plant size, and other firms will enter the industry.
  **e.** increase its plant size, and other firms will exit from the industry.

**21.** Refer to Fig. 1. The long-run equilibrium price and quantity combination is
   **a.** $6 and 7 units.
   **b.** $6 and 17 units.
   **c.** $8 and 9 units.
   **d.** $8 and 18 units.
   **e.** $9 and 7 units.

**22.** If an industry experiences external economies as the industry expands in the long run, the long-run industry supply curve will
   **a.** be perfectly inelastic.
   **b.** be perfectly elastic.
   **c.** have a positive slope.
   **d.** have a negative slope.
   **e.** have allocative inefficiency.

**23.** Which of the following is *not* true of a new long-run equilibrium resulting from a new technology in a perfectly competitive industry?
   **a.** Price will be lower.
   **b.** Industry output will be greater.
   **c.** Firm profits will be greater.
   **d.** All firms in the industry will be using the new technology.
   **e.** Average total cost will be lower.

## Competition and Efficiency

**24.** A long-run equilibrium in a perfectly competitive industry would *not* be efficient if
   **a.** firms are price takers.
   **b.** new technologies are developed.
   **c.** there are external economies or external diseconomies.
   **d.** there are external costs or external benefits.
   **e.** there is free entry to the industry.

**25.** Resources are used efficiently when

    **a.** consumers are on their marginal social benefit curves.

    **b.** firms are economically efficient.

    **c.** price = marginal social benefit = marginal social cost.

    **d.** there are no external benefits or external costs.

    **e.** all of the above are true.

## Short Answer Problems

**1.** Why will a firm in a perfectly competitive industry choose *not* to charge a price either above or below the market price?

**2.** Why will economic profit tend to be zero in long-run equilibrium in a perfectly competitive industry?

**3.** Table 1 gives the total cost structure for one of many identical firms in a perfectly competitive industry.

| TABLE 1 | | | | | |
| --- | --- | --- | --- | --- | --- |
| Quantity (units per day) | Total Cost ($) | Total Variable Cost ($) | Average Total Cost ($) | Average Variable Cost ($) | Marginal Cost ($) |
| 0 | 12 | | | | ... |
| 1 | 24 | | | | ... |
| 2 | 32 | | | | ... |
| 3 | 42 | | | | ... |
| 4 | 54 | | | | ... |
| 5 | 68 | | | | ... |
| 6 | 84 | | | | |

| TABLE 2 | | | |
| --- | --- | --- | --- |
| Quantity (units per day) | Profit $p = \$9$ | Profit $p = \$11$ | Profit $p = \$15$ |
| 0 | | | |
| 1 | | | |
| 2 | | | |
| 3 | | | |
| 4 | | | |
| 5 | | | |
| 6 | | | |

**a.** Complete the table by computing total variable cost, average total cost, average variable cost, and marginal cost at each level of output. (*Remember:* As in the problems in Chapter 11, marginal cost should be entered *midway* between rows.)

**b.** Complete Table 2 by computing the profit (per day) for the firm at each level of output if the price of output is $9; $11; $15.

**c.** Consider the profit-maximizing output decision of the firm at alternative prices. How much will the firm produce if the price of output is $9? $11? $15? Explain each of your answers.

**4.** A firm will maximize profit if it produces every unit of output for which marginal revenue exceeds marginal cost. This is called the *marginal analysis* of profit maximization. Using marginal analysis, determine the profit-maximizing level of output for the firm in Short Answer Problem **3** when the price of output is $15. How does your answer here compare with your answer in Short Answer Problem **3c**?

**5.** This problem concerns a hypothetical pottery manufacturing firm that produces ceramic mugs for sale in a purely competitive market. With a plant of given size, the firm can turn out the quantities of ceramic mugs shown in Table 3 by varying the amount it uses of a single variable input, labour.

**TABLE 3**

| Number of Mugs | Labour-Hours (per-day) |
|---|---|
| 20 | 6.50 |
| 40 | 11.00 |
| 60 | 14.50 |
| 80 | 17.50 |
| 100 | 20.50 |
| 120 | 23.75 |
| 140 | 27.50 |
| 160 | 32.00 |
| 180 | 37.50 |
| 200 | 44.50 |
| 220 | 53.50 |
| 240 | 65.00 |
| 260 | 79.50 |
| 280 | 97.50 |

Suppose the firm can hire all the labour it would ever want at the going wage of $8 per labour-hour. The firm's total fixed costs are $64 per day.

**a.** In the space below, draw a table showing output, total variable cost (*TVC*), total cost (*TC*), average variable cost (*AVC*), average total cost (*ATC*), and marginal cost (*MC*). (*Remember:* Marginal cost should be entered *midway* between rows of output.)

**b.** On the grid below, on a graph with *Mugs (per day)* on the horizontal axis, draw the three "per-unit" cost curves, *AVC*, *ATC*, and *MC*. (Note that the marginal cost values from your table should be plotted on the graph *midway* between the corresponding units of output.)

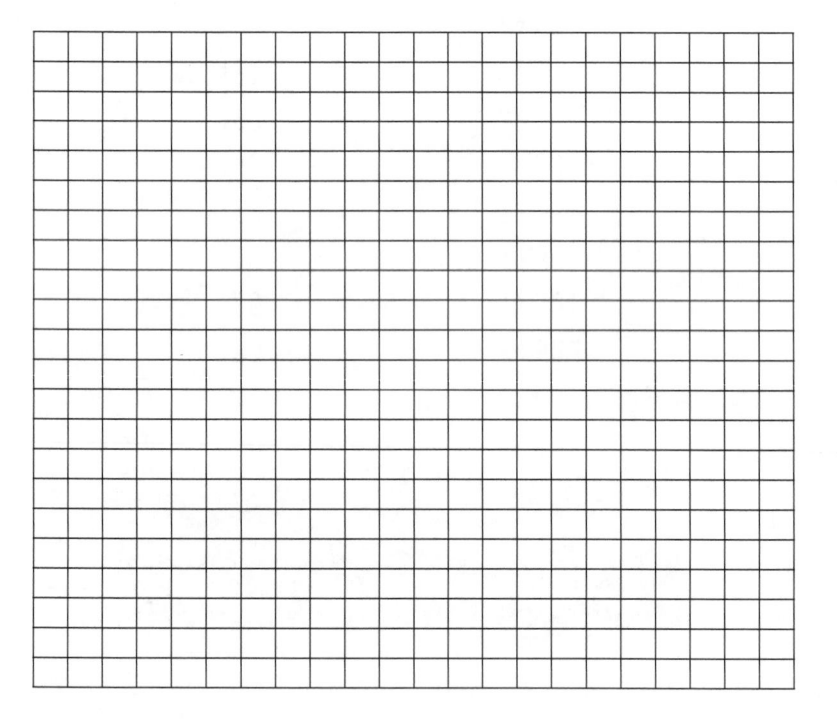

**c.** Consider (separately) the following alternative market prices that the firm might face:

$$P = \$3.20, P = \$2, P = \$1.65, P = \$1.40.$$

Assuming that the firm wants to maximize its profit, for *each* of the above prices answer the following questions: Approximately how many mugs per day would the firm produce? How do you know? Is the firm making a profit at that price? And if so, approximately how much?

6. Suppose that the ceramic pottery mug industry consists of 60 firms, each identical to the single firm discussed in Short Answer Problem **5**. Table 4 represents some points on the industry demand schedule for ceramic pottery mugs.

| TABLE 4 | |
| --- | --- |
| Price ($) | Quantity Demanded |
| 1.00 | 15,900 |
| 1.60 | 14,400 |
| 2.20 | 12,900 |
| 2.80 | 11,400 |
| 3.40 | 9,900 |
| 4.00 | 8,400 |
| 4.60 | 6,900 |
| 5.20 | 5,400 |
| 5.80 | 3,900 |
| 6.40 | 2,400 |
| 7.00 | 900 |

**a.** On the grid below, graph the industry short-run supply curve. Draw the industry demand curve on the same graph.

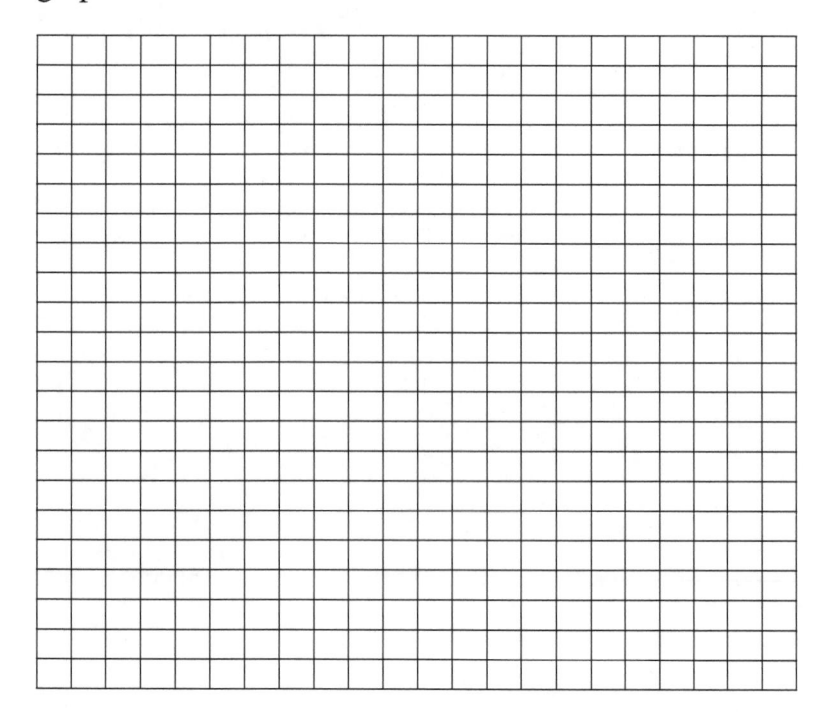

**b.** What is the short-run equilibrium price of ceramic pottery mugs?

**c.** Is the ceramic pottery mug industry in long-run equilibrium? Explain your answer.

**7.** A perfectly competitive industry has 100 identical firms in the short run, each of which has the short-run cost curves listed in Table 5.

| TABLE 5 | | | |
|---|---|---|---|
| Output (units) | Average Total Cost ($) | Average Variable Cost ($) | Marginal Cost ($) |
| 11 | 20.5 | 13.1 | |
| | | | 12 |
| 12 | 19.8 | 13.0 | |
| | | | 14 |
| 13 | 19.3 | 13.1 | |
| | | | 16 |
| 14 | 19.1 | 13.3 | |
| | | | 18 |
| 15 | 19.0 | 13.6 | |
| | | | 20 |
| 16 | 19.1 | 14.0 | |
| | | | 22 |
| 17 | 19.2 | 14.5 | |
| | | | 24 |
| 18 | 19.5 | 15.0 | |
| | | | 26 |
| 19 | 19.8 | 15.6 | |
| | | | 28 |
| 20 | 20.3 | 16.2 | |
| | | | 30 |
| 21 | 20.7 | 16.9 | |

This short-run average total cost curve touches the long-run average cost curve at the minimum point on the long-run average cost curve as the point "Long-run competitive equilibrium." The industry demand schedule is the same in the long and the short run. Table 6 represents some points on the demand schedule.

| TABLE 6 | |
|---|---|
| Price ($) | Quantity Demanded |
| 11 | 3,200 |
| 13 | 3,000 |
| 15 | 2,800 |
| 17 | 2,600 |
| 19 | 2,400 |
| 21 | 2,200 |
| 23 | 2,000 |
| 25 | 1,800 |
| 27 | 1,600 |
| 29 | 1,400 |
| 31 | 1,200 |

**a.** What is the quantity of output corresponding to the firm's break-even point? the shutdown point? Explain your answers.

**b.** What is the short-run equilibrium price in this market? Show how you found your answer.

**c.** What amount of profit or loss is being made by each firm at the short-run equilibrium price? Is this industry in long-run equilibrium at its present size? Why or why not?

**d.** Exactly how many firms will exist in this industry in the long run? Explain your answer. How much economic profit will each firm earn in the long run?

**8.** Consider a perfectly competitive industry in long-run equilibrium. All firms in the industry are identical.

   **a.** On the grid, draw a two-part graph illustrating the long-run equilibrium for the industry—part (a) on the top half of the grid—and for the typical firm—part (b) on the bottom half of the grid. The graph of the firm should include the *MC*, *ATC*, *MR*, and *LRAC* curves. Assume that the *LRAC* curve is U-shaped. Label the equilibrium price $P_0$, the equilibrium industry quantity $Q_0$, and the output of the firm $q_0$.

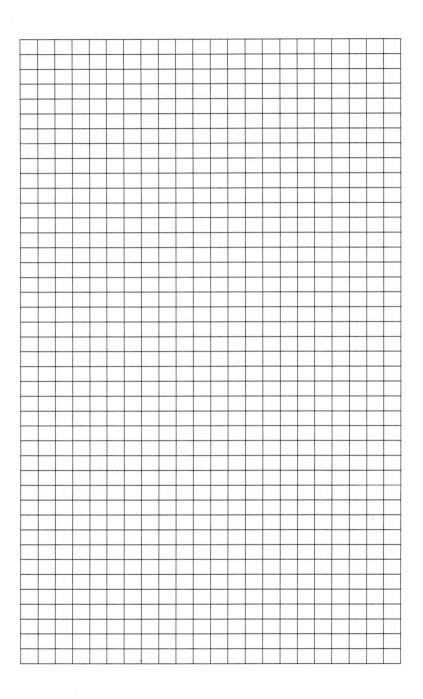

**b.** Now, suppose there is a decline in industry demand. Using your graphs from part **a**, show what happens to market price, firm output, firm profits, and industry equilibrium quantity in the short run (assume that the shutdown point is not reached).

    Then show what happens to market price, firm output, firm profits, and industry equilibrium quantity in the long run (assume that there are no external economies or diseconomies). What has happened to the number of firms?

# Answers

## True/False and Explain

1. **T** Each firm is a price taker. (274–275)

2. **F** Individual firm demand curve is horizontal. Industry demand curve is downward sloping. (274–275)

3. **F** Maximize economic profit. (274–275)

4. **F** Losses in the short run but not the long run. (276–279)

   5. **F** True if $P <$ minimum $AVC$. False if $P >$ minimum $AVC$ but $<$ minimum $ATC$. (276–279)

6. **F** As long as $P >$ minimum $AVC$. (280–283)

7. **T** Otherwise the firm is driven out of business by lower-cost firms. (283–285)

   8. **T** $ATC$ shifts upward with no $\Delta MC$. Economic losses cause exit. (283–285)

9. **F** As new firms enter, supply shifts rightward, price falls, and output of each existing firm decreases. (283–285)

10. **T** Price rises above $ATC$, creating economic profit. (286–289)

11. **F** Short-run economic losses cause firms to exit, shifting supply leftward, raising price until economic losses eliminated. (286–289)

12. **F** Negatively sloped. (286–289)

13. **F** Efficient when $MB = MC$. (290–291)

14. **F** Efficient when sum of consumer surplus and producer surplus is maximized. (290–291)

15. **T** $P = MB = MC$ and maximum sum of consumer and producer surpluses. (290–291)

## Multiple-Choice

1. **d** Identical products. (274–275)

2. **d** So there is room for many (efficient) firms in the industry. (274–275)

3. **d** Firm can increase $Q$ without $\Delta P$, so $MR$ from additional $Q = P$. (274–275)

   4. **c** Draw graph. Firm should choose lower $Q$ where $P = MC$. If $AVC$ at current $Q = \$10$, minimum $AVC$ must be $< \$10$, so new $Q$ at $P >$ minimum $AVC$. (276–279)

5. **b** Since $MR = AR$, $AR > ATC$. Multiplying by $Q$ yields $TR > TC$, so there is economic profit. (276–279)

6. **b** Firm stays shut down ($Q = 0$) until $P$ reaches minimum $AVC$. (276–279)

   7. **a** **a** implies shutdown. Other answers possible with losses (**b**, **d**) or profits (**c**, **e**). (276–279)

8. **d** ($MC = P =$) $AR > ATC$. **a**, **b**, **c** not consistent with profit maximization. **e** implies losses. (276–279)

9. **e** If the firm couldn't pay variable costs then below shutdown. If paying all variable and fixed costs, then breaking even. (280–283)

10. **a** Definition. **c** is momentary supply curve. **d** is demand curve facing individual firm. (280–283)

**11. a** For one firm: $7 = 1 + 2Q_S$; $2Q_S = 6$; $Q_S = 3$. For 100 firms, $3 \times 100 = 300$. (280–283)

**12. c** Profit $= TR$ ($15 \times 10$) $- TC$ ($100 + $50$) = 0. (280–283)

ⓒ **13. d** $TR$ ($10 \times 10$) $- TC$ ($100 + $50$) = -$50$. Shutting down would bring bigger loss of $100 (fixed costs). (280–283)

ⓒ **14. c** He is making a long-run decision. **a**, **b** refer to the short run. **d** is false because *losses* are a signal to move resources. (280–283)

**15. a** Definition of long-run equilibrium includes zero economic profit. (283–285)

**16. b** Long-run equilibrium is at intersection of *ATC*, *MC*, and *LRAC* curves. (283–285)

**17. e** Product produced in short and long run, revenues exactly cover all costs (including implicit costs). (283–285)

**18. b** As firms exit, supply shifts left, decreasing industry *Q* and raising *P*. In response to higher *P*, remaining firms increase *Q*. (286–289)

**19. c** Choose *Q* where $P = MC$. (286–289)

**20. d** Economic profit attracts new entry, causing falling *P* and increased output creates incentive to build larger, lower-cost plant. (286–289)

**21. b** Long-run equilibrium is at intersection of *SRAC*, *MC*, and *LRAC* curves. (286–289)

**22. d** Because decreasing costs as industry *Q* increases. (286–289)

**23. c** In long-run equilibrium, economic profit is always zero. (286–289)

**24. d** **a**, **e** are conditions of perfect competition. **b**, **c** affect the shape of the long-run supply curve but not efficiency. (290–291)

**25. e** When there are no external benefits or external costs, **a** and **b** are true; **c** is the equilibrium between demand and supply. (290–291)

## Short Answer Problems

**1.** If a firm in a perfectly competitive industry charged a price even slightly higher than the market price, it would lose all of its sales. Thus it will not charge a price above the market price. Since it can sell all it wants at the market price, it would not be able to increase sales by lowering its price. Thus it would not charge a price below the market price since this would decrease total revenue and profits.

**2.** In a perfectly competitive industry, the existence of positive economic profit will attract the entry of new firms, shifting the industry supply curve rightward, causing the market price to fall and firm profits to decline. This tendency will exist as long as there is positive economic profit. Similarly, the existence of economic losses will cause firms to exit from the industry, shifting the industry supply curve leftward, causing the market price to rise and firm profits to rise (losses to decline). This tendency will exist as long as losses are being incurred. Thus, the only point of rest in the long run (the only equilibrium) occurs when economic profits are zero.

**3. a.** Completed Table 1 is shown here as Table 1 Solution.

**TABLE 1  Solution**

| Quantity (units per day) | Total Cost ($) | Total Variable Cost ($) | Average Total Cost ($) | Average Variable Cost ($) | Marginal Cost ($) |
|---|---|---|---|---|---|
| 0 | 12 | 0 | — | — | |
| | | | | | ....... 12 |
| 1 | 24 | 12 | 24.00 | 12.00 | |
| | | | | | ....... 8 |
| 2 | 32 | 20 | 16.00 | 10.00 | |
| | | | | | ....... 10 |
| 3 | 42 | 30 | 14.00 | 10.00 | |
| | | | | | ....... 12 |
| 4 | 54 | 42 | 13.50 | 10.50 | |
| | | | | | ....... 14 |
| 5 | 68 | 56 | 13.60 | 11.20 | |
| | | | | | ....... 16 |
| 6 | 84 | 72 | 14.00 | 12.00 | |

**b.** Completed Table 2 is given here as Table 2 Solution. The values for profit are computed as total revenue minus total cost, where total revenue is price times quantity and total cost is given in Table 1.

**c.** If the price is $9, profit is maximized (actually, loss is minimized) when the firm shuts down and produces zero units. If the firm chooses to produce, its loss will be at least $14, which is greater than the fixed cost loss of $12. If the price is $11, the firm is still unable to make a positive economic profit. The loss is minimized (at $9) if the firm produces 3 units.

**TABLE 2  Solution**

| Quantity (units per day) | Profit p = $9 | Profit p = $11 | Profit p = $15 |
|---|---|---|---|
| 0 | −12 | −12 | −12 |
| 1 | −15 | −13 | −9 |
| 2 | −14 | −10 | −2 |
| 3 | −15 | −9 | 3 |
| 4 | −18 | −10 | 6 |
| 5 | −23 | −13 | 7 |
| 6 | −30 | −18 | 6 |

At this price, all of variable cost and part of fixed cost can be recovered. At a price of $15, the firm will maximize profit (at $7) at an output of 5 units per day.

**4.** The marginal analysis of profit maximization states that the firm should produce all units of output for which marginal revenue exceeds marginal cost. For a perfectly competitive firm, marginal revenue equals price, so (equivalently) the firm should produce every unit for which price exceeds marginal cost. If the price of output is $15, we can see from Table 2 Solution that the firm should produce 5 units. Since the marginal cost of moving from the 4th to the 5th unit ($14) is less than price ($15), the 5th unit should be produced. The marginal cost of moving to the 6th unit ($16), however, is greater than price. It should not be produced. The answer here is the same as the answer in **3c**.

**5. a.** With only one variable input (labour), *AVC* (for any level of output) = (labour hours × wage rate). The requested table is Table 7.

| **TABLE 7** | | | | | |
|---|---|---|---|---|---|
| Output (per day) | TVC ($) | TC ($) | AVC ($) | ATC ($) | MC ($) |
| 0 | 0 | 64 | — | — | |
| | | | | | 2.60 |
| 20 | 52 | 116 | 2.60 | 5.80 | |
| | | | | | 1.80 |
| 40 | 88 | 152 | 2.20 | 3.80 | |
| | | | | | 1.40 |
| 60 | 116 | 180 | 1.93 | 3.00 | |
| | | | | | 1.20 |
| 80 | 140 | 204 | 1.75 | 2.55 | |
| | | | | | 1.20 |
| 100 | 164 | 228 | 1.64 | 2.28 | |
| | | | | | 1.30 |
| 120 | 190 | 254 | 1.58 | 2.12 | |
| | | | | | 1.50 |
| 140 | 220 | 284 | 1.57 | 2.03 | |
| | | | | | 1.80 |
| 160 | 256 | 320 | 1.60 | 2.00 | |
| | | | | | 2.20 |
| 180 | 300 | 364 | 1.67 | 2.02 | |
| | | | | | 2.80 |
| 200 | 356 | 420 | 1.78 | 2.10 | |
| | | | | | 3.60 |
| 220 | 428 | 492 | 1.95 | 2.24 | |
| | | | | | 4.60 |
| 240 | 520 | 584 | 2.17 | 2.43 | |
| | | | | | 5.80 |
| 260 | 636 | 700 | 2.45 | 2.69 | |
| | | | | | 7.20 |
| 280 | 780 | 844 | 2.79 | 3.01 | |

**b.** The graph appears in Fig. 2. It also illustrates the answers to part **c**.

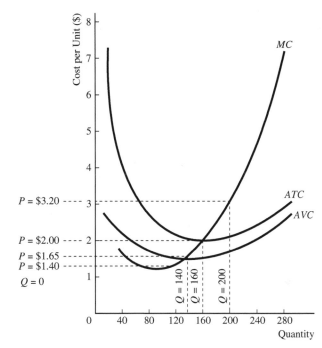

▲ **FIGURE 2**

**c.** In every case, at the profit-maximizing output, marginal revenue (which, for a price-taking firm in a perfectly competitive market, is the same as market price) is equal to marginal cost, provided that price is greater than average variable cost.

Profit "per unit of output" is the difference between average revenue (price) and average total cost at the level of output. Total profit is "per unit profit" × number

**TABLE 8**

| Price ($) | Output Chosen | Per Unit Profit ($) | Total Profit ($) |
|---|---|---|---|
| 3.20 | 200 | 1.10 | 220.00 |
| 2.00 | 160 | 0 | 0 |
| 1.65 | 140 | −0.38 | −53.20 |
| 1.40 | 0 | 0 | −64.00 |

Note the following:

1.  Marginal cost is $3.20 at approximately 200 units.
2.  The per unit profit is $P - ATC$.
3.  160 units is the "break-even" level of output, where $MC$ = minimum $ATC$ and the firm is just covering all its opportunity costs.
4.  At an output of 140 units, the firm continues to produce in the short run because it can more than cover its variable costs. If it produced zero units, its loss would be greater, $64, which is the amount of its fixed costs.
5.  Any positive output increases losses when the price is below the shutdown price, which here is approximately $1.57. When price is less than minimum $AVC$, the firm would not only lose its fixed costs, it would also lose additional money on every unit it produced.

**TABLE 9**

| Price ($) | Quantity Supplied by 1 Firm | Quantity Supplied by 60 Firms |
|---|---|---|
| 1.57 | 134 | 8,040 |
| 1.80 | 150 | 9,000 |
| 2.20 | 170 | 10,200 |
| 2.80 | 190 | 11,400 |
| 3.60 | 210 | 12,600 |
| 4.60 | 230 | 13,800 |
| 5.80 | 250 | 15,000 |
| 7.20 | 270 | 16,200 |

**a.** The graph of the industry supply curve appears in Fig. 3, together with the industry demand curve.

of units of output. Economic profit might be zero or negative (a loss) and still be the best the firm can attain in the short run. The calculations of total profit at each price appear in Table 8.

**6.** There are 60 identical price-taking firms.

For every possible price (above minimum $AVC$ of approximately $1.57), each firm will supply the quantity at which $P = MC$. We can derive (in Table 9) the industry supply schedule from the $MC$ curve of an individual firm.

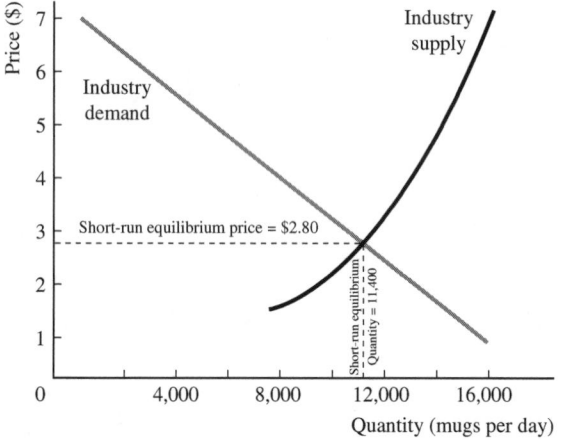

▲ **FIGURE 3**

**b.** The short-run equilibrium price is $2.80 (where a total of 11,400 mugs per day are supplied and sold; or 190 mugs per day supplied by each firm at $MC$ of $2.80).

**c.** At a price of $2.80 and output of 190, for each firm, $P > ATC$ where $ATC = $2.06$. So all existing firms are making an economic profit after covering all opportunity costs including a normal profit. (See Helpful Hint **3**.) The industry will attract new entrants because it offers more than normal profit. Even though the industry is in short-run equilibrium, it is *not* in long-run equilibrium because the number of firms has not "stabilized." New firms will enter the industry, the industry supply curve will shift rightward, and price will fall until no firm is making economic profit.

ⓒ **7. a.** The break-even point occurs at 15 units of output. At this level of output, $ATC$ is at its minimum ($19) and is equal to $MC$. Since the $MC$ of moving from the 14th to the 15th unit is $18, and the $MC$ of moving from the 15th to the 16th unit is $20, we can interpolate the $MC$ exactly at 15 units as midway between $18 and $20, or as $19. The shutdown point occurs at 12 units of output. At this level of output, $AVC$ is at its minimum ($13) and is equal to $MC$. The interpolated value of $MC$ at exactly 12 units of output is midway between $12 and $14, or is $13.

**b.** The short-run equilibrium price is $25. This is the price at which industry quantity supplied equals quantity demanded, as shown in Table 10.

| TABLE 10 | | | |
|---|---|---|---|
| $P = MC$ ($) | Quantity Supplied by 1 Firm | Quantity Supplied by 100 Firms | Quantity Demanded |
| 13 | 12 | 1,200 | 3,000 |
| 15 | 13 | 1,300 | 2,800 |
| 17 | 14 | 1,400 | 2,600 |
| 19 | 15 | 1,500 | 2,400 |
| 21 | 16 | 1,600 | 2,200 |
| 23 | 17 | 1,700 | 2,000 |
| **25** | **18** | **1,800** | **1,800** |
| 27 | 19 | 1,900 | 1,600 |
| 29 | 20 | 2,000 | 1,400 |

**c.** At a price of $25, each firm produces 18 units of output. At 18 units, $ATC$ is $19.50, so economic profit is being earned. The amount of profit is ($25 − $19.50 per unit =) $5.50 per unit. Total economic profit per firm is $5.50/unit × 18 units = $99. This means that new entrants will be attracted to the industry. We conclude that the industry is not in long-run equilibrium.

**d.** Entry continues until economic profit is competed away, and all firms are operating at the minimum point of the $LRAC$ curve (which, in this problem, is also the minimum point of the given short-run average total cost curve).

Minimum $ATC$ for each firm occurs at 15 units of output, when $ATC = MC = $19$, so price in the long run must be $19. At a price of $19, consumers demand 2,400 units (from Table 12.10). It follows that when the industry is in long-run equilibrium, there must be 2,400 units/15 units per firm = 160 firms in the industry, each producing 15 units of output at zero economic profit.

**8. a.** A long-run equilibrium in a perfectly competitive industry is illustrated in Fig. 4.

Part (a) illustrates industry equilibrium at the intersection of industry demand ($D_0$) and industry supply ($S_0$): point $a$. The equilibrium industry quantity is labelled $Q_0$ and the equilibrium market price is labelled $P_0$.

Part (b) illustrates the situation for a single firm in long-run equilibrium. The firm is at point $a'$, the minimum point of both the short-run average total cost curve ($ATC$) and the long-run average cost curve ($LRAC$). The firm is producing the output labelled $q_0$ and earning zero economic profit.

**b.** The new short-run equilibrium is also illustrated Fig. 4. The decrease in demand shifts the market demand curve leftward, from $D_0$ to $D_1$. The new market equilibrium is at point $b$. The price has fallen from $P_0$ to $P_1$ and the industry equilibrium quantity has fallen from $Q_0$ to $Q_1$. The fall in price induces firms to reduce output as shown by the move from point $a'$ to point $b'$ on the $MC$ curve in part (b). Since $P_1$ is less than minimum $ATC$, firms are incurring losses in the new short-run equilibrium.

The new long-run equilibrium is also illustrated in Fig. 4. With short-run losses, firms will exit from the industry in the long run. This causes the industry supply curve to shift leftward, causing the price to rise and thus reducing losses. Firms continue to leave until the industry supply curve has shifted enough to eliminate losses, from $S_0$ to $S_1$. This gives a new long-run industry equilibrium at point $c$ and the price has returned to its initial level, $P_0$, but industry quantity has fallen to $Q_2$.

As firms exit and the market price rises, remaining firms will increase their output (moving up the $MC$ curve from point $b'$ to point $a'$) and their losses will be reduced. When sufficient firms have left the industry, the price will have risen (returned) to $P_0$ and firms will have returned to point $a'$ in part (b). At this point, each firm is again earning zero economic profit and firm output has returned to $q_0$. But, since there are now fewer firms, industry equilibrium quantity is less.

(a) **Industry**

(b) **Firm**

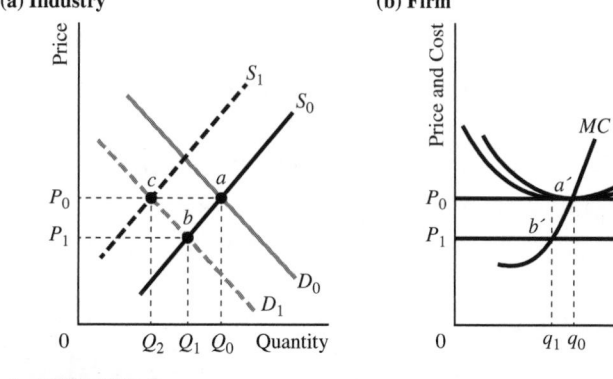

▲ **FIGURE 4**

# 13 Monopoly

## Key Concepts

### Monopoly and How It Arises

**Monopoly** is a model of market structure where the force of *competition* is absent and there is only one supplier with market power. Monopoly arises when there are

- no close substitutes for the product.
- **barriers to entry**—constraints protecting the firm from competition from potential new entrants.
  - Natural barriers to entry—a **natural monopoly** occurs when, due to economies of scale, one firm can supply the market at lower *LRAC* than multiple firms can.
  - Ownership barriers to entry—one firm owns a significant portion of a key resource.
  - Legal barriers to entry—for a **legal monopoly**, competition and entry are restricted by *public franchise*, *government licence*, *patent*, or *copyright*

Price-setting strategies depend on type of monopoly:

- **Single-price monopoly**—must sell each unit of output at the same price to all customers.
- **Price discrimination**—selling different units of output for different prices.

## A Single-Price Monopoly's Output and Price Decision

Single-price monopoly charges the same price for every unit output.

- Monopoly's demand curve is industry demand curve.
- Marginal revenue ($MR$) < price ($P$). To sell additional output, must lower $P$ on *all* output.
- In moving down the monopoly's demand curve
  - when total revenue ($TR$) is increasing, $MR$ is positive, $\eta > 1$.
  - when $TR$ maximum, $MR$ is zero, $\eta = 1$.
  - when $TR$ decreasing, $MR$ is negative, $\eta < 1$.
- Monopoly's technology and costs are like a firm in perfect competition.
- Profit-maximizing monopoly chooses output at which $MR = MC$, charges maximum price consumers are willing to pay (on demand curve).
- Monopoly never operates in inelastic range of demand curve. Monopoly has no supply curve.
- Monopoly can make economic profit even in the long run because barriers prevent entry of new firms.

## Single-Price Monopoly and Competition Compared

Output and price:

- Single-price monopoly $Q$ < competitive $Q$.
- Single-price monopoly $P$ > competitive $P$.

Efficiency:

- Single-price monopoly is inefficient compared to efficiency of perfect competition. Monopoly prevents gains from trade: restricts output, captures some consumer surplus, but creates *deadweight loss*—total loss of *consumer surplus* and *producer surplus* (revenue – opportunity cost production) below efficient levels.

- Social cost of monopoly is greater than deadweight loss because of **rent seeking**—attempt to capture **economic rent** (consumer surplus, producer surplus, or economic profit).

  - If no barriers to rent seeking, cost of resources used rent seeking = value monopoly profit (with no rent seeking), so no economic profit.

  - Social cost of monopoly = deadweight loss + resources used rent seeking

# Price Discrimination

Price discrimination (selling different units of output for different prices) converts consumer surplus into economic profit for the monopoly. Examples include charging lower per-unit price on large order than small; discriminating among groups with different average willingness to pay.

Price discrimination requires:

- Product cannot be resold.
- Charge lower $P$ to lower willingness-to-pay group. Charge higher $P$ to higher willingness-to-pay group.

**Perfect price discrimination**—different price for each unit sold; obtains maximum price each consumer is willing to pay; converts *all* consumer surplus into economic profit.

- *MR* curve is the same as demand curve.
- Same output and efficiency (zero deadweight loss) of perfectly competitive industry, but

  - all consumer surplus is captured as economic profit.

  - rent seeking occurs that might eliminate economic profit.

# Monopoly Regulation

*Natural monopolies* may be regulated to operate in the social interest: to achieve gains from monopoly (economies of scale) but avoid worst inefficiencies, higher prices, and restricted output.

- **Regulation**—government rules influencing prices, quantities, and entry.
- **Deregulation**—removing government regulation.

Two theories about how regulation works:

- **Social interest theory**—predicts regulations serve the social interest to eliminate dead-weight loss and efficiently allocate resources.
- **Capture theory**—predicts regulations serve self-interest of producers, who "capture" the regulator, for maximum economic profit and deadweight loss.

Possible regulation rules:

- **Marginal cost pricing rule**—set price equal to marginal cost. Maximizes total surplus and is efficient, but not viable because firm incurs economic loss.
- **Average cost pricing rule**—set price equal to average total cost. Firm earns normal profit only. Inefficient, but better than unregulated monopoly.
- **Rate of return regulation**—set price to achieve target rate of return on capital.
  - Ideally, yields normal profit only; same outcome as average cost pricing rule.
  - But problem of incentives for firm to inflate cost (of capital) to yield economic profit.
- **Price cap regulation**—set price ceiling to achieve target rate of return on capital.
  - Gives firm incentive to keep costs under control. Replacing rate of return regulation.
  - Often combined with earnings sharing regulation that forces firms to share profits above a target level with consumers.

# Helpful Hints

1. The opposite extreme of perfect competition is monopoly. While in perfect competition there are many firms that can decide only on quantity produced but not on price, a monopoly is a single firm with the ability to set both quantity and price. These differences create differences in the revenue situation facing the monopoly. The cost curves for the two market structures are assumed to be the same.

   Because there is only one firm, the industry demand curve is also the firm demand curve. Facing a negatively sloped demand curve, if a single-price monopoly wants to sell one more unit of output, it must lower its price. This has two effects on revenue. First, the sale of an additional unit will increase revenue by the amount of the price. However, since the firm must also *drop the price on previous units*, revenue on these will decrease. The net change in revenue, the marginal revenue, will be less than price and the marginal revenue curve will lie below the demand curve.

   Combining this new revenue situation with our familiar cost curves from Chapter 11 yields the important Fig. 1. Notice the following points about this graph.

   The profit-maximization rule for a single-price monopoly is to find the quantity of output where $MR = MC$. This is the same rule that applies to a perfectly competitive firm.

   For a perfectly competitive firm $MR$ is also equal to price, so the intersection of $MR$ and $MC$ yields the profit-maximizing output and price. That is not true for the monopolist. $MR$ is not equal to price, and once the profit-maximizing output is identified, the monopolist still has to set the price.

   To find the profit-maximizing price, draw an imaginary vertical line up to the demand

▲ **FIGURE 1  Monopoly Output & Price**

curve from the intersection of *MR* and *MC*. Then draw an imaginary horizontal line to the price axis to read the price.

Understanding what the vertical and horizontal distances of the economic profit area represent will make you less likely to make mistakes in drawing that area. The vertical distance is between the demand (or average revenue) curve and the average total cost curve. That distance measures average revenue minus average total cost, which equals average economic profit, or economic profit per unit. The horizontal distance is just the number of units produced. So the area of the rectangle (vertical distance × horizontal distance) = economic profit per unit × number of units = total economic profit. Do *not* make the mistake of drawing the vertical distance down to the intersection of *MC* and *MR*. That intersection has no economic meaning for the calculation of total economic profit.

2. There is an easy trick for drawing the marginal revenue curve corresponding to any linear demand curve. The price intercept (where $Q = 0$) is the same as for the demand curve, and the quantity intercept (where $P = 0$) is exactly *half* of the output of the demand curve. The marginal revenue curve is, therefore, a downward-sloping straight line whose slope is twice as steep as the slope of the demand curve.

3. Price discrimination can be profitable for a monopoly only if different consumer groups have different willingness to pay for the product. If such differences exist, the price-discriminating monopolist treats the groups as different markets. The profit-maximization rule for a price-discriminating monopoly is to find the quantity of output where *MR in each market = MC*. Then, in each market, charge the maximum price the consumer group is willing to pay for that output (on demand curve). Different willingness to pay translates into different elasticities of demand between groups, yielding different prices in the two markets.

4. The absence of entry barriers into a perfectly competitive industry is the basis for the prediction that any short-run economic profit in perfect competition will be competed away in the long run. Conversely, the presence of entry barriers in monopoly is the basis for the prediction that monopoly profits can persist in the

Notes:

long run. However, when rent-seeking activity is taken into account, there may be no long-run economic profit, even in monopoly. Rent seeking is any activity aimed at obtaining existing monopoly rights or creating new monopoly rights. Competition among rent seekers bids up the cost of rent seeking until it just equals the value of the potential monopoly profits, leaving the rent-seeker-turned-monopolist with little or no economic profit.

**5.** Fig. 2 depicts revenue and marginal cost curves for an industry. Use this figure to think of regulation as determining the division of the potential total surplus (the area of triangle *abc*) among consumer surplus, producer surplus, and deadweight loss.

   If the industry is perfectly competitive, then output will be $Q_c$ and the market price will be $P_c$. Total surplus is maximized and is given by the area of triangle *abc*. Total surplus is equal to the sum of consumer surplus (triangle *dbc*) and producer surplus (triangle *adc*). There is no deadweight loss so efficiency is achieved.

   If the industry is a profit-maximizing monopoly, output will be $Q_m$ and the price will be $P_m$. In this case, total surplus is represented by the area of trapezoid *abfg*. Because of monopoly restriction of output, total surplus under monopoly is less than under competition. The difference is the deadweight loss from monopoly—the amount of total surplus that is lost when we go from competition to monopoly. The deadweight loss is given by the area of triangle *gfc*. Total surplus can be divided into consumer surplus (triangle *ebf*) and producer surplus (trapezoid *aefg*). Consumer surplus is quite small, but producer surplus is at a maximum.

   Actual output is likely to be between these bounds. As output moves from $Q_c$ to $Q_m$, consumer surplus decreases while producer surplus and the deadweight loss both increase. If this industry is regulated, the social interest theory of intervention predicts output will be close to $Q_c$, while the capture theory of intervention predicts output closer to $Q_m$.

**▲ FIGURE 2**

# Self-Test
## True/False and Explain

### Monopoly and How It Arises

1. Monopoly can arise when there are close substitutes for a product.

2. If one firm can supply the market at a lower cost than multiple firms can, then there are natural barriers to entry.

3. Barriers to entry are essential to a monopoly.

### A Single Price Monopoly's Output and Price Decision

4. Over the output range where total revenue is decreasing, marginal revenue is positive.

5. The supply curve of a monopoly firm is its marginal cost curve.

6. Once a single-price monopoly chooses its output, average revenue always equals price.

### Single-Price Monopoly and Competition Compared

7. In moving from perfect competition to single-price monopoly, part of the deadweight loss is due to a reduction in producer surplus.

8. When rent seeking is taken into account, economic profits from monopoly are guaranteed in the long run.

## Price Discrimination

**9.** Price discrimination only works for goods that can be readily resold.

**10.** Price discrimination is an attempt by a monopolist to capture the producer surplus.

**11.** For a perfect price-discriminating monopolist, the demand curve is also the marginal revenue curve.

## Monopoly Regulation

**12.** If a regulator applies an average total cost pricing rule, a natural monopoly will earn normal profits only.

**13.** According to the capture theory, government regulatory agencies eventually capture the profits of the industries they regulate.

**14.** Under rate of return regulation, firms can get closer to maximizing producer surplus if they inflate their costs.

**15.** Price cap regulation gives firms incentives to keep costs under control, and is replacing rate of return regulation

# Multiple-Choice

## Monopoly and How It Arises

1. Which of the following is a *natural* barrier to the entry of new firms in an industry?
   a. licensing of professions
   b. economies of scale
   c. issuing a patent
   d. a public franchise
   e. all of the above

## A Single-Price Monopoly's Output and Price Decision

2. In order to increase sales from 7 units to 8 units, a single-price monopolist must drop the price from $7 per unit to $6 per unit. What is marginal revenue in this range?
   a. $48
   b. $6
   c. $1
   d. −$1
   e. none of the above

3. Four monopolists were overheard talking at an expensive restaurant. Which of their statements below is a correct strategy for maximizing profits?
   a. "In my company, we don't increase output unless we know that the larger output will raise total revenue."
   b. "I think cost minimization is the key to maximizing profits."
   c. "We try to make the most of our equipment by producing at maximum capacity."
   d. "I don't really keep close tabs on total profits, but I don't approve any business deal unless it increases my revenue more than it increases my costs."
   e. None of the above.

4. A profit-maximizing monopoly will never produce at an output level
   a. where it would incur economic losses.
   b. where marginal revenue is less than price.
   c. where average cost is greater than marginal cost.
   d. in the inelastic range of its demand curve.
   e. in the inelastic range of its marginal revenue curve.

**5.** For the single-price monopoly shown in Fig. 3, when profit is maximized, quantity is

**a.** 3 and price is $3.

**b.** 3 and price is $6.

**c.** 4 and price is $4.

**d.** 4 and price is $5.

**e.** 5 and price is $4.

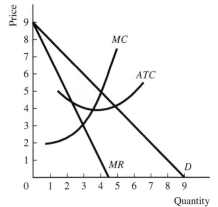

▲ **FIGURE 3**

**6.** If the single-price monopoly shown in Fig. 3 is maximizing profit, what is total economic profit?

**a.** $3

**b.** $4

**c.** $6

**d.** $9

**e.** none of the above

**7.** A single-price monopolist will maximize profits if it produces the output where

**a.** price equals marginal cost.

**b.** price equals marginal revenue.

**c.** marginal revenue equals marginal cost.

**d.** average revenue equals marginal cost.

**e.** average revenue equals marginal revenue.

**8.** If a profit-maximizing monopoly is producing an output at which marginal cost exceeds marginal revenue, it

**a.** should raise price and lower output.

**b.** should lower price and raise output.

**c.** should lower price and lower output.

**d.** is incurring losses.

**e.** is maximizing profit.

## Single-Price Monopoly and Competition Compared

**9.** Table 1 lists marginal costs for the XYZ firm. If XYZ sells 3 units at a price of $6 each, what is its producer surplus?

a. $2

b. $6

c. $7

d. $9

e. $12

**TABLE 1**

| Quantity | Marginal Cost |
|----------|---------------|
| 1 | 2 |
| 2 | 3 |
| 3 | 4 |
| 4 | 5 |

**10.** Which of the following is true for a producing single-price monopolist but not for a producing perfect competitor?

a. The firm maximizes profit by setting marginal cost equal to marginal revenue.

b. The firm is a price taker.

c. The firm can sell any level of output at any price it sets.

d. The firm's marginal cost is less than average revenue.

e. None of the above.

**11.** Activity for the purpose of creating monopoly is

a. called rent seeking.

b. illegal in Canada.

c. called price discrimination.

d. called legal monopoly.

e. costless.

**12.** Taking rent-seeking activity into account, the social cost of monopoly is equal to the

**a.** deadweight loss from monopoly.

**b.** monopoly profit.

**c.** deadweight loss plus monopoly profit.

**d.** deadweight loss minus monopoly profit.

**e.** consumer surplus lost plus producer surplus lost.

**13.** Consider the industry demand curve in Fig. 4. If the industry operates under perfect competition, which area in the diagram indicates consumer surplus?

**a.** *aek*

**b.** *dhk*

**c.** *dik*

**d.** *dih*

**e.** none of the above

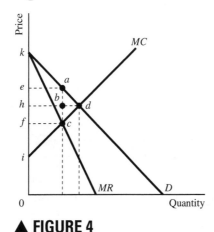

▲ **FIGURE 4**

**14.** Consider the industry demand curve in Fig. 4. If the industry operates under perfect competition, which area in the diagram indicates producer surplus?

**a.** *aek*

**b.** *dhk*

**c.** *dik*

**d.** *dih*

**e.** none of the above

**15.** Consider the industry demand curve in Fig. 4. Which area in the diagram indicates the deadweight loss from a single-price monopoly?

**a.** *eacf*

**b.** *acd*

**c.** *abd*

**d.** *bcd*

**e.** none of the above

## Price Discrimination

**16.** Which area in Fig. 4 indicates the deadweight loss from a perfect price-discriminating monopoly?

   **a.** *eacf*

   **b.** *acd*

   **c.** *abd*

   **d.** *bcd*

   **e.** none of the above

**17.** When perfect price discrimination occurs, which of the following statements is *false*?

   **a.** Buyers cannot resell the product.

   **b.** The firm can distinguish between buyers.

   **c.** The firm sets prices.

   **d.** The firm captures consumer surplus.

   **e.** Efficiency is worse than with a single-price monopoly.

**18.** The output of a (not perfect) price-discriminating monopoly will be

   **a.** less than a single-price monopoly.

   **b.** more than a single-price monopoly, but less than a perfectly competitive industry.

   **c.** the same amount as a perfectly competitive industry.

   **d.** more than a perfectly competitive industry.

   **e.** none of the above.

**19.** Many video stores charge a lower rental for Wednesday nights compared with weekends. This price discrimination is profitable only if the average willingness to pay for DVDs on Wednesdays is

   **a.** greater than the average willingness to pay for DVDs on weekends.

   **b.** less than the average willingness to pay for DVDs on weekends.

   **c.** positive and the average willingness to pay for DVDs on weekends is negative.

   **d.** negative and the average willingness to pay for DVDs on weekends is positive.

   **e.** equal to one.

## Monopoly Regulation

**20.** A natural monopoly has

   **a.** low fixed cost and low marginal cost.

   **b.** low fixed cost and high marginal cost.

   **c.** high fixed cost and low marginal cost.

   **d.** high fixed cost and high marginal cost.

   **e.** high fixed cost and increasing marginal cost.

**21.** Fig. 5 gives revenue and cost curves for an industry. This industry is a natural monopoly because

   **a.** one firm can supply the entire market at a lower price than can two or more firms.

   **b.** there are decreasing returns to scale over the entire range of demand.

   **c.** there are diseconomies of scale over the entire range of demand.

   **d.** even a single firm will be unable to earn a positive profit in this industry.

   **e.** all of the above are true.

▲ **FIGURE 5**

**22.** Consider the natural monopoly in Fig. 5. If regulators set a price just sufficient for the firm to earn normal profits, what output will it produce?

   **a.** 0, because the firm incurs economic losses when $P = MC$

   **b.** $Q_0$

   **c.** $Q_1$

   **d.** $Q_2$

   **e.** $Q_3$

**23.** Consider the natural monopoly in Fig. 5. If regulators use a marginal cost pricing rule, what line segment gives the amount of subsidy (per unit of output) required to keep the monopolist in business?

   **a.** $ba$

   **b.** $ea$

   **c.** $fc$

   **d.** $gd$

   **e.** $eb$

**24.** Consider the natural monopoly in Fig. 5. Under price cap regulation, regulators will set the price at

**a.** $P_0$.

**b.** $P_1$.

**c.** $P_2$.

**d.** $P_3$.

**e.** $P_4$.

**25.** A monopolist under rate of return regulation has an incentive to

**a.** inflate costs.

**b.** produce more than the efficient quantity of output.

**c.** charge a price equal to marginal cost.

**d.** maximize consumer surplus.

**e.** maximize shareholder profits.

# Short Answer Problems

**1.** A single-price monopoly is the only seller of skyhooks in the Canadian market. The firm's total fixed cost is \$112 per day. Its total variable costs and total costs (both in dollars per day) are shown in Table 2 on the next page.

**a.** Complete the table by computing marginal cost, average variable cost, and average total cost. (*Remember:* Marginal cost should be entered *midway* between rows of output.) If you need to, use the space below for your computations.

| TABLE 2 | | | | | |
|---|---|---|---|---|---|
| Quantity | Total Variable Cost (*TVC*) | Total Cost (*TC*) | Marginal Cost (*MC*) | Average Variable Cost (*AVC*) | Average Total Cost (*ATC*) |
| 9 | 135 | 247 | | | |
| 10 | 144 | 256 | | | |
| 11 | 155 | 267 | | | |
| 12 | 168 | 280 | | | |
| 13 | 183 | 295 | | | |
| 14 | 200 | 312 | | | |
| 15 | 219 | 331 | | | |
| 16 | 240 | 352 | | | |
| 17 | 263 | 375 | | | |
| 18 | 288 | 400 | | | |
| 19 | 315 | 427 | | | |
| 20 | 344 | 456 | | | |

**b.** Table 3 on the next page lists some points on the demand curve facing the firm, as well as the total cost information from part **a**. Complete the table by copying your values for marginal cost from Table 2 and by computing total revenue, marginal revenue, and economic profit. (*Remember:* Marginal revenue, like marginal cost, should be entered *midway* between rows of output.) If you need to, use the space below for your computations.

What is the firm's profit-maximizing quantity of output? At what price will it sell skyhooks? What will be its total economic profit? Explain your answers.

## TABLE 3

| Price (P) | Quantity Demanded ($Q_D$) | Total Revenue (TR) | Marginal Revenue (MR) | Total Cost (TC) | Marginal Cost (MC) | Economic Profit (TR-TC) |
|---|---|---|---|---|---|---|
| 57 | 9 | | | 247 | | |
| 56 | 10 | | | 256 | | |
| 55 | 11 | | | 267 | | |
| 54 | 12 | | | 280 | | |
| 53 | 13 | | | 295 | | |
| 52 | 14 | | | 312 | | |
| 51 | 15 | | | 331 | | |
| 50 | 16 | | | 352 | | |
| 49 | 17 | | | 375 | | |
| 48 | 18 | | | 400 | | |
| 47 | 19 | | | 427 | | |
| 46 | 20 | | | 456 | | |

**c.** On the graph in Fig. 6, plot the demand curve and the *MR*, *AVC*, *ATC*, and *MC* curves corresponding to the data in parts **a** and **b**. Show the equilibrium output and the area of economic profit on your diagram.

▲ **FIGURE 6**

**d.** The firm's cost curves are unchanged, but consumer demand shifts. Table 4 lists points on the new demand curve, as well as the total cost information from part **a**. Complete the table by copying your values for marginal cost from Table 2, and by computing the new values for total revenue, marginal revenue, and economic profit.

| TABLE 4 | | | | | | |
|---|---|---|---|---|---|---|
| Price (P) | Quantity Demanded ($Q_D$) | Total Revenue (TR) | Marginal Revenue (MR) | Total Cost (TC) | Marginal Cost (MC) | Economic Profit (TR-TC) |
| 24.50 | 9 | | | 247 | | |
| 24.00 | 10 | | | 256 | | |
| 23.50 | 11 | | | 267 | | |
| 23.00 | 12 | | | 280 | | |
| 22.50 | 13 | | | 295 | | |
| 22.00 | 14 | | | 312 | | |
| 21.50 | 15 | | | 331 | | |
| 21.00 | 16 | | | 352 | | |
| 20.50 | 17 | | | 375 | | |
| 20.00 | 18 | | | 400 | | |
| 19.50 | 19 | | | 427 | | |
| 19.00 | 20 | | | 456 | | |
| 18.50 | 21 | | | 487 | | |

What is the firm's new profit-maximizing quantity of output? At what price will it now sell skyhooks? What will be its total economic profit? Explain.

**e.** On the graph in Fig. 7, plot the new demand curve and *MR* curve. Copy the *AVC*, *ATC*, and *MC* curves from Fig. 6. Show the new equilibrium output and the area of economic profit on your diagram.

▲ **FIGURE 7**

**f.** Suppose demand falls even further so that the new demand curve equation is $P = 19 - 1/2Q_D$. On the graph in Fig. 8, plot this demand curve and copy the *AVC* curve from Fig. 8. Explain why the monopolist will shut down in the short run.

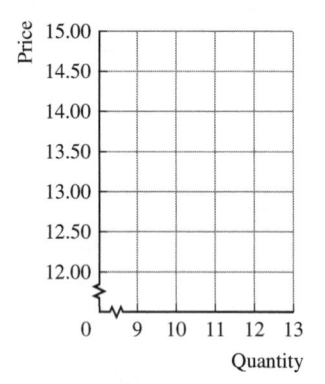

▲ **FIGURE 8**

@ **2.**  You are given the following information about an industry consisting of 100 identical firms.

The demand curve facing the industry is

$$P = 36 - 0.01Q$$

The marginal revenue curve facing the industry is

$$MR = 36 - 0.02Q$$

The marginal cost curve of an individual firm is

$$MC = -12 + 2Q$$

The horizontal sum of the marginal cost curves of all of the firms in the industry is

$$MC = -12 + 0.02Q$$

Use this information to answer the following questions.

**a.** Suppose all 100 firms are controlled by a single-price monopolist. Calculate the profit-maximizing quantity of output for the monopolist. Calculate the price per unit of output that the monopolist will charge.

**b.** Suppose instead that the 100 firms operate independently as a perfectly competitive industry. Calculate the short-run equilibrium quantity of output for the industry as a whole. Calculate the short-run equilibrium price for the industry.

**c.** *Without* using your answer about industry output in part **b**, calculate the short-run equilibrium output per firm.

**d.** Compare the monopoly price and quantity outcomes with the perfect competition price and quantity outcomes.

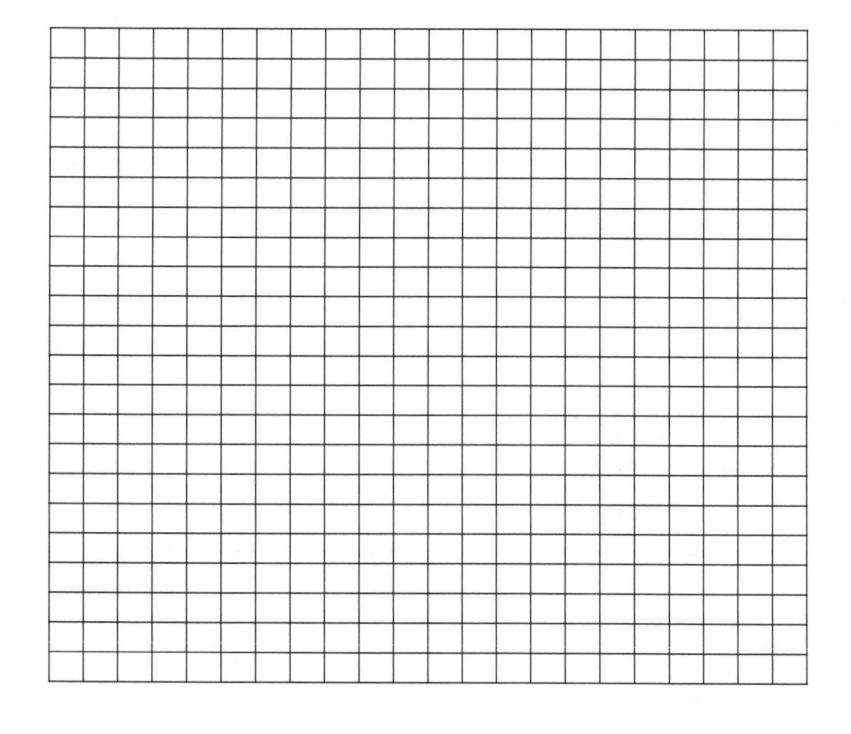

**3.** Before every Olympic Games, the International Olympic Committee (IOC) auctions off the monopoly rights to televise the Games to the highest bidder. NBC won the bid for the Summer 1996 Olympics, paying US$456 million. Yet analysts (correctly) predicted that NBC would not make a profit, since NBC did not profit from telecasts of the 1988 and 1992 Olympics. The questions below will help to understand this apparent paradox.

**a.** What kind of monopoly does NBC have?

**b.** NBC earns revenue by selling airtime to commercial sponsors. Assume that NBC faces a normal, downward-sloping demand curve in selling 30-second commercial spots. Let's ignore for the moment the payment to the IOC and assume that marginal cost and average total cost of delivering the airtime are equal and constant. On the grid, draw a graph representing NBC's profit-maximizing decision. Although you do not have enough information to calculate precise numbers, indicate generally the quantity of commercial spots sold and the price per commercial spot.

**c.** On your graph, indicate the area representing economic profit. If the analysts' predictions were correct, what is the value of this area?

**d.** Why did NBC fail to realize this economic profit?

**4.** Barney's Bistro has two kinds of customers for lunch: stockbrokers and retired senior citizens. The demand schedules for lunches for the two groups are given in Table 5.

Barney decides to price discriminate between the groups by treating each demand separately and charging the price that maximizes profit in each of the two submarkets. Marginal cost and average total cost are equal and constant at $2 per lunch.

## TABLE 5

| | Stockbrokers | | | Senior Citizens | | |
|---|---|---|---|---|---|---|
| Price $(P)$ | Quantity Demanded $(Q_D)$ | Total Revenue $(TR_{SB})$ | Marginal Revenue $(MR_{SB})$ | Quantity Demanded $(Q_D)$ | Total Revenue $(TR_{SC})$ | Marginal Revenue $(MR_{SC})$ |
| 8 | 0 | | | 0 | | |
| 7 | 1 | | | 0 | | |
| 6 | 2 | | | 0 | | |
| 5 | 3 | | | 1 | | |
| 4 | 4 | | | 2 | | |
| 3 | 5 | | | 3 | | |
| 2 | 6 | | | 4 | | |
| 1 | 7 | | | 5 | | |
| 0 | 8 | | | 6 | | |

ⓐ **a.** Complete Table 5 on the previous page by computing the total and marginal revenue associated with stockbroker demand ($TR_{SB}$ and $MR_{SB}$) as well as the total and marginal revenue associated with senior citizen demand ($TR_{SC}$ and $MR_{SC}$). (*Remember:* Marginal revenue should be entered *midway* between rows.) If you need to, use the space below for your computations.

**b.** What are the profit-maximizing output and price for stockbrokers?

**c.** What are the profit-maximizing output and price for senior citizens?

**d.** What is total economic profit?

**e.** Show that the total economic profit in part **d** is the maximum by comparing it with total economic profit if instead Barney served 1 additional lunch *each* to stockbrokers and senior citizens, and 1 less lunch *each* to stockbrokers and senior citizens.

**f.** What is the consumer surplus for stockbrokers? for senior citizens? for all customers?

**5.** The price of the last unit sold and the quantity sold are exactly the same in an industry under perfect competition and under a perfect price-discriminating monopoly. Are consumers therefore indifferent between the two? Explain.

**6.** Fig. 9 gives the demand, marginal revenue, and marginal cost curves for a certain industry. Your task is to illustrate how consumer and producer surplus are distributed under each of four ways of organizing the industry. In each case redraw any relevant part of Fig. 9 and then (1) indicate the region of the graph corresponding to consumer surplus by drawing horizontal lines through it; (2) indicate the region corresponding to producer surplus by drawing vertical lines through it; and (3) indicate the region (if any) corresponding to deadweight loss by putting dots in the area.

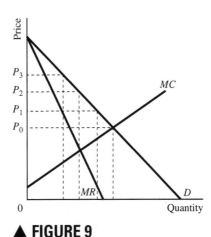

▲ **FIGURE 9**

**a.** The industry consists of many perfectly competitive firms.

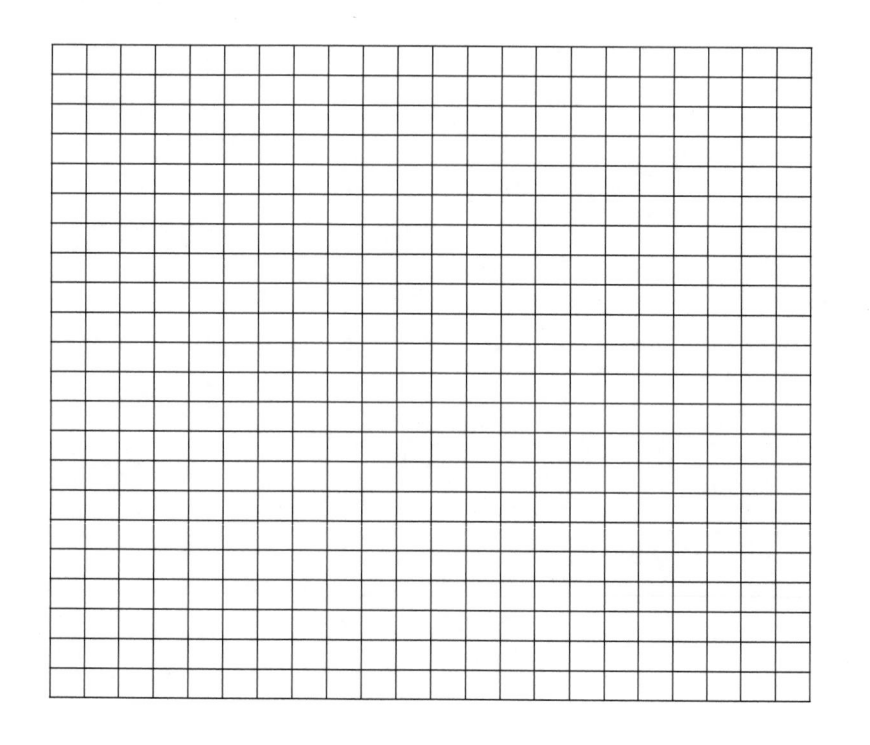

**b.** The industry is a single-price monopoly.

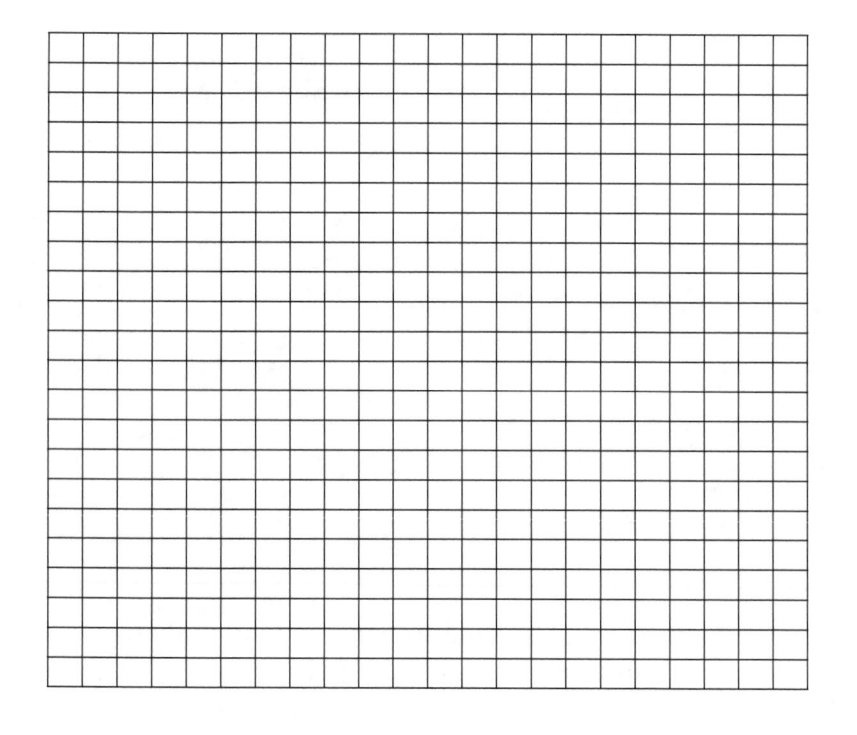

**c.** The industry is a perfect price-discriminating monopoly.

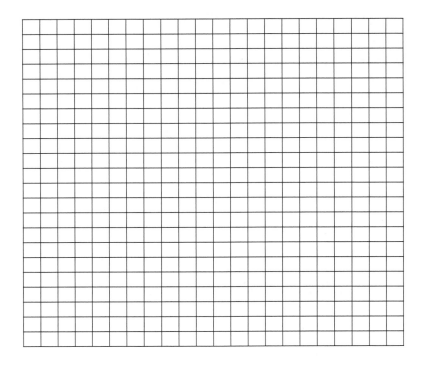

**7. a.** Why is rate of return regulation equivalent to average cost pricing?

**b.** Why is rate of return regulation being increasingly replaced by price cap regulation?

**8.** Fig. 10 illustrates the industry demand, marginal revenue (*MR*), and marginal cost (*MC*) curves in a monopoly. The industry is regulated.

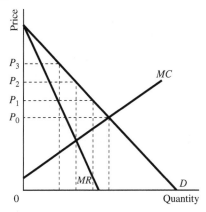

▲ **FIGURE 10**

**a.** What price and quantity are predicted by the public interest theory of regulation? Why?

**b.** What price and quantity are predicted by the capture theory of regulation? Why?

# Answers

## True/False and Explain

1. **F** When there are *no* close substitutes. (300–301)
2. **T** Definition of natural monopoly. (300–301)
3. **T** Without barriers to entry, other firms will enter industry, creating competition. (300–301)
4. **F** *MR* is negative. (302–305)
5. **F** Monopolist has no supply curve. (302–305)
ⓒ 6. **T** Average of all (equal) prices of product = price. (302–305)
7. **T** Area below competitive price and above *MC* for reduced output. (306–309)
8. **F** In equilibrium, economic profit may be totally eliminated by rent-seeking costs. (306–309)
9. **F** Can*not* be readily resold. (309–312)
10. **F** To capture consumer surplus and convert to economic profit. (309–312)
11. **T** Demand curve gives revenue for each successive unit sold (at different price). (309–312)
12. **T** $P = AR = ATC$. Outcome is inefficient because there is deadweight loss, but more efficient than an unregulated monopoly. (313–315)
13. **F** Industry captures more of total surplus. (313–315)
14. **T** Increased costs yield increased profits. (313–315)
15. **T** Specifies highest price firms are allowed to charge; used in electricity and telecommunications industries. (313–315)

## Multiple-Choice

1. **b** Others are legal barriers. (300–301)
2. **d** *TR* ($P = \$7$) = $\$7 \times 7 = \$49$. *TR* ($P = \$6$) = $\$6 \times 8 = \$48$. $MR = \Delta TR = \$48 - \$49$. (302–305)
3. **d** *MR*–*MC* comparisons are key. Revenue **a** and cost **b** are important, but must be *compared* for profitability. (302–305)
4. **d** *TR* would be decreased needlessly. Monopolist could decrease *Q* and raise *P* to increase *TR*. (302–305)
5. **b** *Q* where *MR* = *MC*. Highest *P* consumers will pay for 3 units. (302–305)
ⓒ 6. **c** $(AR - ATC) \times Q = (\$6 - \$4) \times 3$. (302–305)
7. **c** Rule for choosing output. (302–305)
8. **a** Draw graph. $Q_{current} > Q$ corresponding to $MR = MC$. (302–305)
ⓒ 9. **d** Sum of $(P - MC)$ for each unit of output. (306–309)
ⓒ 10. **d** **a** is true for both. **b** is true for competitor only. **c** is false for both. (306–309)
11. **a** Definition. Activity has costs. (306–309)
12. **c** Monopoly profit = resources used rent seeking. (306–309)
13. **b** Area above price but below demand (willingness to pay). (306–309)
14. **d** Area below price but above *MC*. (306–309)

15. **b** Sum of lost producer (*bcd*) and consumer (*abd*) surplus compared to competitive outcome. (306–309)

16. **e** Deadweight loss is zero. (309–312)

17. **e** Efficiency the same as perfect competition. (309–312)

18. **b** c is true for perfect price discrimination. (309–312)

19. **b** Charge lower price with higher $\eta$ and higher price with lower $\eta$. (309–312)

20. **c** Yielding an always downward-sloping *LRAC*. (313–315)

21. **a** Definition of natural monopoly. (313–315)

22. **d** Where $P = ATC$. (313–315)

23. **d** To cover loss per unit of output. (313–315)

24. **c** (313–315)

25. **a** To increase profits. (313–315)

## Short Answer Problems

1. **a.** Completed Table 2 is given here as Table 2 Solution.

**TABLE 2  Solution**

| Quantity | Total Variable Cost (*TVC*) | Total Cost (*TC*) | Marginal Cost (*MC*) | Average Variable Cost (*AVC*) | Average Total Cost (*ATC*) |
|---|---|---|---|---|---|
| 9 | 135 | 247 | | 15.00 | 27.44 |
| | | | ... 9 | | |
| 10 | 144 | 256 | | 14.40 | 25.60 |
| | | | ... 11 | | |
| 11 | 155 | 267 | | 14.09 | 24.27 |
| | | | ... 13 | | |
| 12 | 168 | 280 | | 14.00 | 23.33 |
| | | | ... 15 | | |
| 13 | 183 | 295 | | 14.08 | 22.69 |
| | | | ... 17 | | |
| 14 | 200 | 312 | | 14.29 | 22.29 |
| | | | ... 19 | | |
| 15 | 219 | 331 | | 14.60 | 22.07 |
| | | | ... 21 | | |
| 16 | 240 | 352 | | 15.00 | 22.00 |
| | | | ... 23 | | |
| 17 | 263 | 375 | | 15.47 | 22.06 |
| | | | ... 25 | | |
| 18 | 288 | 400 | | 16.00 | 22.22 |
| | | | ... 27 | | |
| 19 | 315 | 427 | | 16.58 | 22.47 |
| | | | ... 29 | | |
| 20 | 344 | 456 | | 17.20 | 22.80 |

**b.** Completed Table 3 is shown here as Table 3 Solution.

**TABLE 3  Solution**

| Price (P) | Quantity Demanded ($Q_D$) | Total Revenue (TR) | Marginal Revenue (MR) | Total Cost (TC) | Marginal Cost (MC) | Economic Profit (TR-TC) |
|---|---|---|---|---|---|---|
| 57 | 9 | 513 | | 247 | | 266 |
| | | | ⋯ 47 | | ⋯ 9 | |
| 56 | 10 | 560 | | 256 | | 304 |
| | | | ⋯ 45 | | ⋯ 11 | |
| 55 | 11 | 605 | | 267 | | 338 |
| | | | ⋯ 43 | | ⋯ 13 | |
| 54 | 12 | 648 | | 280 | | 368 |
| | | | ⋯ 41 | | ⋯ 15 | |
| 53 | 13 | 689 | | 295 | | 394 |
| | | | ⋯ 39 | | ⋯ 17 | |
| 52 | 14 | 728 | | 312 | | 416 |
| | | | ⋯ 37 | | ⋯ 19 | |
| 51 | 15 | 765 | | 331 | | 434 |
| | | | ⋯ 35 | | ⋯ 21 | |
| 50 | 16 | 800 | | 352 | | 448 |
| | | | ⋯ 33 | | ⋯ 23 | |
| 49 | 17 | 833 | | 375 | | 458 |
| | | | ⋯ 31 | | ⋯ 25 | |
| 48 | 18 | 864 | | 400 | | 464 |
| | | | ⋯ 29 | | ⋯ 27 | |
| 47 | 19 | 893 | | 427 | | 466 |
| | | | ⋯ 27 | | ⋯ 29 | |
| 46 | 20 | 920 | | 456 | | 464 |

Equilibrium output occurs where $MC = MR = 28$, $Q = 19$, $P = \$47$, economic profit = \$466 per day.

The profit-maximizing quantity of output occurs where marginal cost equals marginal revenue, at 19 units. The maximum price the firm can charge and still sell 19 units is \$47. This combination of quantity and price yields a total economic profit of \$466, which, as can be seen from the table, is the maximum possible profit.

**c.** The requested diagram appears in Fig. 6 Solution.

▲ **FIGURE 6  Solution**

**d.** Completed Table 4 is given here as Table 4 Solution.

| Price (P) | Quantity Demanded ($Q_D$) | Total Revenue (TR) | Marginal Revenue (MR) | Total Cost (TC) | Marginal Cost (MC) | Economic Profit (TR-TC) |
|---|---|---|---|---|---|---|
| **TABLE 4** Solution | | | | | | |
| 24.50 | 9 | 220.50 | | 247 | | −26.50 |
| | | | ··· 19.50 | | ··· 9 | |
| 24.00 | 10 | 240.00 | | 256 | | −16.00 |
| | | | ··· 18.50 | | ··· 11 | |
| 23.50 | 11 | 258.50 | | 267 | | −8.50 |
| | | | ··· 17.50 | | ··· 13 | |
| 23.00 | 12 | 276.00 | | 280 | | −4.00 |
| | | | ··· 16.50 | | ··· 15 | |
| 22.50 | 13 | 292.50 | | 295 | | −2.50 |
| | | | ··· 15.50 | | ··· 17 | |
| 22.00 | 14 | 308.00 | | 312 | | −4.00 |
| | | | ··· 14.50 | | ··· 19 | |
| 21.50 | 15 | 322.50 | | 331 | | −8.50 |
| | | | ··· 13.50 | | ··· 21 | |
| 21.00 | 16 | 336.00 | | 352 | | −16.00 |
| | | | ··· 12.50 | | ··· 23 | |
| 20.50 | 17 | 348.50 | | 375 | | −26.50 |
| | | | ··· 11.50 | | ··· 25 | |
| 20.00 | 18 | 360.00 | | 400 | | −40.00 |
| | | | ··· 10.50 | | ··· 27 | |
| 19.50 | 19 | 370.50 | | 427 | | −56.50 |
| | | | ··· 9.50 | | ··· 29 | |
| 19.00 | 20 | 380.00 | | 456 | | −76.00 |

Equilibrium output occurs where $MC = MR = 16$. $Q = 13$. $P = \$22.50$. economic profit $= -\$2.50$.

The profit-maximizing quantity of output occurs where marginal cost equals marginal revenue, now at 13 units. The maximum price the firm can charge and still sell 13 units is $22.50. This combination of quantity and price yields a total economic profit of −$2.50 (an economic loss). As can be seen from the table, this is the minimum possible loss. The firm will continue to produce in the short run, because this loss is less than its shutdown loss, which would be $112, the amount of its fixed cost.

**e.** The requested diagram appears in Fig. 7 Solution.

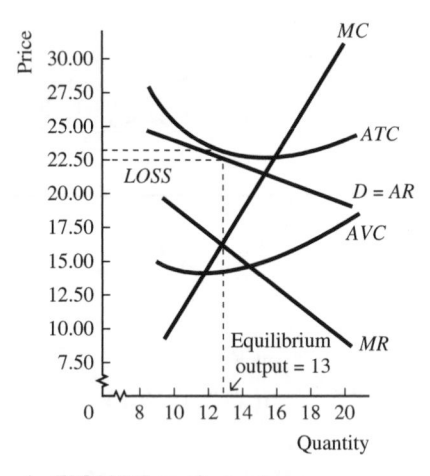

▲ **FIGURE 7  Solution**

**f.** The requested diagram appears in Fig. 8 Solution. Since the demand curve is everywhere below the *AVC* curve, no matter what quantity of output the firm might produce, price will be less than *AVC*. This means that the firm will lose money on every unit produced in addition to losing its total fixed cost. The monopolist will minimize loss in this case by shutting down and losing just its fixed cost ($112).

▲ **FIGURE 8  Solution**

ⓒ **2.  a.** The monopolist will choose the quantity of output where marginal revenue equals marginal cost. To calculate this quantity, set the equation for marginal revenue equal to the equation for industry marginal cost (since the monopolist controls all of the firms).

$$36 - 0.02Q = -12 + 0.02Q$$
$$48 = 0.04Q$$
$$1,200 = Q$$

To calculate the price that the monopolist will charge, substitute the quantity 1,200 into the demand equation. This is the mathematical equivalent of graphically, after finding the quantity corresponding to the intersection of $MC$ and $MR$, moving your eye up to the demand curve to read the price.

$$P = 36 - 0.01Q$$
$$P = 36 - 0.01(1,200)$$
$$P = 36 - 12$$
$$P = 24$$

**b.** The perfectly competitive industry's short-run equilibrium quantity of output occurs where industry demand intersects industry supply. Set the industry demand equation equal to the industry supply equation, which is the horizontal sum of the marginal cost curves of all firms in the industry.

$$36 - 0.01Q = -12 + 0.02Q$$
$$48 = 0.03Q$$
$$1,600 = Q$$

To calculate the short-run equilibrium price for the industry, we can substitute the quantity 1,600 into either the industry demand equation or the industry supply equation. Using the industry demand equation yields

$$P = 36 - 0.01Q$$
$$P = 36 - 0.01(1,600)$$
$$P = 36 - 16$$
$$P = 20$$

Using the industry supply equation yields the same result:

$$P = -12 + 0.02Q$$
$$P = -12 + 0.02(1,600)$$
$$P = -12 + 32$$
$$P = 20$$

**c.** If industry output is 1,600 units and there are 100 identical firms, then obviously the output per firm is 1,600 units/100 firms equals 16 units/firm. But the question specifically asks you *not* to use the information about industry output.

The other way to calculate the short-run equilibrium output per firm is to substitute the equilibrium price of 20 into the individual firm's marginal cost curve, which is also its short-run supply curve:

$$P = -12 + 2Q$$
$$20 = -12 + 2Q$$
$$20 = 2Q$$
$$16 = Q$$

**d.** The monopoly price ($24) is higher than the perfect competition price ($20) and the monopoly quantity of output (1,200) is lower than the perfect competition quantity of output (1,600).

**3. a.** NBC had a legal monopoly, based on a public franchise—an exclusive right granted to a firm to supply a good or service.

**b.** The requested diagram is shown in Fig. 11. The quantity of commercial spots sold is $Q_{CS}$ and the price is $P_{CS}$.

**c.** The shaded rectangle above *ATC* and below $P_{CS}$ in Fig. 11 represents economic profit. That profit, which is based on costs that exclude the US$456 million payment to the IOC, will be US$456 million if the analysts are correct.

**d.** NBC fails to make an economic profit because of the costs of rent seeking. NBC competes for the monopoly rights to televise the Olympics. Bidders continue

**▲ FIGURE 11**

to offer a higher price for those rights until the price equals the value of the economic profit to be earned from owning the rights

**4. a.** The completed table is Table 5 Solution.

**b.** The profit-maximizing output for stockbrokers occurs when $MC = \$2 = MR_{SB}$. This is at 3 lunches and the price is $5 per lunch to stockbrokers.

**c.** The profit-maximizing output for senior citizens occurs when $MC = \$2 = MR_{SC}$. This occurs at 2 lunches and the price to senior citizens is $4 per lunch.

**d.** Total revenue is $15 from stockbrokers, $8 from senior citizens, or $23. Since average total cost is $2 per lunch, total cost is $2 × 5 lunches = $10. Total economic profit is $13.

**e.** If Barney served 1 more lunch each to stockbrokers and senior citizens, that would be 4 lunches for stockbrokers ($4 per lunch) and 3 lunches for senior citizens ($3 per lunch). Since average total cost is $2 per lunch, total

## TABLE 5  Solution

| | Stockbrokers | | | Senior Citizens | | |
|---|---|---|---|---|---|---|
| Price $(P)$ | Quantity Demanded $(Q_D)$ | Total Revenue $(TR_{SB})$ | Marginal Revenue $(MR_{SB})$ | Quantity Demanded $(QD)$ | Total Revenue $(TR_{SC})$ | Marginal Revenue $(MR_{SC})$ |
| 8 | 0 | 0 | | 0 | 0 | |
| | | | .... 7 | | | .... 0 |
| 7 | 1 | 7 | | 0 | 0 | |
| | | | .... 5 | | | .... 0 |
| 6 | 2 | 12 | | 0 | 0 | |
| | | | .... 3 | | | .... 5 |
| 5 | 3 | 15 | | 1 | 5 | |
| | | | .... 1 | | | .... 3 |
| 4 | 4 | 16 | | 2 | 8 | |
| | | | .... −1 | | | .... 1 |
| 3 | 5 | 15 | | 3 | 9 | |
| | | | .... −3 | | | .... −1 |
| 2 | 6 | 12 | | 4 | 8 | |
| | | | .... −5 | | | .... −3 |
| 1 | 7 | 7 | | 5 | 5 | |
| | | | .... −7 | | | .... −5 |
| 0 | 8 | 0 | | 6 | 0 | |

cost is $2 \times 7$ lunches $= \$14$. Total revenue is $16 from stockbrokers, $9 from senior citizens, or $25. Total economic profit is $11, less than the $13 in part **d**.

If Barney served 1 less lunch each to stockbrokers and senior citizens, that would be 2 lunches for stockbrokers ($6 per lunch) and 1 lunch for senior citizens ($5 per lunch). Since average total cost is $2 per lunch, total cost is $2 \times 3$ lunches $= \$6$. Total revenue is $12 from stockbrokers, $5 from senior citizens, or $17. Total economic profit is $11, less than the $13 in part **d**.

**f.** The consumer surplus of stockbrokers is

$$(\$7 - \$5) + (\$6 - \$5) + (\$5 - \$5) = \$3$$

The consumer surplus of senior citizens is

$$(\$5 - \$4) + (\$4 - \$4) = \$1$$

The consumer surplus of all customers is

$$\$3 + \$1 = \$4$$

**5.** While the quantity sold and the price charged to the last customer are the same for perfect competition and a perfect price discriminator, the distribution of consumer surplus is not the same. Since a perfect price discriminator charges each customer the most she is willing to pay, there is no consumer surplus. Any consumer surplus that would have occurred under perfect competition now accrues to the monopoly. Consumers would like to obtain more consumer surplus, and therefore pay less for the same amount. Consequently, consumers prefer perfect competition.

**6. a.** Under perfect competition, price equals marginal cost. The amount of consumer surplus is given by the area under the demand curve but above the price $(P_0)$ while the amount of producer surplus is given by the area above the $MC$ curve but below the price; see Fig. 9 Solution (a) on the next page.

**b.** If the industry is a single-price monopoly, price will be greater than $MC$ and output will be less than under competition. Consumer surplus is still given by the area under the demand curve but above the price ($P_2$), while producer surplus is given by the area above the $MC$ curve but below

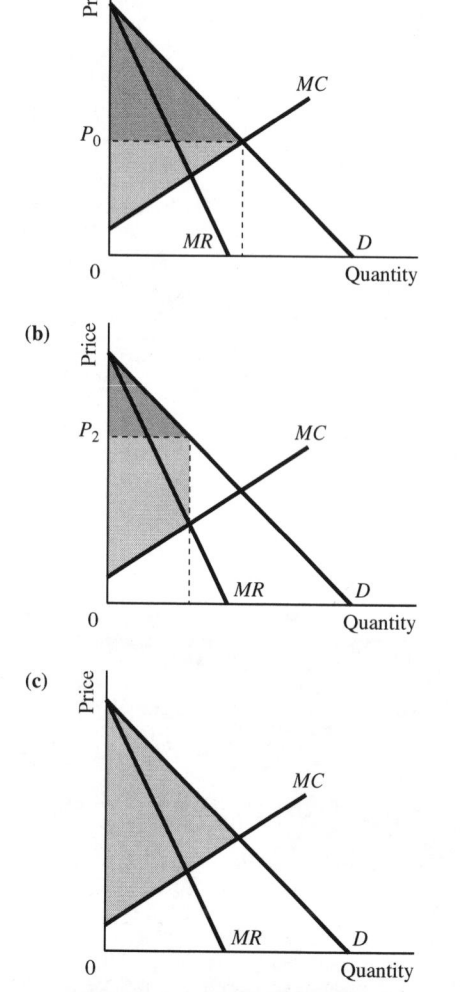

▲ **FIGURE 9** Solution

the price up to the monopoly level of output. The remaining part of the large triangle is a deadweight loss—the amount of surplus under competition that is lost under a single-price monopoly; see Fig. 9 Solution (b).

**c.** Under perfect price discrimination, all of the potential surplus is captured by the producer and there is no deadweight loss (or consumer surplus). See Fig. 9 Solution (c).

**7. a.** The key here is to recall that economic cost includes a normal rate of return. Because rate of return regulation sets a price that allows a normal rate of return, it is setting the price equal to average total cost.

**b.** Under rate of return regulation, firms have an incentive to inflate their costs, since they are guaranteed a normal rate of return on all costs. A price ceiling in price cap regulation gives firms an incentive to operate efficiently and keep costs under control. Regulators try and set a price ceiling that yields the same output as (uninflated) average cost pricing. In case the price is set too high, price cap regulation is often combined with earnings sharing regulation, so profits above a target level must be shared with firms' customers.

**8. a.** Social interest theory predicts that regulators set price and quantity to maximize total surplus. This means they choose quantity (and price) where $MC$ is equal to demand. This corresponds to a quantity of 500 units and a price of $4 per unit.

**b.** Capture theory predicts that regulators choose quantity and price to maximize the ˜profit of the industry. This is the quantity a profit-maximizing monopolist would choose, 300 units, where $MC = MR$. The highest price that could be charged and still sell that quantity can be read from the demand curve: $6 per unit.

# 14 Monopolistic Competition

## Key Concepts
### Monopolistic Competition
**Monopolistic competition** is a model of market structure in which many firms compete; there is **product differentiation** (firms make similar but slightly different products) giving firms some monopoly power; firms compete on product quality, price, and marketing; there is free entry and exit.

- Firm ignores other individual firms and collusion is impossible because all firms have a small market share.
- Firm faces a downward-sloping demand curve.
- Marginal revenue curve $\neq$ demand curve.
- Firm can choose price and output.

## Price and Output and in Monopolistic Competition
Outcomes:

- Profit maximization (or loss minimization): choose $Q$ where $MC = MR$, charge highest possible price (on demand curve).
- Short-run economic profit possible, attracts entry, causing leftward shift of demand (and $MR$) curves facing each firm.

- Short-run economic loss possible, some firms exit, causing rightward shift of demand (and *MR*) curves facing each remaining firm.
- Long-run economic profit $= 0$, $P = ATC$. But

  - *ATC* not at minimum. Firm has **excess capacity**, producing *below* its **efficient scale** where $ATC =$ minimum.

  - $P > MC$ by amount of **markup**.

- Inefficiency of monopolistic competition must be weighed against gain of greater product variety.

# Product Development and Marketing

To restore economic profits, monopolistically competitive firms must continuously innovate and develop new products. New firms enter with similar products, compete away economic profits—the cycle continues.

Marketing expenditures on advertising and packaging (selling costs) are used to *create perception* of product differentiation even when actual product differences are small, and to **signal** quality.

- Selling costs are fixed costs that increase total costs, but average total cost might decrease if output increases enough.
- Selling costs might increase demand for a firm's product, but might also decrease demand by increasing competition.

Inefficiencies of monopolistic competition (selling costs and excess capacity) must be weighed against gain of greater product variety.

# Helpful Hints

1. Most industries are neither perfectly competitive nor pure monopolies; they lie somewhere between these two extremes. This does not mean that the last two chapters have been wasted. By examining firms under these extreme market structures, we now can discuss the wide range of industries between them in just two chapters.

   The intermediate forms of market structure share many characteristics of perfect competition and/or monopoly. Consider the profit-maximizing rule of choosing the output where $MC = MR$. The rule applies not only in perfect competition and monopoly, but also in monopolistic competition and many of the oligopoly models we will see in Chapter 15. Free entry leads to zero long-run economic profit in both perfect competition and monopolistic competition. The downward-sloping demand and marginal revenue curves of monopoly also apply to monopolistic competition, a kinked demand curve, and dominant firm oligopoly models.

   The extreme and unrealistic assumptions of models of perfect competition and monopoly allow us to isolate the impact of important forces like profit maximization and important constraints like competition and market demand. These forces and constraints also operate in more realistic market structures. But it was necessary to isolate these forces and constraints beforehand rather than attempt to immediately analyse "realistic" market structures like monopolistic competition and oligopoly, which would have been a confusing jumble of details and possible outcomes. It would have been like driving in a strange, large city without a road map.

2. In graphing a monopolistically competitive firm in long-run equilibrium, be sure that the $ATC$ curve is tangent to the demand curve at the same level of output at which the $MC$ and $MR$ curves intersect. Also be sure that the $MC$ curve intersects the $ATC$ curve at the minimum point on the $ATC$ curve.

# Self-Test

## True/False and Explain

### What Is Monopolistic Competition?

1. Barriers to entry give monopolistically competitive firms some monopoly power.

2. Product differentiation gives monopolistically competitive firms some monopoly power.

3. Monopolistically competitive firms compete only on price.

4. Monopolistically competitive firms pay close attention to the actions of other individual firms.

5. Monopolistically competitive firms do not collude with other firms to fix higher prices.

### Price and Output in Monopolistic Competition

6. In monopolistic competition, short-run profits attract new entry, shifting each individual firm's demand curve rightward.

7. Free entry is the key characteristic of monopolistic competition that produces excess capacity.

8. When a monopolistically competitive industry is in long-run equilibrium, economic profit is zero and price equals minimum average total cost.

**9.** In monopolistic competition, price exceeds marginal cost.

**10.** Monopolistically competitive firms can earn an economic profit in the long run.

## Product Development and Marketing

**11.** Firms in monopolistic competition must innovate continuously to enjoy economic profits.

**12.** Selling costs always increase average total costs.

**13.** Advertising by monopolistic competitors is always efficient.

**14.** Advertising can signal product quality.

**15.** Advertising makes a monopolistically competitive firm's demand curve more elastic.

# Multiple-Choice

## What Is Monopolistic Competition?

1. In monopolistic competition, firms
   a. can collude.
   b. strategically interact with other firms.
   c. have an element of monopoly power.
   d. face a kinked demand curve.
   e. do all of the above.

2. A monopolistically competitive firm is like a *monopoly* because
   a. both face perfectly elastic demand.
   b. both earn an economic profit in the long run.
   c. both have *MR* curves that are below their demand curves.
   d. neither is protected by high barriers to entry.
   e. both are protected by high barriers to entry.

3. A monopolistically competitive firm is like a *perfectly competitive* firm because
   a. both face perfectly elastic demand.
   b. both earn an economic profit in the long run.
   c. both have MR curves that are below their demand curves.
   d. neither is protected by high barriers to entry.
   e. both are protected by high barriers to entry.

4. With product differentiation
   a. monopolistically competitive firms can compete on quality and marketing.
   b. a firm makes a product that is slightly different from its competitors products.
   c. a firm's demand curve is more inelastic compared to identical products.
   d. a firm faces a downward-sloping demand curve.
   e. all of the above are true.

**5.** In monopolistic competition,
   **a.** the size of firms is small relative to the size of the industry.
   **b.** the size of firms is large relative to the size of the industry.
   **c.** the size of firms is the same as the size of the industry.
   **d.** there are two firms in the industry.
   **e.** there is one firm in the industry.

**6.** A monopolistically competitive firm can set the price of what it sells because of
   **a.** barriers to entry.
   **b.** economies of scale.
   **c.** many buyers.
   **d.** inelastic demand.
   **e.** product differentiation.

**7.** Brand name products are an example of
   **a.** economies of scope.
   **b.** economies of scale.
   **c.** product differentiation.
   **d.** collusion.
   **e.** none of the above.

## Price and Output in Monopolistic Competition

**8.** For a monopolistically competitive firm in long-run equilibrium,
   **a.** $P = MC$.
   **b.** $MC = ATC$.
   **c.** $AR = ATC$, but $P > MC$.
   **d.** $MC = AR$, but $ATC > AR$.
   **e.** none of the above is true.

**9.** Fig. 1 represents a monopolistically competitive firm in short-run equilibrium. What is the firm's level of output?

    **a.** $Q_1$

    **b.** $Q_2$

    **c.** $Q_3$

    **d.** $Q_4$

    **e.** zero

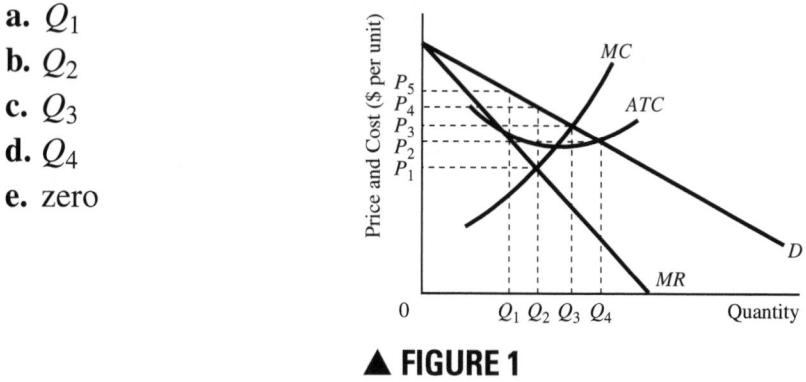

**▲ FIGURE 1**

**11.** Fig. 1 represents a monopolistically competitive firm in short-run equilibrium. In the long run,

    **a.** new firms will enter, and each existing firm's demand shifts leftward.

    **b.** new firms will enter, and each existing firm's demand shifts rightward.

    **c.** existing firms will leave, and each remaining firm's demand shifts leftward.

    **d.** existing firms will leave, and each remaining firm's demand shifts rightward.

    **e.** there will be no change from the short run.

**10.** Fig. 1 represents a monopolistically competitive firm in short-run equilibrium. What is the firm's economic profit *per unit*?

    **a.** $P_4 - P_2$

    **b.** $P_4 - P_1$

    **c.** $P_4$

    **d.** $P_3$

    **e.** None of the above

**12.** Under monopolistic competition, long-run economic profit tends toward zero because of

    **a.** product differentiation.

    **b.** the lack of barriers to entry.

    **c.** excess capacity.

    **d.** inefficiency.

    **e.** downward-sloping demand curves facing each firm.

**13.** In the long run, a monopolistically competitive firm will earn the same economic profit as

**a.** a monopolistically competitive firm in the short run.

**b.** a member of a cartel.

**c.** a pure price-discriminating monopolist.

**d.** a perfectly competitive firm.

**e.** none of the above.

**14.** Which of the following is true for perfect competition, monopolistic competition, and single-price monopoly?

**a.** homogeneous product

**b.** zero long-run economic profit

**c.** short-run profit-maximizing quantity where $MC = MR$

**d.** easy entry and exit

**e.** none of the above

**15.** In the long run, the firm in monopolistic competition will

**a.** face a perfectly elastic demand curve.

**b.** produce more than the quantity that minimizes *ATC*.

**c.** produce less than the quantity that minimizes *ATC*.

**d.** produce the quantity that minimizes *ATC*.

**e.** earn economic profit.

**16.** In the long run, a monopolistically competitive firm will produce the output at which price equals

**a.** marginal cost.

**b.** marginal revenue.

**c.** average variable cost.

**d.** average total cost.

**e.** **b** and **d**.

**17.** Which of the following characteristics is *not* shared by a single-price monopoly and monopolistic competition?

   **a.** firms face a downward-sloping demand curve

   **b.** profit-maximizing quantity where $MC = MR$

   **c.** equilibrium $ATC$ above minimum $ATC$

   **d.** positive long-run economic profit

   **e.** positive long-run normal profit

**18.** When firms in a monopolistically competitive industry incur economic losses, firms will

   **a.** enter the industry, and demand increases for the original firms.

   **b.** enter the industry, and demand decreases for the original firms.

   **c.** exit the industry, and demand increases for the original firms.

   **d.** exit the industry, and demand decreases for the original firms.

   **e.** exit the industry, and supply increases for the original firms.

**19.** In the long run, all firms in a monopolistically competitive industry earn

   **a.** zero accounting profit.

   **b.** zero normal profit.

   **c.** zero economic profit.

   **d.** positive economic profit.

   **e.** negative economic profit.

## Product Development and Marketing

**20.** Selling costs

   **a.** are variable costs that increase total cost.

   **b.** always increase demand for a firm's product.

   **c.** always decrease demand by increasing competition.

   **d.** always provide consumers with valuable services.

   **e.** include marketing expenditures on advertising and packaging.

**21.** Because consumers value product variety,

    **a.** monopolistic competition is more efficient than perfect competition.

    **b.** similar products will not have the same price.

    **c.** the inefficiencies of monopolistic competition must be weighed against the benefits of variety.

    **d.** monopolistically competitive firms earn long-run economic profits.

    **e.** brand names are inefficient.

**22.** Monopolistically competitive firms constantly develop new products in order to

    **a.** make the demand for their product more elastic.

    **b.** increase demand for their product.

    **c.** increase the quantity demanded of their product

    **d.** increase supply of their product

    **e.** do all of the above.

**23.** A firm's decision about how much to spend on product development depends on

    **a.** only marginal revenue from product development.

    **b.** only marginal cost of product development.

    **c.** both marginal revenue from and marginal cost of product development.

    **d.** both marginal social revenue from and marginal social cost of product development.

    **e.** both average revenue from and average cost of product development.

**24.** In monopolistic competition, firms

    **a.** have high selling costs.

    **b.** have deficient capacity in the long run.

    **c.** rarely advertise.

    **d.** avoid brand names to keep costs down.

    **e.** produce the efficient quantity of output.

**25.** An advantage of monopolistic competition over perfect competition is
   **a.** economic profit.
   **b.** product variety.
   **c.** excess capacity.
   **d.** efficiency.
   **e.** economies of scale.

## Short Answer Problems

**1.** Consider a single firm in a monopolistically competitive industry in the short run. Using axes like those shown in Fig. 2, on the grid below draw a new graph for a firm making an economic profit.

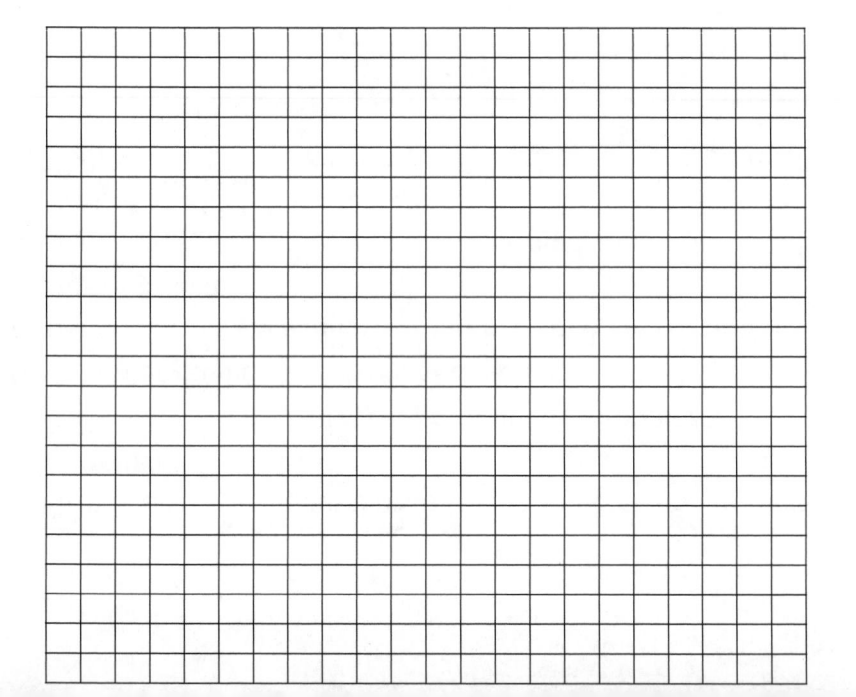

▲ **FIGURE 2**

**2.** Consider a single firm in a monopolistically competitive industry in the short run. Using axes like those shown in Fig. 2, on the grid below draw a new graph for a firm incurring a loss that will cause shutdown.

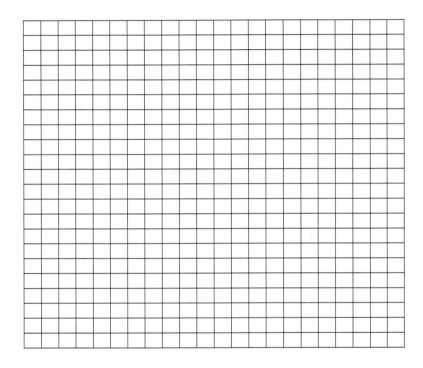

**3.** Consider a single firm in a monopolistically competitive industry in the short run. Using axes like those shown in Fig. 2, on the grid below draw a new graph for a firm that is incurring a loss, but is still producing.

**4.** Starting from the situation in Short Answer Problem **3**, explain what will happen in this industry and how your graph in Problem **3** will be affected. (No new graph is required.)

**5.** Using axes like those shown in Fig. 2, on the grid below draw a new graph for a firm in a monopolistically competitive industry in long-run equilibrium.

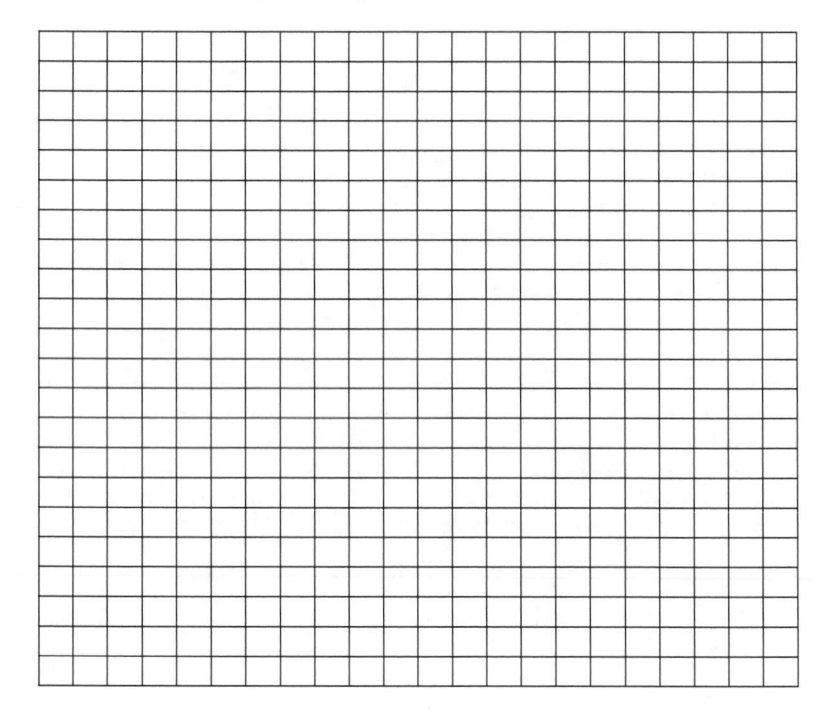

<sup>Ct</sup> **6.** Consider a monopolistically competitive industry in long-run equilibrium. Firm *A* in this industry attempts to increase profits by advertising.

**a.** On the grid below, draw a graph like the one in Fig. 3 to show what will happen in the short run as a result of the decision to advertise. Briefly explain your graph in the space provided in the right column.

▲ **FIGURE 3**

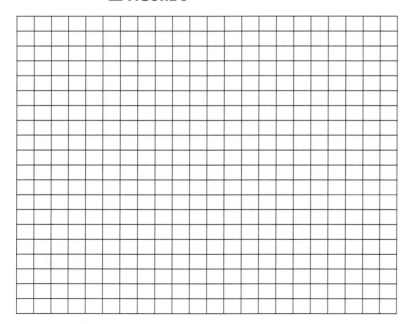

**b.** If the firm is successful in raising profits in the short run, what will happen in the long run?

7. When all firms in a monopolistically competitive industry advertise, it makes the demand curve facing each firm more elastic. Explain why, using the concept of substitutes in consumption.

8. You are driving along an unfamiliar highway and you are hungry. There are many unfamiliar restaurants and a McDonald's. Even if you don't like McDonald's, explain why you might choose to eat there.

# Answers

## True/False and Explain

1. **F** Free entry and exit in monopolistic competition. (324–325)

2. **T** Creates a downward-sloping demand curve; there is some ability to raise price without sales going to zero. (324–325)

3. **F** With differentiated products, also compete on quality and marketing. (324–325)

4. **F** Sensitive to average market price, but not individual competitors, as in oligopoly in Chapter 15. (324–325)

5. **T** With many firms, coordination is difficult and collusion is not possible. (324–325)

6. **F** New entry shifts individual firm demand (and marginal revenue) curves leftward. (326–329)

7. **F** Product differentiation creates downward-sloping demand tangent to $ATC$ below full capacity output. (326–329)

8. **F** Zero economic profit, but $P \neq$ minimum $ATC$. (326–329)

9. **T** Difference between $P$ and $MC$ is markup (326–329)

10. **F** Without barriers to entry, new firms cause price to fall until economic profits = 0. (326–329)

11. **T** With existing products, new firms enter and compete away economic profits. (330–333)

12. **F** Selling costs are fixed costs that increase total costs, but if output increases enough, average total cost may decrease. (330–333)

ⓒⓣ 13. **F** Depends on information versus persuasion content of advertising and gains from increased product variety. (330–333)

14. **T** Advertising can be used to signal quality to consumers. (330–333)

15. **T** (330–333)

## Multiple-Choice

1. **c** All other answers describe oligopoly, which is coming in Chapter 15. (324–325)

2. **c** Both have downward-sloping demand curves, so both have $MR$ curves that are below demand curves. (324–325)

3. **d** Both have no entry barriers, which allows a large number of firms. (324–325)

4. **e** All are definitions or results of product differentiation. (324–325)

5. **a** Many firms, each with a small market share. (324–325)

6. **e** Product differentiation creates pricing power. Demand is not perfectly elastic. (324–325)

7. **c** See text discussion. (324–325)

ⓒⓣ 8. **c** Demand curve ($AR = P$) tangent to $ATC$ and above $MC$. (326–329)

9. **b** Where $MC = MR$. (326–329)

©t 10. **a** At $Q2$, $AR - ATC$. (326–329)

11. **a** With new entrants due to economic profit, industry demand is divided among more firms, so each firm's demand curve shifts leftward. (326–329)

12. **b** **a** and **e** create possibility of economic profit, **c** and **d** are outcomes, not forces leading to zero economic profit. (326–329)

13. **d** Zero economic profit. (326–329)

14. **c** **b** and **d** are false for monopoly. **a** is false for monopolistic competition. (326–329)

15. **c** Excess capacity at $Q$ where demand is tangent to downward slope $ATC$. (326–329)

16. **d** Where demand curve is tangent to $ATC$. (326–329)

©t 17. **d** Zero long-run economic profit for monopolistic competition. (326–329)

18. **c** With exit, market demand is divided among a smaller number of firms. Demand and quantity supplied increase for originals. (326–329)

19. **c** Positive normal profits, positive accounting profits. (326–329)

20. **e** Selling costs are fixed costs that may increase or decrease demand, and may persuade consumers about exaggerated differences between products rather than provide valuable information. (330–333)

21. **c** Disadvantages of excess capacity and advertising costs versus gains from variety. (330–333)

22. **b** Increased demand allows short-run economic profit. New products make demand more inelastic. (330–333)

23. **c** Always compare $MR$ and $MC$. Firms don't consider social costs or revenues. (330–333)

24. **a** Selling costs are used to differentiate products. Have inefficient, excess capacity and use brand names. (330–333)

25. **b** Variety provides choice. (330–333)

## Short Answer Problems

1. Fig. 2 Solution (a) illustrates a monopolistically competitive firm making an economic profit in the short run. The important feature of the graph is that at the profit-maximizing output, price is greater than average total cost. Economic profit is the shaded area.

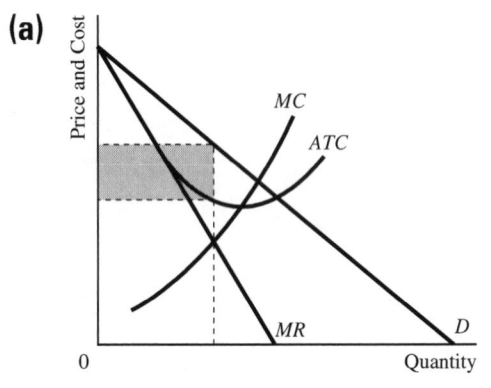

▲ **FIGURE 2 Solution**

**2.** Fig. 2 Solution (b) illustrates a firm that will shut down in the short run since price is less than average variable cost at the profit-maximizing (loss-minimizing) level of output.

**(b)**

▲ **FIGURE 2 Solution**

**3.** Fig. 2 Solution (c) illustrates a firm incurring a loss but continuing to produce. The loss is the shaded area. Note that, at the profit-maximizing output, price is less than *ATC* but greater than *AVC*.

**(c)**

▲ **FIGURE 2 Solution**

**4.** Since firms are incurring a loss, firms will leave the industry. The demand curves facing each remaining firm will shift rightward as they each attract some customers of departing firms. As firms' demand curves shift rightward, losses are reduced. Firms continue to have an incentive to leave until losses are eliminated. Thus remaining firms' demand curves continue to shift until they are tangent to the *ATC* curve.

**5.** Fig. 2 Solution (d) illustrates a monopolistically competitive firm in long-run equilibrium. The demand curve facing the firm is tangent to the *ATC* curve at the profit-maximizing output. Thus the firm is making zero economic profit.

**(d)**

▲ **FIGURE 2 Solution**

**6. a.** Advertising will increase firm *A*'s cost, but also increase demand (it hopes). If the increase in demand (revenue) is greater than the increase in cost, firm *A* will increase its profit. Fig. 3 Solution on the next page illustrates this situation. The initial curves are given by $D_0$, $ATC_0$, and $MR_0$.

Initially the firm is producing $Q_0$ and selling at price $P_0$ and making zero economic profit. Advertising, which is a fixed cost, raises the *ATC* curve to $ATC_1$ (*MC* does not shift), but also increases the demand and marginal revenue curves to $D_1$ and $MR_1$, respectively. The shift in the demand curve is sufficiently great that there is now positive economic profit at the new profit-maximizing level of output ($Q_1$). Economic profit is the shaded area.

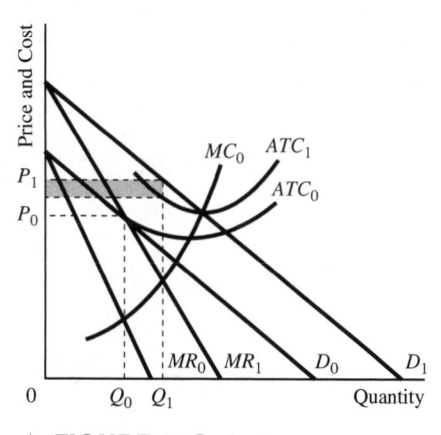

▲ **FIGURE 3  Solution**

**b.** Other firms will also begin to advertise to attempt to increase their profit (or recover lost profit). As all other firms advertise, the demand curve for our firm will shift back to the left as it loses some customers it gained. In the long run, once again, all firms will be making zero profit even after advertising.

**7.** Advertising by all firms in a monopolistically competitive industry makes consumers more aware of substitutes. From Chapter 4, we know that elasticity of demand depends on the substitute available for a product. The more substitutes consumers become aware of, the greater their choices, and the easier it is to switch to another product if the price rises.

**8.** McDonald's is a brand name, and you know from experience that, whatever you think of their food, the quality is consistent (and the washrooms are clean). You know what to expect. Since you have no information about the unfamiliar restaurants, you use the "information" provided by the brand name to make your choice.

# 15 Oligopoly

## Key Concepts

### What Is Oligopoly?

**Oligopoly** is a model of market structure where few firms compete and *strategically interact*. A firm considers the effects of its actions on behaviour of others and actions of others on its own profit.

- Natural or legal barriers prevent entry new firms.
- **Duopoly**—oligopoly market with two firms.
- **Cartel**—group of firms in collusive agreement.

### Oligopoly Games

**Game theory** analyses strategic behaviour. Games have

- rules—specify permissible actions by players.
- **strategies**—actions such as raising or lowering price, output, advertising, or product quality.
- payoffs—profits and losses of players. A **payoff matrix** shows payoffs for every possible action by each player.
- outcome—determined by players' choices. In a **Nash equilibrium**, *A* takes best possible action given *B*'s action, and *B* takes best possible action given *A*'s action.

A "prisoners' dilemma" is a one-time, two-person game with a **dominant strategy equilibrium**. Each player has a dominant strategy (unique best strategy independent of other player's action) of cheating, that is, confessing.

- Prisoners' dilemma yields a Nash equilibrium outcome that is *not* in the best interests of the players.

In a duopoly game, each firm can *comply* with a **collusive agreement** to restrict output and raise price, or it can *cheat*.

- In one-time price-fixing game, prisoners' dilemma solution occurs—each firm has a dominant strategy of cheating, even though both firms would be better off if they could trust each other and comply.
- Unlike prisoners' dilemma game, a game of "chicken" has a Nash equilibrium that is *not* a dominant strategy equilibrium.

Game theory can be used to analyse other choices for firms—how much to spend on research and development, on advertising, whether to enter or exit an industry.

## Repeated Games and Sequential Games

In a repeated game, other strategies can create **cooperative equilibrium** in which each firm complies with collusive agreement and makes monopoly profits. Requires firms to punish cheating in previous period.

- *Tit-for-tat strategy*—taking the same action the other player took last period. Lightest punishment.
- *Trigger strategy*—cooperating until the other player cheats, then cheating forever. Most severe punishment.

Game tree—shows decisions made at first and second stages of sequential game—can be used to analyse sequential entry-deterrence game. In a **contestable market** there are few firms but free entry and exit, so existing firms face competition from *potential* entrants. Existing firms may use strategies of

- set monopoly price, but risk entry of new firm.
- set competitive price and earn normal profit to keep out a potential competitor.
- **limit pricing**—set highest price that just inflicts loss on entrant. Compared to monopoly outcome, charge lower price and produce greater quantity to deter entry.

# Anti-Combine Law

**Anti-combine law** regulates oligopolies; seeks to prevent them from becoming or behaving like monopolies.

Competition Act of 1986 distinguishes between

- criminal actions (conspiracy to fix prices, bid-rigging, false advertising), dealt with by courts.
- noncriminal actions (mergers, abuse of market position, exclusive dealing), dealt with by Competition Tribunal.

Evidence suggests anti-combine laws have served the social interest.

# Helpful Hints

1. This chapter uses elementary game theory to explain oligopoly. The prisoners' dilemma game illustrates the most important game theory concepts (rules, strategies, payoffs, outcome), which are then used in more complex game theory models like repeated and sequential games.

   It is important to learn how to find the Nash equilibrium of a prisoners' dilemma–type game. Take the example of players *A* and *B*, where each player has to choose between two strategies—confess or deny. First set up the payoff matrix. Then look at the payoff matrix from *A*'s point of view. *A* does not know if *B* is going to confess or deny, so *A* asks two questions: (1) Assuming that *B* confesses, do I get a better payoff if I confess or deny? (2) Assuming that *B* denies, do I get a better payoff if I confess or deny?

   If *A*'s best strategy is to confess, regardless of whether *B* confesses or denies, confessing is *A*'s dominant strategy. Next, look at the payoff matrix from *B*'s point of view. Let *B* ask the equivalent two questions, and find *B*'s dominant strategy. The combination of *A*'s dominant strategy and *B*'s dominant strategy comprises the Nash equilibrium outcome of the game.

2. The key insight of the prisoners' dilemma game is the *tension* between the Nash equilibrium outcome (where both players' best strategy is to confess because they can't trust each other) and the fact that both players could make themselves better off if only they would cooperate. All of the equilibrium situations we have examined up until now have been stable outcomes where all agents' self-interests (utility and profit) have been maximized. Remember, equilibrium is defined as a situation where there is no tendency to change. The Nash equilibrium of the prisoners' dilemma is different. Even though both players confess, their individual self-interests are not maximized. It is the additional possibility of strategic interaction (to trust or not to trust the other player) that creates the instability of outcomes.

   The instability of outcomes in this simple game helps us to understand more complex market phenomena such as gasoline price wars. When gasoline station owners trust each other, prices remain relatively high and profits are maximized. But there is always an incentive to cheat on a collusive agreement. Once cheating begins, trust breaks down and owners are driven to the equilibrium outcome where all owners cheat, prices fall, and profits are reduced. Eventually, reduced profits lead owners to take a chance on trusting each other again, since they figure it couldn't be worse than existing low prices and profits. All stations raise their prices, and the cycle begins again. This instability of price and profit outcomes stems from the cycle of trust and non-trust. In other words, instability arises from strategic interaction between station owners.

# Self-Test

## True/False and Explain

### What Is Oligopoly?

**1.** An oligopolist will consider the reaction of other firms before it decides to cut its price.

**2.** There are no barriers to entry in oligopoly.

**3.** Cartels are legal associations of firms acting together to limit output, raise price, and increase economic profit.

**4.** The Herfindahl–Hirschman Index (HHI) that divides oligopoly from monopolistic competition is 1,000.

### Oligopoly Games

**5.** A Nash equilibrium occurs when $A$ takes the best possible action given the action of $B$, and $B$ takes the best possible action given the action of $A$.

**6.** If duopolists agree to collude, they can (jointly) make as much profit as a single monopoly.

**7.** For colluding duopolists in a nonrepeated game, the equilibrium is always for both firms to cheat.

**8.** The Nash equilibrium in a game of "chicken" is a dominant strategy equilibrium.

## Repeated Games and Sequential Games

9. For colluding duopolists in a repeated game, the equilibrium is always for both firms to cheat.

10. A limit-pricing strategy sets the price that inflicts the highest loss on a new entrant.

11. Repeated games are more likely to have a cooperative equilibrium than one-time only games.

12. If an oligopoly operates in a contestable market, one potential outcome is competitive prices and normal profits.

## Anti-Combine Law

13. According to Canada's anti-combine laws, mergers and abuse of a dominant market position are criminal offences.

14. Anti-combine laws can work in the social interest or in the self-interest of producers.

15. The Competition Act distinguishes between business practices that are criminal and noncriminal.

# Multiple-Choice

## What Is Oligopoly?

1. If the efficient scale of production only allows three firms to supply a market, the market is called a
   a. three-firm monopoly.
   b. cost-based oligopoly.
   c. natural oligopoly.
   d. monopolistic competition.
   e. competitive monopoly.

2. Each of the following is a characteristic of monopolistic competition. Which is *not* a characteristic of oligopoly?
   a. Each firm faces a downward-sloping demand curve.
   b. Firms are profit-maximizers.
   c. The sales of one firm will not have a significant effect on other firms.
   d. There is more than one firm in the industry.
   e. Firms set prices.

3. A cartel is a group of firms that agree to
   a. behave competitively.
   b. raise the price of their products.
   c. lower the price of their products.
   d. increase the amount they produce.
   e. cheat on each other.

4. Because an oligopoly has a small number of firms
   a. each firm can act like a monopoly.
   b. the firms may legally form a cartel.
   c. the HHI for the industry is small.
   d. the four-firm concentration ratio for the industry is small.
   e. the firms are interdependent.

**5.** Fig. 1 shows the daily demand (*D*) for limousine rides in Moose Jaw, Saskatchewan, and the average total cost (*ATC*) of a limousine company. The limousine market in Moose Jaw is

**a.** a natural duopoly.

**b.** a natural monopoly.

**c.** a natural oligopoly with three firms.

**d.** monopolistically competitive.

**e.** perfectly competitive.

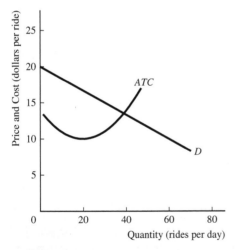

▲ **FIGURE 1**

## Oligopoly Games

**6.** Which of the following is *not* common to all games?

**a.** rules

**b.** collusion

**c.** strategies

**d.** payoffs

**e.** the analysis of strategic interaction

**7.** In the prisoners' dilemma with players Art and Bob, each prisoner would be best off if

**a.** both prisoners confess.

**b.** both prisoners deny.

**c.** Art denies and Bob confesses.

**d.** Bob denies and Art confesses.

**e.** none of the above occurs.

**8.** If a duopoly with collusion maximizes profit,

    **a.** each firm must produce the same amount.

    **b.** each firm must produce its maximum output possible.

    **c.** industry marginal revenue must equal industry marginal cost at the level of total output.

    **d.** industry demand must equal industry marginal cost at the level of total output.

    **e.** total output will be greater than without collusion.

**TABLE 1**

| | | Firm B | | | |
|---|---|---|---|---|---|
| | | **Low Price** | | **High Price** | |
| Firm A | Low Price | A: | $2 | A: | $20 |
| | | B: | $5 | B: | −$15 |
| | High Price | A: | −$10 | A: | $10 |
| | | B: | $25 | B: | $20 |

**9.** Table 1 gives the payoff matrix of profits for firms *A* and *B* when there are two strategies for each firm: (1) charge a low price or (2) charge a high price. The equilibrium in this game (played once) is a Nash equilibrium, because

    **a.** firm *B* will reduce profit by more than *A* if both charge a lower price.

    **b.** firm *B* is the dominant firm.

    **c.** the best strategy for each firm does not depend on the strategy chosen by the other.

    **d.** there is no credible threat by either firm to punish the other if it breaks the agreement.

    **e.** all of the above are true.

**10.** Refer to the nonrepeated game in Table 1. In Nash equilibrium, what are firm *A*'s profits?

    **a.** −$10

    **b.** $2

    **c.** $10

    **d.** $20

    **e.** indeterminate

**11.** Refer to the nonrepeated game in Table 1. If both firms could agree to collude, what would be firm *A*'s profits?

    **a.** −$10

    **b.** $2

    **c.** $10

    **d.** $20

    **e.** indeterminate

**12.** Refer to the nonrepeated game in Table 1. The equilibrium of the game is called a

    **a.** dominant firm equilibrium.

    **b.** cooperative equilibrium.

    **c.** duopoly equilibrium.

    **d.** credible strategy equilibrium.

    **e.** Nash equilibrium.

**13.** The firms Trick and Gear form a cartel to collude to maximize profit. If this game is nonrepeated, the Nash equilibrium is

    **a.** both firms cheat on the agreement.

    **b.** both firms comply with the agreement.

    **c.** Trick cheats, while Gear complies with the agreement.

    **d.** Gear cheats, while Trick complies with the agreement.

    **e.** indeterminate.

**14.** If an R&D game between two firms is a game of chicken, then the equilibrium is

    **a.** both firms conduct R&D.

    **b.** neither firm conducts R&D.

    **c.** only one of the two firms conducts R&D.

    **d.** flawed because R&D must be done, but the game's equilibrium is that it might be done.

    **e.** none of the above.

**15.** Table 2 gives the payoff matrix of profits for Player One and Player Two. There are two strategies for each player. Player One can choose Up or Down. Player Two can choose Left or Right. In this nonrepeated game,

    **a.** Player One has a dominant strategy to choose Up.

    **b.** Player One has a dominant strategy to choose Down.

    **c.** Player Two has a dominant strategy to choose Left.

    **d.** Player Two has a dominant strategy to choose Right.

    **e.** neither player has a dominant strategy.

**TABLE 2**

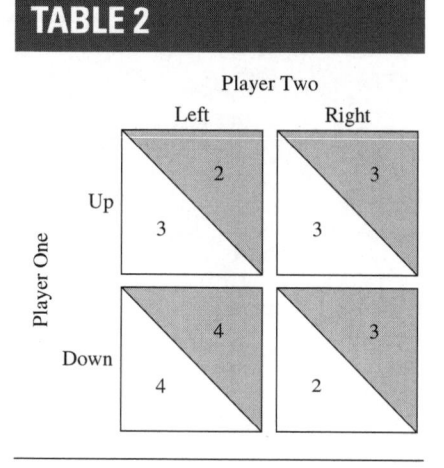

## Repeated Games and Sequential Games

**16.** Consider the same cartel consisting of Trick and Gear from Question 13. Now, however, the game is repeated indefinitely and each firm employs a tit-for-tat strategy. The equilibrium is

    **a.** both firms cheat on the agreement.

    **b.** both firms comply with the agreement.

    **c.** Trick cheats, while Gear complies with the agreement.

    **d.** Gear cheats, while Trick complies with the agreement.

    **e.** indeterminate.

**17.** The equilibrium in Question **16** is called a

    **a.** credible strategy equilibrium.

    **b.** dominant player equilibrium.

    **c.** duopoly equilibrium.

    **d.** trigger strategy equilibrium.

    **e.** cooperative equilibrium.

**18.** When a firm cooperates if the other cooperates, but plays the Nash equilibrium strategy forever if the other cheats, that is a

a. dominant strategy.

b. trigger strategy.

c. tit-for-tat strategy.

d. wimp's strategy.

e. cooperative strategy.

**19.** Limit pricing refers to

a. the highest price a monopolist can set.

b. the highest price that just inflicts a loss on a potential entrant.

c. a strategy used by entering firms in contestable markets.

d. the price determined in a kinked demand curve model.

e. none of the above.

**20.** Which of the following quotes illustrates a *contestable market* in the transporter industry?

a. "I am producing extra transporters even though it results in lower short-run profits, to keep Tommy's Transporters from expanding into my market."

b. "I am producing more transporters than Tommy and I agreed to in business negotiations last week."

c. "If Tommy and I could agree on a higher transporter price, we would both make more profits."

d. "I have been spending more on research and development of a new two-way transporter."

e. None of the above.

**21.** A trigger strategy can be used

a. in a nonrepeated game or a repeated game.

b. in a nonrepeated game but not in a repeated game.

c. in a repeated game but not in a nonrepeated game.

d. only when there is no Nash equilibrium.

e. only in a contestable market.

## Anti-Combine Law

**22.** Anti-combine laws attempt to
  **a.** support prices.
  **b.** establish Crown corporations.
  **c.** prevent monopoly practices.
  **d.** establish fair trade laws.
  **e.** deregulate monopolies.

**23.** Canada's anti-combine law dates back to the
  **a.** 1880s.
  **b.** 1910s.
  **c.** 1930s.
  **d.** 1960s.
  **e.** 1980s.

**24.** The Competition Act distinguishes between business practices that are criminal and noncriminal. Which of the following are criminal practices?
  **a.** conspiracy to fix prices
  **b.** bid-rigging
  **c.** anti-competitive price-fixing actions
  **d.** false advertising.
  **e.** all of the above

**25.** Under the Competition Act, the Competition Tribunal may do all of the following *except*
  **a.** force firms to lower prices.
  **b.** prevent mergers.
  **c.** dissolve mergers.
  **d.** prohibit persons from controlling a class of business.
  **e.** prohibit persons from practising anti-competitive acts.

# Short Answer Problems

**b.** Construct the payoff matrix in the space provided below.

**1.** A small prairie town has two bakeries—Always Fresh and Never Stale. Transportation costs are high relative to the price of bread, so the bakeries do not get any out-of-town competition; the local bread industry is a duopoly. Always Fresh and Never Stale have the same cost curves, and each currently makes an annual profit of $2,000.

    Suppose that a new advertising service, Philomena's Flyers, starts up. If one bakery advertises in Philomena's Flyers, its annual profits will increase to $5,000, while the other bakery will lose $2,000. If both advertise, each will make a zero profit. If neither advertises, each bakery will continue to make an annual profit of $2,000.

**a.** Represent this duopoly as a game by identifying the players, strategies, and possible outcomes.

**c.** What is the Nash equilibrium outcome? Explain.

**2.** Fig. 2(a) gives the identical average total cost (*ATC*) curve for Always Fresh and Never Stale. Fig. 2(b) gives the town's market demand curve for bread and the firms' joint marginal cost curve. Suppose that the two bakeries collude to maximize profit and agree to divide output equally for a single year.

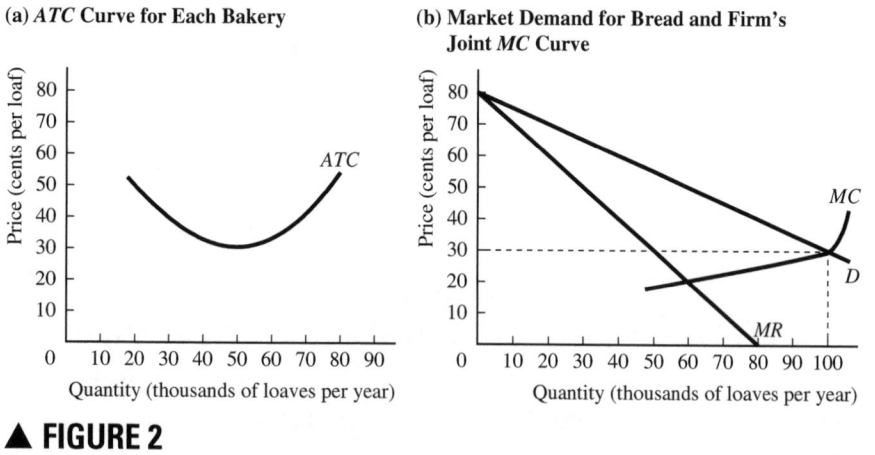

(a) *ATC* Curve for Each Bakery

(b) **Market Demand for Bread and Firm's Joint *MC* Curve**

▲ **FIGURE 2**

**a.** How much will each bakery produce and what price per loaf will they charge?

**b.** What is each bakery's average total cost and profit?

ℂ **3.** Now suppose that Never Stale convinces Always Fresh that demand has decreased and they must reduce their price by 10 cents per loaf in order to sell their agreed-upon quantity. Of course, demand has not decreased, but Always Fresh produces its agreed amount and charges 10 cents less per loaf. Never Stale, the cheater, also charges 10 cents less than before, but increases output sufficiently to satisfy the rest of demand at this price.

**a.** How many loaves of bread does Never Stale produce?

**b.** What is Always Fresh's average total cost and profit?

**c.** What is Never Stale's average total cost and profit?

**4.** Return to the initial situation. The firms are preparing to enter into a *long-term* collusive agreement. Always Fresh credibly assures Never Stale that if Never Stale cheats in a repeated game, Always Fresh will undercut Never Stale's price as soon as the cheating is discovered. Would Never Stale want to cheat on the agreement now? Why or why not?

**5.** Two firms—Katie's Cabs and Madeleine's Movers—are the only two taxicab companies in a small town. These firms are playing a duopoly game. If they both comply with a collusive cartel agreement to restrict the number of their cabs and raise their prices, each can earn an economic profit of $2 million. But if one firm cheats on the agreement—by cutting its prices just a little and quietly acquiring more taxis—and the other complies with the agreement, the cheater earns an economic profit of $2.5 million and the complier suffers an economic loss of $1 million. If both firms cheat, both earn only normal profits and $0 economic profit.

**a.** Use this information to complete the payoff matrix of economic profits in Fig. 3. Put Katie's Cabs' payoffs in the shaded triangles and Madeleine's Movers' payoffs in the clear triangles.

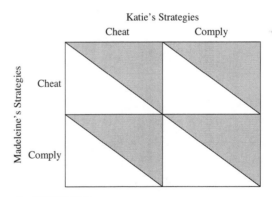

▲ **FIGURE 3**

**b.** If this game is played only once, what is Katie's best strategy? What is Madeleine's best strategy? What will be the equilibrium outcome?

**6.** Suppose the taxi firm duopoly game in Short Answer Problem **5** changes. The payoffs are the same as before when both players choose the same strategy (both cheat or both comply). But when one player cheats and the other complies, the payoffs are now a $2.5 million economic profit for the cheater and a $0.5 million economic profit for the complier.

**a.** Complete the payoff matrix in Fig. 4.

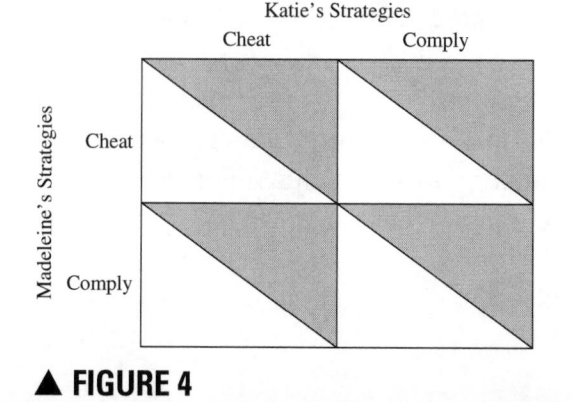

**▲ FIGURE 4**

**c.** When is the joint total profit the largest? When is Katie's profit the largest? Madeleine's profit?

**b.** Does Katie have a clear-cut best strategy? Does Madeleine? Is there a clear equilibrium outcome for this new game?

**▲ FIGURE 5**

**a.** If Madeleine cheats this period, what is her profit? If she cheats this period, what is the maximum profit she can earn next period? What is her maximum two-period profit if she cheats?

**7.** The taxi firm duopoly game changes again so that the payoff matrix is shown in Fig. 5. Madeleine and Katie now see that they will be playing a repeated game. Madeleine knows that Katie has adopted a tit-for-tat strategy. Last period, Madeleine complied with the cartel agreement.

**b.** If Madeleine complies with the agreement, what is her profit this period? If she complies next period, what will be her profit? If she does not cheat in either period, what is the two-period profit she earns?

**c.** Is Katie likely to cheat this period? Why?

**8.** After reading about the major anti-combine cases on pages 356–359 of the text, does it appear that Canada's anti-combine law works in the social interest or in the self-interest of producers?

# Answers

## True/False and Explain

1. **T** Oligopoly involves strategic behaviour. (342–343)

2. **F** Small number of firms because of barriers to entry. (342–343)

3. **F** Cartels take those actions, but they are illegal. (342–343)

4. **T** Below 1,000 = monopolistic competition; above = oligopoly. (343)

5. **T** Definition. (346–347)

6. **T** With collusion, act exactly like monopoly. (348–349)

7. **T** True for nonrepeated game but may be false for repeated game. (349–352)

8. **F** Unlike prisoners' dilemma, *not* a dominant strategy equilibrium (346–354)

ⓒⓣ 9. **F** Tit-for-tat strategy yields cooperative equilibrium in repeated game. (355–357)

10. **F** Sets highest price that just inflicts (smallest) loss, since any loss deters entry. (356–357)

11. **T** Extra strategies like tit-for-tat in repeated games support cooperative equilibrium. (354–357)

12. **T** Possible strategy to keep out competitors. (354–357)

13. **F** Noncriminal offences. Criminal offences include price fixing and false advertising. (358)

14. **T** See text discussion. (358–361)

15. **T** See text discussion. (358–361)

## Multiple-Choice

1. **c** Economies of scale create natural oligopoly. (342–343)

ⓒⓣ 2. **c** Oligopoly involves interdependence between firms. (342–343)

3. **b** Raise price and restrict output. (342–343)

4. **e** Each firm's actions affect the others. (342–343)

5. **c** Efficient scale of 1 firm is 20, so 3 firms satisfy market demand (60) at lowest price (10). (342–343)

6. **b** No collusion in prisoners' dilemma. (346–354)

7. **b** Both denying would yield lesser jail terms, but doesn't happen because players cannot trust each other enough to collude. (346–347)

8. **c** (349)

9. **c** Dominant strategy for each. (351–352)

10. **b** Both firms charge low price. (351–352)

11. **c** Both firms charge high price. (351–352)

12. **e** Each player takes the best possible action, given the action of the other player. (346–354)

13. **a** Similar to prisoners' dilemma outcome. (348–352)

14. **c** In the Nash equilibrium, one firm conducts R&D even though the non-R&D firm has higher profit. (354)

15. **e** Each player's strategy changes as the other player's strategy changes. (346–352)

16. **b** Cooperative equilibrium; each player responds rationally to the credible threat of the other. (355–357)

17. **e** Definition. (355–357)

18. **b** Definition. (355)

19. **b** Definition. **c** would be true for existing firms. (355–357)

20. **a** Produce greater quantity and charge lower price to deter entry. (355–357)

21. **c** Trigger strategy requires more than one game to change from cooperation to cheating. (355–357)

22. **c** See text discussion. (358–361)

23. **a** 1889—see text discussion. (358–361)

24. **e** See text discussion. (358)

25. **a** (358)

## Short Answer Problems

1. **a.** The players are Always Fresh and Never Stale. Each firm has two strategies: to advertise or not to advertise. There are four possible outcomes: (1) both firms advertise, (2) Always Fresh advertises but Never Stale does not, (3) Never Stale advertises but Always Fresh does not, and (4) neither firm advertises.

   **b.** The payoff matrix is given in Fig. 6. The entries give the profit earned by Always Fresh (clear triangles) and Never Stale (shaded triangles) under each of the four possible outcomes.

   **c.** First, consider how Always Fresh decides which strategy to pursue. If Never Stale advertises, Always Fresh can advertise and make zero profit or not advertise

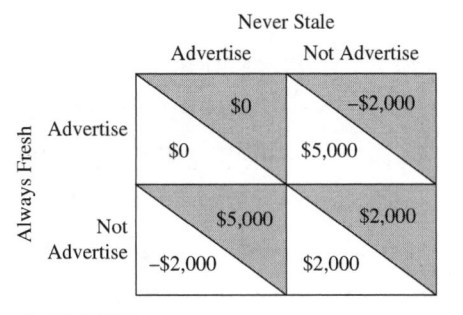

▲ **FIGURE 6**

and make a $2,000 loss. Thus Always Fresh will want to advertise if Never Stale does.

If Never Stale does not advertise, Always Fresh can advertise and make a $5,000 profit or not advertise and make a $2,000 profit. Therefore Always Fresh will want to advertise whether Never Stale advertises or not. Never Stale will come to the same conclusion. The Nash equilibrium is that both firms advertise.

2. **a.** The firms will agree to produce 30,000 loaves each and sell at a price of 50 cents per loaf. We determine this by noticing (Fig. 2(b)) that the profit-maximizing (monopoly) output is 60,000 loaves for the industry (*MR* = *MC* at 60,000), and the industry price is 50 cents per loaf. Since the firms have agreed to divide output equally, each will produce 30,000 loaves.

   **b.** From Fig. 2(a) we determine that, at 30,000 loaves, each firm's average total cost is 40 cents per loaf. Since price is 50 cents per loaf, profit will be $3,000 for each firm.

3. **a.** At the new price of 40 cents per loaf, total quantity demanded is 80,000 loaves. Since Always Fresh continues to produce 30,000 loaves, this means that Never

Stale will produce the remaining 50,000 loaves demanded.

**b.** Since Always Fresh continues to produce 30,000 loaves, its average total cost continues to be 40 cents per loaf. With the new price also at 40 cents, Always Fresh will make a zero economic profit.

**c.** Never Stale has increased output to 50,000 loaves, which implies average total cost of 30 cents per loaf. Thus, given a price of 40 cents, Never Stale's economic profit will be $5,000.

4. Given that the agreement is long term, Never Stale would almost surely not cheat. The reason is that, while Never Stale could increase short-term profit by cheating, it would lose much more future profit if Always Fresh retaliates in a repeated game.

The key point is that Never Stale's behaviour changes, not because cost or demand has changed, but rather because Always Fresh's behaviour has changed in the repeated game. In duopoly and oligopoly, the best strategy for any firm depends on the behaviour of other firms.

5. **a.** The payoff matrix appears in Fig. 3 Solution.

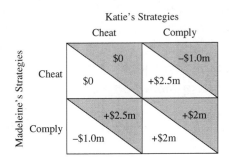

Katie's Strategies

▲ **FIGURE 3  Solution**

**b.** Katie's best strategy is to cheat no matter what Madeleine does. If Madeleine complies with the agreement and does not cheat, Katie will cheat because her profit from cheating ($2.5 million) is greater than her profit from complying ($2 million). If Madeleine cheats, Katie will also cheat because her profit ($0) is higher than the loss she would incur by complying (−$1 million). Katie has a dominant strategy to cheat. Similarly, Madeleine's profits are higher if she cheats, no matter what Katie does. So Madeleine also has a dominant strategy to cheat. The Nash equilibrium outcome is for both players to cheat on the agreement.

**c.** The taxicab industry's profits are highest ($4 million) when both Katie and Madeleine comply with the agreement. Katie's individual profit is highest if she cheats and Madeleine complies. Madeleine's individual profit is highest if she cheats and Katie complies. Though each player's *individual* interest is to cheat, their *joint* interest is to comply.

6. **a.** The payoff matrix appears in Fig. 4 Solution.

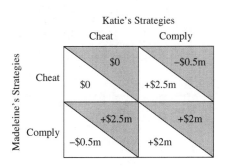

Katie's Strategies

▲ **FIGURE 4  Solution**

**b.** Katie and Madeleine no longer have a dominant strategy. If Madeleine complies, Katie wants to cheat because her profit from cheating ($2.5 million) is greater than her profit from complying ($2 million). But if Madeleine cheats, Katie will want to comply. If Madeleine cheats, Katie earns a profit of $0.5 million by complying but $0 by cheating. So Katie's best strategy now depends on what Madeleine does. Madeleine is in the same situation. Her best strategy depends on what Katie does. Unlike the game in Short Answer Problem **5**, the outcome is not clear-cut. The equilibrium depends on which strategies Madeleine and Katie decide to pursue.

**7. a.** Last period Madeleine complied, so Katie's tit-for-tat strategy means that Katie will comply this period. With Katie complying, Madeleine's profit this period by cheating is $2.5 million. Next period Katie will cheat because Madeleine cheated this period. So next period the most profit that Madeleine can earn is $0 by also cheating. (If Madeleine complied with the agreement when Katie cheated,

Madeleine loses −$2 million.) Over two periods, Madeleine's total profit if she cheats in the first period is $2.5 million.

**b.** Last period Madeleine complied, so Katie's tit-for-tat strategy means that Katie will comply this period. If Madeleine complies this period, she earns $2 million. Because Madeleine complies this period, Katie's tit-for-tat strategy means that next period Katie will comply. Then, if Madeleine also complies next period, she will earn $2 million. By complying each period Madeleine earns a total of $4 million over two periods.

**c.** Madeleine is not likely to cheat. If she does, her total profits over the two periods are much less than if she complies over the two periods. Players in a repeated game are more likely to reach the cooperative equilibrium than are players in a one-time game.

**8.** Since the results of the cases are largely to increase competition and reduce prices to consumers, the Competition Act seems to work in the social interest. Most economists agree.

# 16 Externalities

## Key Concepts

### Externalities in Our Lives

**Externality** is cost or benefit from production activities or consumption activities that affects people who are not part of the original activity. Externalities may be negative or positive.

- **Negative externality**—imposes external cost.
  - Negative production externality (pollution)
  - Negative consumption externality (tobacco smoke)
- **Positive externality**—provides external benefit.
  - Positive production externality (honeybees pollinating nearby fruit orchard)
  - Positive consumption externality (flu vaccination)
- Externalities create market failure (*in*efficiency). Markets overproduce goods/services with negative externalities and underproduce goods/services with positive externalities.

### Negative Externality: Pollution

Many people assume all pollution must be stopped. Economic analysis of pollution, however, evaluates costs and benefits to identify efficient amounts of pollution.

- **Marginal private cost** *(MC)*—cost of producing additional unit of good/service paid by producer.

- **Marginal external cost**—cost of producing additional unit of good/service that falls on people other than the producer.
- **Marginal social cost** *(MSC)*—*MC* incurred by entire society; $MSC = MC +$ Marginal external cost.

Fig. 1 shows the marginal private cost curve, which is also the supply curve ($S = MC$), and the marginal social cost curve (*MSC*). For any quantity produced, marginal external cost = vertical distance between $S = MC$ and *MSC* curves. Demand curve is the same as the marginal social benefit curve ($D = MSB$).

- Efficient equilibrium (where $D = MSB$ intersects *MSC*) takes into account all (private + external) costs.
- Private market equilibrium is inefficient (where $D = MSB$ intersects $S = MC$) because does not take into account marginal external cost.
- Private market equilibrium produces too much of a good with an external cost and creates deadweight loss (from $MSC > MSB$ for all units beyond efficient quantity).

▲ **FIGURE 1  Inefficiency with an External Cost**

Inefficiency from externalities can sometimes be reduced by establishing property rights.

- **Property rights** are a legally established title to ownership, use, and disposal of factors of production and goods and services.
- **Coase theorem**—If property rights exist and **transactions costs** (opportunity costs of conducting transactions) are low, there will be no externalities and private transactions are efficient. Who has property rights will *not* affect the efficiency of the outcome.

Where property rights cannot be established or transactions costs are high, other government actions can achieve efficiency even with negative externalities.

- Taxes—to create incentives for producers to cut back negative externalities, government can impose **Pigovian tax** equal to the external marginal cost.

  - This makes *MSC* curve the relevant *MC* curve for polluting producer's decision, yielding output where *MSC* = *MSB*.

- Emission charges—set price per unit of pollution that polluter pays.

  - In practice, difficult to determine correct price.

- Marketable permits—each polluter given pollution limit (permit) that can be bought and sold.

  - Firms reducing pollution below their limit can sell "excess" reduction to other firms who then can pollute more. In a competitive market for permits, price of permits = marginal external cost of pollution, yielding an efficient outcome where *MSC* = *MSB*.

# Positive Externality: Knowledge

Knowledge from education and research creates private and social benefits.

- **Marginal private benefit** *(MB)*—benefit from one additional unit of good/service received by consumer.

- **Marginal external benefit**—benefit from one additional unit of good/service enjoyed by people other than the consumer.

- **Marginal social benefit** *(MSB)*—*MB* enjoyed by entire society; *MSB* = *MB* + Marginal external benefit.

Fig. 2 shows the marginal private benefit curve, which is also the demand curve (*D* = *MB*), and the marginal social benefit curve (*MSB*). For any quantity consumed, marginal external

▲ **FIGURE 2  Inefficiency with an External Benefit**

benefit = vertical distance between $D = MB$ and $MSB$ curves. Supply curve is same as marginal social cost curve ($S = MSC$).

- Efficient equilibrium (where $MSB$ intersects $S = MSC$) takes into account all (private + external) benefits.
- Private market equilibrium is inefficient (where $D = MB$ intersects $S = MSC$) because does not take into account marginal external benefit.
- Private market equilibrium produces too little of a good with external benefit and creates deadweight loss (from lost $MSB > MSC$ for all units below efficient quantity).

Government actions can achieve efficiency even with positive externalities.

- **Public provision**—government provides the good/service (public education) and charges price below cost that equals marginal private benefit at the efficient quantity.
  - Additional cost paid by taxpayers, to yield total cost = $S = MSC$.
- **Subsidies**—payment by government to private producers of goods/services.
  - If subsidy is equal to external marginal benefit, supply curve becomes $S = MSC -$ subsidy, yielding efficient equilibrium quantity.
- **Vouchers**—government-provided tokens to households for buying specified goods/services.
  - Value of voucher = marginal external benefit, making $MSB$ curve the market demand curve and yielding efficient equilibrium outcome.
- **Patents** and **copyrights**—provide creators of knowledge with **intellectual property rights** in their discoveries; help ensure creator profits.
  - Patents and copyrights encourage development of new knowledge, but create temporary monopoly, so gains from increased knowledge must be balanced against loss from monopoly.

# Helpful Hints

1. A competitive market will produce the quantity of output at which marginal private cost is equal to marginal private benefit. The allocatively efficient quantity is the quantity at which marginal social cost is equal to marginal social benefit.

    The difference between *marginal social cost* and *marginal private cost* is marginal external cost, and the difference between *marginal social benefit* and *marginal private benefit* is marginal external benefit.

    In most economic activities, people who are not part of the original activity are not affected, so there are no external costs or benefits. This means private and social costs and benefits coincide and competitive markets are efficient. However, when third parties are affected, there are external costs or benefits and competitive markets are *not* efficient. Markets overproduce goods/services with external costs (negative externalities) and underproduce goods/services with external benefits (positive externalities).

2. Competitive markets with externalities are not efficient because some of the costs or benefits are *external*. If those costs or benefits could be *internalized* somehow, then the market would be efficient. There are two main approaches to internalizing externalities discussed in this chapter.

    The first is to establish and strictly enforce property rights. Then, costs imposed on people who are not part of the original activity can be recovered through the legal process and will be paid by those involved in the activity: the costs become internal (private).

    The second approach to internalizing externalities is to tax activities that generate external costs and subsidize activities that generate external benefits. By charging a tax equal to the external costs, the entire cost becomes internal. Similarly, by paying a subsidy equal to the external benefits, the entire benefit becomes internal.

3. Fig. 1 in the Key Concepts shows the production of a good with a negative externality (pollution). Note that *the efficient level of pollution is not zero*—efficient $Q$ is *not* $Q = 0$. Generally, costs saved by reducing pollution to zero are less than the benefits lost (benefits from consuming goods whose production created pollution as a by-product).

# Self-Test

## True/False and Explain

### Externalities in Our Lives

1. Externalities arise only from production.

2. Flu vaccination is an example of a positive production externality.

3. A negative production externality imposes an external cost.

### Negative Externality: Pollution

4. If the production of a good involves no external cost, then marginal social cost is equal to marginal private cost.

5. If negative externalities exist, marginal social cost and marginal external cost are equivalent.

6. Externalities often arise from the absence of private property rights.

7. Assigning property rights always solves the problem of a negative externality.

8. Pigovian taxes create incentives for producers to cut back negative externalities.

**9.** Firms with a low marginal cost of reducing pollution will buy marketable pollution permits.

**10.** When external costs are present, the private market produces more than the efficient level of output.

**11.** The efficient quantity of pollution is zero.

## Positive Externality: Knowledge

**12.** The existence of external benefits means that marginal social cost is greater than marginal private cost.

**13.** The private market equilibrium for goods with external benefits has deadweight loss, but the private market outcome with external costs has no deadweight loss because too many goods are produced.

**14.** Patents encourage invention and innovation.

**15.** Copyrights contribute to the development of knowledge, so they have no economic cost.

# Multiple-Choice

## Externalities in Our Lives

1. An externality is a cost or benefit arising from an economic activity that falls on
   a. consumers but not producers.
   b. producers but not consumers.
   c. free riders.
   d. rivals.
   e. none of the above.

2. The production of too few goods with positive externalities is an example of
   a. market failure.
   b. government failure.
   c. producer sovereignty.
   d. consumer sovereignty.
   e. external costs.

3. Which of the following illustrates the concept of external cost?
   a. Bad weather reduces the size of the wheat crop.
   b. A reduction in the size of the wheat crop causes income of wheat farmers to fall.
   c. Smoking harms the health of the smoker.
   d. Smoking harms the health of nearby nonsmokers.
   e. Public health services reduce the transmission of disease.

## Negative Externality: Pollution

4. The income elasticity of demand for a better environment is
   a. negative.
   b. zero.
   c. positive.
   d. trendy.
   e. impossible to know without additional information.

**5.** Levels of acid rain caused by air pollution are
  **a.** less than efficient levels due to external costs.
  **b.** less than efficient levels due to external benefits.
  **c.** more than efficient levels due to external costs.
  **d.** more than efficient levels due to external benefits.
  **e.** decreasing the earth's average temperature.

**6.** Fig. 3 shows demand for good *A* as well as the marginal private cost (*MC*) and marginal social cost (*MSC*) associated with production of good *A*. Production of the sixth unit of output generates an *external*
  **a.** cost of $1.50.
  **b.** cost of $3.00.
  **c.** cost of $6.00.
  **d.** benefit of $3.00.
  **e.** benefit of $6.00.

▲ **FIGURE 3**

**7.** In Fig. 3, how many units of good *A* will be produced in an unregulated market?
  **a.** 0 units
  **b.** 5 units
  **c.** 6 units
  **d.** 8 units
  **e.** impossible to calculate without additional information

**8.** In Fig. 3, what is the efficient quantity of good *A*?
  **a.** 0 units
  **b.** 5 units
  **c.** 6 units
  **d.** 8 units
  **e.** impossible to calculate without additional information

**9.** At the current level of production of buckyballs, marginal social benefit is less than marginal social cost. To achieve allocative efficiency,

**a.** buckyballs should be taxed.

**b.** buckyballs should not be produced.

**c.** output of buckyballs should increase.

**d.** output of buckyballs should decrease.

**e.** property rights in buckyballs should be established.

**10.** The production of too many goods with negative externalities is an example of

**a.** redistribution.

**b.** consumer sovereignty.

**c.** producer sovereignty.

**d.** public failure.

**e.** market failure.

**11.** An externality is

**a.** the amount by which price exceeds marginal private cost.

**b.** the amount by which price exceeds marginal social cost.

**c.** the effect of government regulation on market price and output.

**d.** someone who consumes a good without paying for it.

**e.** a cost or benefit that arises from an activity but affects people not part of the original activity.

**12.** The marginal private cost curve (*MC*) is a positively sloped straight line starting at the origin. If marginal external costs per unit of output are constant, the marginal social cost curve is a positively sloped straight line

**a.** parallel to and above *MC*.

**b.** parallel to and below *MC*.

**c.** starting at the origin and above *MC*.

**d.** starting at the origin and below *MC*.

**e.** identical to *MC*.

13. A market economy tends to _____ goods with negative externalities and _____ goods with positive externalities.
   a. overproduce; overproduce
   b. overproduce; underproduce
   c. underproduce; overproduce
   d. underproduce; underproduce
   e. produce; consume

14. Policies for correcting problems of negative externalities include all of the following *except*
   a. emission charges.
   b. patents.
   c. quantitative limits.
   d. Pigovian taxes.
   e. marketable permits.

15. A battery acid producer pollutes the water upstream from nude swimmers belonging to the Polar Bear Club. If transactions costs are low, the quantity of pollution will be efficient
   a. only if Ronald Coase is a member of the Polar Bear Club.
   b. only if Ronald Coase is not a member of the Polar Bear Club.
   c. only if water property rights are assigned to the producer.
   d. only if water property rights are assigned to the Polar Bear Club.
   e. if water property rights are assigned either to the producer or the Polar Bear Club.

**16.** Refer to Table 1. If the fertilizer market is perfectly competitive and unregulated, output (in tonnes) is

a. 1.

b. 2.

c. 3.

d. 4.

e. 5.

**17.** Refer to Table 1. Fertilizer has a per-unit marginal external

a. cost of $100.

b. benefit of $100.

c. cost of $30.

d. benefit of $30.

e. cost of $0.

| TABLE 1 Chemical Fertilizer Market | | | | |
|---|---|---|---|---|
| Output (tonnes) | Marginal Private Benefit ($) | Marginal Social Benefit ($) | Marginal Private Cost ($) | Marginal Social Cost ($) |
| 1 | 140 | 140 | 50 | 80 |
| 2 | 120 | 120 | 60 | 90 |
| 3 | 100 | 100 | 70 | 100 |
| 4 | 80 | 80 | 80 | 110 |
| 5 | 60 | 60 | 90 | 120 |

**18.** Refer to Table 1. The efficient output of fertilizer (in tonnes) is

a. 1.

b. 2.

c. 3.

d. 4.

e. 5.

## Positive Externality: Knowledge

**19.** The marginal private benefit curve (*MB*) is a negatively sloped straight line. If marginal external benefits per unit of output are positive and decreasing with additional output, the marginal social benefit curve is a negatively sloped straight line
   **a.** parallel to and above *MB*.
   **b.** parallel to and below *MB*.
   **c.** above and steeper than *MB*.
   **d.** above and flatter than *MB*.
   **e.** below and flatter than *MB*.

**20.** Fig. 4 shows the demand curve for good *B*, the marginal social benefit (*MSB*) curve, and marginal private and social cost (*MC* = *MSC*) curve. How many units of good *B* will be produced and consumed in an unregulated market?
   **a.** 0
   **b.** 3
   **c.** 5
   **d.** 6
   **e.** 9

▲ **FIGURE 4**

**21.** In Fig. 4, what is the efficient quantity (in units) of good *B*?
   **a.** 0
   **b.** 3
   **c.** 5
   **d.** 6
   **e.** 9

**22.** In Fig. 4, which of the following government policies would induce the market to achieve allocative efficiency?
   **a.** Tax the production of *B* at $3 per unit.
   **b.** Tax the production of *B* at $4 per unit.
   **c.** Provide vouchers for consumption of *B* at $1 per unit.
   **d.** Provide vouchers for consumption of *B* at $3 per unit.
   **e.** Provide vouchers for consumption of *B* at $4 per unit.

**23.** Policies to achieve allocative efficiency when there are external benefits include
   **a.** intellectual property rights.
   **b.** subsidies.
   **c.** public provision.
   **d.** all of the above.
   **e.** none of the above.

**24.** Knowledge, as a factor of production,
   **a.** displays diminishing marginal productivity.
   **b.** creates external costs.
   **c.** has costs totalling those paid to the patent holder.
   **d.** is encouraged by intellectual property rights.
   **e.** is all of the above.

**25.** When market failure occurs, government will act to reduce inefficiency. This is a prediction of a
   **a.** fair results theory of government behaviour.
   **b.** fair rules theory of government behaviour.
   **c.** social interest theory of government behaviour.
   **d.** public choice theory of government behaviour.
   **e.** rent-seeking theory of government behaviour.

## Short Answer Problems

℗ **1.** Your roommate is an environmentalist who is appalled at the economic concept of an "efficient" level of pollution. She argues that since everyone agrees pollution is "bad," society must work toward eliminating all pollution. How would you, as an economics major, convince her that it is not in society's best interests to eliminate all pollution?

**2.** The production of steel also produces pollution and generates external costs. Suppose government attempts to solve the problem by imposing a tax on steel producers. At the after-tax level of output, we observe the original marginal social cost curve is below the demand curve. Is the after-tax level of output efficient? If not, should steel production, and therefore pollution production, be increased or decreased?

**3.** Two prairie pioneers, Jethro and Hortense, have adjacent fields. Because they get along so well and always work out any problems that arise, they have not bothered to put up a fence. Then one day Jethro buys a new pig, Babe. Babe sometimes wanders into Hortense's field and eats her corn. If Babe would only stay on Jethro's farm, he would eat valueless garbage. Suppose that Babe eats $500 worth of Hortense's corn per year (a negative externality imposed on Hortense) and that to build a fence between the farms costs $300. No property rights to keep animals off the fields have been established yet.

    **a.** If the property right is given to Jethro so Babe can continue to wander, will Hortense build a fence? Explain.

**b.** If, instead, the property right is given to Hortense, so that she can charge Jethro for the corn Babe eats, will Jethro build a fence? Explain.

**c.** Explain how this example illustrates the Coase theorem.

The marginal social cost (*MSC*) is

$$MSC = 3/2Q_S$$

The demand curve for Flatulost (there are no external benefits) is

$$P = 12 - 1/2Q_D$$

$Q_S$ is the quantity of Flatulost supplied, $P$ is the price of Flatulost in dollars, and $Q_D$ is the quantity demanded.

**a.** In an unregulated market, what is the equilibrium quantity of Flatulost? the equilibrium price?

ct **4.** Lever Sisters Company produces Flatulost, a popular room deodorizer. Unfortunately, the production process releases sulphur dioxide into the atmosphere. The marginal private cost (*MC*) to Lever Sisters of producing Flatulost is

$$MC = 1Q_S$$

**b.** To achieve allocative efficiency, what should be the equilibrium quantity of Flatulost? the equilibrium price?

**c.** Compare the unregulated market quantity and price with the allocatively efficient quantity and price.

**d.** The government wants to impose a tax on Flatulost to achieve the allocatively efficient quantity of output. What should the tax be?

**5.** The first two columns of Table 2 give the demand schedule for education in Hicksville, while the third column gives the marginal social cost. Since education generates external benefits, marginal social benefit given in the last column is greater than marginal private benefit.

**TABLE 2  Education in Hicksville**

| Quantity (number of students) | Marginal Private Benefit ($) | Marginal Social Cost ($) | Marginal Social Benefit ($) |
|---|---|---|---|
| 100 | 500 | 200 | 800 |
| 200 | 400 | 250 | 700 |
| 300 | 300 | 300 | 600 |
| 400 | 200 | 350 | 500 |
| 500 | 100 | 400 | 400 |
| 600 | 0 | 450 | 300 |

**a.** On the grid, represent the data in Table 2 graphically.

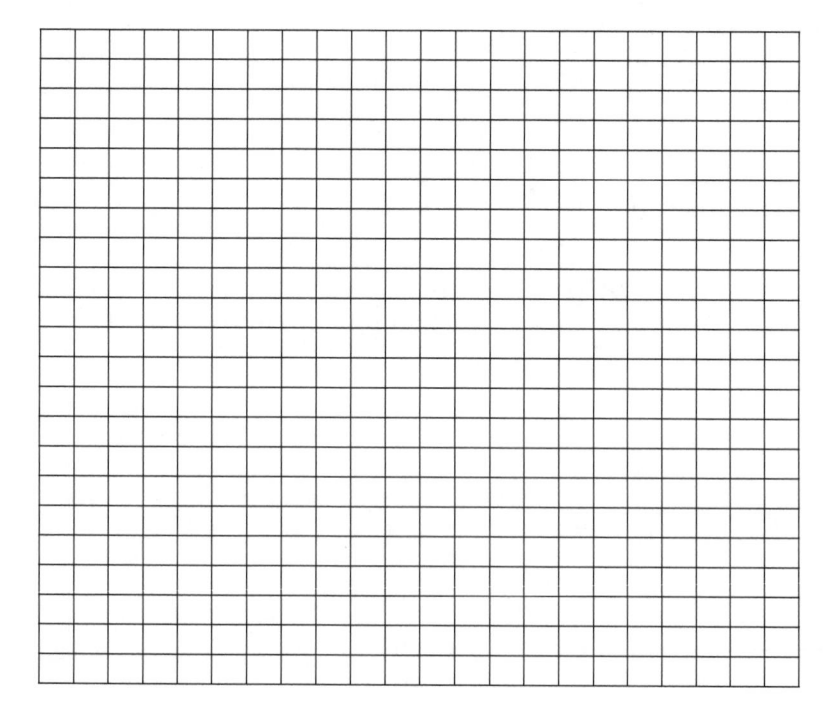

**b.** What equilibrium price and quantity would result if the market for education is unregulated?

**c.** What is the allocatively efficient quantity of students in Hicksville?

**6.** In an attempt to address the inefficient level of education in Hicksville, the town council decides to publicly support schooling. The council offers a $200 voucher to each student who buys a year of education.

    **a.** Draw the new marginal private benefit curve, which includes the voucher, on your graph and label it $MB_1$.

    **b.** What are the approximate new equilibrium price and quantity?

**7.** The Hicksville town council increases the voucher to $400.

    **a.** Draw another marginal private benefit curve, which includes the voucher, on your graph and label it $MB_2$.

    **b.** What are the approximate corresponding equilibrium price and quantity?

    **c.** What level of voucher will achieve the efficient quantity of education?

**8.** What are the benefits and costs of creating intellectual property rights for the creation of new knowledge?

# Answers

## True/False and Explain

1. **F** Externalities can arise from production or consumption and be negative or positive. (372–374)

2. **F** Positive consumption externality. (372–374)

3. **T** Positive production or consumption externality provides external benefit. (372–374)

4. **T** $MSC = MC$ + marginal external cost. (375–379)

5. **F** $MSC = MC$ + marginal external cost. (375–379)

6. **T** Property rights allow recovery of (external) costs. (375–379)

7. **F** True if transactions costs are low; false otherwise. (375–379)

8. **T** See text discussion. (375–379)

9. **F** Firms with low marginal cost of reducing pollution sell permits; firms with high marginal cost of reducing pollution buy. (375–379)

10. **T** Where $MC$ (instead of $MSC$) intersects demand. (375–379)

11. **F** Efficient quantity where $D = MSB$ intersects $MSC$ production (including pollution). (375–379)

ⓒⓣ 12. **F** External benefits affect $MSB$, not $MSC$; $MSB = MB$ + marginal external benefit. (379–383)

ⓒⓣ 13. **F** Both have deadweight loss; with external costs, deadweight loss is excess $MSC$ over $MSB$ for units produced beyond the efficient quantity. (379–383)

14. **T** Intellectual property rights overcome the positive externality problem of knowledge. (379–383)

15. **F** Copyrights are monopolies with associated inefficiencies; but the benefits of new knowledge are presumed to outweigh the costs of monopoly. (379–383)

## Multiple-Choice

1. **e** Falls on people who are not part of the original activity. (372–374)

2. **a** Markets fail to produce efficient quantity of goods with positive externalities. (372–374)

3. **d** Cost falls on people who are not part of the original activity. (372–374)

4. **c** Better environment is a normal good, so $\eta_y > 0$. (375–379)

5. **c** Market overproduction of good with negative externalities (external costs). (375–379)

6. **b** Vertical distance between $MSC$ and $MC$ at $Q = 6$. (375–379)

7. **d** Where $MC$ intersects demand. (375–379)

8. **b** Where $MSC$ intersects demand. (375–379)

9. **d** Draw graph. We don't know if positive, negative, or any externality. (375–379)

10. **e** Failure to achieve allocative efficiency because external costs not taken into account in private, market decisions. (375–379)

11. **e** Definition. (375–379)

**12. a** *MC* shifts leftward by vertical distance equal to marginal external cost per unit. (375–379)

**13. b** Outcomes of market failure. (375–379)

**14. b** Patents correct problems of positive externalities. (375–379)

**15. e** This is the Coase theorem. (375–379)

**16. d** Where *MB* = *MC* = 80. (375–379)

**17. c** *MSC* – *MC* is constant. (375–379)

**18. c** Where *MSB* = *MSC*. (375–379)

ⓒ⫶ **19. c** (379–383)

**20. b** Where *MC* intersects demand. (379–383)

**21. c** Where *MC* intersects *MSB*. (379–383)

**22. d** Value voucher = marginal external benefit = vertical distance between *MB* and *MSB*. (379–383)

**23. d** All move output to where *MSB* = *MSC*. (379–383)

**24. d** No diminishing marginal productivity; creates external benefits; patent monopoly creates loss from restricted use. (379–383)

**25. c** It is in the public interest to achieve efficiency. (379–383)

## Short Answer Problems

ⓒ⫶ **1.** We all want to eliminate pollution, *ceteris paribus*, but every action, including reducing pollution, has a cost. Once again, the key concept underlying the economic argument is opportunity cost. What is the opportunity cost of reducing pollution, or what does society have to give up to achieve a pollution-free environment?

Small reductions in pollution are relatively inexpensive—eliminating lead from gasoline and paint, conserving energy to reduce output from coal-fired electrical plants, etc. But to eliminate all pollution would mean eliminating all cars and airplanes, outlawing all power except solar and hydroelectric power, shutting down most factories, etc. The cost of eliminating *all* pollution is enormous, and that additional cost is far greater than the additional benefits from further reductions in pollution. Therefore some level of pollution is efficient. Pollution is part of the opportunity cost of the benefits we receive from driving or flying instead of walking, from enjoying the comfort of air conditioning in hot weather, and from enjoying goods produced in factories. The efficient level of pollution balances the marginal social cost of the pollution against the marginal social benefit of the production and consumption associated with that level of pollution.

**2.** Since the marginal social cost curve is below the demand curve at the after-tax output, marginal social cost is less than marginal benefit. This means that the tax has been set too high; it has been set at a level in excess of the external cost. As a result, the after-tax level of steel production will be less than the efficient level. The level of steel production and pollution production should be increased by decreasing the amount of the tax.

**3. a.** Hortense will build a fence. Although the fence costs $300 per year, it saves her the $500 in lost corn that Babe would otherwise eat.

**b.** Jethro will build a fence. $300 per year is less than the $500 per year he would have to pay Hortense for Babe's wanderings.

**c.** The Coase theorem states that if transactions costs are low, property rights are established and there are no externalities—an efficient outcome occurs regardless of who is assigned the property right. Because Jethro and Hortense can work out their problems amicably, transactions costs are low. Building a fence eliminates the negative externality of the wandering pig and occurs regardless of which pioneer is assigned the property right. The outcome is efficient because, for this one decision, the $300 cost to society of the fence is less than the $500 cost of consumed corn.

**4. a.** In an unregulated market, the equilibrium quantity would be determined by the intersection of the supply ($MC$) and demand curves. In equilibrium, $Q_S = Q_D = Q^*$. Setting the $MC$ equation equal to the demand equation yields

$$1Q^* = 12 - 1/2Q^*$$
$$3/2Q^* = 12$$
$$Q^* = 8$$

To solve for the equilibrium price ($P^*$), substitute $Q^*$ into the demand (or into the $MC$) equation:

$$P^* = 12 - 1/2Q^*$$
$$P^* = 12 - 1/2Q \; (8)$$
$$P^* = 8$$

**b.** In order to achieve efficiency, $MSC$ must equal marginal social benefit ($MSB$). Since there are no external

benefits, the demand curve is also the $MSB$ curve. In equilibrium, $Q_S = Q_D = Q^*$. To find the equilibrium quantity, set the $MSC$ equation equal to the demand equation:

$$3/2Q^* = 12 - 1/2Q^*$$
$$2Q^* = 12$$
$$Q^* = 6$$

To solve for the equilibrium price ($P^*$), substitute $Q^*$ into the demand (or into the $MSC$) equation:

$$P^* = 12 - 1/2Q^*$$
$$P^* = 12 - 1/2Q \; (6)$$
$$P^* = 9$$

**c.** Compared with the efficient outcomes, the unregulated market produces too much Flatulost (8 units versus 6) and the product sells at too low a price ($8 versus $9).

**d.** The tax should be equal to the cost differential ($MSC - MC$) at the optimum output of 6 units. Since the $MSC$ curve $= 1.5 \times MC$ curve, the tax should be 50 percent.

**5. a.** Fig. 5 graphically represents the data in Table 2. The demand for education is given by the marginal private benefit curve ($MB$), the marginal social cost curve is $MSC$, and the marginal social benefit curve is $MSB$. Ignore the other curves for now.

**b.** In an unregulated market, equilibrium price and quantity are determined by intersecting $MB$ and $MC$

curves. Equilibrium price is $300; equilibrium quantity is 300 students.

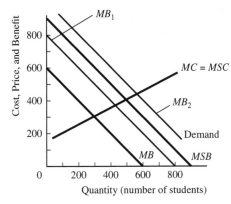

▲ **FIGURE 5**

c. Since there are no external costs, the efficient quantity is determined by the intersection of the *MSC* and *MSB* curves. Efficiency is attained at a quantity of 500 students.

**6. a.** The voucher increases the marginal private benefit to each student by the amount of the voucher, $200. The new *MB* curve, labelled $MB_1$, is included in Fig. 5.

**b.** The new equilibrium after the $200 voucher is at the intersection of the *MSC* and $MB_1$ curves. The price of a unit of education is approximately $370 and there are approximately 430 students.

**7. a.** With a voucher of $400 per student, the *MB* curve shifts to $MB_2$ in Fig. 5.

**b.** With this voucher the equilibrium is at the intersection of the *MSC* and $MB_2$ curves. The corresponding price of a unit of education is approximately $430 and the number of students is approximately 570.

**c.** In order to achieve an efficient outcome, the voucher must make the *MB* curve coincide with the *MSB* curve. This requires a voucher of $300 per student.

**8.** Intellectual property rights create incentives for individuals to create new knowledge by granting the inventor a limited monopoly to benefit from the application of her idea. Without the property right, anyone could freely use the idea and there would be little profit to the inventor. The limited monopoly, although necessary as an incentive to produce knowledge, has a social cost—the restriction of knowledge-based output below the efficient, competitive quantity.

# 17 Public Goods and Common Resources

## Key Concepts

### Classifying Goods and Resources

A good/service/resource is either

- **excludable**—can prevent others from consuming it, or
- **nonexcludable**—can*not* prevent others from consuming it and is either
- **rival**—one person's consumption decreases amount available for others, or
- **nonrival**—one person's consumption does *not* decreases amount available for others

These characteristics are used to classify all goods/services/resources into four types:

- **Private good**—rival and excludable. Example: a hot dog.
- **Public good**—nonrival and nonexcludable; can be consumed simultaneously by everyone; no one can be excluded. Example: national defence.
- **Common resource**—rival and nonexcludable; a unit can be used only once, but no one can be excluded from using other available units. Example: ocean fish.
- **Natural monopoly good**—nonrival and excludable; with economies of scale and low marginal cost, increased consumption reduces cost, but buyers can be excluded. Example: cable television.

# Public Goods

Public goods create **free-rider** (someone who consumes without paying) **problem**—no one has an incentive to pay for a public good.

Efficient quantity of public good occurs at the quantity where marginal social benefit equals marginal social cost.

- Private provision of a public good creates a free-rider problem and provides less than the efficient quantity of the good.
- Government provision can provide an efficient quantity of a public good, where politicians compete for votes of well-informed voters.

The quantity of government provision of a public good generally depends on political marketplace and actions of voters, politicians, and bureaucrats.

- Politicians follow **principle of minimum differentiation**—tendency for competitors to make themselves identical to appeal to maximum number voters/clients.
- Voters may be **rationally ignorant**—deciding *not* to acquire information because cost of acquisition > expected benefit. Then politicians, influenced by bureaucrats and special interest lobbyists, may allow inefficient overprovision of a public good.

Types of political equilibrium:

- Social interest theory—predicts governments achieve efficiency because voters are fully informed.
- Public choice theory—predicts governments create inefficiency because voters are rationally ignorant.

# Common Resources

Commonly owned resources create **tragedy of the commons**—overuse of a common resource because no one has an incentive to conserve and use it sustainably. Overfishing of Atlantic cod is an example.

- Sustainable catch is the quantity that can be caught year after year without depleting the stock.
- Overfishing occurs where maximum sustainable catch starts decreasing. Page 398 of the text shows the maximum sustainable catch at 300,000 tonnes per year.

Fig.1 shows the tragedy of the commons outcome (overfishing equilibrium) and the efficient use outcome. The marginal cost curve (MC) shows the additional cost of keeping a boat and crew at sea long enough to catch an additional tonne of fish. The marginal social cost (MSC) curve shows the MC plus the external cost of stock depletion that makes it harder and more costly for others to catch fish. The marginal social benefit (MSB) curve shows the price consumers are willing to pay for an additional tonne of fish.

▲ **FIGURE 1**

- Overfishing equilibrium—the unregulated equilibrium use of a common resource, is the quantity where $MC = MSB$. Overfishing occurs because the equilibrium of 800,000 tonnes is greater than the maximum sustainable production of 300,000 tonnes.
- Efficient equilibrium—the efficient use of a common resource is the quantity where $MSC = MSB$, or 300,000 tonnes.

Efficient use of a common resource requires incentives that confront users with marginal *social* consequences of their actions. Three main incentive methods:

- Property rights—assigning private property rights to a resource makes the *MSC* curve the same as the owner's *MC* curve, so owner will use the resource efficiently. But difficult to assign enforceable property rights to the ocean or the atmosphere.

- Quota—government sets quota at efficient quantity. Problems include incentives to cheat by increasing output and differing marginal costs among producers, so efficient producers might not get proper share of quotas.
- **Individual transferable quota (ITQ)**—production limit assigned to an individual, who can sell the quota to someone else. Market price of ITQ will equal marginal social benefit minus marginal cost at the efficient quantity, so producers with higher marginal costs will not produce.

# Helpful Hints

1.  All goods provided by the government are not necessarily public goods. A public good is defined by being *nonrival* and *nonexcludable*, not by whether or not it is publicly provided. For example, many communities provide swimming pools and residential garbage pickup. Neither of these is a pure public good despite the fact that each may be provided by the government. In other communities, the same services are provided by the private market.

2.  The nonrival and nonexcludable properties of pure public goods imply that we obtain the marginal benefit curve for the economy as a whole differently than for private goods.

    For a private good, to obtain the demand curve for the whole economy, we sum the individual marginal benefit (demand) curves *horizontally*. For example, at a price of $7, suppose Max demands 5 units of a private good, Lisa demands 5 units, and total demand is 10 units. Because the private goods are rival and excludable, the units Max consumes must be different from the units Lisa consumes, and therefore must be added together to get total market demand.

    But for a public good, to obtain the economy's marginal benefit curve we sum the individual marginal benefit curves *vertically*. For example, for the fifth unit of a public good, suppose Max is willing to pay $7 and Lisa is willing to pay $7. Because public goods are nonrival and nonexcludable, both Max and Lisa can consume the fifth unit simultaneously. The total benefit from consuming the fifth unit is $7 + $7 = $14.

# Self-Test

## True/False and Explain

### Classifying Goods and Resources

**1.** Cable television service is nonrival and excludable.

**2.** A movie you watch in a mostly empty theatre is both non-rival and nonexcludable.

**3.** Common resources are rival and nonexcludable.

### Public Goods

**4.** Goods supplied by government are defined as public goods.

**5.** The excludability feature of goods leads to the free-rider problem.

**6.** The existence of public goods gives rise to the free-rider problem.

**7.** The economy's marginal benefit curve for a public good is obtained by adding the marginal benefits of each individual at each quantity of provision.

**8.** The private market will produce much less than the efficient quantity of pure public goods.

**9.** According to public choice theory, not only is there the possibility of market failure, there is also the possibility of "government failure."

**10.** Political parties tend to propose fundamentally different policies to give voters a clearer choice.

## Common Resources

**11.** If the quantity of fish caught is less than the sustainable catch, the fish stock shrinks.

**12.** As the quantity of fish caught increases, the marginal social benefit of consuming fish decreases.

**13.** For a common resource, marginal social benefit is greater than marginal private benefit.

**14.** The efficient use of a common resource is the quantity where $MSC = MSB$.

**15.** Individual differences in marginal cost prevent an ITQ system from delivering an efficient outcome.

# Multiple-Choice

## Classifying Goods and Resources

1. When a city street is not congested, it is like a(n)
   **a.** external good.
   **b.** internal good.
   **c.** rival good.
   **d.** private good.
   **e.** public good.

2. A private good is
   1 rival.
   2 nonrival.
   3 excludable.
   4 nonexcludable.
   **a.** 1 and 3
   **b.** 1 and 4
   **c.** 2 and 3
   **d.** 2 and 4
   **e.** 1 only

3. A common resource is
   1 rival.
   2 nonrival.
   3 excludable.
   4 nonexcludable.
   **a.** 1 and 3
   **b.** 1 and 4
   **c.** 2 and 3
   **d.** 2 and 4
   **e.** 2 only

4. A public good is
   1 rival.
   2 nonrival.
   3 excludable.
   4 nonexcludable.
   **a.** 1 and 3
   **b.** 1 and 4
   **c.** 2 and 3
   **d.** 2 and 4
   **e.** 4 only

**5.** Which of the following goods is nonexcludable?

**a.** city bus

**b.** toll bridge

**c.** lighthouse

**d.** art museum

**e.** all of the above

## Public Goods

**6.** Governments provide pure public goods like national defence because

**a.** governments are more efficient than private firms at producing such goods.

**b.** of free-rider problems that result in underproduction by private markets.

**c.** people do not value national defence very highly.

**d.** of the potential that private firms will make excess profits.

**e.** of external costs.

**7.** The quantity of public goods produced by an unregulated market tends to be

**a.** less than the efficient quantity.

**b.** equal to the efficient quantity.

**c.** greater than the efficient quantity.

**d.** that which maximizes total public benefit.

**e.** that which maximizes net public benefit.

**8.** The market demand curve for a *private* good is obtained by summing the individual marginal

**a.** cost curves horizontally.

**b.** cost curves vertically.

**c.** benefit curves horizontally.

**d.** benefit curves vertically.

**e.** benefit curves diagonally.

**9.** The economy's total demand curve for a *public* good is obtained by summing the individual marginal

   **a.** cost curves horizontally.

   **b.** cost curves vertically.

   **c.** benefit curves horizontally.

   **d.** benefit curves vertically.

   **e.** benefit curves diagonally.

**10.** The efficient scale of provision of a public good occurs where

   **a.** total benefit is at a maximum.

   **b.** total benefit is at a minimum.

   **c.** marginal social benefit is at a maximum.

   **d.** marginal social benefit minus marginal social cost equals zero.

   **e.** marginal social cost is at a minimum.

**11.** Refer to Fig. 2, which shows the marginal social cost and marginal social benefit of defence satellites, which are a public good. The number of satellites a private market would supply is

   **a.** 0.

   **b.** 1.

   **c.** 2.

   **d.** 3.

   **e.** 4.

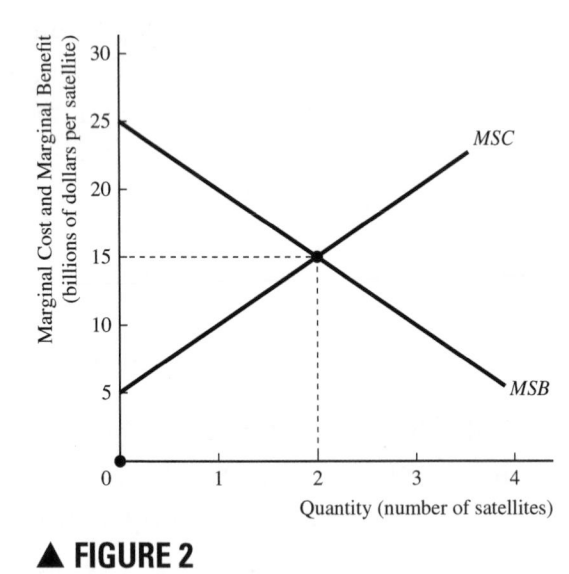

▲ **FIGURE 2**

**12.** Refer to Fig. 2, which shows the marginal social cost and marginal social benefit of defence satellites, which are a public good. The efficient number of satellites is

**a.** 0.

**b.** 1.

**c.** 2.

**d.** 3.

**e.** 4.

**13.** Refer to Fig. 2, which shows the marginal social cost and marginal social benefit of defence satellites, which are a public good. The number of satellites bureaucrats (who want to maximize their department's budget) would press for is

**a.** 0.

**b.** 1.

**c.** 2.

**d.** 3.

**e.** the efficient number.

**14.** According to public choice theory, a voter will favour a candidate whose political program is

**a.** perceived to offer the greatest personal benefit to the voter.

**b.** best for the majority of the people.

**c.** closest to the efficient use of resources.

**d.** favoured by the median voter.

**e.** all of the above.

**15.** Competitors who make themselves identical to appeal to the maximum number of voters illustrate the principle of

**a.** maximum differentiation.

**b.** minimum differentiation.

**c.** rational ignorance.

**d.** nonrivalry.

**e.** excludability.

**16.** Competition between two political parties will cause those parties to propose policies
  **a.** that are quite different.
  **b.** that are quite similar.
  **c.** of rational ignorance.
  **d.** that reduce the well-being of middle-income families and increase the well-being of the rich and the poor.
  **e.** that equate total costs and total benefits.

**17.** Rational ignorance
  **a.** results when the cost of information exceeds the benefits of having the information.
  **b.** allows special interest groups to exert political influence.
  **c.** combined with special interest groups can yield inefficient provision of public goods.
  **d.** results in all of the above.
  **e.** results in none of the above.

**18.** If voters have similar views and are well informed, the quantity of national defence provided by the government will tend to be
  **a.** greater than the efficient quantity.
  **b.** less than the efficient quantity.
  **c.** the least costly quantity.
  **d.** the quantity that maximizes net benefit.
  **e.** the quantity that maximizes the Ministry of Defence budget.

**19.** On any given spending issue subject to a vote, the median voter is the one who favours
  **a.** the least spending.
  **b.** the most spending.
  **c.** the efficient level of spending.
  **d.** the average level of spending.
  **e.** spending more than the level favoured by half the voters and less than the level favoured by half the voters.

## Common Resources

**20.** The tragedy of the commons is the absence of incentives to
- **a.** reduce marginal cost of common resources.
- **b.** prevent underuse of common resources.
- **c.** prevent overuse of common resources.
- **d.** discover new common resources.
- **e.** export wool in sixteenth-century England.

**21.** In the equilibrium for a common resource with no government regulation, marginal social
- **a.** benefit is greater than marginal benefit.
- **b.** cost is less than marginal cost.
- **c.** benefit equals marginal social cost.
- **d.** benefit is greater than marginal cost.
- **e.** benefit equals marginal cost.

**22.** In the equilibrium for a common resource, efficiency requires that marginal social
- **a.** benefit is greater than marginal benefit.
- **b.** cost is less than marginal cost.
- **c.** benefit equals marginal social cost.
- **d.** benefit is greater than marginal cost.
- **e.** benefit equals marginal cost.

**23.** ITQs are issued that will yield efficient output in the fishing market. ITQs will be traded at a market price equal to the marginal
- **a.** cost of producing the efficient output.
- **b.** social cost of producing the efficient output.
- **c.** social benefit of producing the efficient output minus the marginal cost.
- **d.** social benefit of producing the efficient output plus the marginal cost.
- **e.** social cost of producing the efficient output plus the marginal cost.

**24.** With a production quota for a common resource like fish,

    **a.** the common resources is always used efficiently.

    **b.** the marginal cost for each boat owner is the same.

    **c.** each boat owner has an incentive to stick to the production quota.

    **d.** each boat owner has an incentive to cheat on the production quota.

    **e.** none of the above.

**25.** Which of the following methods is *not* used to achieve the efficient use of a common resource?

    **a.** assigning property rights

    **b.** quotas

    **c.** subsidies

    **d.** individual transferable quotas

    **e.** all of the above are used to achieve the efficient use of a common resource

# Short Answer Problems

**1.** What is the free-rider problem?

**2.** Heritage Apartments has 100 residents who are concerned about security. Table 1 gives the total cost of hiring a 24-hour security guard service as well as the marginal benefit to each of the residents.

| TABLE 1 | | | |
|---|---|---|---|
| Number of Guards | Total Cost per Day ($) | Marginal Benefit per Resident ($) | Marginal Benefit to All Residents ($) |
| 1 | 300 | 10 | |
| 2 | 600 | 4 | |
| 3 | 900 | 2 | |
| 4 | 1,200 | 1 | |

**a.** Why is a security guard a public good for the residents of Heritage Apartments?

**b.** Why will zero guards be hired if each of the residents must act individually?

**c.** Complete the last column of Table 1 by computing the marginal benefit of security guards to all of the residents together.

⊕ **3.** Now suppose that the residents form an Apartment Council that acts as a governing body to address the security issue.

**a.** What is the optimal (allocatively efficient) number of guards? What is the net benefit at the optimal number of guards?

**b.** Show that net benefit is less for either one less guard or for one more guard than for the optimal number of guards.

**c.** How might the Apartment Council pay for the guards?

**4.** Two candidates are competing in an election for president of the Economics Club. The only issue dividing them is how much will be spent on the annual Economics Club party. It is well known that the seven voting members of the club (*A* through *G*) have the preferences in Table 2. These are strongly held preferences about exactly how much should be spent on the party.

| TABLE 2  Economics Club Preferences | |
| --- | --- |
| **Voting Member** | **Proposed Amount ($)** |
| *A* | 10 |
| *B* | 20 |
| *C* | 30 |
| *D* | 40 |
| *E* | 50 |
| *F* | 60 |
| *G* | 70 |

**a.** How much will each candidate propose to spend?

**b.** To demonstrate that your answer to part **a** is correct, consider the outcome of the following two contests:
  **i.** Candidate 1 proposes the amount you gave in part **a** and candidate 2 proposes $1 less. Which candidate will win? Why?

  **ii.** Candidate 1 proposes the amount you gave in part **a** and candidate 2 proposes $1 more. Which candidate will win? Why?

**c.** Suppose the Sociology Club is also electing a president and the same single issue prevails. It is well known that the seven voting members of the Sociology Club have the following strongly held preferences regarding exactly how much should be spent on their party (see Table 3).

| TABLE 3 Sociology Club Preferences | |
|---|---|
| **Voting Member** | **Proposed Amount ($)** |
| T | 0 |
| U | 0 |
| V | 0 |
| W | 40 |
| X | 41 |
| Y | 42 |
| Z | 43 |

How much will each of the two candidates propose in this case?

5. Explain why it may be rational for voters to be ignorant.

6. Table 4 gives three alternative income distributions for five individuals, *A* through *E*. Currently, income is distributed according to distribution 1 (the first column of the table). Consider alternative proposed distributions 2 and 3, one at a time.

| TABLE 4 | | | |
|---|---|---|---|
| **Individual** | **Distribution 1 ($)** | **Distribution 2 ($)** | **Distribution 3 ($)** |
| A | 0 | 200 | 150 |
| B | 200 | 300 | 250 |
| C | 400 | 350 | 450 |
| D | 700 | 600 | 600 |
| E | 1,000 | 850 | 850 |

a. If distribution 2 is proposed as an alternative to distribution 1, will it have majority support? Why or why not?

b. If distribution 3 is proposed as an alternative to distribution 1, will it have majority support? Why or why not?

**7.** What is the tragedy of the commons problem, and why does it occur? Use the example of ocean fisheries to illustrate your explanation.

**8.** Fig. 3 shows the marginal social cost, marginal private cost, and marginal social benefit curves for Atlantic Halibut fish, a common resource.

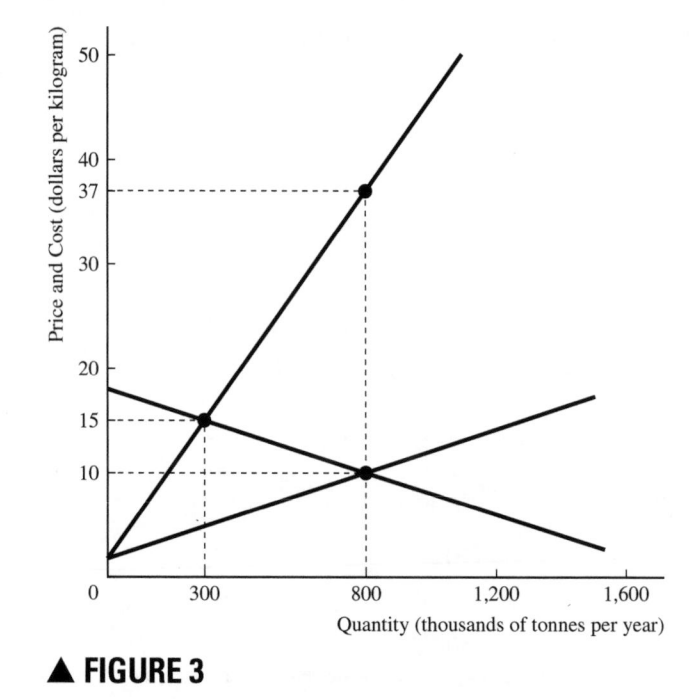

▲ **FIGURE 3**

**a.** Label each curve.

**b.** What is the private equilibrium quantity of fish caught? What is the efficient quantity of fish caught? Illustrate the deadweight loss.

**c.** If the government were to set a production quota, what quota achieves the efficient outcome?

**d.** If the government issues individual transferable quotas (ITQs), what is the market price of an ITQ?

# Answers

## True/False and Explain

1. **T** Your use of cable does not affect me, but buyers can be excluded from service. (392)

2. **F** Nonrival because your attendance does not affect others' access to tickets, but those not paying can be excluded. (392)

3. **T** Taking more fish from the ocean leaves less for others (rival), but no one can be prevented from fishing (nonexcludable). (392)

4. **F** By definition, public goods are *nonrival* and *nonexcludable*. But governments also supply swimming pools, which are rival and excludable goods (see Helpful Hint **1**). (393–397)

5. **F** Nonexcludability creates a free-rider problem. (393–397)

6. **T** Nonexcludability means there is no incentive for anyone to pay. (393–397)

7. **T** See Helpful Hint **2**. (393–397)

8. **T** Because there is no accounting for external benefits. (393–397)

9. **T** Believe government agents act in own interest, not necessarily the public interest. (393–397)

10. **F** Propose similar policies as vote-maximizing strategy appealing to the median voter. (393–397)

11. **F** The fish stock grows. (398–403)

12. **T** Consumers are willing to pay less for additional fish, according to the law of demand. (398–403)

13. **F** Marginal social and private benefits from consuming fish are equal. Marginal social *cost* is greater than marginal private *cost*. (398–403)

14. **T** Efficient use of a common resource is sustainable. (398–403)

15. **F** Low cost producers are willing and able to pay more for quotas, so producers with higher marginal costs will not produce. (398–403)

## Multiple-Choice

1. **e** Nonrival and nonexcludable. Congestion creates rivalry. (392)

2. **a** (392)

3. **b** A unit of a common resource can be used only once, but no one can be excluded from using other available units. (392)

4. **d** Can be consumed simultaneously by everyone; no one can be excluded. (392)

5. **c** Can't prevent ships from seeing the light. (392)

6. **b** Would not be profitable for private firms. (393–397)

7. **a** Private production is unprofitable because of the free-rider problem. (393–397)

8. **c** Because private goods are rival and excludable, quantities consumed by each individual at each price are different and must be added to get total market demand. (393–397)

9. **d** Because public goods are nonrival, can sum marginal benefit to each individual. (393–397)

10. **d** Equivalent to $MSB = MSC$. (393–397)

11. **a** Because of free-rider problem, no one is willing to pay for production. (393–397)

12. **c** Where $MSB$ intersects $MSC$. (393–397)

13. **d** Best for bureaucrats, even though $MSC > MSB$. Possible only if voters are not well informed. (393–397)

14. **a** Voters, like consumers, are assumed to be concerned only with their own self-interest. (393–397)

15. **b** Definition of principle. (393–397)

16. **b** Vote maximizing by using principle of minimum differentiation. (393–397)

17. **d** a definition, **b**, **c** are outcomes of rational ignorance. (393–397)

18. **d** Government will respond to demands of voters. (393–397)

19. **e** Median = exactly halfway between. (393–397)

20. **c** Prevent overuse and depletion because common resources are rival and nonexcludable. (400–405)

21. **e** $MSB$ and $MB$ are the same. (398–403)

22. **c** (398–403)

23. **c** (398–403)

24. **d** $MC$ is not the same for all. (398–403)

25. **c** Common resources are overused because they are too inexpensive, so subsidies would make overuse worse. (398–403)

## Short Answer Problems

1. The free-rider problem is the problem of unregulated markets producing too little of a pure public good because there is little incentive for individuals to pay for the good. There is nothing to prevent the person from being excluded from consuming the good, or from getting a free ride.

2. **a.** A security guard is a public good because, in this case, it is nonrival and non-excludable. It is nonrival because one resident's *consumption* of the security provided by a guard does not reduce the security of anyone else. It is nonexcludable because once a security guard is in place, all residents enjoy the increased security; none can be excluded.

   **b.** If each resident must act individually in hiring a security guard none will be hired because each resident receives only $10 in benefit from the first guard, which costs $300 per day.

   **c.** The entries in the last column of Table 1 Solution are obtained by multiplying the marginal benefit per

**TABLE 1  Solution**

| Number of Guards | Total Cost per Day ($) | Marginal Benefit per Resident ($) | Marginal Benefit to All Residents ($) |
|---|---|---|---|
| 1 | 300 | 10 | 1,000 |
| 2 | 600 | 4 | 400 |
| 3 | 900 | 2 | 200 |
| 4 | 1,200 | 1 | 100 |

resident by the number of residents, 100. This multiplication is the numerical equivalent of summing the individual marginal benefit curves vertically for each quantity of guards.

**3. a.** If the Apartment Council hires each guard for whom the marginal benefit exceeds the marginal cost, they will hire the optimal number of guards. The marginal cost of each additional guard is $300. The marginal benefit of the first guard is $1,000, so he will be hired. Similarly, the marginal benefit of the second guard is $400, and she will be hired.

   The marginal benefit of the third guard is only $200, which is less than marginal cost. Therefore the efficient (optimal) number of guards is two. For two guards, the net benefit is $800: total benefit ($1,400) minus total cost ($600).

**b.** For one guard, net benefit is $700: total benefit ($1,000) minus total cost ($300). For three guards, net benefit is also $700: total benefit ($1,600) minus total cost ($900). Thus the net benefit of $800 is greatest for two guards.

**c.** The Apartment Council might pay for the guards by collecting a security fee of $6 per day from each of the 100 residents in order to hire two security guards.

**4. a.** Each candidate will propose spending $40 since that is the preference of the median voter (voter *D*).

**b. i.** Candidate 1 will win because *D*, *E*, *F*, and *G* will vote for that candidate, because $40 comes closer to matching their preferences than the $39 proposed by candidate 2. Only *A*, *B*, and *C* will vote for candidate 2.

**ii.** Candidate 1 will win because *A*, *B*, *C*, and *D* will vote for that candidate; only *E*, *F*, and *G* will vote for candidate 2.

**c.** Candidates will both propose spending $40 on the party since that is what the median voter prefers. In this case, the median voter's view is not "average."

**5.** Most issues have only a small and indirect effect on most voters. In such cases it is irrational for a voter to spend much time and effort to become well informed because the additional cost would quickly exceed any additional benefit. Only if the voter is significantly and directly affected by an issue will it pay to become well informed. As a result, most voters will be rationally ignorant on any given issue.

**6. a.** Only *A* and *B* are better off under distribution 2. Distribution 2 will receive the support of only *A* and *B* with *C*, *D*, and *E* opposed. Note that the median voter (*C*) is worse off under distribution 2.

**b.** Distribution 3 will receive majority support since it makes the median voter better off. It will be supported by *A*, *B*, and *C* and opposed by *D* and *E*.

**7.** The tragedy of the commons—the overuse and depletion of a common resource—occurs because no one has an incentive to conserve and use a shared resource sustainably. In the fishing example, each fisherman has an incentive to continue fishing until the marginal benefit (revenue from selling an additional tonne of fish) equals his marginal cost—the additional cost of keeping a boat and crew at sea long enough to catch an additional tonne of fish. But for each tonne he catches, he doesn't take into account the external cost of stock depletion that makes it harder and more costly for others to catch fish.

8. **a.** See Fig. 3 Solution. It shows the marginal social cost, marginal private cost, and marginal social benefit curves for Atlantic Halibut fish, a common resource.

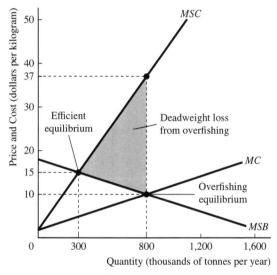

▲ **FIGURE 3  Solution**

**b.** The private equilibrium quantity is determined by the intersection of the *MC* and *MSB* curves, 800,000 tonnes. The efficient sustainable catch, 300,000 tonnes, is determined by the intersection of the *MSC* and *MSB* curves. The deadweight loss is shaded.

**c.** The quota that achieves the efficient outcome is set for the quantity at which *MSC* equals *MSB*—300,000 tonnes.

**d.** The market price of an individual transferable quota (ITQ) equals the *MSC* − *MC* at the efficient level of fish, or $37 − $10 = $27 per tonne of fish.

# 18 Markets for Factors of Production

## Key Concepts

### The Anatomy of Factor Markets

Factors of production, or resources (labour, capital, land, entrepreneurship) are hired by firms to produce output.

- Price of labour services (for **jobs**) is the wage rate.
- Price of capital services (for use of capital goods) is a rental rate.
- Price of land (all natural resources) services, including **nonrenewable natural resources**, is a rental rate.
- Entrepreneurs receive the economic profit/loss from their business decisions.

### The Demand for a Factor of Production

Demand for factors is a **derived demand**, stemming from demand for goods and services produced by a factor and driven by a firm's profit-maximizing objective.

- **Value of marginal product** (*VMP*) is extra revenue from employing one more unit of factor.
  - $VMP = MP \times P_{\text{output}}$
- Profit-maximizing firm hires additional units of labour up to the quantity of factor where $VMP$ = wage rate ($W$).

- Firm's demand curve for labour is downward-sloping value of marginal product curve of labour.
- Firm's long-run demand for labour curve (*VMP* curve) shifts rightward if
  - increased $P_{output}$.
  - technological change increases *MP* labour.
  - increased price of substitute factor of production.
  - decreased price of complement factor of production.

## Labour Markets

Market demand curve for labour is the horizontal sum of quantities of labour demanded by all firms at each wage rate.

Supply of labour determined by households' decisions allocating time between labour supply (work) and leisure.

- Wage rate is *opportunity cost of leisure*.
- At wage rates above a household's *reservation wage*, household supplies labour.
- *Substitution effect* from higher wage induces increased quantity of labour supplied.
- *Income effect* from higher wage induces decreased quantity of labour supplied.
- When wage rises, quantity of labour supplied increases when substitution effect > income effect.
- Individual household labour supply curve is *backward bending* when income effect > substitution effect.

Market supply of labour curve is the horizontal sum of all household supply curves. Upward sloping over normal range of wage rates.

**Labour unions** are organized groups of workers, with objectives of increasing wage rate and influencing working conditions.

Methods of achieving objectives include

- restricting supply of labour.
- increasing demand for union labour by
    - increasing value of marginal product of union members.
    - encouraging import restrictions.
    - supporting minimum wage laws.
    - supporting immigration restrictions.

**Monopsony**—a market structure in which there is a single buyer. Firm that is the only employer in town is a monopsonist in the labour market.

- To hire more labour, a monopsonist must pay a higher wage. Marginal cost of labour curve (*MCL*) for monopsonist is upward sloping and above and steeper than the market supply curve of labour.
- Profit-maximizing rule for monopsonist is to hire quantity of labour where *MCL* curve intersects *VMP* curve, then offer lowest wage for which labour will work (on supply curve).
- For a monopsonist, employment and wage are lower than for competitive labour market. More elastic supply of labour means less *opportunity* for monopsony to cut wages, to reduce employment, or to increase economic profit.

Adding a union to a monopsony labour market can create **bilateral monopoly**, in which wage is determined by the relative bargaining strength of the firm and of the union.

- Highest possible wage where *MCL* intersects *VMP*. Lowest possible wage is pure monopsony wage.
- Adding a minimum wage law to a monopsony labour market can actually increase wages and increase employment.

# Capital and Natural Resource Markets

Demand for capital is derived from value of marginal product of capital. Firms hire additional units of capital up to quantity where *VMP* of capital equals the rental rate of capital.

Firms decide whether to buy versus rent physical capital by evaluating present value.

- **Discounting** is conversion of a future amount of money to its present value.
- **Present value** of future amount of money is amount that, if invested today, will grow as large as future amount, taking account of earned interest.

$$\text{Present value} = \frac{\text{Amount money available } n \text{ years}}{(1 + r)^n}$$

- If present value of future rental payments exceeds cost of buying capital equipment, firm buys capital equipment.
- If present value of future rental payments is less than cost of buying capital equipment, firm rents capital equipment.

Economists call all natural resources *land*.

Supply of land is perfectly inelastic, so price is determined by demand alone. Demand for land is derived from value of marginal product of land. Firms hire additional units of land up to quantity where *VMP* of land equals the rental rate of land.

Price of nonrenewable natural resources depends on demand and supply.

- Demand is determined by value of marginal product (*VMP*) and expected future price.
- Supply is determined by marginal cost of extraction (*MC*), expected future price and scale of production facilities.

**Hotelling Principle**—price of natural resource expected to rise at rate = interest rate.

- If expected rate of price rise > interest rate, demand increases, supply decreases, and price of resource rises.
- If expected rate of price rise < interest rate, demand decreases, supply increases, and price of resource falls.

# Helpful Hints

1. Be careful to distinguish between the value of marginal product of a factor of production and the marginal revenue of a unit of output. The value of marginal product of a factor of production is calculated by multiplying marginal product and price of output ($VMP = MP \times P_{\text{output}}$). The intuition is this: marginal product tells us how much more output we receive from using more of a factor, and price of output tells us the value or revenue we receive from selling each unit of that additional output. Therefore $MP$ times $P_{\text{output}}$ tells us the value we receive (the $VMP$) from using more of the factor of production.

2. This chapter gives a broad overview of characteristics common to competitive markets for the factors of production labour, capital, and land. Profit-maximizing firms will hire factors up to the point where the value of marginal product ($VMP$) is equal to the price of the factor service.

3. The most important graph in this chapter is reproduced here as Fig. 1. Using the example of Angelo's Bakery, the figure demonstrates that a firm's demand for labour curve is the same as its value of marginal product curve of labour.

   Part (a) shows the value of marginal product curve ($VMP$) based on the example in the textbook on page 418. Notice that the values for $VMP$ are plotted midway between the labour inputs used in their calculation. For example, the

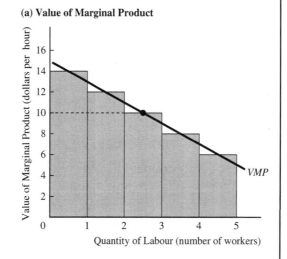

**(a) Value of Marginal Product**

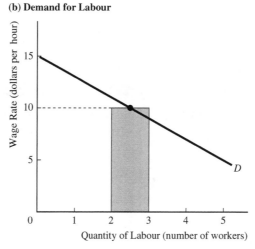

**(b) Demand for Labour**

▲ **FIGURE 1**

*MRP* of moving from 0 to 1 labourer is 14, so the value of 14 on the *VMP* curve is plotted midway between 0 and 1 labourers.

Part (b) constructs Angelo's demand for labour by asking how much labour Angelo will hire at alternative wage rates. Since Angelo is a profit maximizer, he will hire labour up to the point where the value of marginal product of labour is equal to the wage rate. For example, if the wage rate is $10 per hour, Angelo will hire 3 workers since the value of marginal product is $10 when 3 workers are hired. Other points on the labour demand curve can be obtained in similar fashion. The result is that the labour demand curve is the same as the *VMP* curve.

4.  The concept of present value is essential in thinking about the value today of an investment or of future amounts of money. It gives us a method of comparing investments that have payments at different points in time. The intuition behind present value is a dollar today is worth more than a dollar in the future because today's dollar can be invested to earn interest. To calculate the value today of an amount of money that will be paid in the future, we must discount that future amount to compensate for the forgone interest. The present value of a future amount of money is the amount that, if invested today, will grow as large as the future amount, taking into account the interest that it will earn.

5.  The profit-maximizing condition of hiring the services of a factor of production until *VMP* = price of factor service, must be adapted when a firm buys capital equipment instead of renting the equipment services.

    If the present value of future rental payments exceeds the cost of buying the capital equipment, the firm buys the capital equipment instead of renting. If the present value of the future rental payments is less than the cost of buying the capital equipment, the firm rents instead of buying.

6.  This chapter introduces the concept of a monopsonist, a firm that is the only buyer in a market, such as labour. The monopsonist faces an upward-sloping supply curve of labour. As a result, its marginal cost of labour curve (*MCL*) is different from the labour supply curve.

    There is a close parallel between (a) the relationship between the labour supply curve and the *MCL* curve for the monopsonist and (b) the already familiar relationship

**Notes:**

(Chapter 13) between the demand curve and the marginal revenue curve (*MR*) for the monopolist. Both sets of relationships stem from the assumption of a single price for labour or output in the relevant market.

The monopolist, as the only seller in an output market, faces a downward-sloping demand curve. The marginal revenue from the sale of an additional unit of output is *less* than the selling price because the monopolist must *lower* the price on all previous units as well. Thus the *MR* curve lies *below* the demand curve for the single-price monopolist.

For the monopsonist in a labour market, the marginal cost of hiring an additional unit of labour is *higher* than the wage because the monopsonist must *raise* the wage on all previous units of labour as well. Thus the *MCL* curve lies *above* the supply of labour curve for the monopsonist.

Another way to think about this parallel is that the supply and *MCL* relationship (and the resulting wage versus *VMP* relationship) is just the demand and *MR* relationship (and the resulting price versus *MC* relationship) flipped upside-down.

# Self-Test

## True/False and Explain

### The Anatomy of Factor Markets

**1.** Profit is the factor price of capital.

**2.** Farmland is a nonrenewable natural resource.

### The Demand for a Factor of Production

**3.** A firm's average revenue product curve is also its demand for labour curve.

**4.** A factor's value of marginal product equals the marginal product of the factor multiplied by the price of output.

**5.** A firm's demand for labour decreases when the price of a substitute for labour rises.

### Labour Markets

**6.** A household supplies no labour at wage rates below its reservation wage.

**7.** A backward-bending supply of labour curve occurs when the income effect dominates the substitution effect.

**8.** Unions support minimum wage laws in part because they increase the cost of low-skill labour, a substitute for skilled union labour.

**9.** For a firm that is a monopsonist in the labour market, the supply curve of labour is the marginal cost of labour curve.

**10.** In a monopsonistic labour market, the introduction of a minimum wage that is above the current wage will raise the wage but reduce employment.

**11.** In the case of bilateral monopoly in a labour market, the wage depends on the bargaining strength of the two traders.

## Capital and Natural Resource Markets

**12.** If the present value of future rental payments for capital equipment is less than the cost of buying the capital equipment, the firm should buy the capital equipment.

**13.** The market supply of a particular piece of land is perfectly elastic.

**14.** For oil, the value of marginal product is the fundamental determinant of demand, and the marginal cost of extraction is the fundamental determinant of supply.

**15.** The Hotelling Principle states that the price of hotel stocks is expected to rise at a rate equal to the interest rate.

# Multiple-Choice

## The Anatomy of Factor Markets

1. Which price for a factor of production is determined differently from the rest?
   a. wages for labour services
   b. rental rates for capital services
   c. rental rates for land services
   d. profit rates for entrepreneurial services
   e. none of the above—all are determined similarly

## The Demand for a Factor of Production

2. An example of derived demand is the demand for
   a. sweaters derived by an economics student.
   b. sweaters produced by labour and capital.
   c. labour used in the production of sweaters.
   d. sweater brushes.
   e. none of the above.

3. A profit-maximizing firm will continue to hire units of a factor of production until the
   a. marginal cost of the factor equals its marginal product.
   b. marginal cost of the factor equals its average revenue product.
   c. average cost of the factor equals its value of marginal product.
   d. marginal cost of the factor equals its value of marginal product.
   e. factor's value of marginal product equals zero.

4. A firm's value of marginal product of labour curve is also its
   a. marginal cost curve for labour.
   b. labour demand curve.
   c. labour supply curve.
   d. output supply curve.
   e. average revenue curve.

5. If the price of its output falls, a firm will employ
   a. less labour, causing the wage to fall.
   b. less labour, causing the marginal product of labour to rise.
   c. less labour, causing the marginal product of labour to fall.
   d. more labour, causing the marginal product of labour to rise.
   e. more labour, causing the marginal product of labour to fall.

6. A technological change that increases the marginal product of labour will shift the labour
   a. demand curve leftward.
   b. demand curve rightward.
   c. supply curve leftward.
   d. supply curve rightward.
   e. supply and demand curves rightward.

## Labour Markets

7. If the wage rate increases, the *substitution* effect will give a household an incentive to
   a. raise its reservation wage.
   b. increase leisure and decrease work.
   c. increase work and decrease leisure.
   d. increase both work and leisure.
   e. decrease both work and leisure.

8. If the wage rate increases, the *income* effect will give a household an incentive to
   a. raise its reservation wage.
   b. increase leisure and decrease work.
   c. increase work and decrease leisure.
   d. increase both work and leisure.
   e. decrease both work and leisure.

**9.** As the wage rate rises, a household will have a backward-bending labour supply curve if
  **a.** the income effect reinforces the substitution effect.
  **b.** the wage rate rises above the reservation wage.
  **c.** the substitution effect dominates the income effect.
  **d.** the income effect dominates the substitution effect.
  **e.** leisure is an inferior good.

**10.** The market supply curve of labour is
  **a.** upward sloping.
  **b.** backward bending.
  **c.** first upward sloping and then backward bending as the wage increases.
  **d.** vertical.
  **e.** horizontal.

**11.** If the desire for leisure increased, the wage rate would
  **a.** rise and employment would fall.
  **b.** rise and employment would rise.
  **c.** fall and employment would fall.
  **d.** fall and employment would rise.
  **e.** fall and employment may rise or fall.

**12.** Which of the following would unions be *least* likely to support?
  **a.** increasing the legal minimum wage
  **b.** restricting immigration
  **c.** encouraging imports
  **d.** increasing demand for the goods their workers produce
  **e.** increasing the marginal product of union labour

**13.** A union is formed to restrict labour supply in a previously competitive labour market. If the union succeeds in raising the wage,

a. employment will fall.

b. employment will rise.

c. employment will not change.

d. the total wage bill will rise.

e. the total wage bill will fall.

**14.** Fig. 2 illustrates a monopsonist in the labour market ($MCL$ = marginal cost of labour). The profit-maximizing wage rate and quantity of labour hired will be

a. $4 per hour and 800 hours of labour.

b. $4 per hour and 400 hours of labour.

c. $7 per hour and 600 hours of labour.

d. $9 per hour and 400 hours of labour.

e. none of the above.

▲ **FIGURE 2**

**15.** If the labour market illustrated in Fig. 2 became competitive, the equilibrium wage rate and quantity of labour hired would be

a. $4 per hour and 800 hours of labour.

b. $4 per hour and 400 hours of labour.

c. $7 per hour and 600 hours of labour.

d. $9 per hour and 400 hours of labour.

e. none of the above.

**16.** If a union forms to face the monopsonist in Fig. 2, the situation is one of

a. binding arbitration.

b. derived demand.

c. duopoly.

d. collusive oligopoly.

e. bilateral monopoly.

**17.** If a union and the monopsonist in Fig. 2 agree to collective bargaining, the outcome will be an hourly wage

  **a.** of $7.

  **b.** between $4 and $7.

  **c.** between $4 and $9.

  **d.** between $7 and $9.

  **e.** of $9.

**18.** Compared to a competitive labour market with the same value of marginal product and labour supply curves, a monopsonist market has a(n)

  **a.** lower wage and lower employment.

  **b.** lower wage and higher employment.

  **c.** higher wage and lower employment.

  **d.** higher wage and higher employment.

  **e.** indeterminate outcome.

**19.** For the monopsonist employer in Fig. 3, the profit-maximizing wage rate and quantity of labour hired will be

  **a.** $9 per hour and 300 hours of labour.

  **b.** $8 per hour and 350 hours of labour.

  **c.** $8 per hour and 500 hours of labour.

  **d.** $7 per hour and 400 hours of labour.

  **e.** $6 per hour and 300 hours of labour.

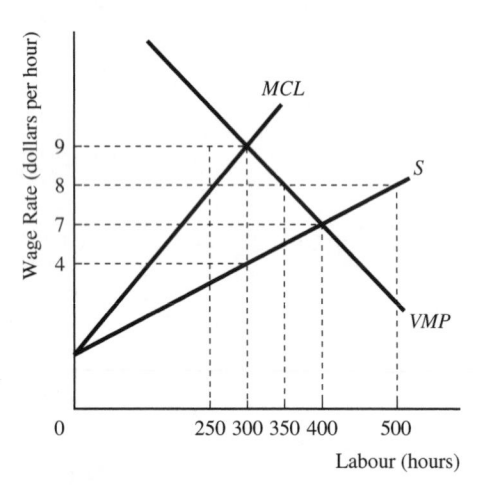

▲ **FIGURE 3**

**20.** Suppose the government passes a minimum wage law that prohibits anyone from hiring labour at less than $8 per hour. In Fig. 3, the marginal cost of labour (*MCL*) for the monopsonist

   **a.** is not affected.

   **b.** equals $8 only from 0 to 250 hours of labour.

   **c.** equals $8 only from 0 to 350 hours of labour.

   **d.** equals $8 only from 0 to 500 hours of labour.

   **e.** shifts up by a vertical distance of $8.

## Capital Markets

**21.** The supply curve of capital is

   **a.** upward sloping.

   **b.** downward sloping.

   **c.** perfectly elastic.

   **d.** perfectly inelastic.

   **e.** backward bending.

**22.** If the present value of $300 received one year from now is $200, what is the annual interest rate?

   **a.** 25 percent (0.25)

   **b.** 33.3 percent (0.333)

   **c.** 50 percent (0.5)

   **d.** 66.7 percent (0.667)

   **e.** none of the above

**23.** Technological advances increase both the demand for capital and the supply of capital by the same amount. As a result, the rental rate _____ and the quantity of capital _____.

   **a.** rises; increases

   **b.** remains constant; increases

   **c.** increases; remains constant

   **d.** falls; increases

   **e.** remains constant; decreases

## Natural Resource Markets

**24.** Which of the following is a nonrenewable natural resource?

 **a.** coal

 **b.** land

 **c.** water

 **d.** trees

 **e.** none of the above

**25.** If the market for a nonrenewable natural resource is currently in equilibrium, the price of the resource

 **a.** is equal to the value of marginal product of the resource.

 **b.** is expected to rise at a rate equal to the interest rate.

 **c.** is expected to fall at a rate equal to the interest rate.

 **d.** will actually rise at a rate equal to the interest rate.

 **e.** will actually fall at a rate equal to the interest rate.

# Short Answer Problems

**1.** Table 1 gives the total and marginal product schedules for a firm that sells its output and buys labour in competitive markets. Initially the price at which the firm can sell any level of output is $5 per unit and the wage rate at which it can purchase any quantity of labour is $15 per unit.

 **a.** Complete the first two blank columns in Table 1 by computing the *TR* and $VMP_L$ corresponding to a price of output = $5.

**TABLE 1**

|  |  |  | P = $5 | | P = $3 | |
|---|---|---|---|---|---|---|
| Quantity Labour (L) | Output (Q) | Marginal Product ($MP_L$) | Total Revenue (TR) | Value of Marginal Product ($VMP_L$) | Total Revenue (TR) | Value of Marginal Product ($VMP_L$) |
| 0 | 0 | | | | | |
| | | ... 12 | | | | |
| 1 | 12 | | | | | |
| | | ... 10 | | | | |
| 2 | 22 | | | | | |
| | | ... 8 | | | | |
| 3 | 30 | | | | | |
| | | ... 6 | | | | |
| 4 | 36 | | | | | |
| | | ... 4 | | | | |
| 5 | 40 | | | | | |
| | | ... 2 | | | | |
| 6 | 42 | | | | | |

**b.** The value of marginal product of labour ($VMP_L$) can be computed by either of the following formulas:

$$VMP_L = \Delta TR / \Delta L$$

$$VMP_L = MP_L \times P_{output}$$

where $\Delta TR$ = the change in total revenue, $\Delta L$ = the change in labour, $P_{output}$ = price of output, and $MP_L$ = marginal product of labour. Show that these two formulas are equivalent for the case when the quantity of labour changes from 1 to 2 units.

**c.** If the firm maximizes profit, what quantity of labour will it employ? How much output will it produce?

**d.** If total fixed cost is $125, what is the amount of profit?

**e.** What is its profit if the firm hires one more unit of labour than the profit-maximizing quantity? one less unit of labour than the profit-maximizing quantity?

**f.** On the grid, draw a graph of the firm's demand for labour and the supply of labour to the firm and illustrate the profit-maximizing labour decision.

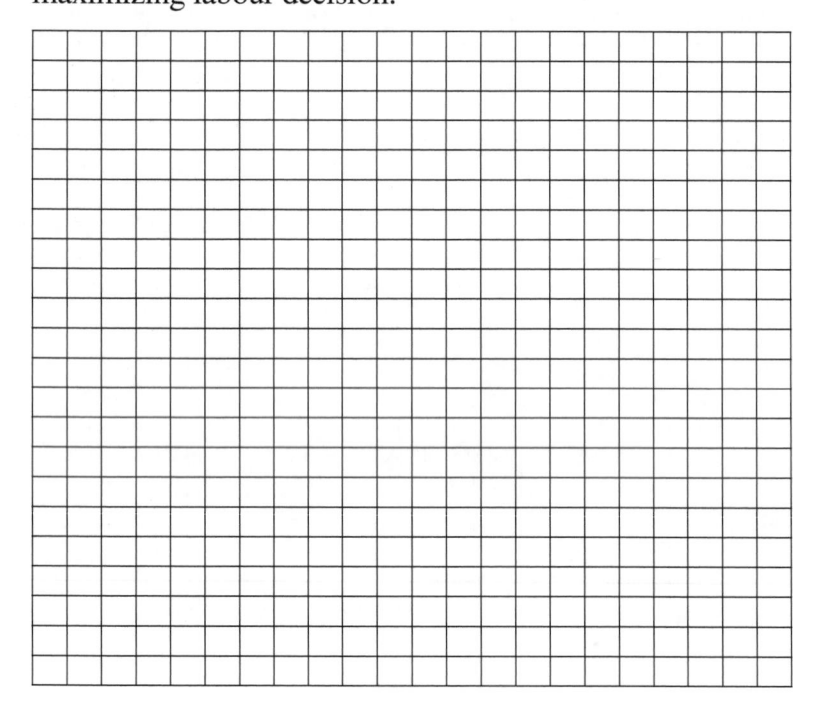

**2.** Now, suppose that the market demand for the output of the firm in Short Answer Problem **1** decreases, causing the price of output to decrease to $3 per unit. The total and marginal product schedules remain unchanged.

**a.** Complete the last two blank columns in Table 1 on page 520 by computing the $TR$ and $VMP_L$ corresponding to price of output = $3.

**b.** If the wage remains at $15 per unit of labour, what is the profit-maximizing quantity of labour that the firm will hire? How much output will it produce? (Write your answers in the space provided on the next page.)

**e.** On the grid, draw a new graph of the firm's demand for labour and supply of labour and illustrate the new profit-maximizing labour decision.

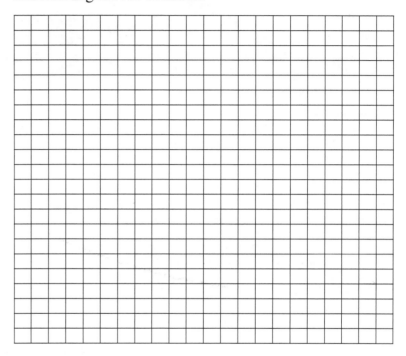

**c.** Total fixed cost continues to be $125. What is the amount of profit?

**d.** Will the firm shut down in the short run? Explain.

**3.** The price of output for the firm in Short Answer Problem **2** remains at $3, but the wage now rises to $21 per unit of labour. The total and marginal product schedules remain unchanged.

**a.** What happens to the demand curve for labour (the *VMP* of labour curve)?

**b.** Under these circumstances, what is the profit-maximizing quantity of labour that the firm will employ? How much output will it produce?

**d.** On the grid, draw a graph of the firm's demand for labour and supply of labour and illustrate the new profit-maximizing labour decision.

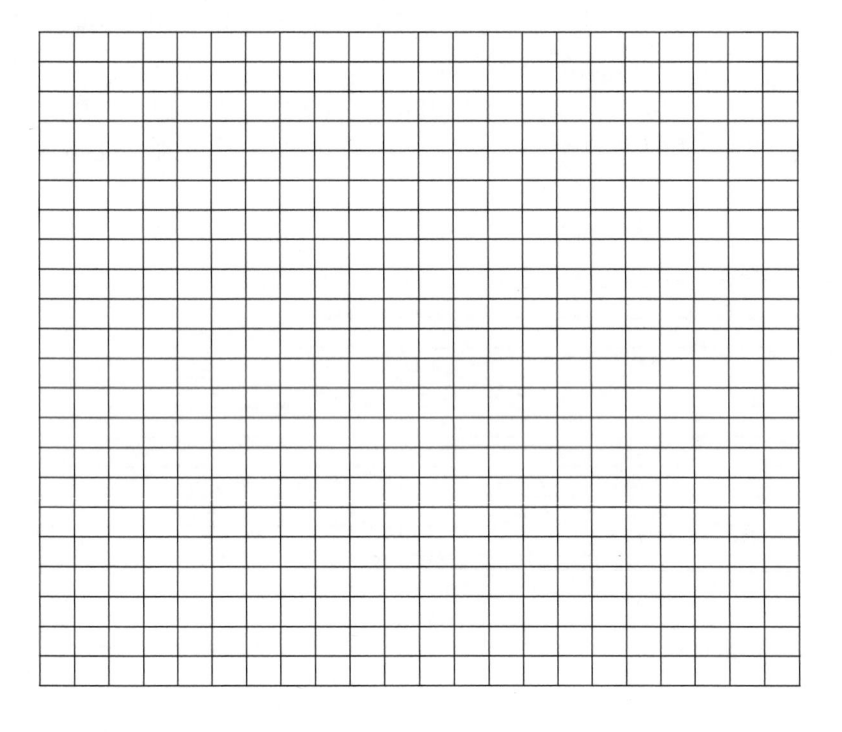

**c.** Total fixed cost continues to be $125. What is the amount of profit?

**4.** A perfectly competitive firm in long-run equilibrium produces flubits using only two factors of production—labour and capital. Each factor is sold in a perfectly competitive factor market. Labour costs $30 per unit and capital costs $50 per unit.

**a.** Assuming the firm has hired the profit-maximizing quantity of capital in part **b** of this question, the value of marginal revenue product of labour curve is

$$VMP_L = 110 - 8/5Q_L$$

where $VMP_L$ is the value of marginal product of labour and $Q_L$ is the quantity (in units) of labour employed. How many units of labour does the firm employ?

**b.** Assuming the firm has hired the profit-maximizing quantity of labour in part **a** of this question, the value of marginal product of capital curve is

$$VMP_K = 125 - 75/40Q_K$$

where $VMP_K$ is the value of marginal product of capital and $Q_K$ is the quantity (in units) of capital employed. How many units of capital does the firm employ?

**c.** The price of a flubit is $10.

   **i.** How many flubits is the firm producing? (*Hint:* Remember that the firm is in long-run equilibrium.)

   **ii.** What is the marginal (physical) product of the 25th unit of labour hired?

**5.** Initially we observe an industry facing a competitive labour market in which the supply of labour comes from two sources: domestic workers and foreign workers. All workers have similar skills. Also assume that the output of the industry competes with imported goods.

**a.** In Fig. 4, graphically represent the initial competitive labour market. Draw the labour demand and supply curves and identify the equilibrium wage rate and level of employment.

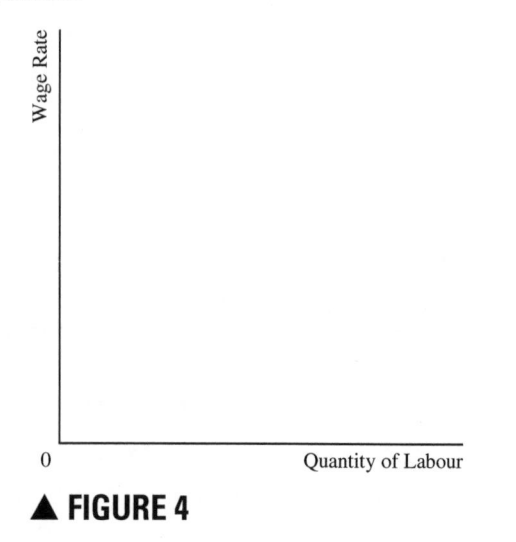

▲ **FIGURE 4**

**b.** Now suppose a union consisting of domestic workers is formed. Through its support a law is passed that prohibits firms from hiring foreign workers. What effect will this have on employment and the wage rate? Illustrate graphically using the graph in part **a**.

**c.** Finally, the industry and union support the passage of a law that legally restricts imports that compete with industry output. Using the same graph, show the consequences for the wage rate and employment.

**6.** Pollutionless Paper is a pulp and paper mill that employs almost all of the labour in a small town in New Brunswick. The town's labour market, which approximates a monopsony, is illustrated in Fig. 5, where $S$ is the supply curve of labour, and $VMP$ and $MCL$ are Pollutionless Paper's value of marginal product of labour and marginal cost of labour curves, respectively.

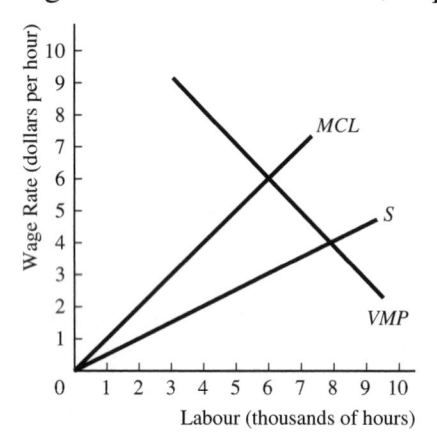

▲ **FIGURE 5**

**a.** If Pollutionless Paper is a profit-maximizing monopsonist, what wage rate will it pay and how much labour will it employ? What is the $VMP$ of labour at this level of employment?

**b.** If the town had a competitive labour market with the same *VMP* curve, what would the equilibrium wage rate and the level of employment be? Compare these outcomes with the monopsony outcomes in part **a**.

**7.** Consider the following alternatives for the labour market in Fig. 5.

**a.** Suppose the government imposes a minimum wage of $4 per hour. What wage rate will Pollutionless Paper pay and how much labour will it employ? Compare these outcomes with the monopsony outcomes in Short Answer Problem **6a**.

**b.** Suppose there is no legal minimum wage, but the workers form a union. If the union tries to negotiate a higher wage rate while maintaining employment at the monopsony level, what is the maximum wage rate that Pollutionless Paper will be willing to pay? What is the minimum wage rate that the union will accept?

**8.** Consider the negotiations between Pollutionless Paper and the union in Short Answer Problem **7b**.

**a.** What determines the wage rate that will actually be paid?

**b.** If Pollutionless Paper and the union are equally strong and realize it, what will the wage rate likely be?

**c.** If Pollutionless Paper and the union are equally strong, but the union mistakenly believes it is stronger, what is the likely outcome of negotiations?

**d.** If Pollutionless Paper and the union are equally strong, but Pollutionless Paper mistakenly believes it is stronger, what is the likely outcome of negotiations?

# Answers

## True/False and Explain

1. **F** Economic profit is residual income to the entrepreneur. (416)

2. **F** Nonrenewable natural resources (oil, natural gas, coal) can only be used once. (416)

3. **F** Value of marginal product curve is demand for labour curve. (417–419)

4. **T** Value of marginal product curve is demand for labour curve. (417–419)

5. **F** If price of capital rises, firms will demand more labour as a cheaper way of producing. (417–419)

6. **T** Reservation wage minimum needed for labour supply. (420–425)

7. **T** Versus upward sloping when substitution effect > income effect. (420–425)

8. **T** Increased price of substitute creates increased demand for union labour. (420–425)

9. **F** *MCL* curve is above supply curve of labour. (420–425)

10. **F** Wages and employment both increase; true for competitive labour market. (420–425)

11. **F** Firm should rent. (420–425)

12. **F** Reverse is true. (426–429)

13. **F** Perfectly inelastic. (426–429)

14. **T** Expected future prices are secondary determinant. (426–429)

15. **F** Definition applies to price of natural resources. (426–429)

## Multiple-Choice

1. **d** Economic profit is a residual. Entrepreneurial services are not traded in markets. (416)

2. **c** Factor used as input to production. (417–419)

3. **d** Where supply curve of factor to firm (*MC*) intersects demand curve for factor (*VMP*). (417–419)

4. **b** Shows quantity of labour demanded at each wage rate. (417–419)

5. **b** Labour demand curve shifts leftward. Because of diminishing *MP*, *decreased* quantity *L* causes *rise* in *MP*. (417–419)

6. **b** At a given wage, firm will demand increased quantity of labour because *VMP* is now higher (since *MP* has increased). (417–419)

7. **c** Substitute work for leisure because opportunity cost of leisure increases. (420–425)

8. **b** Consume more normal goods, including leisure, so working less. (420–425)

9. **d** Income and substitution effects work in opposite directions, so increase leisure dominates decrease work. (420–425)

10. **a** See text discussion. (420–425)

11. **a** Labour supply would shift leftward. (420–425)

12. **c** Increasing imports that are substitutes for domestically produced goods, decreasing demand for domestic, union labour. (420–425)

ⓒᵗ **13. a** Leftward shift in supply decreases employment. Impact on wage bill depends on elasticity of demand for labour. (420–425)

**14. b** *QL* where *MCL* intersects *VMP*. Firm pays lowest wage required for labour to supply that *QL* (on supply curve). (420–425)

**15. c** Where *S* intersects *VMP*. (420–425)

**16. e** Firm is only buyer of labour, union is only seller of labour. (420–425)

**17. c** Between minimum firm can achieve ($4) and maximum union can achieve ($9). (420–425)

**18. a** (420–425)

**19. e** *QL* where *MCL* intersects *VMP*. Firm pays lowest wage required for labour to supply that *QL* (on supply curve). (420–425)

ⓒᵗ **20. d** *MCL* is horizontal at minimum wage until it intersects *S*. Firm must then raise wage to get increased quantity supplied labour. (426)

**21. a** (426–429)

**22. c** Solve $200 = $300/(1 + r)$ for $r$. (426–429)

**23. b** Equal rightward shifts of both demand and supply curves. (426–429)

**24. a** Others are renewable natural resources. (426–429)

**25. b** This is the Hotelling Principle. For current equilibrium, *actual* future prices may or may not follow *expected* prices. (426–429)

## Short Answer Problems

**1. a.** The completed columns for *TR* and $VMP_L$ corresponding to a price of output = $5 are shown in Table 1.

### TABLE 1 Solution

| Quantity Labour (L) | Output (Q) | MVMP Marginal Product (MP_L) | P = $5 Total Revenue (TR) | P = $5 Value of Marginal Product (VMP_L) | P = $3 Total Revenue (TR) | P = $3 Value of Marginal Product (VMP_L) |
|---|---|---|---|---|---|---|
| 0 | 0 | | 0 | | 0 | |
| | | .... 12 | | .... 60 | | .... 36 |
| 1 | 12 | | 60 | | 36 | |
| | | .... 10 | | .... 50 | | .... 30 |
| 2 | 22 | | 110 | | 66 | |
| | | .... 8 | | .... 40 | | .... 24 |
| 3 | 30 | | 150 | | 90 | |
| | | .... 6 | | .... 30 | | .... 18 |
| 4 | 36 | | 180 | | 108 | |
| | | .... 4 | | .... 20 | | .... 12 |
| 5 | 40 | | 200 | | 120 | |
| | | .... 2 | | .... 10 | | .... 6 |
| 6 | 42 | | 210 | | 126 | |

Solution. The values for *TR* come from multiplying the quantity of output by the price of output ($5). The values for $VMP_L$ between any two quantities of labour come from dividing the change in *TR* by the change in quantity of labour, or by multiplying the price of output ($5) by $MP_L$.

**b.** From part **a**, the formula $VMP_L = \Delta TR/\Delta L$ yields a value of marginal product of labour of 50 when the quantity of labour changes from 1 to 2 units. To confirm that the second formula ($VMP_L = MP_L \times P_{output}$) gives the same answer when the quantity of labour changes from 1 to 2 units, substitute in the values for $P_{output}$ ($5, the price of an additional unit of output) and $MP_L$ (10 units of output). This yields the same value of marginal product of labour as above; $5 \times 10$ units $= 50$.

c. The firm maximizes profit by employing labour up to the point where the *VMP* of labour is equal to the marginal cost of labour (the wage rate). That point occurs at 5 units of labour. The *VMP* of moving from 4 to 5 units of labour is 20, and the *VMP* of moving from 5 to 6 units of labour is 10. In moving from 4 to 5 units, *VMP* > *MC* so the firm should hire the 5th unit. But in moving from 5 to 6 units, *VMP* < *MC*, so the firm should not hire the 6th unit. Thus, by interpolation, the *VMP* at exactly 5 units of labour is 15 (midway between 20 and 10). So when 5 units of labour are employed, the *VMP* of labour is equal to the wage rate ($15). Given that 5 units of labour are employed, the profit-maximizing output will be 40 units (from Table 1 Solution).

d. To calculate profit, first calculate total revenue and then subtract total cost. Total revenue is $200 (40 units of output $\times$ $5 per unit) and total cost is also $200—sum of total variable (labour) cost of $75 (5 units of labour $\times$ $15 per unit) and total fixed cost of $125. Thus profit is zero.

e. If the firm employs one more unit of labour (6 units), total revenue will be $210 (42 units of output $\times$ the $5 price). Total cost will be the $125 fixed cost plus $90 in total variable cost (6 units of labour $\times$ $15 wage rate) or $215. Thus profit will be negative $5 ($5 loss).

If the firm employs one less unit of labour (4 units), total revenue will be $180 (36 units of output $\times$ the $5 price). Total cost will be the $125 fixed cost plus $60 in total variable cost (4 units of labour $\times$ $15 wage rate) or $185. Thus profit will be negative $5 ($5 loss).

f. The graph of the firm's labour employment decision appears in Fig. 6. The demand for labour is the firm's $VMP_L$ curve, which is labelled $D_0$ ($D_1$ will be discussed in Short Answer Problem **2**).

Notice that the values for *VMP* are plotted midway between the corresponding quantities of labour. For example, *VMP* of 60 is plotted midway between 0 and 1 units of labour.

Since the firm purchases labour in a perfectly competitive labour market, the supply of labour to the firm is perfectly elastic at the market wage rate. The labour supply curve is labelled $W = $15$. The profit-maximizing decision is at the intersection of these curves, corresponding to a wage rate of $15 quantity of labour of 5 units.

▲ **FIGURE 6**

**2. a.** The completed columns for $TR$ and $VMP_L$ corresponding to price of output = $3 are shown in Table 2 Solution. The values for $TR$ come from multiplying the quantity of output by the price of output ($3). The values for $VMP_L$ between any two quantities of labour come from dividing the change in $TR$ by the change in quantity of labour, or by multiplying the price of output ($3) by $MP_L$.

**b.** If the wage rate remains at $15, the profit-maximizing quantity of labour will fall to 4 units since $VMP_L$ equals the wage rate at 4 units of labour. The $VMP$ of moving from 3 to 4 units of labour is 18, and the $VMP$ of moving from 4 to 5 units of labour is 12. Thus, by interpolation, the $VMP$ at exactly 4 units of labour is 15 (midway between 18 and 12). Given that 4 units of labour are employed, the profit-maximizing output will be 36 units (from Table 2 Solution).

**c.** Profit equals total revenue minus total cost. Total revenue is $108 (36 units of output × $3 per unit) and total cost is $185—sum of total variable (labour) cost of $60 (4 units of labour × $15 per unit) and total fixed cost of $125. Thus profit is –$77, or a loss of $77.

**d.** The firm will not shut down since total revenue ($108) is enough to cover total variable cost ($60) and part of fixed cost. If the firm shuts down, it would lose $125 of fixed cost rather than just $77.

**e.** The graph of the firm's labour employment decision appears in Fig. 6. The new demand for labour is given by the firm's new $VMP_L$ curve, labelled $D_1$. The supply of labour has not changed; it continues to be horizontal at $15, the competitive market wage. The new

these curves and corresponds to a wage rate of $15 and quantity of labour employed of 4 units.

**3. a.** Since the price of output and the marginal product of labour are unaffected by a change in the wage rate, the demand curve for labour (the $VMP$ of labour) will remain at $D_1$.

**b.** If the wage rate rises to $21, the profit-maximizing quantity of labour will fall to 3 units since $VMP_L$ equals the wage rate at 3 units of labour. Given that 3 units of labour are employed, the profit-maximizing output will be 30 units (from Table 2 Solution).

**c.** Profit equals total revenue minus total cost. Total revenue is $90 (30 units of output × $3 per unit) and total cost is $188—sum of total variable (labour) cost of $63 (3 units of labour × $21 per unit) and total fixed cost of $125. Thus profit is –$98, or a loss of $98.

**d.** See Fig. 6. The relevant labour demand curve continues to be $D_1$, but the labour supply curve reflects the rise in the competitive wage rate; it is now horizontal at a wage rate of $21 (labelled $W = $21). The new profit-maximizing decision is at the intersection of these curves and corresponds to a wage rate of $21 and a quantity of labour employed of 3 units.

**4. a.** By assuming that the firm has already hired its capital, we know (in principle) fixed costs and can calculate the profit-maximizing quantity of the variable factor of production (labour) by setting the $VMP_L$ equal to the wage rate ($30).

$$30 = 110 - 8/5Q_L$$
$$8/5Q_L = 80$$
$$Q_L = 50$$

**b.** By assuming that the firm has already hired its labour, we can treat labour as the fixed cost and treat capital as the variable factor of production. Calculate the profit-maximizing quantity of the capital by setting the $VMP_K$ equal to the cost of a unit of capital ($50).

$$50 = 125 - 75/40Q_K$$
$$75/40Q_K = 75$$
$$Q_L = 40$$

**c. i.** The fact that the firm is in long-run equilibrium provides the key to calculating the quantity of flubits produced. In long-run equilibrium, the firm earns zero economic profit, so total revenue is exactly equal to total cost.

We can calculate total cost by adding the costs of the (only) two factors of production. Labour cost is 50 units of labour × $30 per unit or $1,500. Capital cost is 40 units of capital × $50 per unit or $2,000. Total cost is therefore $3,500.

Total revenue must also be equal to $3,500. Since total revenue ($TR$) is just the price of output ($P$) times quantity sold ($Q$), we can calculate $Q$ by substituting in the values we have for $TR$ ($3,500) and $P$ ($10).

$$TR = P \times Q$$
$$\$3,500 = \$10 \times Q$$
$$Q = 350$$

**ii.** To calculate the marginal product of the 25th unit of labour, we begin by calculating the *value* of marginal product of the 25th unit of labour. Substituting $Q_L = 25$ into the equation for $VMP_L$ yields

$$VMP_L = 110 - 8/5(25)$$
$$= 110 - 40$$
$$= 70$$

One definition of the value of marginal product of labour is the marginal product of labour ($MP_L$) times the price of output ($P_{output}$) or $VMP_L = MP_L \times P_{output}$. Rearranging to solve for $MP_L$ yields

$$MP_L = VMP_L/P_{output}$$

Substituting in the values for the value of marginal product of the 25th unit of labour (70) and for the price of output ($10) yields

$$MP_L = 70/10$$
$$MP_L = 7$$

**5. a.** The initial competitive demand for labour and supply of labour curves are $D_C$ and $S_C$, respectively, in Fig. 4 Solution (ignore the other curves for now). The equilibrium wage rate is $W_C$ and the competitive equilibrium level of employment is $QL_C$.

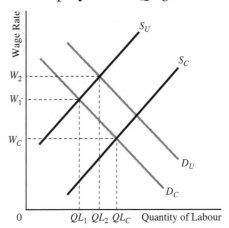

▲ **FIGURE 4   Solution**

**b.** If a law is passed prohibiting firms from hiring foreign workers, the labour supply curve (now under a union) will shift leftward (to $S_U$ in Fig. 4 Solution). This will raise the wage rate to $W_1$ and decrease the quantity of labour employed to $QL_1$.

**c.** Restrictions on imports will increase demand for the product produced in the industry and thus increase the derived demand (*VMP*) of labour in the industry. In Fig. 4 Solution this is a shift from $D_C$ to $D_U$. The result is a further increase in the wage rate to $W_2$ and increase in employment to $QL_2$. Whether the quantity of labour hired now exceeds the initial competitive quantity depends on the magnitude of the shift in the labour demand curve.

**6. a.** A profit-maximizing monopsonist will hire additional labour up to the point where *MCL* equals *VMP*. Referring to Fig. 5, this means that Pollutionless Paper will hire 6,000 hours of labour. To hire that quantity of labour, the labour supply curve *S* tells us that the wage rate must be $3 per hour. This is less than the $6 per hour value of marginal product of labour.

**b.** In a competitive labour market, the wage rate would be $4 per hour and 8,000 hours of labour would be employed. The competitive labour market results in a higher wage rate and a higher level of employment than the monopsony outcomes.

**7. a.** If the government establishes a minimum wage at $4 per hour, the marginal cost of labour to Pollutionless

Paper becomes constant at $4 per hour (up to 8,000 hours of labour). Thus, equating the marginal cost of labour and the value of marginal product of labour leads to a wage rate of $4 and 8,000 hours of labour employed. The addition of a minimum wage to the monopsony labour market results in a higher wage rate and a higher level of employment.

**b.** The maximum wage rate Pollutionless Paper is willing to pay for 6,000 hours of labour is $6 per hour (the *VMP* of that amount of labour). The minimum wage rate that the union will accept for 6,000 hours of labour is $3 per hour (the supply price of that amount of labour).

**8. a.** The wage rate that will actually be paid as the outcome of bargaining depends on the relative bargaining strengths of the firm and the union. Bargaining strength depends on costs (from lockouts and strikes) that each side can inflict on the other if there is a failure to agree.

**b.** Pollutionless Paper and the union will split the difference between $6 and $3 and agree on a wage rate of $4.50.

**c.** If the union holds out for more than a $4.50 wage rate, Pollutionless Paper will likely lock out the workers.

**d.** If Pollutionless Paper holds out for less than a $4.50 wage rate, the union will likely strike. When lockouts or strikes occur, it is usually because one side has misjudged the situation.

# 19 Economic Inequality

## Key Concepts

### Measuring Economic Inequality

Measures of economic inequality look at

- **market income**—wages, interest, rent, and profit before paying income taxes.
- **total income**—market income + cash payments to households by governments.
- **after-tax income**—total income − tax payments by households to governments.

Distribution of after-tax household income in Canada in 2009 was positively skewed.

- *Mode* (most common) income was $30,000–$34,999.
- *Median* income was $48,300.
- *Mean* income was $59,700.

There is a great deal of inequality of income and wealth. The degree of inequality is measured by the Lorenz curve.

- **Lorenz curve** for income (wealth) graphs the cumulative percentage of income (wealth) against the cumulative percentage of households.
- The 45° "line of equality" represents a hypothetically equal distribution of income (wealth).
- The farther the Lorenz curve from the line of equality, the more unequal the distribution.

- **Gini ratio** is the ratio of the area between the line of equality and the Lorenz curve, to the entire area beneath the line of equality. For equally distributed income, Gini ratio $= 0$. If 1 person has all income and others none, Gini ratio $= 1$.
- The distribution of wealth in Canada is even more unequal than the distribution of income.

**Wealth** is the *stock* of assets owned by an individual. Wealth includes *human capital* as well as financial assets. *Income* is the *flow* of earning received by an individual from his or her stock of wealth.

- Data used to construct wealth distributions do not include human capital and therefore overstate wealth inequalities.
- Distributions of annual income and wealth are more unequal than distributions of lifetime income and wealth.
- Even correcting for these factors, there are significant inequalities in distributions of income and wealth in Canada, with the income shares of the richest 20 percent of households rising since 1980.

**Poverty** exists when families cannot buy adequate food, shelter, and clothing.

- Poverty is a relative concept and is measured by the **low-income cutoff** (families spending 64 percent or more of their income on food, shelter, and clothing). On average in Canada since 1980, 17 percent of families have incomes below the low-income cutoff.

# Inequality in the World Economy

Income inequality in Canada is

- more equal than distributions in Brazil and South Africa
- more unequal than distributions in Finland, Sweden, and many European countries.

Global distribution of income across countries is becoming more equal, while income distributions within countries are becoming more unequal.

# The Sources of Economic Inequality

Income inequality arises from differences in human capital, or skill differentials in labour markets.

- Demand—high-skilled labour has higher value of marginal product (*VMP*) and demand curve than low-skilled labour.
- Supply—high-skilled labour has more *human capital*, which is costly to acquire. Supply curve for high-skilled labour is above the supply curve for low-skilled labour.
- Wages (equilibrium of demand and supply) are higher for high-skilled labour.

Wage differentials can be partly explained by

- human capital differences—differences in schooling, work experience, job interruptions, and effects of technological change and globalization.
- discrimination—results in lower wages and employment for those discriminated against.
- contests among superstars—result in extremely high incomes for winners. Globalization has increased the sizes of the talent pool and the income "prizes."

Wealth inequality increases between generations because

- assets can be inherited but debt cannot.
- of *assortative mating* (marrying within one's own socioeconomic class).

# Income Redistribution

Income is redistributed by governments through income taxes, income maintenance programs, and subsidized services.

- Income taxes can be
  - **progressive**—marginal tax rate increases with higher-level income.
  - **regressive**—marginal tax rate decreases with higher-level income.
  - **proportional** (*flat-rate tax*)—marginal tax rate is constant at all levels income.

- Income maintenance programs include social security, employment insurance, and welfare.
- Subsidized services (provision of goods and services below cost) such as education and health-care services reduce inequality.

Income distribution *after taxes and benefits* redistributes income to the very poor considerably, reducing the inequality of the *market income* distribution.

Income redistribution creates a **big tradeoff** between equity and efficiency. Redistribution uses scarce resources and weakens incentives, so a more equally shared pie results in a smaller pie.

# Helpful Hints

1. Statistics used to construct Lorenz curves and Gini ratios do not always give an accurate picture of inequality. You should understand why a distribution of wealth that excludes the value of human capital gives a distorted picture relative to the distribution of income. You should also understand why the distribution of annual (static) income gives a distorted picture relative to the distribution of lifetime (dynamic) income. Finally, you should understand why the distribution of before-tax, before-benefits income gives a distorted picture relative to the distribution of after-tax, after-benefits income.

# Self-Test

## True/False and Explain

### Measuring Economic Inequality

**1.** The farther the Lorenz curve from the 45° line, the more equal the distribution of income.

**2.** In Canada, measured income is more equally distributed than measured wealth.

**3.** Wealth distribution data exclude human capital and thus *overstate* inequality.

**4.** Income is a stock of earnings.

**5.** The lifetime distribution of income is more equal than the annual distribution of income.

### Inequality in the World Economy

**6.** The global distribution of income across countries is becoming more equal, while income distributions within countries are become more unequal.

### The Sources of Economic Inequality

**7.** The demand for low-skilled workers is to the left of the demand for high-skilled workers.

**8.** Globalization has increased the salary received by the "winner" of a contest to become the top executive of a large multinational company.

**9.** The larger the value of marginal product of skill and the more costly it is to acquire, the smaller the wage differential between high-skilled and low-skilled workers.

**10.** Assortative mating makes the distribution of wealth more unequal over time.

## Income Redistribution

**11.** Under a proportional income tax, total taxes rise as income rises.

**12.** Under a progressive income tax, the marginal tax rate does not change as income rises.

**13.** A regressive income tax redistributes income from the rich to the poor.

**14.** Compared with the market distribution of income, government taxes and benefits reduce the inequality of income distribution.

**15.** In general, reducing income inequality by redistributing income from the rich to the poor will lead to greater production of goods and services.

# Multiple-Choice

## Measuring Economic Inequality

**1.** Which diagram is used by economists to illustrate the distribution of income or wealth?

   **a.** Lorenz curve

   **b.** normal bell-shaped distribution

   **c.** Sophia Loren curve

   **d.** low-income cutoff curve

   **e.** none of the above

**2.** In Fig. 1, the richest 20 percent of all households receive what share of all income?

   **a.** 10 percent

   **b.** 20 percent

   **c.** 30 percent

   **d.** 40 percent

   **e.** none of the above

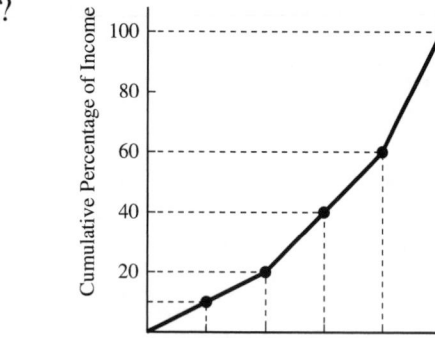

▲ **FIGURE 1**

**3.** In Fig. 1, the poorest 20 percent of all households receive what share of income?

   **a.** 10 percent

   **b.** 20 percent

   **c.** 30 percent

   **d.** 40 percent

   **e.** none of the above

**4.** In Fig. 1, the middle 20 percent of all households receive what share of income?

   **a.** 10 percent

   **b.** 20 percent

   **c.** 30 percent

   **d.** 40 percent

   **e.** none of the above

**5.** The curve in Fig. 1 represents the

   **a.** line of fairness.

   **b.** line of equality.

   **c.** learning curve.

   **d.** wage differential curve.

   **e.** Lorenz curve.

**6.** Consider the Lorenz curves in Fig. 2. Which Lorenz curve corresponds to the greatest income *inequality*?

   **a.** *A*

   **b.** *B*

   **c.** *C*

   **d.** *D*

   **e.** impossible to tell without additional information

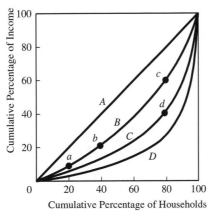

▲ **FIGURE 2**

**7.** In Fig. 2, what is curve *A* (a straight line) called?

   **a.** market distribution line

   **b.** line of equality

   **c.** fairness line

   **d.** low-income cutoff line

   **e.** none of the above

**8.** Which point in Fig. 2 indicates that the richest 20 percent of households earn 40 percent of the income?

   **a.** *a*

   **b.** *b*

   **c.** *c*

   **d.** *d*

   **e.** none of the above

**9.** The distribution of *annual income*

   **a.** understates inequality because it does not take into account the household's stage in its life cycle.

   **b.** understates inequality because it does not take into account the distribution of human capital.

   **c.** overstates inequality because it does not take into account the household's stage in its life cycle.

   **d.** overstates inequality because it does not take into account the distribution of human capital.

   **e.** is an accurate measure of inequality.

**10.** The distribution of *wealth*

   **a.** understates inequality because it does not take into account the household's stage in its life cycle.

   **b.** understates inequality because it does not take into account the distribution of human capital.

   **c.** overstates inequality because it does not take into account the household's stage in its life cycle.

   **d.** overstates inequality because it does not take into account the distribution of human capital.

   **e.** is an accurate measure of inequality.

**11.** Which distribution would show the most *equality*?

   **a.** stock of financial wealth

   **b.** stock of human capital

   **c.** annual income

   **d.** lifetime income

   **e.** all show the same degree of equality

**12.** Wealth differs from income in that

   **a.** income is a stock, wealth is a flow.

   **b.** wealth is derived from income.

   **c.** income is what you earn, wealth is what you own.

   **d.** income is what you own, wealth is what you earn.

   **e.** wealth is preferable to income.

**13.** The Gini ratio for a perfectly equal distribution of income is
  **a.** equal to zero.
  **b.** equal to 1.
  **c.** equal to 100.
  **d.** equal to infinity.
  **e.** named after Gini Lollobrigida

## Inequality in the World Economy

**14.** Recently, the distribution of income within most countries has become ____ equal and the distribution of income in the world has become ____ equal.
  **a.** less; less
  **b.** less; more
  **c.** more; less.
  **d.** more; more
  **e.** progressively; regressively

## The Sources of Economic Inequality

**15.** Refer to Fig. 3. For any given quantity of labour employed,
  **a.** the elasticity of demand is lower for high-skilled workers than for low-skilled workers.
  **b.** wages will be lower for high-skilled workers than low-skilled workers.
  **c.** wages will be higher for high-skilled workers than low-skilled workers.
  **d.** the vertical distance between the curves is the compensation for the cost of acquiring skill.
  **e.** the vertical distance between the curves is the present value of human capital.

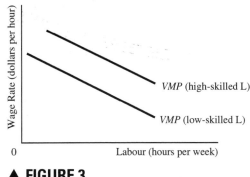

▲ **FIGURE 3**

**16.** The vertical distance between the two supply curves in Fig. 4

   **a.** is the compensation for the cost of acquiring skill.

   **b.** is the *VMP* of skill.

   **c.** is the result of discrimination against low-skilled workers.

   **d.** is the result of subsidies for high-skilled workers.

   **e.** will disappear if there is free entry in the high-skilled market.

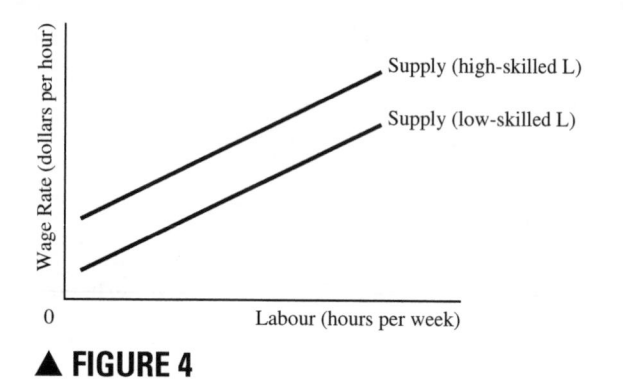

▲ **FIGURE 4**

**17.** Refer only to the information in Fig. 4. For any given wage rate, more hours of

   **a.** low-skilled labour will be demanded than high-skilled labour.

   **b.** high-skilled labour will be demanded than low-skilled labour.

   **c.** low-skilled labour will be supplied than high-skilled labour.

   **d.** high-skilled labour will be supplied than low-skilled labour.

   **e.** low-skilled labour will be supplied if the *VMP* of skill increases.

**18.** Wage differentials between males and females can be explained by

   **a.** educational differences.

   **b.** human capital differences.

   **c.** degree of specialization differences.

   **d.** discrimination.

   **e.** all of the above.

**19.** If discrimination restricts a group's access to education and training, the effect will be to shift their

**a.** *VMP* curve rightward and increase the wage.

**b.** *VMP* curve leftward and decrease the wage.

**c.** *VMP* curve rightward and decrease the wage.

**d.** supply of labour curve up and decrease the wage.

**e.** supply of labour curve down and decrease the wage.

**20.** Assortative mating means that

**a.** poor men tend to marry rich women.

**b.** rich men tend to marry rich women.

**c.** rich men tend to marry poor women.

**d.** same-sex marriages occur because "like attracts like."

**e.** same-sex marriages are prohibited.

## Income Redistribution

**21.** If the marginal tax rate increases as income increases, the income tax is defined as

**a.** progressive.

**b.** proportional.

**c.** negative.

**d.** regressive.

**e.** excessive.

**22.** In Table 1, which tax plan is proportional?

**a.** Plan *A*

**b.** Plan *B*

**c.** Plan *C*

**d.** Plan *D*

**e.** impossible to calculate without additional information

| TABLE 1 | | | | |
|---|---|---|---|---|
| Current Market Income | Tax Payment Plan *A* | Tax Payment Plan *B* | Tax Payment Plan *C* | Tax Payment Plan *D* |
| 0 | 0 | 0 | 0 | 200 |
| 1,000 | 100 | 100 | 200 | 200 |
| 2,000 | 200 | 400 | 200 | 200 |
| 4,000 | 400 | 1,600 | 200 | 200 |

**23.** In Table 1, which tax plan is progressive?

　**a.** Plan *A*

　**b.** Plan *B*

　**c.** Plan *C*

　**d.** Plan *D*

　**e.** impossible to calculate without additional information

**24.** Which of the following *reduces* the inequality of income or wealth relative to the market distribution?

　**a.** government payments to the poor

　**b.** a regressive income tax

　**c.** large inheritances

　**d.** assortative mating

　**e.** all of the above

**25.** Redistribution of income from the rich to the poor will lead to a reduction in total output. This is known as the

　**a.** market distribution.

　**b.** Robin Hood principle.

　**c.** inheritance principle.

　**d.** big tradeoff.

　**e.** capitalist dilemma.

# Short Answer Problems

1. Consider the worlds of Vulcan and Klingon. The Vulcan Lorenz curve is given in Fig. 5, and the Klingon income distribution data are given in Table 2.

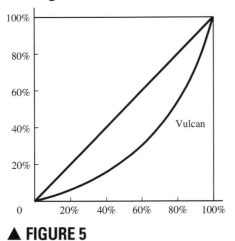

▲ FIGURE 5

| TABLE 2  Klingon Income Distribution | |
|---|---|
| **Household Income Rank** | **Percentage Share Total Income** |
| Lowest 20% | 10% |
| Second 20% | 10% |
| Middle 20% | 20% |
| Fourth 20% | 30% |
| Highest 20% | 30% |

**a.** Label the axes of Fig. 5 and explain what the diagonal line represents.

**b.** Using the data from Table 2, draw the Klingon Lorenz curve on Fig. 5.

2. Chapter 5 describes two approaches to ideas about fairness—fair results and fair rules.

**a.** Describe briefly each idea about fairness.

**b.** Using only the information in Short Answer Problem **1**, which idea(s) about fairness can be used to judge Vulcan and Klingon? Which world is more fair according to the idea(s)?

**3.** Table 3 gives information regarding the distribution of income in an economy that generates $100 billion in total annual income.

### TABLE 3  Total Household Income

| Percentage of Households | Total Income (billions of $) | Income Share (%) | Cumulative Percentage of Households | Cumulative Percentage of Income |
|---|---|---|---|---|
| Poorest 20% | 5 | | | |
| Second 20% | 10 | | | |
| Third 20% | 15 | | | |
| Fourth 20% | 20 | | | |
| Richest 20% | 50 | | | |

**a.** Complete the last three columns in Table 3.

**b.** On the grid, draw the Lorenz curve for income in this economy and label it *A*.

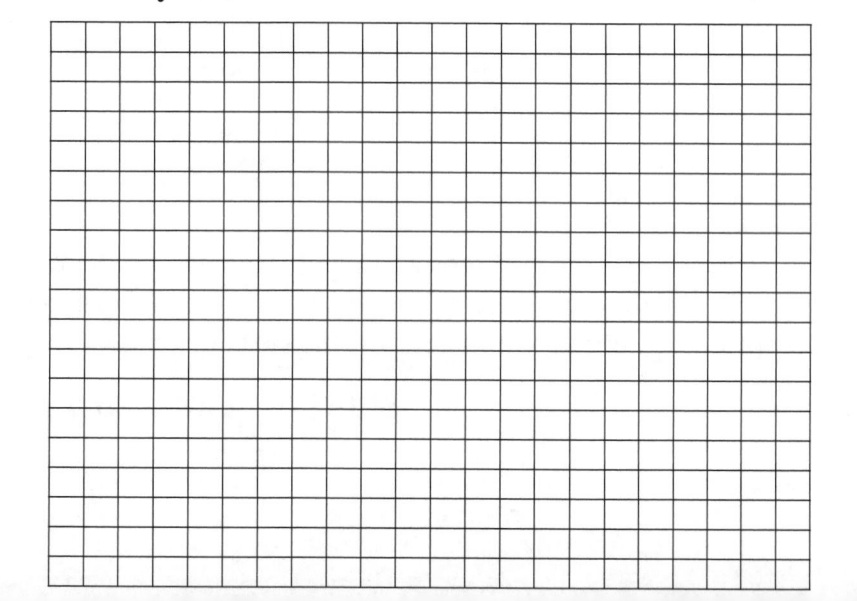

**4.** Now suppose a progressive income tax is levied on the economy. The distribution of after-tax income is given in Table 4. We assume none of the revenue is redistributed to families in the economy. Note that total after-tax income is $71 billion.

### TABLE 4  After-Tax Household Income

| Percentage of Households | After-Tax Income (billions of $) | After-Tax Income Share (%) | Cumulative Percentage of Households | Cumulative Percentage of After-Tax Income |
|---|---|---|---|---|
| Poorest 20% | 5 | | | |
| Second 20% | 9 | | | |
| Third 20% | 12 | | | |
| Fourth 20% | 15 | | | |
| Richest 20% | 30 | | | |

**a.** Complete Table 4.

**b.** Draw the Lorenz curve for after-tax income on the same graph you used for Short Answer Problem **3b** and label it *B*.

**c.** What effect has the progressive income tax had on inequality?

**d.** What is the size of the "big tradeoff" in this case?

**TABLE 5  After-Benefits Household Income**

| Percentage of Households | After-Benefits Income Share (billions of $) | After-Benefits Income Share (%) | Cumulative Percentage of Households | Cumulative Percentage of After-Benefits Income |
|---|---|---|---|---|
| Poorest 20% | 15 | | | |
| Second 20% | 16 | | | |
| Third 20% | 18 | | | |
| Fourth 20% | 20 | | | |
| Richest 20% | 31 | | | |

**5.** Finally, suppose that, in addition, the government redistributes all revenue so that the after-benefits (after-tax) income distribution is given in Table 5. For example, those in the poorest group receive benefits income of $10 billion so their after-benefits income becomes $15 billion.

**a.** Complete Table 5.

**b.** Draw the Lorenz curve for after-benefits income on the same graph you used for Short Answer Problems **3b** and **4b** and label it *C*.

**c.** What effect has income redistribution through benefits payments had on inequality?

**6.** Consider an economy consisting of 100 individuals who are identical in every way. Each lives to be 80 years of age and no older. Between birth and the age of 20 years they earn zero income; between the ages of 21 and 35 each earns an annual income of $30,000; between the ages of 36 and 50 each earns an annual income of $40,000; between the ages of 51 and 65 each receives an annual income of $60,000; and between the ages of 66 and 80 each receives an annual income of $20,000. At any given time there are 20 individuals in each of the five age groups. For simplicity, assume there are no bequests. This information is summarized in Table 6 on the next page.

**TABLE 6  Lifetime Income Patterns**

| Age Group (years) | Number in Age Group | Individual Annual Income ($) |
|---|---|---|
| 0–20 | 20 | 0 |
| 21–35 | 20 | 30,000 |
| 36–50 | 20 | 40,000 |
| 51–65 | 20 | 60,000 |
| 66–80 | 20 | 20,000 |

**b.** Draw the Lorenz curve for annual income in this economy and label it *B*.

**c.** Which of these is a better measure of the inequality among individuals in this economy? Why?

**a.** On the grid, draw the Lorenz curve for lifetime income in this economy and label it *A*.

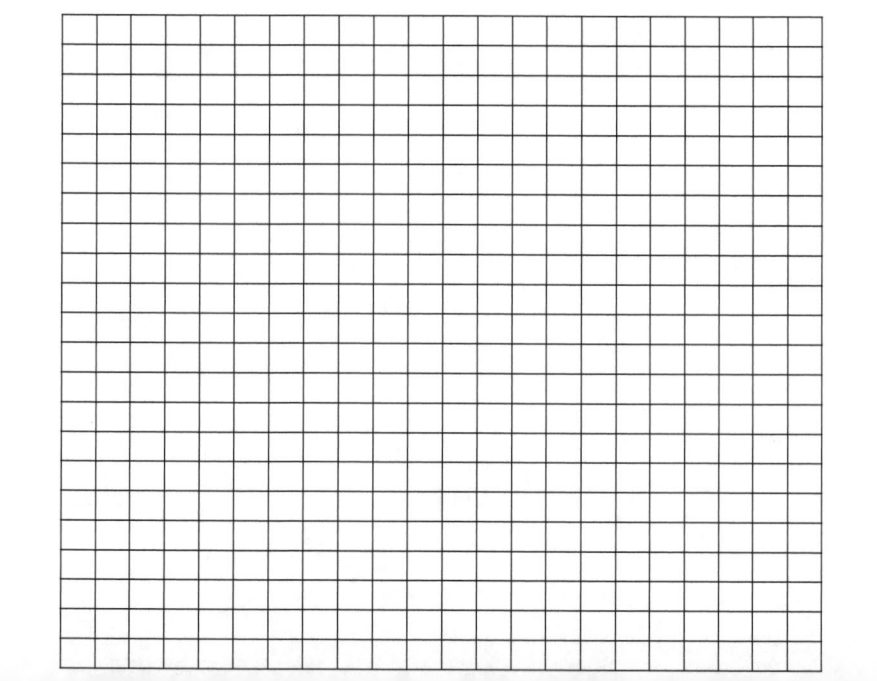

**7.** Fig. 6 shows the demand and supply of low-skilled and high-skilled labour. $D_L$ and $D_H$ are the demand curves for low-skilled and high-skilled workers, respectively, and $S_L$ and $S_H$ are the supply curves for low-skilled and high-skilled workers, respectively.

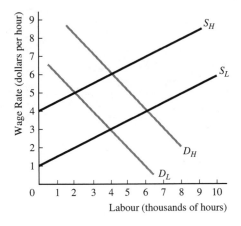

▲ **FIGURE 6**

**a.** What is the *VMP* of skill if 5,000 hours of each kind of labour are hired?

**b.** What amount of extra compensation per hour is required to induce the acquisition of skill at the same level of hiring?

**c.** What are the equilibrium wage and quantity of labour in the market for high-skilled labour?

**d.** What are the equilibrium wage and quantity of labour in the market for low-skilled labour?

**8.** Why is there a "big tradeoff" between equity and efficiency?

# Answers

## True/False and Explain

1. **F** More unequal. (440–445)

2. **T** See text discussion. (440–445)

3. **T** Human capital wealth is more equally distributed than financial wealth. (440–445)

4. **F** Income is a flow of earning from a stock of wealth. (440–445)

5. **T** Differences in life cycle stages make annual income more unequal. (440–445)

6. **T** Because average incomes in poor countries are rising faster than average incomes in rich countries. (446–447)

7. **T** Because the value of marginal product of low-skilled workers is lower than that of high-skilled workers. (448–452)

8. **T** Globalization increases the size of the pool of job candidates, increasing the size of winner's "prize." (448–452)

9. **F** The larger the wage differential. (448–452)

10. **T** Wealthy people seek wealthy partners, increasing concentration of wealth. (448–452)

11. **T** Marginal tax rate is constant, but total taxes increase. (453–455)

12. **F** Marginal tax rate rises with higher incomes. (453–455)

13. **F** From poor to rich. (453–455)

14. **T** See text page 454. (453–455)

15. **F** Lower production due to the big tradeoff. (453–455)

## Multiple-Choice

1. **a** Definition. (440–445)

2. **d** 100 percent – 60 percent of cumulative income. (440–445)

3. **a** 10 percent – 0 percent of cumulative income. (440–445)

4. **b** 40 percent – 20 percent of cumulative income. (440–445)

5. **e** Definition. (440–445)

6. **d** Curve farthest from 45° line. (440–445)

7. **b** Definition. (440–445)

8. **c** Moving from 80 percent to 100 percent of households (richest 20 percent) moves income from 60 percent to 100 percent of total (40 percent). (440–445)

9. **c** Human capital affects distribution of wealth, not income. (440–445)

10. **d** Life cycle biases distribution income, not wealth. (440–445)

11. **d** Lifetime income is more equally distributed than annual income or than any wealth distribution in a given year. (440–445)

12. **c** Wealth is a stock, income is a flow derived from wealth. (440–445)

13. **a** Since no area inside the Lorenz curve. (440–445)

14. **b** (446–447)

15. **c** Reverse of **a** is true. **d** applies to supply. **e** is nonsense. (448–452)

16. **a** (448–452)

**17. c** No demand curves on figure. Increased *VMP* skill shifts demand, not supply. (448–452)

**18. e** All can contribute to differentials. (448–452)

**19. e** Education and training would increase human capital and shift supply curve labour up. (448–452)

**20. b** Marriage within a socioeconomic class. (448–452)

**21. a** Definition. (453–455)

**22. a** Taxes are always 10 percent of income. (453–455)

**23. b** With higher income, tax rate increases from 0 percent, to 10 percent, to 20 percent, to 40 percent. (453–455)

**24. a** Others increase inequality. (453–455)

**25. d** See text discussion. (453–455)

## Short Answer Problems

**1. a.** See Fig. 5 Solution. The diagonal line represents hypothetical income equality.

**b.** See Fig. 5 Solution.

**2. a.** According to the fair-results idea, there should be equality of incomes. According to the fair-rules idea, there should be equality of opportunity.

**b.** Since we have information only on income outcomes and not on the processes or opportunities leading to those incomes, only the fair-results idea can be used to judge Vulcan and Klingon. Since the Klingon Lorenz curve is closer to the line of equality, the Klingon world is more fair according to the fair-results idea.

**3. a.** Table 3 is completed as Table 3 Solution. The income share for each group of families is the total income of that group as a percentage of total income in the economy ($100 billion). The cumulative percentage of income (last column) is obtained by adding the percentage income share of the group (from the third column) to the total percentage income share of all poorer groups of families.

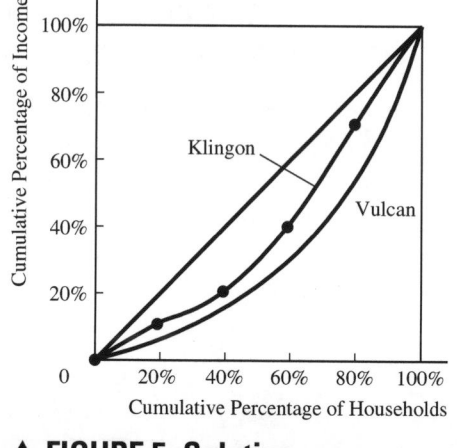

▲ **FIGURE 5 Solution**

| TABLE 3 Solution Total Household Income | | | | |
|---|---|---|---|---|
| Percentage of Households | Total Income (billions of $) | Income Share (%) | Cumulative Percentage of Households | Cumulative Percentage of Income |
| Poorest 20% | 5 | 5 | 20 | 5 |
| Second 20% | 10 | 10 | 40 | 15 |
| Third 20% | 15 | 15 | 60 | 30 |
| Fourth 20% | 20 | 20 | 80 | 50 |
| Richest 20% | 50 | 50 | 100 | 100 |

**b.** The curve labelled *A* in Fig. 7 is the Lorenz curve for total family income. This simply plots the values in the last two columns of Table 3 Solution.

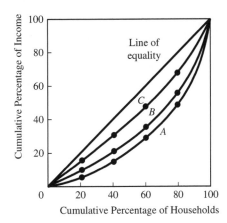

▲ **FIGURE 7**

**4. a.** Table 4 is completed as Table 4 Solution.

**TABLE 4  Solution After-Tax Household Income**

| Percentage of Households | After-Tax Income (billions of $) | After-Tax Income Share (%) | Cumulative Percentage of Households | Cumulative Percentage of After-Tax Income |
|---|---|---|---|---|
| Poorest 20% | 5 | 7 | 20 | 7 |
| Second 20% | 9 | 13 | 40 | 20 |
| Third 20% | 12 | 17 | 60 | 37 |
| Fourth 20% | 15 | 21 | 80 | 58 |
| Richest 20% | 30 | 42 | 100 | 100 |

**b.** The curve labelled *B* in Fig. 7 is the Lorenz curve for after-tax household income.

**c.** The progressive income tax has reduced inequality by taking a larger percentage of income from higher income groups.

**d.** The "big tradeoff" is the fact that a more equally shared pie results in a smaller pie. While the after-tax distribution is now more equal, total income has been reduced from $100 billion to $71 billion. The $29 billion loss is the cost of the big tradeoff, due to the costs of administering the redistribution program and the deadweight loss from weakened work incentives.

**5. a.** Table 5 is completed as Table 5 Solution.

**TABLE 5  Solution After-Benefits Household Income**

| Percentage of Households | After-Benefits Income Share (billions of $) | After-Benefits Income Share (%) | Cumulative Percentage of Households | Cumulative Percentage of After-Benefits Income |
|---|---|---|---|---|
| Poorest 20% | 15 | 15 | 20 | 15 |
| Second 20% | 16 | 16 | 40 | 31 |
| Third 20% | 18 | 18 | 60 | 49 |
| Fourth 20% | 20 | 20 | 80 | 69 |
| Richest 20% | 31 | 31 | 100 | 100 |

**b.** The curve labelled *C* in Fig. 7 is the Lorenz curve for after-tax, after-benefits household income.

**c.** Income redistribution through benefits payments has reduced inequality.

**6. a.** Since each individual in the economy earns exactly the same lifetime income, the Lorenz curve for lifetime income coincides with the line of equality and is labelled *A* in Fig. 8.

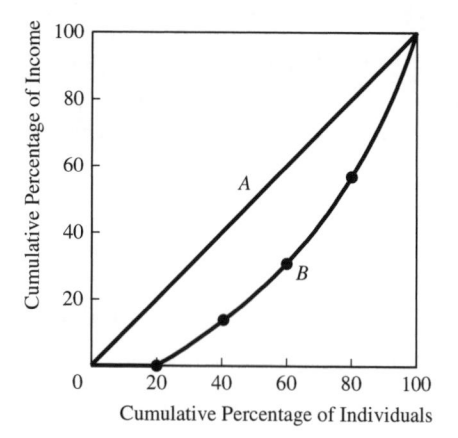

**▲ FIGURE 8**

**b.** The Lorenz curve for annual income is labelled *B* in Fig. 8. It reflects that the poorest 20 percent of individuals, those aged 0–20 years, receive 0 percent of the annual income; the second-poorest 20 percent, 60–80 years, 13 percent; the third-poorest 20 percent, 21–35 years, 20 percent; the fourth-poorest 20 percent, 36–50 years, 27 percent; and the richest 20 percent, 51–65 years, 40 percent.

**c.** The distribution of lifetime income is a better measure of the degree of inequality. In this imaginary economy all individuals are identical (equal), a fact reflected in equal lifetime incomes. The only reason annual income distribution in this economy is not equal is because individuals are at different stages of identical life cycles.

**7. a.** The *VMP* of skill is the difference between the *VMP* of high-skilled versus low-skilled labour; the vertical distance between the demand curves for high-skilled and low-skilled labour. In Fig. 6, the *VMP* of skill is $3 per hour when 5,000 hours of each kind of labour are employed.

**b.** Since labour supply curves give the minimum compensation workers are willing to accept in return for supplying a given quantity of labour, the extra compensation for skill is the vertical distance between the supply curves of high-skilled and low-skilled labour. At 5,000 hours of employment for both kinds of labour, this is $3 per hour.

**c.** In equilibrium in the market for high-skilled labour, the wage rate will be $6 per hour and employment will be 4,000 hours of labour. This occurs at the intersection of the $D_H$ and $S_H$ curves.

**d.** In equilibrium in the market for low-skilled labour, the wage rate will be $3 per hour and employment will be 4,000 hours of labour. This occurs at the intersection of the $D_L$ and $S_L$ curves.

**8.** If greater equity means increasing the equality of income, it can only be achieved by income redistribution; the income of some must be taxed in order to make transfer payments to others. However, there are incentive effects that reduce the total amount of income available to be distributed.

If productive activities such as work are taxed, there will be a tendency to reduce time spent in those activities. Furthermore, any redistribution program would require resources to administer it and thus leave fewer resources for other productive activities. Thus we arrive at the insight that a more equally shared pie results in a smaller pie.